A PRACTICAL GUIDE TO LAWYERING SKILLS

Third Edition

The College of Law
of England and Wales

The College of Law of England and Wales
Temple Circus
Temple Way
Bristol   BS1 6HG
Tel   01483 216220
E-mail   library-bristol@lawcol.co.uk

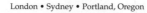

Cavendish
Publishing
Limited

London • Sydney • Portland, Oregon

A PRACTICAL GUIDE TO LAWYERING SKILLS

Third Edition

Fiona Boyle, BSc, Cert Ed

Solicitor and Senior Lecturer in Law

Deveral Capps, LLB, LLM, Cert Ed

Barrister and Principal Lecturer in Law

Philip Plowden, BA, LLM

Barrister, Solicitor and Associate Dean

all at the University of Northumbria, Newcastle upon Tyne

Clare Sandford, MA, Cert Ed

Solicitor and formerly Senior Lecturer in Law

Cavendish
Publishing
Limited

London • Sydney • Portland, Oregon

Fifth edition published in Great Britain 2005 by Cavendish Publishing Limited,
Routledge-Cavendish
2 Park Square, Milton Park, Abingdon, Oxon, OX14 4RN

Simultaneously published in the USA and Canada
by Routledge-Cavendish
270 Madison Avenue, New York, NY 10016

Routledge-Cavendish is an imprint of the Taylor & Francis Group, an informa business

British Library Cataloguing in Publication Data

A practical guide to lawyering skills – 3rd ed
1 Practice of law – Great Britain
I Boyle, Fiona
340'.023'41

ISBN 13: 978-1-859-41975-5
ISBN 10: 1-85941-975-5

Printed and bound in Great Britain by CPI Antony Rowe, Chippenham, Wiltshire

PREFACE

Lawyering skills are increasingly part of the curriculum, whether on undergraduate law degrees, on joint honours degrees, on the postgraduate diploma in law, and (most obviously) on the postgraduate vocational law courses, such as the Legal Practice Course (LPC) and the Bar Vocational Course (BVC).

Once, there was a view that the study of practical lawyering skills was somehow separate from and lesser than the study of 'proper' law – the 'Pericles and the plumber' debate, as it became known.[1] In other jurisdictions, such as America and Australia, that debate is now of historical interest only: law is taught in all its forms – the academic, the practical, the socio-political, the clinical. No one form needs to be seen as more important than any other; no one form needs to be seen as undermining the study of any other. We hope very much that this book will contribute to that process in this jurisdiction.

This book is intended as a practical guide to the development of certain core lawyering skills for all students – whether in the context of undergraduate or postgraduate courses. We have been guided by the skills content of the two main postgraduate courses (the LPC for solicitors and the BVC for barristers), but we have tried to look more widely at the other skills that are demanded of those who undertake legal work in practice – in particular, at written communication skills, mediation skills and at information technology skills.

We know that many students who read law at undergraduate level have no intention of carrying on into legal practice. We also know from our own experience, teaching on both vocational and undergraduate courses (and, in particular, the Northumbria Exempting Degree which combines both elements), that the study of black letter law is invariably enhanced by an understanding of the application of that law in its practical context. The skills that are developed in this book are the core skills that underlie the law that is taught at both undergraduate and vocational levels.

The hardest part of writing a book on lawyering skills is in deciding where to stop. All of the authors can draw on experiences of law in practice, and invariably our experiences are reflected in what we see as the core skills that students need to develop. As authors, we must acknowledge our sources, and in this book those sources are not simply the writings of the many learned authors on the practice of law, from the classical writers on rhetoric to the many contemporary analyses of different aspects of legal skills; nor are our sources simply our colleagues and students who have contributed so much to this book; we also have to acknowledge our clients and our fellow practitioners, who, for better or worse, have provided the foundation for this book.

The Bar's Code of Conduct requires that all barristers:

> ... promote and protect fearlessly and by all proper and lawful means the lay client's best interests and do so without regard to his own interests or to any consequences to himself or to any other person.[2]

It is a principle that must underlie all legal work. It is our hope that this book will help to develop the skills that will enable all students to do exactly that.

---

1   'A university is not a trade school for the production of plumbers': Twining, W, 'Pericles and the plumber' (1967) 83 LQR 396, p 404.

2   Bar Council, *Code of Conduct of the Bar of England and Wales*, para 303. A similar provision governs the conduct of solicitor-advocates.

CONTENTS

TABLE OF CASES

TABLE OF STATUTES

STATUTORY INSTRUMENTS

European Legislation

TABLE OF ACRONYMS

BVC	Bar Vocational Course
CPR	Civil Procedure Rules 1998
LPC	Legal Practice Course
IATC	Inns Advocacy Training Committee
NITA	National Institute of Trial Advocacy
OSS	Office for the Supervision of Solicitors
PLR	Practical Legal Research
SCCCIC	Solicitors' Client Care and Costs Information Centre

CHAPTER 1

LEGAL WRITING: BASIC PRINCIPLES, PLANNING, PLAIN ENGLISH AND PRESENTATION

INTRODUCTION

Legal writing and lawyers

Writing is at the heart of what lawyers do. Whether as solicitors or barristers or lawyers in other employment, we are asked to scrutinise the written word, to analyse the written word and, above all, to advise using the written word.

Books about writing tend to start with a simple proposition: writing is about communication. But communication can take different forms. When you write to a client you may be advising, clarifying, reassuring, confirming. When you write to an opponent you may be threatening, negotiating, informing or arranging. Sometimes you may write simply in order to send out a message that you have not forgotten about the case. Communication is not always in what is written, but may arise from the fact of writing.

In this chapter, we first consider the special features of legal communication and the basic principles that underpin all effective legal writing. In the following chapter, we will look at the process of writing: how to use first and second drafts, how to review your own work, and the particular requirements of such elements of legal writing as letters of advice, internal and external memoranda, attendance notes, reports and briefs. We also touch on particular issues that arise from the rise in electronic communication – and particularly the use of email.

Writing in practice and in law school

Legal writing does not occur in a vacuum. When you are in practice, you will be adjusting the style and content of your legal writing to fit in with the demands of a particular area of legal work, with its own conventions, and with the conventions of the firm that you are working for.

A letter from a senior partner at one of the large law firms in the City to Margot Costanzo makes the point that different areas of work seem to have their own unspoken conventions:

> Writing style in the firm is dictated by custom and practice, tempered by partners' individual styles and preferences. Trainees also receive an extensive note on drafting, but this covers mainly agreements.
>
> Typically, property and litigation lawyers write letters in the first person plural, often adopting a more formal tone than is necessary. We would advise that this is not a style which generally meets the approval of the writer of this letter.
>
> Typically, a corporate lawyer adopts a less formal style with assistants, just as partners, writing letters in their own name and in the first person singular. I approve of this, as I am sure you do too, Margot.[1]

---

1   Costanzo, M, *Legal Writing*, 1993, London: Cavendish Publishing, p 7.

On undergraduate law courses, you may be writing essays, coursework or exams, where the primary assessment will be of your legal knowledge, rather than directly focusing on your communication skills. Alternatively, the assessment may be a more skills-oriented one, and the primary assessment criteria may be your ability to write effectively or to draft appropriately. On the Legal Practice Course (LPC) and the Bar Vocational Course (BVC) (the two postgraduate vocational courses for students who wish to qualify as solicitors or barristers in England and Wales), writing and drafting are formally assessed as 'skills'.

On the LPC, skills are simply assessed on a competent/non-competent basis. On the BVC, the skills assessments are graded: outstanding, very competent, competent and fail. In an academic environment, therefore, you will find a variety of different criteria which are used to assess your ability; in practice, the criteria will rarely be overt.

In these two chapters, therefore, we also need to consider both the practical and the academic aspects of legal writing as a legal skill.

However, although academic assessments may be part of the development of an effective legal writing style, they are not the ultimate goal. Effective legal writing must take account of the demands of the particular task and the needs of the particular client, and it is for this reason that this chapter starts by looking at the different functions of communication for lawyers.

Why are these chapters about legal writing rather than drafting?

Most legal skills books now recognise that legal writing is a skill with a different focus from legal drafting. For this reason, the Essential Legal Skills series has separate books on the two separate areas. In her book, *Legal Writing*, Margaret Costanzo defines the difference in the following way:

> Legal writing is essentially a process of *solving problems* and *proposing options*. Legal drafting is a process of *defining relationships* and *setting out procedures*. Much of legal drafting is about *adapting precedents*: more of legal writing is about *original composition*.[2]

In this book we use 'legal writing' to refer to informal communications, such as letters, memoranda, attendance notes and even briefs (the more formally drafted communications from solicitor to barrister). In Chapters 5 and 6 (on opinion writing and on drafting), we consider the more formal legal documents, such as contracts, wills, pleadings in litigation matters, affidavits, and barristers' written opinions on cases; all of these tend to require the writer to comply with certain formal procedural requirements which go beyond the mere process of communication itself.

WRITING AND COMMUNICATION

Being able to write effectively will not make you a lawyer. But if you cannot write effectively, it will always hamper your progress as a lawyer. Here is the stumbling block: most lawyers in practice believe they write effectively. The trouble is that their clients do not agree.

---

2   *Op cit*, Costanzo, fn 1, p 3.

Lawyers have a reputation for communicating very badly with their clients, in the same way that doctors have a reputation for indecipherable handwriting. Both reputations seem to be justified. The Office for the Supervision of Solicitors lists poor communication as a primary cause of consumer dissatisfaction with legal services, and many complaints to the Bar Council about barristers seem to have their roots in poor communication between lawyers and their clients.

What is the function of lawyers?

One pragmatic definition is that the function of a lawyer is to assist a client in protecting or asserting those rights that are defined by law. Lawyers acting as advocates, whether solicitors or barristers, are generally under a professional duty to say for the client what the client would, if he or she possessed the requisite skill and knowledge, say for himself or herself. This is a good example of the principle that the primary duty of any lawyer is to provide his or her clients with the legal knowledge and skill that will enable them to look after their affairs.

Ultimately, the lawyer's duty is to communicate effectively with the client so that the client can decide what steps to take. Because of this duty, the emphasis is on informing, advising and assisting the client. Often, clients may be very dependent on the advice and analysis provided by their lawyer; often, clients, even when they are themselves lawyers (as will generally be the case where barristers are advising their professional clients, solicitors), will be keen to off-load the responsibility for making decisions back on to the adviser – but, as lawyers, we all ultimately act on the basis of 'instructions', on what our clients tell us they want us to do. In order to be able to give sensible instructions, the clients must be in a position where they have been fully and properly informed and advised. And this is the reason why communication is at the heart of a lawyer's skills.

Why communicate by writing?

Legal writing may have any number of different purposes. You may be writing to a lay client (that is, a non-lawyer) to advise, or you may be writing to them to confirm advice which you have already given face to face or on the telephone. You may be writing to another lawyer, whether friendly or hostile, to set out your client's position. You may be drafting a memorandum to inform colleagues about relevant aspects of a case, or an attendance note to record what steps have been taken on a particular case. Increasingly all of these things may happen by email, making the process of communicating by writing a far speedier affair.

What each of these scenarios has in common is that you are being required to communicate in writing. But why is this the case? If you have already seen your client, and indeed spent a long time talking to them about their case, why then write to them simply in order to repeat all this information? Why do you need to write to another lawyer to set out your client's position when you can simply telephone them? Why draft an attendance note when you know perfectly well what is going on in this case? Are all these simply examples of lawyers creating extra work – extra *billable* work? The answer may well be different in each case. But the underlying purpose of using written communication, rather than relying upon oral or visual communication, can be summarised as follows:

Written communication enables information to be recorded in a format which may be accessible to other people, at other places, and at other times. As a consequence of this, a written communication will often later be treated as evidence of what was done or said at an earlier place and time.

In order to see how well this definition holds up to reality, let's consider the functions of a standard letter to a client, confirming advice given during an interview. Why does the lawyer write this letter?

Part of the reason is to provide your client with a record of your earlier advice. It is, therefore, a way of making sure that your client has remembered all the advice. What is more, having the advice set out or summarised in written form will give the client a chance to go over the information as often as they wish in order to make sure that they understand what is being proposed and why. Moreover, the letter serves as a permanent record of the advice, so that the client can go back to it at some later date to remind himself or herself why a certain course of action has been taken. The letter may also be given to other interested parties so that they can see what the lawyer has advised, even though they themselves may not have been present at the original interview or conference. From the lawyer's point of view, the written communication provides a valuable safeguard against any future claim for negligent advice; the lawyer can point to the letter as a record of what was advised, sometimes many years earlier, and often by a different lawyer.

Does all communication have the same purpose?

Writing is always about communication at some level, but you can come up with long lists of different reasons for communication. If you think about some of the different reasons why lawyers may need to communicate, you would probably include:

(a) to advise;

(b) to record;

(c) to inform;

(d) to confront;

(e) to reply;

(f) to confirm;

(g) to justify;

(h) to reassure.

Indeed, you can probably think of other reasons for communicating. And, if there is such a range of different reasons for communicating, then there cannot be a single rule that defines what will make a communication *effective*. In order to work out if the communication is effective, we need, first, to consider the basic ground rules for all communication.

PLANNING AND WRITING

You learnt to write so long ago you have probably forgotten the process. As you developed, what was required of you in your writing changed. One of the primary focuses of the education process is the development of written communication skills, so that, imperceptibly, you became able to analyse, organise and present material (whether in science, or history, or languages) in increasingly sophisticated ways. Exams and coursework at all stages almost always demanded from you not merely knowledge of the material, but the ability to apply the material and to present it in written form. It becomes easy to forget that, with each piece of writing, you are, whether consciously or not, undertaking a complex preparatory process.

This section looks at a series of questions that can help to make sure that you have prepared effectively:

(a) Why am I writing?

(b) Who am I writing for?

(c) How should I organise what I need to say?

(d) Is my language appropriate?

(e) Are the sentences clear?

(f) Does the letter look clear?

(g) Have I made clear what happens next?

(h) Post or email?

Why are you writing?

The first stage in preparing to write must always be to decide why you are writing. As we have discussed above, that doesn't just mean identifying the functions of the communication (to advise, to confirm, to record, etc), but also considering why you are communicating by writing at all.

Writing isn't always the most effective way of communicating. Indeed, writing places a barrier in the communication process: communication must be reduced to words on a page, and those words must then be read and interpreted by the reader. In contrast, oral communication seems more direct and effective: words are spoken, heard and (with luck) understood. And, of course, oral communication has the advantage of flexibility.

Speech has the advantage of directness in the communication, and speed of delivery. Indeed, the speed at which we talk means that there is more time to discuss possibilities and options in a way that would be confusing in a written communication. But talking, as a form of communication, suffers from an inherent lack of organisation, and also from our poor listening skills. If you have ever seen a transcript of yourself talking, you may be amazed at the apparent chaos of your delivery. Ideas may start with a clear sentence, but often, in speech, sentences will descend into sequences of clauses and phrases, all linked to the main idea, rather like footnotes in a written text.

It isn't simply that we may mis-hear information; we may often misunderstand what is being said. It is perhaps for this reason that we tend to say the same thing in a number of different ways when we are talking to someone, in order to make sure that the message is properly received. Written communication does not need this element of redundancy. In your written communication, you can always aim to make good the defects of oral communication.

Who are you writing for?

You may be writing to a range of possible recipients. So far, we have tended to think about writing in terms of communication between yourself and your client. But not all clients are the same. This is not simply to say that some clients may be better educated, or may have different language skills from other clients. You may find that you use a different style and tone when writing to a corporate client from the one you use when writing to a 'private' client. Certainly, in a letter to a court, you will use a level of formality which would be completely out of place if you were writing to another individual. Similarly, if you are writing to a lawyer representing the other side in a matter, your language and tone will be different from the language you would use if you were writing to a neutral third party.

You must, of course, even in the most hard fought cases, abide by the rules of professional practice, which require a minimum degree of civility even when corresponding with your opponents! Thus, for example, *The Guide to the Professional Conduct of Solicitors* states that:

> A solicitor must maintain his or her personal integrity and observe the requirements of good manners and courtesy towards other members of the profession or their staff, no matter how bitter the feelings between clients. A solicitor must not write offensive letters to other members of the profession.[3]

Even if, for some reason, you were writing the same letter to each of these different recipients, your language and the style of your letter would be different for each one. This partly reflects the fact that the purpose of the letter would probably vary: you might be writing to advise your client, but to confront the other side, and to inform the court, while seeking to reassure a third party. But it is also because there are different conventions (especially in writing the more formal letters to your opponents and to the court) which may affect the principle of simple communication.

As an example, look at the following sentence:

> I am instructed that damages in the sum of £15,000 are sought in this matter.

But before we agree that these are two examples of inappropriate 'officialese', consider the following alternatives:

> We want £15,000.
> They've been told to keep off the grass.

Certainly, the first example is very formal. However, is 'We want £15,000' appropriate? Does it sound like language you would expect a lawyer to use? How would it sound if it was read out in court? The answer is, it depends on whom the letter is intended for and what level of formality is appropriate to that recipient.

This is *not* to encourage you to try and 'write like a lawyer'. Writing like a lawyer – or like you think a lawyer should write – is generally fatal. Being obscure, even when corresponding with other lawyers, doesn't make you seem more like a lawyer; it only confuses and delays matters. But you must always consider your audience. Or to put it another way: know your reader.

---

3   Law Society, *The Guide to the Professional Conduct of Solicitors*, 8th edn, 1999, London: Law Society, p 322, 19.01, para 3.

How should you organise what you need to say?

Your list of what your reader needs to know may start off with a single item, or it may run to 10 or even 20 separate elements of information. If you have just a single item – my reader needs to know what will happen at the police station – you may well find that this then breaks down into a number of smaller items: what happens on arrival at the police station; access to free legal advice; procedure during an interview; the right of silence and the inferences that arise; and so on. Similarly, a long list of items – entitlement to written reasons for dismissal; how to obtain a copy of the contract; time limits for applications to an Employment Tribunal; whether to apply to the county court or the tribunal – may well coalesce into a single main category: what to do after being fired from your job.

Whichever way round the list is in your case, there is still a single guiding principle: information is normally most effectively organised when it moves from the general to the specific.

Consider the following:

> A jury can only draw an inference from your silence if they think it is reasonable to do so. The inference is presumably that you didn't mention the facts at the police station because you have made them up later, or because you didn't feel they would stand up to questioning. If you do not answer the questions at the police station stage, and then you later raise facts in your defence at court, the jury can draw inferences from your earlier failure to mention the facts when questioned. But you do not have to say anything and you cannot be forced to answer the police questions. You have a right to silence. You have a right to free legal advice at the police station and I will be present to advise you during the interview.

The words are relatively clear – perhaps with the exception of the 'inference', although the writer does try to explain what this is. But as a whole, the paragraph is hard to follow. It's true that the law on inferences from silence at the police station is very complex,[4] but the confusion here is made worse because of the way the information has been structured. If you try to analyse the propositions in the paragraph, you will see that they move from the very specific (what is the effect of this inference?) to the more general (you have a right to silence) and, finally, the scene-setting (I will be present to advise you during the interview).

If we reverse the order of the material, we get the following:

> You have a right to free legal advice at the police station and I will be present to advise you during the interview. You have a right to silence. So you do not have to say anything and you cannot be forced to answer the police questions. However, if you do not answer the questions at the police station stage, and then you later raise facts in your defence at court, the jury can draw inferences from your earlier failure to mention these facts when questioned. The inference is presumably that you didn't mention the facts at the police station because you have made them up later, or because you felt they would not stand up to questioning. A jury can only draw an inference from your silence if they think it is reasonable to do so.

---

4   You will find the statutory provisions in the Criminal Justice and Public Order Act 1994, ss 34, 36 and 37.

Apart from a few link words ('so', 'however'), the only difference is the order of the material. This advice moves from the general to the specific. It is a process of a narrowing focus on the material, which some commentators refer to as the *pyramid rule* or *pyramid principle*.[5] This general principle of organisation underlies almost all writing and, indeed, most writers do it without even realising they are doing it. As usual, it is when something goes wrong, when you feel your letter is falling short of its purpose, that you may need to go back to look at how you have prepared the material. Does it flow logically? Does it move from the general to the specific?

Is good organisation the key to effective writing?

Sadly, the answer is 'no'. Good organisation is part of the key to writing effectively, but it is only part of the answer. You need also to think about the language that you are using, the grammatical structures, and even the presentation of your material on the page – or in the questions from the start of this section:

(a) Is my language appropriate?

(b) Are the sentences clear?

(c) Does the letter look clear?

All these need more detailed consideration. They are not simply part of the planning process, but part of the writing itself, and so we will look at these in detail later in the chapter. But, before we move on from the question of how best to prepare to write, there is one final matter that you will always need to consider: have I made clear what happens next?

What happens next?

Consider the extract from the letter concerning police station procedure (above). In its restructured form, it is relatively clear. The language is reasonably appropriate – assuming that this is a letter to a lay client. The content seems accurate enough, and the presentation, as far as one can see, is not obstructing the communication. But if the purpose of the letter is to advise the client, the extract that we have seen is wholly ineffective. Go back and re-read the extract. Based on what it says, should the client exercise his or her right to silence? What defence facts do you think that this client might reasonably be expected to mention? Do you think the jury would be likely to draw an inference?

It is impossible to answer any of these questions. The extract provided simply does not contain this advice.

But is this unfair? What if the letter is simply intended to confirm that the solicitor will be present? After all, maybe, at this stage, the client does not want to know all the intricacies of whether to remain silent or to answer questions. The lawyer may have made the decision to wait until there is more information before dealing with these issues. But, if this is the case, then the communication needs to make this clear. 'What happens next?' Answer:

5　See Minto, B, *The Pyramid Principle: Logic in Writing and Thinking*, 1981, London: Minto International, discussed by Costanzo in *op cit*, fn 1, Chapter 2.

> I will meet you at the police station at 2.00 pm on Thursday 23 March. At this stage, I will see if we can find out more information from the police about the allegations against you. When we have this information, I will then be in a better position to advise you whether to answer the police questions or to exercise your right of silence.

So 'What happens next?' doesn't necessarily mean you have to go on to advise your client. It may simply confirm to your reader how much they are expected to get out of the letter by making clear what action will now follow. Sometimes, the answer to 'What happens next?' may simply be:

> This letter is simply to keep you informed about the progress of the case. I will contact you as soon as I hear from the court with a date for the next hearing.

But even this limited answer is often valuable in explaining to the client that the letter does not require them to do anything at this stage. And the principle is not confined to letters to your clients. If you ask yourself the question when you write to the opposition or to the court, it will remind you to make clear what you now expect to happen in a matter:

> In the light of this, we look forward to receiving your written assurance that the trespass to Mrs Smith's land will stop at once. If we do not receive a satisfactory assurance within 14 days of the date of this letter, we will begin court proceedings.

Or to the court:

> Please find enclosed a copy of the Notice of Appeal in this case. We understand that you will now be listing the case for a full hearing and we will wait to hear from you with the proposed date.

'What happens next?' makes you go back to the first question you asked in your planning: 'What is the purpose of the communication?' It asks you, the writer, whether you have achieved the different purposes for which you initially wrote the letter and whether you are now able, as a result, to move to the next stage in the case.

'What happens next?' is often as applicable to the writing of briefs, and of attendance notes and of memoranda, as it is to letter writing. As we shall see, it is a good principle to use the final paragraph of a brief to counsel to confirm what counsel is being required to do, and what you expect to happen next. Similarly, where there is any significant information in an attendance note, it is worth concluding the note by indicating what action is now required on the case, or what you anticipate the next steps will be. 'What happens next?' prevents communication from simply hanging in the air by re-affirming the purpose of the communication.

And so, the question 'What happens next?' closes the planning circle, and brings you back to the process of actually writing. And that is what the next sections focus on: the language you use in your writing, the grammatical structures that you choose, and the presentation of your material.

Post or email?

The traditional process of written communication was based on letters or reports which were sent by post, or at least which were sent by fax, but which were then read in paper form. There is now fairly widespread use of email, and you can certainly anticipate that some clients will welcome the (normally) instantaneous transmission of information which can be achieved by email. There are a few core considerations which you must bear in mind.

First, email is not normally a secure form of communication. You must draw this to the attention of your client. You must ensure that you have their informed consent to the use of email for communications. If a matter has a fairly high degree of confidentiality, you should probably advise against the use of email unless you and your client are happy that confidentiality can be maintained.

Secondly, you must ensure that there are appropriate records kept of all email communication. Your firm or chambers will have in place systems for keeping track of post which is sent and received. Similar systems need to be in place for email. Where client files are kept in paper format you may need to print out all emails to the file. If files are kept electronically you must ensure that your case management systems copy the emails to the file.

Thirdly, consider whether you need to adjust what you say to fit in with the particular demands of email. Don't use the email itself for lengthy or complex communications – we would suggest that you draft these as a formal letter or report or Advice, even if you then send this electronically by email.

Fourth, email offers huge advantages from almost instantaneous communication. Be careful. The general need to review what you are writing still remains. Don't be pressurised into sending communications which haven't gone through the same careful process of review that you would apply to the rest of your writing.

Finally, beware of emails which contain the text of every preceding email: you may find that you are sending out information which you didn't mean to.

> For example, a client emails you to ask the answer to a planning law matter. You forward the email to a colleague with a request to deal with it quickly as the client is notoriously demanding. Your colleague emails you back the answer, adding that she's glad that you are dealing with the client as she always found the client impossible to deal with. You pass the email on to another colleague to check there are no tax issues. The email chain gets longer. Each exchange is listed below, but is by now well below your screen as you review the most recent message. A few days later you forward the final advice to the client, forgetting that every other email is set out below. Your client reads the full exchange of views! Be careful.

Do you need to send a paper copy if you have sent a letter by email? There is no hard and fast rule here. Be sure you are clear about the formal rules for service if the document is part of a litigation process, or has otherwise to comply with legal rules which govern how a document may be served. Make sure you check the Civil Procedure Rules, or other applicable rules.

PLAIN ENGLISH WRITING

Can legal writing ever be easy to read?

Plain English is not simply the product of using simple words. It requires the organisation of often complex material into a readily comprehensible form: it therefore requires sufficient preparation, effective presentation and accessible expression. You can use the simplest words, but if you are not clear about what you are saying, the message can never be clear. So, using appropriate language is not, by itself, enough. But, if you do not use appropriate language, no matter how clear you are about what you wish to communicate, you will be making the communication process harder.

Faced with the complexity of many elements of the law, it is easy to feel that plain English is simply not possible. However, consider the following paragraph from a decision of the Court of Appeal. In this case, the court was considering one of the most problematic areas of tort law, that of economic loss. The court was being asked to decide whether Martin and Co, who had accidentally cut through an electricity cable, were liable to Spartan Steel, who had had to shut down production of their factory while the supply was restored. In this extract, one judge is listing the various factors which he says have to be considered:

> The second consideration is the nature of the hazard, namely, the cutting of the supply of electricity. This is a hazard which we all run. It may be due to a short circuit, to a flash of lightning, to a tree falling on the wires, to an accidental cutting of the cable, or even to the negligence of someone or other. And when it does happen, it affects a multitude of persons: not as a rule by way of physical damage to them or their property, but by putting them to inconvenience, and sometimes to economic loss. The supply is usually restored in a few hours, so the economic loss is not very large. Such a hazard is regarded by most people as a thing they must put up with – without seeking compensation from anyone. Some there are who install a stand-by system. Others seek refuge by taking out an insurance policy against breakdown in the supply. But most people are content to take the risk on themselves. When the supply is cut off, they do not go running round to their solicitor. They do not try to find out whether it was anyone's fault. They just put up with it. They try to make up the economic loss by doing more work next day. This is a healthy attitude which the law should encourage.[6]

Having read this paragraph, please go back and consciously consider the language that is used. There is nothing here that is not immediately accessible, whether to a lawyer or to a lay person. The content is clear, and the reasoning appears to flow logically from this lucid explanation of the law.

Contrast this with the more traditional language used in another dissenting judgment in the same case:

> Having considered the intrinsic nature of the problem presented in this appeal, and having consulted the relevant authorities, my conclusion, as already indicated, is that an action lies in negligence for damages in respect of purely economic loss, provided that it was a reasonably foreseeable and direct consequence of failure in a duty of care. The application of such a rule can undoubtedly give rise to difficulties in certain sets of circumstances, but so can the suggested rule that economic loss may be recovered *provided* that it is directly consequential upon physical damage.[7]

This is more traditional legal language. It is clear and comprehensible to a lawyer who understands the concepts as expressed, but it makes few concessions to accessibility. The first extract is from the speech by Lord Denning; the second from a similarly respected Court of Appeal judge, Edmund-Davies LJ. Lord Denning, of course, was deliberately using the decision as an attempt to reformulate the law and has consciously chosen to use language that is directly persuasive. He himself states earlier in the decision:

---

6   *Spartan Steel v Martin and Co* [1973] QB 27, p 38E–G.
7   *Ibid.*

> The more I think about these cases, the more difficult I find it to put each into its proper pigeon-hole. Sometimes I say: 'There was no duty.' In others I say: 'The damage was too remote.' So much so that I think the time has come to discard these tests which have proved so elusive.

It is not, therefore, an accident that Denning uses a language and tone which is deliberately simple and which relates directly to everyday experience – what actually happens (lightning, falling trees, etc), and what people actually do (put up with electricity cuts, install stand-by systems, take out insurance). He knows that to win his argument he must persuade the court and subsequent judges who will apply the decision that his restatement of the law is a more logical and comprehensible approach. He therefore deliberately moves away from more abstract language to more concrete, accessible language, recognising that the clarity of his argument gives it a powerful persuasive force. Students generally enjoy the boldness and clarity of a Denning decision, but you should not make the mistake of thinking that this is an innocent simplicity.

Nor is Lord Denning alone in this approach. Over the last decade the language used by the senior judiciary in the judgments has grown increasingly accessible. It is clearly no longer thought that there is any need for points of high legal importance to be written in impenetrable legal language. If anything the reverse is true. Here is an extract from Lord Hoffmann's powerful judgment in the case of the Belmarsh detainees, where the Government had indefinitely detained suspected foreign terrorists who could not be deported because of fears that they would be tortured or killed in the countries to which they were to be returned. Eight of the nine Law Lords ruled that the legislation was not compatible with the European Convention on Human Rights. Alone of the Law Lords, Lord Hoffmann went further in ruling that the Government had acted wrongly in even assuming that the circumstances were such as to permit them to "derogate" (or withdraw) from the fundamental right to liberty:

> Of course the government has a duty to protect the lives and property of its citizens. But that is a duty which it owes all the time and which it must discharge without destroying our constitutional freedoms. There may be some nations too fragile or fissiparous to withstand a serious act of violence. But that is not the case in the United Kingdom. When Milton urged the government of his day not to censor the press even in time of civil war, he said:

> "Lords and Commons of England, consider what nation it is whereof ye are, and whereof ye are the governours"

> This is a nation which has been tested in adversity, which has survived physical destruction and catastrophic loss of life. I do not underestimate the ability of fanatical groups of terrorists to kill and destroy, but they do not threaten the life of the nation. Whether we would survive Hitler hung in the balance, but there is no doubt that we shall survive Al-Qaeda. The Spanish people have not said that what happened in Madrid, hideous crime as it was, threatened the life of their nation. Their legendary pride would not allow it. Terrorist violence, serious as it is, does not threaten our institutions of government or our existence as a civil community. [8]

---

8   *A (FC) and Others (FC) v Secretary of State for the Home Department* [2004] UKHL 56, at [95]–[96]

You will also note from the above extracts that, where the language is clear and to the point, the argument appears to be fully exposed. Thus, for example, where Lord Denning says: 'This is a healthy attitude which the law should encourage,' you are almost encouraged to challenge this assertion. It is not a value judgment which he has concealed under abstract legal argument; he has expressed it directly and unambiguously. This is the price that you pay for being clear in your writing. If people understand what you are saying, then they can challenge it. So if you are not entirely sure of your point, there is always a temptation – sometimes an unconscious temptation – to use more complex language and structures so that you will not be challenged. In legal writing, this tendency must always be avoided.

'This writer is of the opinion that ...': voice and person

Voice

> The use of the passive voice by lawyers is commonplace. Greater formality and distance is achieved by use of the passive. Details may be evaded by using the passive. Clarity is rarely enhanced.

All the sentences above use the passive voice. In a sentence which uses the active voice, the subject acts upon the object: the cat sits on the mat. With the passive voice the order will be reversed: the mat is sat on by the cat.

The greatest problem with the passive is that it is often unspecific. Sometimes, the information which is excluded may not be important. When Lord Denning, in one of the extracts above, says that 'the supply is usually restored in a few hours', it is not clear who restores the supply (presumably the electricity board), but the focus of the sentence is on the fact that the supply will be restored; who will do it is immaterial, and the use of the passive means that the sentence focuses on the important point. However, by using the passive you may inadvertently leave out important information:

> The defendant was observed in the shop. (But by whom?)
>
> You will be notified once the documents are received. (Notified by whom – and received by whom?)
>
> Notice must be served within 14 days. (But who has to serve the notice, and on whom do they serve it?)

Additionally, the passive has the effect of keeping matters relatively impersonal. There may be times when this is entirely appropriate – if, for example, you are trying to present matter in an even-handed way:

> This decision has been criticised in later cases. (Impersonal, non-committal.) My own view is that it is unlikely to apply to your own situation. (Active, personal.)

You may be writing a document where a degree of formality is appropriate. Use of the passive can help:

> The argument as to liability is not accepted. The breach of contract is attributed to the plaintiff's conduct.

Note that recasting this in the active voice does produce a more direct – if more overtly confrontational – tone:

> We do not accept the argument as to liability. It is the plaintiff's conduct that gave rise to the breach of contract.

As a rule, use the active voice for clarity and a more personal approach. The passive has its uses, but be aware of why you are using it and always consider whether you could use the active voice more effectively in its place.

Person

We have talked about the way that use of the passive voice can have the effect of depersonalising communication. This can be further increased by the tendency of lawyers to use the first person plural ('we') when writing letters in the name of the firm. You may even find lawyers who are either so self-effacing or so self-important that they refer to themselves in the third person ('the writer of this letter takes the view that ...'). This level of artificiality is sometimes transferred to the recipient of the letter ('We look forward to receiving instructions from your good self ...'). In other cases, the writer may wholly dehumanise the client by writing about them in the third person as well: for example, consider the following paragraph from a letter to a client who is buying a house:

> The purchaser will have responsibility for arranging insurance from the date of exchange of contracts. The purchaser will therefore need to put matters in hand to ensure that the writer of this letter is in funds should the purchaser wish insurance arrangements to be made by this firm.

There is, we suppose, some original grammatical justification for a letter which is coming from a firm of solicitors (Jones and Co), and which is signed with the firm's name, to be written in the plural, although it effectively undermines the issue of the personal relationship between the solicitor dealing with the case and his or her client. As a general rule, however, no one actually believes that the letter was written by the firm acting as a whole and, unless there are good reasons to the contrary, it is a better idea to draft matters in the first person singular and second person singular:

> As purchaser, you are responsible for insuring the property from the date on which we exchange contracts. If you would like me to arrange the insurance, you will need to make sure that you send me a cheque for ... at least seven days before the exchange takes place.

Barristers, being self-employed, have even less excuse for referring to themselves in the plural – no matter what their size – although some still prefer the element of god-like detachment which can be achieved by terms such as 'the writer of this Opinion' or even 'Counsel's advice therefore is ...'. It goes without saying that this kind of pomposity is equally unnecessary.

Hereby, hereinafter and howsoever caused: jargon, legalese and foreign languages

Jargon and lawyers' language

> Jargon: chatter, twittering; confused talk; slang; artificial or barbarous language; the terminology of a profession, art, group, etc.[9]

---

9   *Chambers English Dictionary*, 1990, London: Chambers.

Every job has its jargon.

It is not just professionals, such as accountants, doctors and management consultants, who take refuge behind a wall of unintelligible terms. Specialist occupations in the criminal underworld have long been the source of long lists of technical terms for the mysteries of lifting (pickpocketing), kiting (passing forged cheques) and blagging (armed robbery) – as any viewer of popular television will know. It appears this has always been the case. The Elizabethan playwright, Thomas Dekker, listed hundreds of examples of criminal argot, including the following list of pickpocketing terms:

> He that cuts the purse is called the *Nip*.
>
> He that is halfe with him is the *Snap* or the *Cloyer*.
>
> The knife is called a *Cuttle-bung*.
>
> He that picks the pocket is called a *Foist*.
>
> He that faceth the man, is the *Stale*.
>
> The taking of the purse is called *Drawing*.
>
> The spying of this villainy is called *Smoking* or *Boiling*.
>
> The purse is the *Bung*.
>
> The money the *Shells*.
>
> The act doing, is called *Striking*.[10]

Lawyers are equally notorious for using language that bewilders lay clients.

It is tempting to say that some solicitors communicate in jargon, because they think that this is how solicitors are supposed to communicate. It is not a disease that is confined to solicitors, nor is it confined to the written word. Barristers, because of the nature of their work, rarely write to their lay clients, and written communications with the solicitors are often couched in the more appropriately formal language of an advice or opinion. But attend court, whether with a solicitor or barrister, and listen in to the inevitable court door negotiations, and you will be amazed at how often the lawyers use legal jargon even when trying to explain the compromise offers to their clients:

> Of course, this is without prejudice; however, I'm minded to recommend settlement on these terms.
>
> Inevitably, someone is going to bear a litigation risk if we continue, but the offer on the table is to let costs lie where they fall.
>
> They're threatening a Part 36 payment, which of course would leave us exposed on costs, and we need to keep the statutory charge in mind.
>
> The settlement would be on a full and final basis, but we would need to adjourn to draft a Tomlin Order, but with liberty to apply.

Sometimes it is just an understandable carry-over from the sort of discussion that has been going on between the opposing lawyers. In that discussion, it is reasonable to expect both sides to understand terms such as 'letting costs lie where they fall', or what is involved in a 'Part 36 payment' or a 'Tomlin Order'. Most lawyers will pick up their client's bewildered look and will change gear and stop using these terms, or will

---

10   From Dekker, T, *The Bel-Man of London*, 1936, London: Dent, p 145.

remember to explain to them that, for example, 'without prejudice' means that the negotiations cannot be referred to in court.

But there can be times when the observer gets the impression that the lawyer is deliberately using the jargon as a form of pressure on the client. It is a way of saying: 'See how little of this you understand. I know what I'm talking about. Put yourself in my hands and agree to my recommendation.' It could be that the lawyer is not fully prepared for the hearing and is eager to take the settlement, or because the lawyer genuinely thinks the settlement is in the client's best interests, but knows that the client wants their day in court. Everyone hates losing a case – and sometimes lawyers seem to try to use the full brunt of The Law (knowledge to which they, and not their clients, have access) to push the client into accepting a compromise.

This is, of course, entirely wrong, whether it happens at the court door, or in the solicitor's office, or at conference in chambers. The case is always the client's. The decisions are made by the client. It is the duty of the lawyer to ensure that the client is fully informed as to the legal strengths and weaknesses of their case, but if a client wishes to fight a case against his or her lawyer's advice, then (subject to making sure that the client acknowledges your advice in writing, often by signing the backsheet of counsel's brief, and subject to any duty to the Community Legal Service) that is for the client to decide.

But the greatest danger of using legal terminology thoughtlessly is that there may be some terms which you forget to explain. Take the expression 'in full and final settlement': to a lawyer, this is a clear and precise expression. It means, among other things, that if the client wanted to re-apply to the court for more compensation, perhaps because a personal injury had got unexpectedly worse, the matter would not be re-opened. It is essential that the client understands how and why the settlement is 'final'.

In the context of legal writing, therefore, the use of jargon comes back to the principle that you must always remind yourself who you are writing to, and why you are writing to them. Language that may be appropriate between lawyers is unlikely to be appropriate for the majority of clients. Do not blind your clients with legal terminology in the hope of impressing them; you are more likely to impress them if you can explain clearly what is happening and why. And if you find that you are using more legalese in a piece of writing than you would normally do, stop and ask yourself why. Often, the answer is that you are not 100% clear about either the facts or the law yourself. It is easy to hide your ignorance by making sure the client won't understand your writing, but it will come back to haunt you! It takes confidence in your abilities as a lawyer to write with the clarity of Lord Denning, but by training yourself to write with that clarity, your abilities as a lawyer will develop.

What's wrong with using 'legal' language?

Dear Mr and Mrs Green,

15 George Crescent

We write further to correspondence with yourself of 13th ult.

The writers have hitherto been proceeding in this matter on the basis that the vendor of the property would undertake and agree to give good and sufficient notice of any pre-existing encumbrance on the property. Inasmuch as it now appears that the situation is otherwise, we would advise that it is not unlikely that the matter in hand will proceed less expeditiously than had been earlier indicated by reason of the above issue.

Unless and until full and complete disclosure as to the said encumbrances is made, no further steps in the purchase of the above property would be advisable.

Or, in ordinary English:

Dear Mr and Mrs Green

15 George Crescent

We had been expecting the seller, Mr Brown, to send us details about who, if anybody, might have any claim over 15 George Crescent. (This would include, for example, a bank or building society with whom the property was mortgaged, or some member of Mr Brown's family with a claim to the house.) He has now told us that he will not be providing this information. This is likely to delay the purchase because, before we can proceed, we will need to make the searches ourselves to find out these details.

Why on earth would anyone write the first version of this letter?

To be honest, we're not sure. Perhaps this is the 'house style' of the firm, and the writer has little choice. If so, why is this the 'house style'? It may just be an example of lawyers doing something one way because it has always been done that way! If it is supposed to remind the reader that they are dealing with a Real Lawyer, it may succeed in doing this – until the client hears about a lawyer from a friend who is said to be approachable and whose advice can be understood. At that point, the client is likely to change lawyer.

The alternative view is that the letter is drafted in this way because the lawyer doesn't know what he or she is doing and is therefore trying to ensure that the client is kept in ignorance too. Just as the use of jargon can sometimes be a danger sign that you yourself are not sure about something, so the use of excessively 'lawyerly' language can signal that the lawyer is similarly trying to blind his or her client with The Law.

Some of the terms which lawyers reach for have their origins in historical legal distinctions; some reflect the dual use of legal French and legal English five or six hundred years ago. Sometimes 'legal pairs' just trip off a lawyer's tongue – or pen, at any rate. Even lawyers who would not dream of telling a client that they have 'made and entered into' an agreement, or that something is a 'good and sufficient' reason for fighting the case, may still inform their clients that an agreement would be 'null and void' or 'each and every' partner must be a 'fit and proper' person to run a business.

The golden rule is to use one word rather than two wherever possible. And it isn't just legal terms that you should bear in mind. Consider the following:

Would you be good enough to ...

We should be grateful if you would ...

We would ask that you ...

As Margot Costanzo points out, what is wrong with 'please'?

Similarly, 'in respect of', 'in connection with', 'in relation to', 'with regard to' could all be replaced by the word 'about' or cut altogether.

However, there is one exception to this golden rule of one word, not two: old and middle English 'portmanteau' words. These are words such as: howsoever, whosoever, whatsoever, hereby, herein, hereunder, herewith, therein, thereby – and so on. Avoid these. Even if you can justify them in your formal drafting of wills, pleadings, leases, contracts and other formal legal documents – and we are not convinced that they are justifiable even within that context – they have no place in legal writing. There is never a good reason why any of these words should appear in your writing. They are simply not necessary. Or, as one lawyer to another, they are otiose, nugatory and to be avoided.[11]

Inter alia *and* prima facie: *lawyers and Latin*

At the turn of the century, it was a safe assumption that a solicitor or barrister would be the product of a particular educational system. That system would have included a thorough grounding in Latin, and very probably Greek. This had two implications: first, the writer could use quotations from the classical authors in letters, opinions and decisions of the court as a way of signalling his education (and in the expectation of being understood); and, secondly, the terms could be used as a means of excluding the less knowledgeable (and, in particular, many lay clients) from the mysteries of the law.

Latin and Greek are clearly no longer mainstream elements of the modern educational system. Lawyers, moreover, are more likely to come from a variety of educational backgrounds. Older practitioners, who learnt Latin at school and who completed their training at a time when the use of Latin and Greek was more widespread in the law, are more likely to continue to use Latin phrases; but the use of the Latin quotations is now chiefly the preserve of senior members of the judiciary, who are presumably continuing to signal their eminence:

> It is a question of degree upon which different minds may reach different opinions. As Terence said long ago: *'Quot homines tot sententiae: suo quoique mos,'* which may be translated: 'So many men, so many opinions; his own a law to each.'[12]

The statute 4 Geo 2 c 26 forbade the use of Latin in court proceedings as long ago as 1730, but as recently as 31 March 1998, the Court of Appeal was still having to instruct lawyers that 'the time has come to abandon all Latin tags'.[13] You might think that the use of Latin would no longer be an issue. In a letter to the *Law Society Gazette*, one lawyer wrote worrying about the public's poor perception of lawyers and their profession and ended his letter with the words *'Quem Jupiter vult perdere dementat prius* – need I say more?', sparking correspondence from trainee solicitors who pointed out that they had no idea what this meant![14] And consider the following: *inter alia; prima facie; ad verbum; pro tem; ipso facto; per se; pari passu.* These phrases are still in relatively regular use in lawyers' correspondence. Why?

In part, it is the same tendency by which we tend to use Latinate words when we want a document to appear more formal: we expedite rather than hurry; we indicate rather than show; we donate rather than give. The use of more formal language signals a certain seriousness to the reader. But sometimes, too, it is simply intended as a signal

---

11 Otiose: unoccupied; indolent; functionless; futile; superfluous. Nugatory: trifling; worthless; inoperative; unavailing; futile. Both definitions again courtesy of *Chambers* (*op cit*, fn 9).

12 *R v National Insurance Commissioner ex p Secretary of State for Social Services*, R (A) 2/80 (Appendix), *per* Lord Denning.

13 *Re O and Others* (1998) unreported, 31 March, CA, *per* May LJ, quoted in (1998) 148 NLJ 1228.

14 (1998) 95 Law Soc Gazette 31.

of our own (comparative) status: doctors may have stethoscopes; we have our own language.

There may be times when Latin words or phrases are justified: *prima facie* seems to us a useful and relatively accessible phrase and we wouldn't normally object to it in a letter. But will your reader understand its strict legal meaning – in other words, that there is sufficient material to establish a proposition, subject to the production of contrary evidence? The problem is that *prima facie* can also mean 'at first glance'. So if you write to a client and say that '*Prima facie* I believe we have a case', it is not clear whether you simply mean that at first sight you think there is a case or that there is sufficient material to support a case.

Sometimes it is suggested that the best way of checking whether a Latinism has entered the English language is to look in an English dictionary. On this basis, *prima facie* is certainly an English term, but on the same page you can also find pricket, primage, prill, *prie-dieu* and pridian – all of which are causing the spell checker on this word processor to throw up its hands in despair.[15]

Words can be in an English dictionary and still be inappropriate for use in everyday writing. Similarly, words can be in everyday use in legal writing and conversation, but they may not be appropriate for use in communication outside the profession.

To boldly go: spelling and grammar

Throughout this section, the emphasis has been on communication as the central concern of any legal writing. So, at this stage, we could just tell you that spelling and grammar are important only to the extent that they help you to communicate effectively. If you can't spell, you may confuse your reader; worse, you may mislead your reader. If your grammar is defective, it may take the reader longer to work out what you are trying to say – they may even just give up. Or again, you may actively mislead your reader.

But spelling and grammar are not simply about the mechanics of communication. What you write and how you write it also sends out a message about what kind of person you are. This is why your clients will generally respect you more as a lawyer if they receive friendly and accessible letters, since these suggest that the writer must be similarly friendly and accessible. Getting your spelling and your grammar wrong doesn't simply impede your communication with your reader; it can send out a message that you are either ignorant, careless, or both.

The extent to which it sends out such a message depends on the prejudices of the recipient of the letter. So you might feel that a file note or a memorandum to a colleague would be unlikely to be contentious. But, from bitter experience, every lawyer will tell you that it is always those letters and notes that have a way of ending up included in affidavits and in formal court bundles and other public documents, where your inability to spell or to write a grammatical sentence will be revealed to the world.

---

15 Pricket: a fallow deer buck in his second year. Primage: a payment in addition to freight made by shippers for loading. Prill: to turn into pellet form. *Prie-dieu*: a praying-desk or chair. Pridian: pertaining to yesterday.

We're not arguing for a return to the full paraphernalia of grammatical rectitude; the convoluted language of which Churchill said: 'This is the sort of language up with which I will not put.' Customs have changed. It is not that standards have slipped, but that what is now 'standard' is not what was then 'standard'. It is probably no longer wrong to start a sentence with a conjunction (such as 'and', or 'but'). But don't make a habit of it. And every now and then a sentence without a verb may help to emphasise a particular point. But not too often. Remember that senior lawyers and businessmen are likely to remain influenced by the more formal standards of their own training. To them, your lapses will suggest that you are, at best, a careless lawyer. And their prejudices must be borne in mind.

Spelling

In these days of widespread word processing, bad spelling should be becoming a thing of the past. Where there is a spell checker on your computer, then (allowing for its tendency to want to spell everything the American way) there is no excuse for not using it. If you're not working from a computer (and even if you are), you must keep a dictionary to hand. There are only two steps you need to take in eradicating misspellings: the first is to recognise that there are words that you need to check in a dictionary; the second is to do it. And if, when you are in practice, you use a dictaphone, don't assume that the task of checking the material is the typist's. It isn't the typist's name at the bottom of a document; it's yours.

A misspelling may send out a message that you are ignorunt. Or ignorant even. Or it may simply suggest that you can't be bovered to chec your work. You must bother to check. Because the reader's eye is drawn to the mistake, the reader stops concentrating on the content of your letter. Your carefully planned legal advice is lost.

Spell it write. (And remember that there are some mistakes that even a spell checker won't spot for you!)

Grammar

> Most of the prescriptive rules of the language [experts] make no sense on any level. They are bits of folklore that originated for screwball reasons several hundred years ago and have perpetuated themselves ever since. For as long as they have existed, speakers have flouted them, spawning identical complaints about the imminent decline of the language century after century ... The rules conform neither to logic nor to tradition, and if they were ever followed they would force writers into fuzzy, clumsy, wordy, ambiguous, incomprehensible prose, in which certain thoughts are not expressible at all.[16]

The author of this quotation, Steven Pinker, is a professor at MIT, where he studies, among other things, the psychology of language. His view is that the rules we are taught to worry about (don't start sentences with 'But'; don't leave prepositions at the end of sentences; don't split infinitives) are artificial and irrelevant, and can be traced

---

16   Pinker, S, *The Language Instinct*, 1995, London: Penguin, p 373.

back to the etiquette books of the 18th century which were produced to help people to deal with their increased (and unprecedented) social mobility.

It is true that the most important grammatical rules are the ones that ensure that your communication is clear and free of ambiguity – in other words, that you are saying what you intend to say. The rules that help to ensure clarity are simple: keep sentences short; avoid a whole series of dependent clauses and phrases; make sure that your verb has a subject and, generally, an object. These points all relate to your writing style, but, if followed, they should help to give your writing a clarity and precision which come from the correct use of grammar.

But what about the traditional grammatical rules? Can you write to a client telling them 'to boldly go ahead with the purchase' or must you tell them 'boldly to go ahead' or 'to go ahead boldly'? Similarly, is it permissible to write that you are sending a contract 'for you to add your signature to', or must you write 'to which you should add your signature' in order to avoid ending the sentence with a preposition?

There is no single answer to this; much depends on what you think your reader's reaction will be. Margot Costanzo makes the excellent point that:

> The better rule is that the meaning of verbs is understood more readily when all parts of the verb and accompanying prepositions stay together.[17]

If you write that a client 'needs to quickly, but taking care not to overlook any important points, look through the documents', the reader has to make a mental effort to hold the verb 'to ... look through' open, while reading the adverbial clause 'quickly, but taking care not to overlook any important points', before returning to the original verb. It is no surprise that the sentence is easier to read if it is recast with the verb kept together: '... needs to look through the documents quickly, but taking care not to overlook any important points.'

There may be some readers who you suspect will be more upset by a split infinitive than by the rather forced construction you have to adopt to avoid one. Some readers may take such grave offence to a sentence ending in a preposition, that you need to turn the sentence around to avoid it. Communication is the purpose of writing, and, all things being equal, avoiding these arbitrary grammatical shibboleths will make your writing clearer. But, communication is also a social construct, and sometimes you will have to anticipate the prejudices of your reader. After all, if you are writing to a chambers for a pupillage or a firm for a training contract, you would go out of your way to make sure that your spelling and grammar were irreproachable, to try to make the best possible impression. The same has to apply to your legal writing in general.

Non-sexist language

The legal rule that the masculine includes the feminine may justify the use of the word 'he' throughout certain formal legal documents. This does not justify the rule's adoption in legal writing. The masculine does not include the feminine; if you write of the planned director of a company that 'he' must be able to do certain tasks, you are effectively creating or reflecting expectations.

---

17 *Op cit*, Costanzo, fn 1, p 73.

Is there an easy way of avoiding such traps? Consider the following extract from a letter:

> When you next speak to the purchasing manager at the company, he will need to be told that floating charges apply to his recent stock purchases from Milford and Sons.

You could avoid referring to the purchasing manager as 'he' by saying 'he or she', but this can seem very clumsy if you have to keep doing it throughout the letter. You may be able to recast the sentence: 'Floating charges apply to the recent stock purchases from Milford and Sons and you will need to tell the purchasing manager this.' In some books you will find 'he/she' or 's/he', but these are not normally used in legal letters.

One way round this problem which some writers adopt is to use the non-gender-specific 'they'; thus, the sentence would become:

> When you next speak to the purchasing manager at the company, they will need to be told that floating charges apply to their recent stock purchases from Milford and Sons.

This is an extension of the modern tendency to say 'If *anyone* rings me, tell *them* to ...' (rather than 'tell *him* to ...'). Grammarians argue that a single antecedent cannot be followed by a plural pronoun. This is arguable in the case of words such as 'anyone' or 'everyone' – try using the word 'him' in the following sentence: 'I talked to everyone in the room before the police took statements from them.' However, most readers would still probably regard the combination of 'the purchasing manager' and 'they' as being a grammatical lapse rather than an acceptable attempt to use a gender-neutral pronoun. In your legal writing, be aware that 'he' and 'his' do not normally indicate 'she' or 'hers'; try to avoid gender-specific terms, unless you intend them; but also bear in mind that there will be some readers for whom 'Chair' remains a piece of furniture and 'Chairman' the acceptable usage. Remember that, for years after her promotion to the Court of Appeal, Elizabeth Butler-Sloss had to be addressed as Lord Justice Butler-Sloss, simply because there had never been a Lady Justice!

PRESENTATION: MAKING IT LOOK EASY

We have looked at some of the key principles of planning and plain English. The final element of the writing process, however, can easily be overlooked. Yet, presentation is going to be the first aspect of your writing which the reader notices. Is the page covered with a single unending paragraph, the words densely packed together, the sentences riddled with commas and semi-colons? Is the print small and hard to read? Are there any clues as to how the material is organised – which part deals with which problem?

A page of unbroken text is deeply off-putting, and customs in writing have changed so that we tend to set out material in shorter, more compact paragraphs. It is no longer unacceptable to use headings and other forms of signposting in your writing. These changes are reflected even in the presentation of decisions from the higher courts.

Contrast the following two extracts. The first is from *Gorris v Scott*,[18] where the Court of Exchequer is deciding whether damages arose for breach of a statute requiring sheep to be kept in pens while on a ship; the sheep had not been kept in pens and had

---

18   (1874) LR 9 Exch 125.

been swept overboard as a result. However, as Piggott B explained, protecting the sheep from this fate was not the purpose of the statute:

> For the reasons which have been so exhaustively stated by the Lord Chief Baron, I am of opinion that the declaration shews no cause of action. It is necessary to see what was the object of the legislature in this enactment, and it is set forth clearly in the preamble as being 'to prevent the introduction into Great Britain of contagious diseases among cattle, sheep, or other animals', and the 'spread of such diseases in Great Britain'. The purposes enumerated in s 75 are in harmony with this preamble, and it is in furtherance of that section that the order in question was made. The object, then, of the regulations which have been broken was, not to prevent cattle from being washed overboard, but to protect them against contagious disease. The legislature never contemplated altering the relations between the owners and carriers of cattle, except for the purposes pointed out in the Act; and if the Privy Council had gone out of their way and made provisions to prevent cattle from being washed overboard, their act would have been *ultra vires*. If, indeed, by reason of the neglect complained of, the cattle had contracted a contagious disease, the case would have been different. But as the case stands on this declaration, the answer to the action is this: Admit there has been a breach of duty; admit there has been a consequent injury; still the legislature was not legislating to protect against such an injury, but for an altogether different purpose; its object was not to regulate the duty of the carrier for all purposes, but only for one particular purpose.

What is the effect of the presentation of this extract? The content is not especially challenging, but how could the material itself be made more approachable? Would you have found it easier to read if it had been divided into shorter paragraphs, or if Piggott B had been writing his decision at a time when the use of subject headings was appropriate in such legal writing?

In contrast, consider the following extract from the (dissenting) decision of Mummery LJ in the Court of Appeal, dealing with the question of whether Miss Plant, who had survived a suicide pact, could benefit under the will of the other party, Mr Dunbar, who had not been so lucky:

> I conclude that the appeal should be dismissed on this point for the following reasons:
>
> (1) The starting point is the application of the forfeiture rule as a rule of public policy, without regard to whether the consequences flowing from the application of the rule are just or unjust. The discretion introduced by s 2 [Forfeiture Act 1982] is intended to be exercised to modify the consequences of the application of the rule and to produce a result which the justice of the case requires.
>
> (2) One of the material circumstances is that the conduct of Miss Plant was unlawful. She committed a criminal offence which resulted in death. It is difficult to adjudicate on the relative moral culpability of her and Mr Dunbar. Mr Crichton-Gold submitted that she was more morally culpable since it was she who first brought up the question of suicide, leading Mr Dunbar to enter into the pact under which they would both commit suicide. I see the force of that point, but the pact which they made and the relationship between them was such that I find it impossible to adjudicate on the issue of relative moral culpability.
>
> (3) The intention of Mr Dunbar was rightly regarded by the judge as material. Joint beneficial ownership of the house and the fact that the life policy was written for the benefit of Miss Plant, show that his intention was that she, rather than anyone else, should have that property on his death. The intention fact is not, however, determinative of the justice of the case, which must take account of the circumstances in which that intention takes effect. Miss Plant was criminally

implicated in the death which attracts the application of the forfeiture rule and gives rise to the discretion to redirect the destination of the property. Mr Dunbar's intentions must be considered in that context.

(4) The wishes of the father and family of Mr Dunbar are material and should be given weight ... They have a legitimate interest in a decision on the scope of the modification order. Justice requires due weight to be given to their wishes.[19]

Note how the combination of short paragraphs and the use of numbered points helps to organise the material. The facts of the case are far from clear cut, and the legal issues are similarly confused. By summarising the reasons for his decision point by point, Mummery LJ is able to show clearly the different weight he has given to each consideration. The reader is able to follow his reasoning without difficulty.

If this can be done with such brevity and clarity in a Court of Appeal decision in a complex and emotionally charged case, the presentational principles should not be impossible to apply in everyday legal writing. What, then, are the guiding principles of clear and effective presentation in your writing?

Keep it short: sentence length in legal writing

Longer sentences are more taxing to read, as they will tend to contain more information, and that information will need to be organised into clauses, and sub-clauses; some may be linked by punctuation dividers like semi-colons (which at least indicate a pause for the reader), but commas (a much lighter pause) are more frequently used, with brackets and other forms of parentheses – such as dashes – being used to try and break up the flow of material, and, while there is no reason why a long sentence should not be understandable to any reader, most people find it easier to deal with sentences which contain only a single point, and where different subjects are signalled by new sentences, or even new paragraphs, although this stylistic development (along with the use of shorter paragraphs) is very much a development of the second half of the 20th century, and does not reflect the writing and drafting, especially by lawyers, in previous generations.

The previous sentence (and paragraph) contains 160 words. With the use of appropriate punctuation, it is possible to write lengthy sentences and still preserve clarity. However, it is not easy to do so, and such sentences are not easy to read.

It is also possible to write using very short sentences. Few sentences need to be longer than 15 words. If you have a second point which you want to make, you start a second sentence. However, it can get very repetitive. Your writing can become very staccato. You need to be able to recognise the advantages of short sentences. You also need to be able to recognise when they become monotonous and confusing.

Average sentence length in newspapers varies between 23 and 29 words,[20] with the so called 'red top' tabloids, like *The Sun* and *The Mirror*, considerably below this. While legal writing has a wholly different context from newspaper journalism, the underlying need for clarity and accessibility applies equally to both. Sentence length should be used as a general indication, and not an end in itself. If your sentences are consistently long, you are likely to be linking different points within the sentence. The more links

---

19 *Dunbar v Plant* [1997] 4 All ER 289, p 303.
20 See Rylance, P, *Legal Writing and Drafting*, 1994, London: Blackstone.

that there are within a sentence, the greater the likelihood of ambiguity or lack of clarity creeping in.

How can you keep your sentences short?

First, you must check your work. It is easy for longer sentences to creep into your writing without your noticing. If you find that you have written a sentence which is longer than you intended, then you will need to edit it. The easiest way of shortening a sentence is to remove any excess words. The other simple way of reducing sentence length is to remove conjunctions (joining words, such as 'and' and 'but') and to split one sentence into two separate sentences.

In the following sentence the excess words and the conjunctions have been italicised:

> *I would be grateful if you could* please read the *enclosed* documents and then return them to me, *having* signed *them* at the bottom with at least two witnesses present *in the room with you* at the same time, although those witnesses need not *actually* read the documents.

And the sentence can be effectively recast:

> Please read these documents. They should be signed by you at the bottom. At least two witnesses must be present when you sign the documents. However, the witnesses need not read the documents. Please return the signed documents to me.

The first sentence is 48 words long. The second version is still 40 words long, but this is spread out over four sentences. Because sentence beginnings and endings are points of emphasis in a text, the second version gives specific emphasis to many of the points. But, because of this, too many very short sentences can lead to a letter where everything seems to be emphasised, which is rather like writing where everything is underlined or put in bold: it is hard to read.

But what if you have a sentence which needs to contain a large amount of information?

The most common reason why this will occur is that you are listing information within the sentence. Thus, for example:

> The 1991 Practice Direction makes clear that some particular types of case, such as professional negligence actions, fatal accident cases, cases involving fraud and undue influence, defamation actions, malicious prosecution and false imprisonment actions, and cases involving claims against the police, will be considered important and may therefore be tried in the High Court.

In sentences involving lists, always consider whether the material is better set out as a list, rather than being contained in the body of the text.

> The 1991 Practice Direction makes clear that certain categories of case will be considered important and can properly be tried in the High Court. These categories include:
>
> (a) professional negligence actions;
>
> (b) fatal accident cases;
>
> (c) cases involving fraud and undue influence;
>
> (d) defamation actions;
>
> (e) malicious prosecution and false imprisonment actions; and
>
> (f) cases involving claims against the police.

Lists are valuable presentational aids, which help the reader to see information at a glance, without getting bogged down in long, complex sentences.

One point per paragraph? Keeping your paragraphs short

In the extracts from *Gorris v Scott* and *Dunbar v Plant* above, we have seen how the use of paragraphs to break up the flow of text can not only help the reader by identifying the different elements of an argument, but can also make the text appear less daunting to a reader by breaking down the material into more digestible sections.

Are paragraphs, then, simply a visual aid, a way of making your writing seem easier to read, or is there an underlying purpose to paragraphs?

In *Legal Writing*, Margot Costanzo suggests five basic principles for the effective use of paragraphs:

(a) a paragraph should normally contain more than one sentence;

(b) a paragraph should normally contain a sentence indicating the subject of the paragraph, and often this sentence will be placed at the beginning of the paragraph;

(c) a paragraph should have 'unity of subject matter'; it should deal with only one topic, or one aspect of a topic;

(d) a paragraph must have a clear internal structure;

(e) a paragraph may need internal signposting words (therefore, however, on the other hand) to show the relationship between propositions.

Treat these principles as guidelines, rather than rigid rules. If you follow them, you will find that you are using paragraphs effectively as signposts for different parts of the legal content; they will help you to visualise the structure of your communication. But don't feel that you have to follow the principles on every occasion; there are always exceptions.

One sentence paragraphs can give impact to a point that you want to make.

But don't overdo them.

Point by point: using headings in your writing

Most writers seem to feel that headings are out of place in less formal communications, and certainly in letters.

Dear Aunt Mavis

Re: Your Christmas gift

I am writing to thank you for the present which I received on Christmas Day.

Contents of the present

The present was a bright orange scarf. The scarf was some five feet long. It has lime green tassels and the motif: Lawyers Do It In Court.

Reactions to the gift

I was, of course, delighted to receive this attractive and useful item of clothing. I can imagine that it will add considerable impact to my appearance when I wear it to court. As undoubtedly I will.

Future action

etc, etc.

Obviously, headings are inappropriate in ordinary personal letter writing. However, they are an essential tool in legal writing, and in all but the shortest letters you should consider whether to use headings to divide up the points and to guide the reader. In any letter, headings offer a valuable reassurance to your reader. Headings are of particular use where the reader may want to come back to a particular point to make sure that they understand it.

But do you have to use headings? Couldn't you just use short paragraphs instead?

Use of paragraphs helps to break up both the text and the legal content into its constituent elements. The use of headings, however, can signpost the particular issue or issues which the writer is dealing with at any given point. For this reason, it is often a good idea in a letter of advice to couch the headings as questions: 'Can new shares be issued without the agreement of all current shareholders?'; 'How can you call an Emergency General Meeting?'; 'What steps do you need to take to register the transaction?'; and so forth. As Margot Costanzo points out:

> Have you ever watched an audience's reaction to a speaker's question? The eyes unglaze, the shoulders square, legs uncross and attention is re-focused on the speaker. This technique works with the written word, too.

> One of the tenets of Plain English drafting is to use headings in the form of questions. Readers come to the text with questions, seeking answers. If the writer poses the questions that the reader has in mind, then the reader will be able to find the answers more quickly.[21]

For an excellent example of how a combination of headings and lists can help to clarify even the most complex legal argument, you may like to look at the case of *S-T (Formerly J) v J* [1998] 1 All ER 431. In this case, the Court of Appeal is being asked to decide whether the defendant can claim ancillary relief (maintenance) following the breakdown of her marriage. The problem is that the defendant is a transsexual who was born a woman but subsequently 'married' another woman without revealing her original gender. The fact that the defendant was not originally male apparently only became known 17 years later, while the divorce proceedings were in hand, causing considerable shock and distress to all concerned. The result was that the marriage was declared a nullity and the defendant's application for ancillary relief was refused. The defendant appealed against this decision to the Court of Appeal.

The leading judgment is that of Ward LJ, who handed down a 35 page decision, in which he makes full use of headings and lists in order to separate the many novel issues which the court was being asked to address. The headings clearly show how the legal argument is structured and presented:

The Facts

The Preliminary Issue Defined

The Judgment [of the High Court, divided into points 1–7]

The Appeal

(1) Transsexuals and the matrimonial law

(2) The medical condition of transsexualism and its effect on the defendant's state of mind

---

21 *Op cit*, Costanzo, fn 1, p 82.

(3) Was the crime of perjury committed by the defendant?

(4) What was the gravity of his offence and of his conduct in general?

    (a) The gravity of the offence

    (b) The gravity of the defendant's conduct generally

(5) Does perjury debar the defendant's claim on public policy grounds?

    (a) The rule of public policy

    (b) *Whiston v Whiston* (1995)

    (c) Does this rule that no one shall be allowed profit from his crime apply to this perjury?

    (d) Conclusion

(6) Does a wider rule of public policy apply to debar this claim because *ex turpi causa non oritur actio*?[22]

    (a) The basis of the *ex turpi* principle

    (b) The object matter of the public policy protection

    (c) The essence of marriage

    (d) Is the defendant's conduct injurious to this notion of marriage?

Conclusion

(7) Should the claim be dismissed in the exercise of the court's wide statutory discretion under s 25 of the Matrimonial Causes Act 1973?

Note, also, the different impact of those headings which pose questions. They are more than simple signposts; they actively engage the reader in the discussion.

Pauses and longer pauses: punctuating your legal writing

If you try to use short sentences, punctuation will look after itself. Provided, of course, that you remember the very basic principle that a sentence will start with a capital letter and end with a full stop. A sentence must also contain a verb. Normally. It will also, generally, contain a subject; even the sentence 'Thank you' is, in fact, an abbreviation of 'I thank you', and, as such, contains subject, verb and object.

But unrelieved short sentences make for monotonous, and confusing, reading. We are aiming for clarity in legal writing, but an unbroken sequence of short sentences can simply lead to too much emphasis within the writing; the effect can be to obscure clarity. When we speak, we pause: when we write, we use punctuation. The conventions of punctuation tend to reflect this basic principle.

Commas and full stops

If you look at the previous two sentences, you will find some of the general principles illustrated (including the use of colons and semi-colons). Commas are used for a light pause or to serve as a form of parenthesis (bracket) in the writing. Thus, in the sentence, 'But unrelieved short sentences make for monotonous, and confusing, reading', the

---

22 In case you have not yet studied this area of law, it is worth noting that *ex turpi causa non oritur actio* is the legal principle that a wrongdoer should not benefit from his or her wrongdoing, rather than a gratuitous Latin tag from Ward LJ.

commas serve to mark 'and confusing' as an aside. Similarly, it is sometimes said that certain words at the start of sentences, such as 'however', 'although', and even 'similarly', must have a comma to follow them; but this is better thought of as simply indicating the natural pause which you would have in your voice if you spoke the sentence. The comma is a pause; the full stop indicates a stop, marking off the next sentence. If you only used commas and full stops, you would still be able to write clearly and effectively.

Problems arise with both commas and full stops when they are misused. Consider the following two examples:

> You must ensure that any additional papers are attached to your script with the treasury tags which have been provided, if your paper is not attached, it may be lost.

> At the end of the exam you must lay down your pens. Having stopped writing at the invigilator's instruction.

In the first example, there needs to be a full stop rather than a comma after the word 'provided', as the following words move on to a new topic and constitute a sentence in their own right. (You could use a semi-colon if you wished to preserve the link between the two sentences; we will look at this in the paragraphs below.)

In the second example, there is a full stop after 'pens' and there should be a comma. The following sentence, 'Having stopped writing at the invigilator's instruction', is incomplete, as it has no subject or main verb. In order to make it a satisfactory sentence, you would have to add these: 'You must have stopped writing ... etc.' This second example is more common in students' writing than the first. It is as if the writer feels that the sentence is too long, and so has simply ended it by inserting a full stop, but without then considering if the second part of the sentence can properly stand alone.

The other common problem, especially in legal writing, is the overuse of commas:

> When we arrive at the police station, having met earlier in my office, I will ask for the custody sergeant, who will be responsible for ensuring your rights, as laid down by Parliament, are not breached, and I will report, assuming that you are in agreement with this, that you have answered your bail, as, indeed, you are required to do, but that you do not intend, on present instructions at any rate, to co-operate further, at least on a voluntary basis, with police inquiries.

It is not that the use of commas is incorrect; it is simply that they make the sentence unreadable. There are just too many commas, and it is hard for the reader to know which indicate pauses, and which are parentheses, containing little asides. The problem is not, fundamentally, one of punctuation; it is a question of organisation. The writer is writing as he or she might speak, but on the page it is confusing. If the material is more formally organised, the sense becomes more apparent:

> Your present instructions are that you are not prepared to continue to co-operate with the police, at least on a voluntary basis. You must answer your bail by attending the police station. We will meet first in my office and will go to the police station. There I will speak to the custody officer, whose role is to ensure that your rights are not breached, and I will explain the situation.

Note that we have continued to use some commas, but we have reorganised the material so that it flows in a more logical sequence. The effect is that it can now be broken down into sentences. The meaning is somewhat clearer.

Colons and semi-colons

Colons and semi-colons represent slightly different pauses to the comma. Colons are used in particular for creating a break before a list, but are also used before a quotation. More exceptionally, a colon may be used in what is sometimes referred to as 'balancing halves', as in the sentence we used earlier in this section:

When we speak, we pause: when we write, we use punctuation.

Semi-colons may be used where you could otherwise use a conjunction (such as 'and' or 'but'); they are more final than a comma, but preserve the link between what would otherwise be two separate sentences. Use them with caution for this purpose, as it can make for a long sentence.

Semi-colons are also frequently used where you have a list containing long phrases. It is easy to list short things using a comma, as in the following list: bread, butter, milk, orange juice and carrots.

This list becomes unwieldy if the items in the list are slightly longer: wholegrained or granary-style bread, but not white bread; Cornish butter, but it must be unsalted; milk, provided that it is semi-skimmed; fresh pasteurised California or Florida orange juice; and carrots, but they must be organic. Note how semi-colons provide a clearer break between the items.

Colons and semi-colons are extremely useful and can give variety to the rhythm of your writing. But don't get obsessed with them; correct use of commas and full stops is more important.

'Potatoes'' and 'his's': correct use of apostrophes

Apostrophes are something that almost everyone gets wrong from time to time. But just as the word 'Hopefully', as in 'Hopefully, I will see you', can give some people high blood pressure, so the misuse of apostrophes is treated by some readers as a sign that you are probably ignorant and certainly careless.

An apostrophe signals the possessive. It is a short way of saying 'of':

'Richard's pen', or, alternatively, 'the pen of Richard'.

'The woman's bag', or, 'the bag of the woman'.

'Women's Rights', or, 'the Rights of Women'.

Where the word is plural and there is already an 's' on the end, adding another 's' would sound unwieldy. In this case, an apostrophe alone is used:

'Three dogs' kennels', or, 'the kennels of three dogs'.

'Five hundred potatoes' fate', or, 'the fate of five hundred potatoes'.

This only applies where the plural ends in 's'; hence:

Three children's food.

If you are faced with a name – such as Jones – which ends in an 's', you have a choice:

The Jones's car.

The Jones' car.

The latter is the more modern usage; but neither is incorrect.

Apostrophes are also used to signal elisions in words: can't, don't, won't, haven't. Here the apostrophe is being used to signal the missing letter or letters.

Possessive pronouns – his, her, mine, your, our – do not need an apostrophe, as they are already possessives. You can tell this, since you cannot replace them with 'of':

'His car', but not, 'the car of his'.

'Our potato', but not, 'the potato of our'.

It's/its

The classic mistake which writers make arises from the fact that we have two almost identical words in English: 'its' and 'it's'.

'Its' is a possessive already: you can say: 'Its tail is long', but it makes no sense to say: 'The tail of its is long.' On the other hand, 'it's' is a contraction of 'it is', with the apostrophe signalling the missing vowel.

It is, therefore, very easy to make sure that you are using the right word: if you can recast the word as 'it is', then the spelling must be 'it's', with the apostrophe indicating the missing vowel. When it makes no sense to say 'it is' – as in the sentence 'It is tail is long' – it is clear that the possessive 'its' is the correct word.

Some day, people will cease to treat the misuse of the apostrophe as a sign of ignorance, but for now, you must make sure that you use it correctly.

CONCLUSION

This chapter has focused on the basic principles of legal writing. We have looked at the preparation process, the elements of plain English writing, and the related presentation skills. Whether your reader is a lay client, another lawyer or the court itself, these principles will ensure that what you write is precise, clear and accessible. What we now need to consider is how these principles can be applied to the different areas of legal writing which you may encounter in practice, and on which you may be assessed while a student.

FURTHER READING

Costanzo, M, *Legal Writing*, 1993, London: Cavendish Publishing.

Minto, B, *The Pyramid Principle: Logic in Writing and Thinking*, 1981, London: Minto International.

Minto, B, *The Pyramid Principle*, 3rd edn, 1991, London: Pitman.

Pinker, S, *The Language Instinct*, 1995, London: Penguin.

Rylance, P, *Legal Writing and Drafting*, 1994, London: Blackstone.

CHAPTER 2

LEGAL WRITING: APPLYING WRITING SKILLS – LETTERS, MEMORANDA, BRIEFS, ATTENDANCE NOTES, REPORTS

INTRODUCTION

In the previous chapter, we looked at the basic principles of legal writing – preparation, plain English and presentation. In this chapter, we look at the different areas of legal writing, and outline their conventions, any legal or commercial requirements, and the particular issues that may arise in putting into practice the general principles of clarity, precision and accessibility.

You may be writing for any number of different purposes. You may be writing letters that are intended to advise, or to request, to notify or to negotiate. You may be drafting a document such as an attendance note, which is designed purely as a record of steps taken in an action, or a memorandum, which is intended to communicate information in a public way, often to more than one recipient. You may be involved in more formal writing, such as the drafting of a brief to counsel. All of these will have their own requirements.

Sometimes, the requirements may be simply conventions – how people should be addressed, how a communication should be laid out, how it should be signed (if at all). Often, there may be legal requirements – such as the basic client care and costs information which solicitors are required to communicate to their clients in writing and at a preliminary stage in the retainer.[1] Letters before action – that is, the letters which a lawyer will send to warn a person that they are likely to be subject to legal action – must be drafted with certain formal 'protocols' in mind, which lay down what information the other party should be given, and how long they should be allowed in order to decide what action they will take before proceedings are issued. For barristers, communications that contain legal advice to a professional or lay client will often be couched in the very formal language and layout of an advice or opinion, and because of their formality, these are considered separately in this book.

This chapter, therefore, begins by considering the basic conventions which govern letter writing. Then, since few things are ever perfect at first attempt, this chapter considers how you can best use the drafting process to organise and to perfect your writing. The various kinds of legal writing are then considered in turn.

---

1 Solicitors' Client Care and Costs Information Code, and Solicitors' Practice Rules, r 15. The details of these requirements are discussed later in the chapter.

DEAR SIR OR MADAM: THE CONVENTIONS OF LETTER WRITING

Everyone is expected to know how to write formal letters, and yet few people are ever formally taught how to do so. This short section outlines the basic conventions of formal letter writing.

Salutations and closings

Letters that begin 'Dear Sir' or 'Dear Madam' will end 'Yours faithfully'. You may be writing to 'Dear Sir' because you do not know who the person is, or because, although you know their name, you wish to maintain a high degree of formality in the letter.

Letters that open with a person's name, 'Dear Mr Brown' or 'Dear David', will end 'Yours sincerely'. Obviously, your own clients should normally be addressed by name. It would be unusual to address a client by his or her first name at an early stage in your acquaintance, but this may become appropriate.

Letters to a firm or business will often start 'Dear Sirs'. Again, these should conclude 'Yours faithfully'.

Make sure that the closing is consistent with the letter writer: if you have written as 'I', then sign the letter personally and type your name beneath the signature; if the letter has been written as 'we', sign the letter in the firm's name. (Remember not to mix 'I' and 'we' in the text of the letter unless you mean to do so.)

Headings

Almost all legal letters should have a heading at the beginning. Traditionally, this would start 'Re: ...', but this is no longer widespread. The heading should enable the reader to identify the matter. Thus, headings in conveyancing cases may state the names of the buyer and seller (for example, Pepper to Hart: Sale of 29 The Gables) and litigation matters may state the name of the case (*Pepper v Hart*). A letter to a client may be less formal (Re: Your party wall dispute).

As we discussed in the previous chapter, you should consider using headings to guide the reader through a letter, especially if it is a long or otherwise complex letter. Remember that headings which are couched as questions – 'What action should you take?' – are often an effective way of keeping your reader's attention.

References and other headings

Most legal letters will need to contain your reference number, so that the writer and the case file can be traced quickly. Where you are responding to another formal letter, you should check to see if this also has a reference number. If it does, you will need to include:

Your reference ...

Our reference ...

These will normally be set out at the start of the letter, before the date and any salutations.

Similarly, you should also include such headings as 'private and confidential', 'by facsimile only', and 'without prejudice', at this initial point in the letter.

An opening paragraph?

Remember that opening and closing paragraphs will give your letter greater clarity:

> Thank you for your telephone call on 2 September. I am now writing to confirm our discussion.

> Thank you for your letter of 15 September. You ask whether you are entitled to pull down your neighbour's fence.

Please avoid 'traditional' practice (for example, 'Further to your letter of 15th ult'.). Indeed, in many letters – for example, letters to regular business clients – it is normally better to get straight to the point.

Enclosures?

It is normal practice to indicate that there is an enclosure by putting the word 'Enclosure' or abbreviation 'Encl' at the bottom of the letter, beneath the signature. Similarly, if the letter is being copied to anyone else, the abbreviation 'cc' (carbon copy) followed by the names of the recipients is normally included.

Formalities with email?

Email has only relatively recently developed into a widespread means of communication. It has therefore not built up the traditions and formalities of other forms of writing. Indeed, it was initially the case that email was seen as a particularly informal means of communication – so that concerns about spelling and grammar were out of place. Now that you may be using email as a means of formal communication, it makes sense to apply those conventions from letter writing that seem to make sense in this context. You may well find that your firm has an email style policy, but if not, make sure that you adjust the level of formality so that it is appropriate to the recipient.

Above all with email, do remember that although it is a quick means of communication, this does not mean that it is an impermanent one. Copies of your email will remain on your computer, on various servers and on the recipient's computer, and will be capable of being recovered long after the original communication.

IF AT FIRST YOU DON'T SUCCEED … : THE DRAFTING PROCESS

Drafting does not occur in a vacuum. It is part of the legal process which may already have required you to interview and to advise, to undertake advocacy or negotiation, and, above all, to use your powers of fact analysis and legal research. All of these legal skills are considered elsewhere in this book, but the fact remains that almost any piece of legal writing will be the implementation of the analysis and legal research that you have already undertaken. Before you can write a letter to advise a client that they are entitled to return a defective motor car, you will have needed first to analyse the facts of the client's problem, and then to identify and apply the relevant law. Before you can write a memorandum to colleagues to outline new procedures for dealing with conditional fee agreements in personal injury cases, you are going to have researched and analysed how the developments in the funding of such cases will apply to your firm's workload.

Even the most routine letter has its basis in preparatory analysis:

Thank you for your letter of 16 September, receipt of which is acknowledged.

In order to send the letter, you must have read the previous letter and have decided that no more than a mere acknowledgment was required, or that a more detailed response could afford to wait until further steps were taken. In order to make the decision, you need to know the facts of the case and to have considered its likely legal development.

Our point is this: drafting occurs in a particular context, the context of the case concerned. You will invariably be drafting with the product of your research and your fact analysis of the matter to hand. Drafting, therefore, consists of the organisation of this material into a format which is most accessible to the recipient and which most effectively meets the recipient's needs.

What do you need to know? Starting your drafting

By the drafting stage, you should be able to organise your research and analysis so that you are able to answer the two initial questions which will open and close your draft:

(a) Opening: why am I writing?

(b) Closing: what happens next?

Thus, you may be writing in response to a letter from your client asking for advice:

Opening: why am I writing?

Thank you for your letter of 26 February. You ask whether there is any way to compel your colleague to comply with your agreement to share any winnings from the National Lottery.

Closing: what happens next?

If you let me have a copy of your written agreement, I will then be in a position to look into the matter and to advise you in more detail. Please contact me with the agreement as soon as possible.

Alternatively, you may be responding to a 'without prejudice' discussion with the other party in a dispute:

Opening: why am I writing?

I am writing to confirm our conversation at court this morning in which you suggested that the case could be settled by an undertaking from your client and the payment of agreed costs.

Closing: what happens next?

Please confirm that the proposals set out above are acceptable to your client. If I do not hear from you within 14 days of the date of this letter, I will ask for the matter to be set down for trial in order to avoid any further delays.

These opening and closing paragraphs will then determine the remaining content of the letter.

What goes in the middle?

Start by listing all the points that you need to cover. There may be a lengthy series of points that you want to make, or only a few. The points may all relate to a single issue – for example, the basic contract law which will underlie any agreement to share lottery winnings – or may cover a large number of different areas. Once you have made the list, however, pause before you start to organise the material. Look at the points again and remind yourself why you are writing: what was it that this letter needed to communicate? Often, you will find that some of the material which you have listed may be relevant, but is not necessary. You may well need to consider the case law on offer – acceptance and privity of contract in the lottery winnings case – but your client may not need chapter and verse about each principle. So, check the points, and remove any that are not necessary.

The next stage is to categorise – in other words, to collect together those points which logically belong together. Often, this is the stage when you will be able to allocate headings to each separate group of points.

In the previous chapter, we discussed the 'pyramid principle', the general organisational principle that you should move from the general to the specific. This is a particularly useful mechanism for working out the order in which you will put the information in the central part of the letter. Where the information follows a more logical structure, however, such as chronological order, you will find it easier to take advantage of this way of structuring the material.

An example: the lottery inquiry

James is a member of an informal lottery syndicate at work. Each person chips in £1 per week. A member of the syndicate, normally Richard, buys the tickets on Friday evening. The numbers are based on the birthdays of all the different members of the group. Since the group started, two years ago, various members have come and gone. James admits that he often forgets to pay the £1, but tells you that he always pays his arrears whenever Richard asks him for the money. Last week, one of the tickets won £120,000. Richard has told James that only the people who paid for the ticket will share the winnings. James has rung you for advice. He has told you that there is – or was – a written agreement.

Why are you writing?

You know that you need to see the written agreement. This letter is to confirm your initial telephone advice and to remind James to bring the agreement when he comes to see you.

Initial list of points

You start by literally organising your thoughts. You jot down all the various points that occur to you:

- written agreement;
- question of contract;

- who are the parties to the contract?;
- offer and acceptance;
- consideration?;
- intent to be legally binding?;
- verbal terms of agreement;
- variation of the agreement – he paid late?;
- what was agreed about the arrears?;
- what verbal agreement was made?;
- is there any evidence of the payment?

You then start to organise your thoughts. You strike out 'offer and acceptance' and 'consideration': these are certainly all basic contractual principles, but no particular problems seem to arise in relation to them at this point. You therefore decide that you don't need to bother James with them; you are, after all, writing a letter rather than an essay. Similarly, you decide that there is unlikely to be any real issue over whether the agreement was intended to be legally binding: they have gone to the trouble of writing everything down, and it seems likely at this stage that this will not be an issue.

The issue of who is a party to the contract is going to be interesting. You know that the membership of the syndicate has changed over time. Certainly James' argument is that he is still a member, even though he pays his subscription late. You will need to know, however, who the people are who are going to be sharing out the winnings. You will need to ask James to find this out, and to bring the information with him when he comes to see you.

As to whether James is still a member of the syndicate, most of the second half of the list relates directly to this issue. Presumably the syndicate are saying that James is not a member because he did not pay his money on time. James' argument sounds as if it will be that, whatever the written agreement says, there has been a variation (either orally or by conduct), which is evidenced by his having continued to make his payments, albeit in arrears, whenever requested. All these issues can probably be grouped together.

Organising the material

This is a letter where headings will help. Rather than drafting out the whole letter, we have simply set out the headings below. You should be able to see from these how this letter progresses.

Dear James,

Your dispute with the lottery syndicate

Thank you for your letter of 26 February. You ask whether there is any way to compel your colleagues to comply with your agreement to share any winnings from the National Lottery.

The history of the 'syndicate' ...

Was there a legally binding agreement to share any lottery money? ...

What is the effect of your paying your share late? ...

What further information do we need? ...

What happens now?

If you let me have a copy of your written agreement, I will then be in a position to look into the matter and to advise you in more detail. Please contact me with the agreement as soon as possible.

Yours sincerely,

Did I say that? Reviewing your work

You have written your letter, memorandum, report. Now you need to ensure that it achieves the purpose for which it was drafted. Good preparation will help you to prepare a clear and well organised piece of writing, but it will not, of itself, ensure that the writing is error free, and equally importantly, that it is free from ambiguity: in other words, that the writing will communicate exactly what you wish it to communicate. Every piece of writing needs to be checked. Indeed, the more time pressure you are under, the more likely it is that the work will need to be reviewed.

Is it legally accurate?

In some ways, this is the most straightforward part of the review process. What is the problem? What advice, if any, have you given the client? If you have done your research effectively, you should feel confident that this is a question you can answer: Yes.

Is it clear why you are writing?

Start at the beginning. Is it clear to the recipient why you have written? Is there a clear opening paragraph which sets the scene and tells the reader why he or she needs to read the letter and what the reader should be looking for?

Is it clear what you are saying?

Scan the headings – if you have used headings. Are they in a logical order? Do they tell the reader what issues are dealt with in each part?

Within each section, is it clear what the factual and legal position is? Is it clear what issues arise from this? Ambiguity may arise where you fail to separate out the issues:

> Depending on who the parties to the agreement are, it may be possible for you to sue for breach of contract.

This is unclear, because it is conflating a number of different concerns: has James ceased to be a party because he has failed to pay his contribution on time? Is there a contract between James and all the other 'winners' on the syndicate? Who are the members of the syndicate at this point in time?

Alternatively, ambiguity may arise simply because the drafting is unclear:

> Please bring with you the various clauses of the contract, and the names of the members of the syndicate, as we will need to see what they say about the late payment of the contributions.

Here, it is not clear whether the writer means that we will need to see what the clauses say about late payment, or what the members of the syndicate say about it. The sentence needs re-drafting to deal with one matter at a time.

What happens next?

Does the final section of the letter make clear what the writer expects to happen next? As we suggested in the previous chapter, even where you are sending a letter 'for information only' to a client – a very valuable way of ensuring your client continues to feel involved in the progress of the case – it is always worth making clear that your client is not required to do anything. Where you are expecting your client to provide information or to take action on the case, remind your client of this at the close of the letter. If there are a large number of tasks to be done, use a numbered list, so that your client can use it as a checklist. If you are asking for something to be done, have you made clear what the timescale is?

What do you think? Peer review

Your colleagues at work are not going to thank you if you ask them to read all the material that you write. However, there is no better way to check that your communication is clear than to pass it to a third party for them to check. It is human nature that, where you have drafted the material yourself, you are less likely to spot errors, omissions and ambiguities than a dispassionate reader. Alternatively, try to put the material to one side, even if only for a short period; do something else; and then review your writing again with a fresh eye.

RULES OF CLIENT CARE

The principles above govern all writing. However, some of the letters that you write will have a prescribed content. In this section, we touch on the formal rules governing client care which must be observed by all solicitors. The principles which they impose are of value for all lawyers. In the next section, we will look briefly at the principles laid down by the Civil Procedure Rules 1998 (CPR) which must be applied whenever you are writing a letter before action.

Why are there rules of client care?

Both solicitors and barristers are members of professions. One of the features of a profession, as opposed to other types of employment, is that professions tend to be self-governing and will generally be subject to a code of conduct which requires professionals to put their client's needs above their own. In the past, there was perhaps a degree of deference to lawyers, which meant that their clients were loath to challenge the service that they received. This is an attitude which has changed very greatly during the last 20 years, and the volume of complaints against solicitors has swelled accordingly.

While some of these complaints have concerned serious wrongdoing, or serious failures to deal efficiently with legal matters, the majority of complaints have always arisen from poor communication between lawyers and their clients. The failure in communication may be a failure to advise on the costs of a matter, or its likely timescale, or the likelihood of success. Often, the complaints would simply arise from a perceived lack of contact between the solicitor and the client. There may be any number of good reasons for a delay in a case, but if the client isn't told what the reasons are, they will normally assume that the delay is the fault of the lawyers.

Solicitors, in particular, have been slow to recognise the need to introduce good levels of communication with their clients. Sometimes, it has been argued that it is not reasonable to expect the solicitor to outline the timescale of an action at an initial interview, when even the simplest case might turn out to be very much more complex than it first appeared. Similarly, solicitors are reluctant to commit themselves on the likely cost of a matter when they do not know whether it will be simple or hotly contested – but perhaps, also, because they do not want to put clients off by telling them that a matter may be very much more expensive than it actually is.

In response to these failures, the Law Society has imposed a clear code of conduct which solicitors must comply with. Breach of the code will be *prima facie* an inadequate professional service, giving rise to various sanctions (including fines or the remission of fees). A serious breach may be treated as professional misconduct, and may lead to formal disciplinary action against the solicitor concerned. The rules are laid down in the Solicitors' Client Care and Costs Information Code (SCCCIC).[2] This is not the place to look at the rules in detail: they are lengthy, and sometimes complex. However, you need to be aware of the rules since, as you will see, the rules are applying the principles of clear and effective communication with your client.

What must a client care letter contain?

Client care letters must deal with the three Cs: costs, conduct and complaints.

The Code is there to ensure that clients have enough information to understand what is happening with their case, and in particular:

(a) who is dealing with their case;

(b) how the case is progressing;

---

2   See Law Society, *The Guide to the Professional Conduct of Solicitors*, 1999, London: Law Society, Chapter 13.

(c) how much the case is likely to cost (both at the start of the case and as the matter progresses);

(d) what the firm's complaints handling process is.

It is 'good practice' to record in writing all information that the Code requires you to give to your client, as well as any reasons why you have not given particular information in any given case.

Costs information generally

Costs information must be accurate and must not be misleading. You must give the information clearly and 'at a level which is appropriate to the particular client'. In particular, the Code points out that you must explain any unfamiliar terms, such as 'disbursements' – that is, the additional expenses incurred in obtaining items from third parties (such as the cost of medical reports, or property surveys). This is, of course, no more than the principle which we have already considered, that you should ensure that the language that you use is clear and that it is appropriate for your reader.

The information about costs needs to be given at the start of the matter and 'at appropriate stages throughout'. Costs information must be confirmed in writing. In your letter, you must also discuss the cost benefit and the risk of the matter. The Code advises that such advice may need repeating during the case.

Conduct: who is dealing with the case?

In *Pilbrow v Pearless De Rougemont* [1999] 3 All ER 355, CA, P rang a firm of solicitors and asked to see a solicitor about a family matter. The firm dealt with the case and sent the client a bill for £2,600. The client learnt that, in fact, the case had been dealt with by an experienced paralegal, who was neither a solicitor nor a legal executive. The Court of Appeal held that there had been a breach of r 15, that there had been a complete non-performance of the contract, and that there was no obligation to pay the bill.

The case only emphasises the need to comply with the requirement to tell your client not only who will be dealing with their case, but also their status. If you are only a trainee, you must make clear that you are a trainee solicitor; and make clear who will be supervising your work.

Complaints

The Office for the Supervision of Solicitors (OSS) keeps making the point that the majority of complaints could be dealt with easily if solicitors were prepared to talk to their clients and to deal with any problems. The Code requires every principal to make sure that clients are told who to contact in the firm about any problems with the firm's services. The firm must also have a written complaints procedure, which must be given to the client on request.

The complaints procedure must ensure that all complaints are investigated promptly and thoroughly. The client must be given an explanation of the investigation and told of any action taken. If the client is not satisfied, they should be given information about the OSS.

When is 'client care' relevant in your writing?

On one level, client care is always relevant. Client care, in the sense of ensuring that your communication is accurate, accessible and appropriate for your client, is central to the principles of legal writing that we have been considering. However, 'client care' in the narrower sense of the SCCCIC has specific rules.

The Code makes clear that normally, the lawyer will give the information about the three Cs (costs, conduct and complaints) 'at the outset of the matter'. Where it would be 'insensitive or impractical' to do so at that point, the relevant information must be given as soon as reasonably practicable.

With this in mind, you will see that the draft letter to James (about his lottery winnings) may be deficient in practice. It probably needs at least two extra paragraphs:

Costs

As I explained to you on the telephone, my advice so far has been free of charge. I am happy to see you briefly to look at the written agreement concerning the syndicate. If it seems that there may be a claim against the syndicate, we can discuss the likely costs of legal action at that point. I should also be able to give you a clearer estimate of the likely timescale and of the likelihood of success.

Client care

At this point I will be dealing with your inquiry. If it becomes clear that you have a case, I will continue to deal with the matter, but I will also ask my trainee solicitor, Richard Thompson, to assist me. If you have concerns about the work that I do, please could you let me know in the first instance. If I cannot resolve your concern, you should contact Edwina Halpern. Edwina is the senior partner in this firm and she will deal with any complaints. I enclose a copy of the firm's client care brochure which sets out in more detail both the client care systems, and the basis for the firm's charges.

The SCCCIC will often impose additional requirements for your legal writing. However, it doesn't affect the principle that everything that you write must be clear and accessible to your client. If your writing isn't clear, you may find that your clients start using the complaints procedures!

LETTERS BEFORE ACTION

Letters before action – or letters of claim, as they are now known – are another category of legal writing where there are certain prescribed contents, and even organisation, to which you must have regard in your writing.

What is a letter before action?

The normal principle followed by the courts in making an order as to who will pay the costs of a legal action is that 'costs will follow the cause'. In other words, whoever wins the action will normally recover the bulk of their legal costs from the party who lost. Under the Civil Procedure Rules (CPR), this principle is no longer as clear cut as once it was. In particular, it has always been the case that if a person starts a court action without warning the other party, in order to see if the dispute can be settled without the expense of going to court, the claimant would be 'at risk on costs'; in other words, the claimant would need to be able to show that his or her action was reasonable.

In order to show that he or she had tried to resolve the matter without going to the court, the claimant would normally send a letter before action. The idea was that this would put the other party on notice as to the fact of the dispute and its nature, thus enabling them to see whether the dispute could be settled there and then. Over time, however, the purpose of the letter before action was often overlooked; it simply became part of the ritual of litigation. Consider the following, real, letter before action:

Dear Sirs,

Re: Lorraine Elizabeth Donovan

We are instructed by the above named who was formerly in your employ in 1979 to 1980. Your records will reveal Mrs Donovan under her single name, however, we do not have that name upon record at present. Mrs Donovan suffered personal injuries as a result of an accident arising during her employment as a result of your negligence and/or breach of statutory duty. In the near future we shall be issuing a writ against yourselves for personal injuries arising out of the accident and should advise you to pass this letter to your insurers.

Yours faithfully,[3]

The case ended up in the House of Lords because the writ was not issued until after the three year Limitation Act period had passed. The claimant was arguing, among other things, that the letter before action gave the defendants sufficient notice to ensure that they were not prejudiced by any delay. However, as Lord Griffiths remarked in the House of Lords:

> As this letter did not give the maiden name of Mrs Donovan, did not give the date of her accident, did not describe the nature of her injury and did not identify the nature of the alleged negligence or breach of statutory duty it could not possibly enable the defendants to identify the incident in respect of which it was apparently the intention to sue them without more ado.[4]

The court held that Mrs Donovan's remedy was to sue her solicitors.

Letters of claim and the Civil Procedure Rules

Under the CPR, a series of 'protocols' have been developed. These are intended, in the words of Lord Woolf:

> To build on and increase the benefits of early but well informed settlement which genuinely satisfy both parties to a dispute.

The courts will treat the standards which the protocols lay down as being 'the normal reasonable approach to pre-action conduct'. Significant breaches in the terms of the

---

3   Quoted by Lord Griffiths in *Donovan v Gwentoys* [1990] 1 All ER 1018, p 1020.
4   *Ibid*, p 1021.

protocols may lead to 'adverse consequences': costs may be disallowed; applications for extensions of time may be rejected; and so on.

Under the existing protocols, there is an expectation that the claimant, or their legal representative, will notify the potential defendant at an early stage of the likelihood of a claim being made against them. A 'letter of claim' will then follow. The protocols set out specimens of this letter. The letter that follows is taken from the Personal Injury Protocol:

To

Defendant

Dear Sirs

Re: Claimant's full name

       Claimant's full address

       Claimant's Clock or Works Number

       Claimant's Employer (name and address)

We are instructed by the above named to claim damages in connection with *an accident at work/road traffic accident/tripping accident* on day of [*year*] at [*place of accident which must be sufficiently detailed to establish location*].

Please confirm the identity of your insurers. Please note that the insurers will need to see this letter as soon as possible and it may affect your insurance cover and/or the conduct of any subsequent legal proceedings if you do not send this letter to them.

The circumstances of the accident are:

[*brief outline*]

The reason why we are alleging fault is:

[*simple explanation, for example, defective machine, broken ground*]

The rationale for the letter of claim

The CPR make clear the purpose of the letter: it is to provide the defendant and his or her insurer with sufficient information to enable them to commence investigations and to put an initial 'broad valuation' on the case. With this in mind, you must make sure that the letter contains a clear summary of the facts in the case, and of the injuries that have been suffered. In requiring this, the protocols are really only restating the principles of letters before action; but this is in keeping with the spirit of the CPR, which require a 'cards on the table' approach from even the early stages, so that litigation can be avoided wherever possible.

You will note that the specimen letter starts with a clear statement of what the letter is about (the nature of the claim), and that it closes by telling the recipient what is expected of them: to reply within 21 days. The rules suggest that a standard format for these letters should be used, and you should therefore model any letters of claim on the specimen unless there is a very good reason not to do so.

You will note that the language used in drafting this letter is clear and formal, but does not use any explicitly legal terminology. It is drafted so that the person reading it should be able to understand what is alleged and what steps they should take. It is a shame that legal culture is still so ingrained that it obliges rules of court to require lawyers to draft letters in this way!

RECORDING INFORMATION: ATTENDANCE NOTES AND MEMORANDA

Traditionally, attendance notes and memoranda would only be the concerns of solicitors, working in an office environment and with day to day control of case files. For barristers, papers would arrive with particular instructions; that task would then be completed; and the papers would be returned with the opinion or the required drafting. This position is changing, especially as barristers take advantage of their new rights to conduct litigation: the need to keep a central record of all actions in the case will mean that attendance notes become as much part of a barrister's work as a solicitor's.

Attendance notes

What is an attendance note?

An attendance note is no more than a record of 'attendance' on a client, or of work done on the client's case. It may simply record a telephone conversation, or it may be a record of a more lengthy interview, or of an attendance at court.

The advantages and disadvantages of attendance notes can be summarised in a number of propositions:

Proposition 1:   there are far too many pieces of paper. We should reduce paperwork to a minimum.

Proposition 2:   anyone picking up a file should be able to tell what is going on.

Proposition 3:   you may find it hard to justify your bill if you don't have a record of time spent on the case.

Proposition 4:   it is generally too late to write an attendance note when you are being sued for negligence in dealing with a case.

At a minimum your attendance notes will need to contain:

- date;
- time spent on matter;
- client name;
- fee earner name;
- file reference;
- subject matter;
- summary of matter dealt with, including relevant advice;
- note as to whether telephone call out or in, or personal attendance.

In drafting your attendance note, you will need to balance the need for thoroughness (if you are ill, will your colleagues be able to see what they need to do with the case?) against the danger of prolixity (if your attendance notes are all pages long, will your colleagues have time to wade through them to find out what they need to do with the case?). Consider using an 'action list' at the bottom of the note to record what action needs to be taken, by whom, and by when.

Where advice has been given over the telephone or in interview, most solicitors safeguard their position by confirming that advice in writing. This is not only client service; it is also a safeguard against future negligence actions.

Memoranda

A memorandum is a form of report, generally used to communicate matters internally within an organisation. As with an attendance note, there is no formal requirement as to layout or content, although each firm may have its own house style.

Normally, a memorandum will start with an opening distribution and title section:

Halpern Dodds

Internal Memorandum

To:	Jim Dodds
cc:	Edwina Halpern
From:	Tony Smith
Date:	
Re:	Companies House searches – recording disbursements

Where a memorandum relates to client affairs, you will also need to note the file name and file reference, along with the fee earner's reference number. The body of the memorandum may then be set out in paragraphs, generally numbered for ease of reference.

The tone and content will clearly vary depending on the sender and the recipients.

COUNSEL IS INSTRUCTED … : WRITING A BRIEF TO COUNSEL

A brief to counsel is a document instructing a barrister to appear in court on behalf of your client. In practice, you may also be writing to a barrister to ask him or her to write an opinion on a case, to draft documents, or to advise on a matter. In all these cases, there are certain formalities which are still observed. We have used the brief to counsel in order to illustrate the general principles which apply.

Heading, layout and structure

In one obvious respect, a brief to counsel more closely resembles a formal piece of drafting than it does legal writing: the formal heading. In the heading, a brief will reproduce the layout and contents of the formal court documents. A brief in a typical civil matter will therefore start:

In the Westchurch County Court   Case number: 00 39809

Trial listed for: 23 June 200-

James Thompson

Claimant

v

Richard North

Defendant

_____

BRIEF TO COUNSEL

_____

Counsel will find herewith:

1   Statements of case

2   Statement: James Thompson

... etc.

Counsel is instructed by Leslie Carr of Halpern Dodds on behalf of the claimant, James Thompson. As Counsel will note from the statements of case, Mr Thompson is pursuing a claim for damages in the sum of £25,000 against Mr North in respect of moneys owing following a substantial win by a lottery syndicate. Instructing Solicitors have taken a full proof of evidence from Mr Thompson (Document 2), from which Counsel will note the full facts of this case.

In a criminal matter, the heading will be largely the same, although it is more likely that criminal clients will be legally aided. In such cases the words 'Legal Aid' are normally put towards the top left hand corner of the brief. Where a barrister is being asked to advise on a matter where legal proceedings have yet to begin, rather than the names of the parties to the action, the heading will normally say 'In the matter of James Thompson'.

In addition to the formal layout of the heading, a brief will also have a backsheet. This information will largely duplicate the heading, but will be laid out using only the right hand side of the paper:

In the Westchurch County Court

Case number: 00 39809

James Thompson

Claimant

v

Richard North

Defendant

BRIEF TO COUNSEL

Legal Aid

Halpern Dodds and Co

29 Chesterfield Place,

Westchurch

[0071 229 228]

LC/jm/391N

While this may, at first sight, look strange, it makes more sense once you know that the brief and the enclosed documents are normally folded once, lengthways, and then wrapped round with legal ribbon. This leaves half the backsheet setting out the details of the court and the parties to the case; the other half is blank so that a running record can be kept of all actions taken by the barrister or barristers who deal with the matter.

Within the text of the brief, you can lay matters out in any way that seems sensible. Normally you will start by listing the documents which are enclosed with the brief, and then by confirming who is instructing the barrister (it is a good idea to give the barrister your name, as well as the firm's name, so that the barrister knows who to speak to if there is a problem). You need to let the barrister know which of the parties you are asking them to represent, and it is a good idea to confirm at an early stage whether this is a legal aid case, a conditional fee case or is being funded in some other way.

The next logical step is to give a brief summary of what is in issue. You may wish to summarise this in a sentence, and then refer the barrister to the client's statement or proof of evidence. It is normally a good idea to summarise the procedural stages in the matter, so that it is clear why and how the case has progressed to its current stage.

After this, it is a question of structuring the material so that it is as accessible as possible. Clearly, you can rely upon the barrister to be able to analyse the issues for himself or herself; you are not setting out the material as you would need to for a lay person. On the other hand, you should take into account the fact that you may have had conduct of a case for months or even years; you may be entirely at home with a set of facts which would seem very complex to a person coming to them afresh. You may have had the opportunity to talk to witnesses and to draw your own conclusions as to their credibility and their value in the matter. It is true that the barrister should be at least as well informed as to any relevant legal provisions as you are, but if there are any particular issues, it does no harm to highlight these:

Counsel will note that the principal facts in issue relate to any later variation in the written syndicate agreement. It is Mr Thompson's case that there was an oral variation, but also a variation by conduct. Both of these, he will say, are evidenced by his payment of arrears when requested to do so. Instructing Solicitors have taken a statement from Lisa Thompson, the claimant's wife. Counsel will find this at Document 11. In this statement, Mrs Thompson states that on a number of occasions prior to the lottery win she heard her husband talking about having to make payments in arrears. Counsel will of course take into account the hearsay nature of this evidence, and the fact that its credibility must be weakened as it comes from such an interested party. On the other hand, the evidence may be of real assistance in rebutting any allegation that Mr Thompson fabricated his account after the win had been announced.

Language

Apart from the formal layout of the heading and the backsheet of the brief, there is a further formal element to this drafting which you will already have noticed: the use of the third person for both the barrister who is instructed, and the lawyer who is drafting the brief. Thus, rather than writing 'You will note that the principal facts in issue relate to any later variation in the written syndicate agreement', this sentence begins 'Counsel will note …'. Similarly, rather than writing 'I have taken a statement from Lisa Thompson, the claimant's wife', the writer states that 'instructing solicitors' have done this.

Is this language necessary?

The answer must be that it is not. It is a clear relic of a far more formal relationship between the barrister and his or her professional client. The CPR have attempted to sweep away much of the archaic language used in drafting the statements of case (or 'pleadings') in matters that are dealt with by the civil justice system. It is, therefore, strange that this very distant and impersonal language is still felt to be appropriate simply because the communication is between a barrister and a solicitor.

This is an area where the expectations as to how the brief will be drafted will change, and, indeed, they may do so quite quickly in response to the changes under the CPR. However, it would be wrong to say that this means that you should now draft briefs using the first and second person (I and you). There is obviously nothing stopping you from doing this, but your brief might be regarded as somewhat unconventional.

CONCLUSION

In this chapter, we have looked at the application of some of the principles of legal writing which were considered in the previous chapter. In particular, you have considered the drafting process in writing a legal letter, and the formal requirements of 'client care' and of letters before action. Because you have been looking at slightly more specific examples of legal writing, there may be a temptation to feel that the general principles of clarity, of organisation, and of accessibility do not apply. However, we hope that you now recognise that these principles underlie all the writing that you will do – even where, as is perhaps the case with briefs to counsel, a particular level of formality is imposed on the language that you use. No matter what formal requirements you must have regard to, your writing is always ultimately a matter of communication, and you must never lose sight of this principle.

FURTHER READING

For suggested further reading on legal writing, see Chapter 1.

CHAPTER 3

LEGAL RESEARCH

INTRODUCTION

One almost undeniable fact is that no two problems are exactly the same. You will find this is the case with any law problems you will be set throughout your course of study; some may be very similar, but rarely will they be exactly the same. You will also find this is the case when you enter legal practice – no two clients will present you with exactly the same challenges. Each problem will be different on its facts, even if the problems relate to the same area of law. Problems, which could initially appear similar on the facts, may raise different points of law. You will encounter this in any legal practice, whether as a solicitor or barrister.

However, even before then, you will have been made aware of this fact: in the course of your degree, you will be posed many questions, each subtly different. While you may be tempted to 'question spot' in an attempt to identify those subjects which you consider likely to appear on a particular assessment to enable you to avoid revising the entire syllabus, you would not expect to see exactly the same questions appearing word for word as they did on previous exam papers. The subject area covered by the questions may be the same or similar, but the questions will vary, however slightly, on the facts. You expect this and are prepared to adapt your knowledge to answer whatever questions have been posed by the examiner. You should find that you have developed, to some extent, the skills of learning the material and of application, by being able to apply your knowledge of the material to the questions set. Researching a problem requires something of the same process. You are unlikely ever to face exactly the same problem twice. What you are expected to be able to do is develop the skills of locating the relevant material and applying it to the particular facts of the question posed. This locating of the relevant material, in essence, is the skill of research. The application of the relevant material to the particular facts of the question posed by a client in legal practice involves the skill of practical legal research.

In this chapter, we will look at the skill of legal research and, in the next chapter, at its practical application.

THE SKILL OF LEGAL RESEARCH: WHAT SKILLS DO YOU NEED?

When considering what skills you need to acquire to be an effective legal researcher, a good starting point is to attempt to establish: what is legal research? According to Dr Peter Clinch:

> The skill of legal research can mean different things to different people … recently it has been used to describe the skills students need to acquire as part of their degree and professional studies and eventually employ when in legal practice.[1]

---

1   Clinch, P, *Teaching Legal Research*, 1999, Coventry: National Centre for Legal Education, University of Warwick.

This may seem quite overwhelming; however, you are not expected immediately to be able to answer problems of the type you may face when in legal practice. What you are expected to do during your legal education is to acquire the skill of legal research. You may already have experienced or carried out research in your studies without necessarily being aware of having done so: for example, in preparing coursework during your A levels, etc. In the course of your degree or postgraduate professional course, you will be expected to go further, to develop your research skills and to apply them to specific legal problems. During your training contract, should you choose a career as a solicitor, or your pupillage, should you choose to become a barrister, you will draw upon these same skills when addressing a problem posed by a client.

Many students who ultimately embark on a legal career do not take law as their first degree. If this is the route you have chosen, this should not hinder too greatly your ability to carry out legal research. During the course of studying for any degree, you will have been required to undertake research of some description. This could have been preparation for seminars, coursework or a dissertation. You should, therefore, have acquired research skills. These will be useful to you, but may need some adaptation to help you in your legal studies.

This chapter will look at how you can acquire and develop these skills, in the context of legal research. Your existing research skills, whether acquired during your A levels or any other course of study, will take you only part of the way towards solving legal problems. You need to acquire the skill of legal research. However, this should present you with little cause for alarm. After all, as Dr Clinch notes, 'There is very little distinctively "legal" about the skill of legal research'. You can draw upon your existing research skills to help you as legal research involves the 'generic skills of problem analysis, search and retrieval of information and the skill of communication'. You should already have these skills or be in the process of acquiring them during your degree.

So, the skills you need to acquire are fairly easily identified. The essential elements of legal research skills can be expressed as:

- problem analysis, that is, identifying and analysing a problem;
- search and retrieval of information, that is, finding appropriate information to solve the problem;
- communication, that is, presenting the results of the analysis and research in an appropriate and effective manner.

Therefore, this chapter on legal research will consider all these points: problem solving; the search for information; and the presentation of your research.

Problem solving

Problem solving is difficult.

How you address a problem will partly depend upon the type of problem with which you are faced. Put simply, problems can be classified as being either focused or unfocused.

To illustrate the difference, consider the following example. A focused problem might be: what case formulated the current basis of the duty of care in the law of negligence? You, the student, are being required to find a definitive answer to this question; it is a very focused question, requiring a specific and precise answer. Where would you look to find an answer? It is probable that you would know how to take that first step almost instinctively. If that is not yet the case, you will find this becomes easier as you do more research exercises. Simply looking in any textbook on the relevant area of law (here, tort) should produce an answer. You are not being required to offer anything more than that answer; there is no need for any creativity from you.

Try it – try to find the name of the case.[2]

Contrast this with an unfocused problem. You are asked to advise a client who is seeking damages after suffering personal injury and shock when she found a decomposing snail in her drink, which had been poured from an opaque glass bottle. The answer to this problem is not clear. Indeed, the question being posed is not immediately apparent. What do you think it is? You cannot expect a client (or, indeed, an examiner) to reformulate their problem so that it fits neatly into the category of focused problems which you can easily answer.

The unfocused problem is much more demanding of the student. You must first identify what it is that you are being required to answer; you must identify the problem or problems. Here, a number of problems are posed by the single set of facts presented to you by the client. Can she claim damages in these circumstances? Is there any precedent that would suggest damages might be available in these circumstances? If so, who could she claim damages from? On what grounds could she claim damages? None of these questions is presented to you in the problem, but you could not attempt to make anything of the problem unless and until you had identified these questions. This requires a more creative approach than the focused problem. It may also require different research skills.

Many problems lie somewhere between the examples of focused and unfocused problems set out above, or are a combination of both. For example: you could be asked to look into the application of *Donoghue v Stevenson* to a situation where a client suffered shock, but not personal injury, on discovering part of a human finger nail in a gin and tonic which had been served in a clear glass. Here, you are being directed to a particular area of law arising from a specific case – the focused part of the problem – but are also required to apply this to a set of facts which is not exactly in line with those of the case – the unfocused part of the problem, which requires more creative input.

As stated above, how you address a problem will partly depend upon the type of problem with which you are faced. However, it will also depend upon you. Your approach to problem solving partly depends on your character – are you scientifically minded?

---

2   The case is *Donoghue v Stevenson* [1932] AC 562.

Do you blank when you see a 'mind map'?

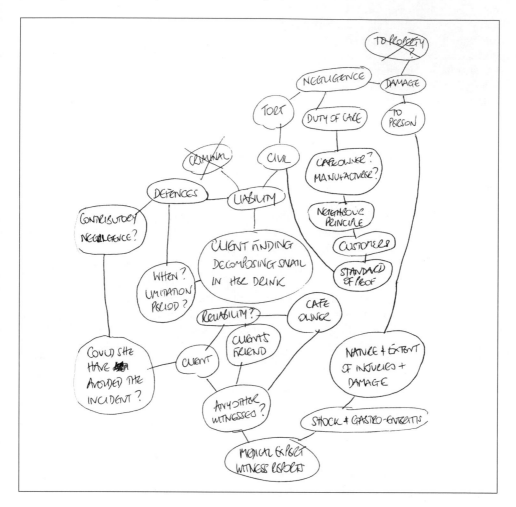

You may find this method of approaching a problem easy to follow. You may find it difficult to follow this mind map, but find it a good way to express your own thought processes. Alternatively, you might find it almost impossible to follow what is going on from the diagram.

Have you the sort of mind which finds it easier if ideas or theories are presented figuratively or diagrammatically? Or do you blank when you see a chart like this?

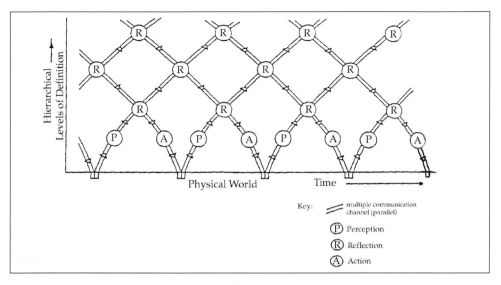

Or even like this?

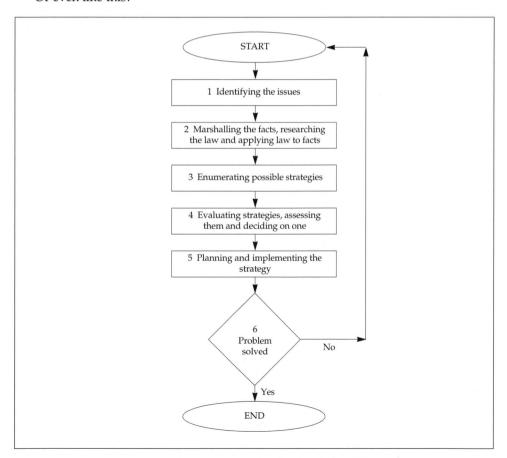

Jacking, Lewis, Brandt and Sell (1990)

Many students will admire the logic and clarity of these charts and will find them useful. Many others will find their eyes skipping over the part of the text containing the diagrams. Which are you?

Have you a more scattergun approach? Would you find it difficult to explain your thought processes in reaching an answer to a problem?

There are many different problem solving theories, one of which may well describe your natural inclination. None is better or worse than any other. You may find above a method which reflects your approach, or you may not. If you are confident that your approach works, then stick with it and learn to refine it by doing practice exercises. If, however, you think that you are not particularly good at problem solving, you might want to consider adapting your methodology to adopt a theory of problem solving that best suits your way of working. You will find that, with practice, you will become more confident and may even develop a few research shortcuts that work for you. Whatever approach you use, concentrate on developing that skill. Practice will not make perfect, in the case of research, but it will make it easier.

There has been much written on how people solve (or attempt to solve) problems. Numerous theories have been put forward attempting to explain or categorise the problem solving process. You might like to look at Margot Costanzo's book on *Problem Solving* in the Essential Legal Skills series.[3] The chapter 'The lawyer inside the problem II' is very accessible. It looks at how the personality of the problem solver may influence the approach they take to solve the problem. Identifying how you attempt to solve a problem may help you identify any defects in your approach.

Consider the following theories of problem solving.

David Kolb[4] produced a model of the four phases of problem solving. He identified four steps that those attempting to solve a problem must go through:

- situation analysis;
- problem analysis;
- solution analysis;
- implementation analysis.

Kolb showed this process in a model.

---

3   Costanzo, M, *Problem Solving*, 1994, London: Cavendish Publishing.
4   Kolb, DA, Rubin, IM and McIntyre, J, *Organisational Psychology: An Experiential Approach to Organisational Behaviour*, 1984, Englewood Cliffs, NJ: Prentice Hall.

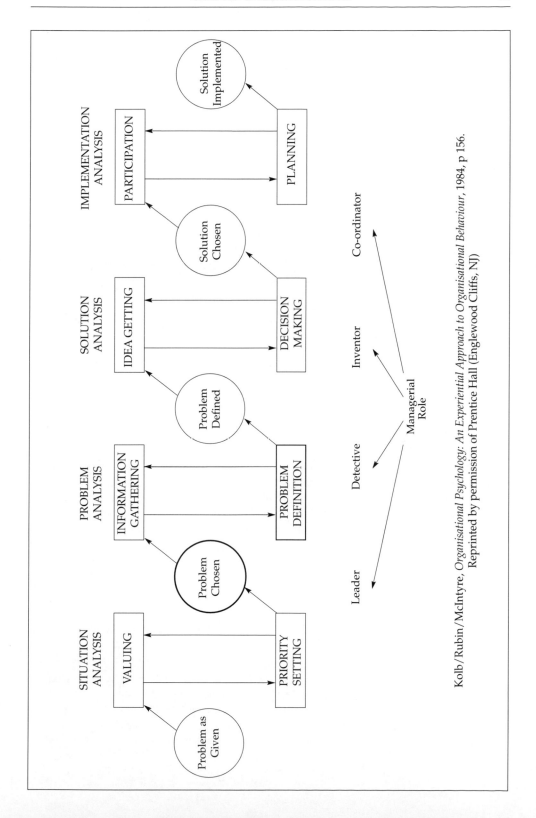

Kolb/Rubin/McIntyre, *Organisational Psychology: An Experiential Approach to Organisational Behaviour*, 1984, p 156.
Reprinted by permission of Prentice Hall (Englewood Cliffs, NJ)

These stages identified by Kolb can also be shown as a cycle, which involves all of these stages, but reflects the fact that the approach of various problem solvers may be different.

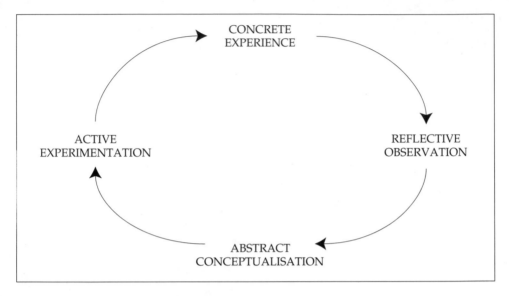

A cycle allows the problem solver to join at any stage and to reach the same end result by following the next steps in the cycle. Each stage can combine creative and analytical thinking.

Try to apply this to any piece of research you have undertaken recently, or have been asked to undertake.

Situation analysis will involve concrete experience. You have been given a problem, typically unfocused. You need to establish exactly what it is that you are being required to answer. You must focus on the relevant parts of the information you have been given – as far as possible, you will attempt to make your unfocused problem a focused problem. You have then chosen the problem you are going to attempt to answer.

The next stage will be problem analysis. This will require you to start to seek a solution to your problem. Taking your focused problem, you will identify the key words which will enable you to start looking at source material to find a solution. We will look at your sources in greater detail later. Kolb refers to this as the information gathering and problem definition stage.

The information you uncover should enable you to move to the next stage: solution analysis. You should by now have some idea of how to answer your problem. Does the solution produced by your research answer the problem? Does your solution work?

Implementation analysis: putting your solution into practice. During your academic stages, this will mean your answering the problem by producing a piece of coursework or a dissertation, or attending and participating in a seminar. During your practical legal training, whether as a trainee solicitor or barrister, this stage may well be out of your hands as it will most likely be up to your supervisor or pupil master to act on the results of your researches.

Although, initially, it might appear that Kolb's model of the four phases of problem solving is too complicated to reflect what you do, you may find that when applying it to your work, you have already undertaken Kolb's experiential learning cycle.

Another theory was put forward by Benjamin Bloom. He argued that educational objectives (and therefore problems set and how to answer them) could be sub-divided in order of increasing sophistication of the mental processes involved. These processes could be:

- evaluation;
- synthesis;
- analysis;
- application;
- comprehension;
- knowledge.

You may go through some or possibly all of these stages in attempting to solve a problem. For example:

- knowledge – this may involve you drawing on existing knowledge to recognise the key facts, enabling you to highlight the key words in a problem;
- comprehension – locating the relevant information in a library, etc, and processing it;
- application – applying the law to the facts of the problem. This requires some level of creativity, using your material in a particular manner;
- analysis – identifying the issues arising from the application of the law to the facts – analyse what you have produced so far;
- synthesis – once you have applied the law to the facts, you can analyse the client's position and draw some conclusions. Synthesis involves gathering together any conclusions you have drawn. It may now be possible to draw a generalisation from the data collected;
- evaluation – assess the client's position as set out in the problem in light of the information you have found and the advice you have suggested and make an appropriate decision on the basis of the data prepared.

Again, try to apply this to any piece of research you have undertaken recently, or have been asked to undertake. This may appear much more complicated than what you have been doing. It is likely that you are going through most, if not all, of the stages identified by Bloom, but that many are 'automatic' in that you are not consciously moving from one stage to another. Alternatively, it may be that the research you are carrying out does not require you to work through all the stages. As the research you undertake becomes more complex, perhaps these other stages will become more evident in your research methodology.

Yet another theory of how we approach the problems we are attempting to solve was developed by Ned Herrmann,[5] who suggested that all problems should be viewed from four perspectives:

---

5   Cited by Costanzo in *op cit*, fn 3.

- A rational analytical perspective: what do we know?
- An organisational perspective: what might we do?
- The perspective of how the situation might affect other people: how will other people behave/react?
- A holistic, conceptual future oriented perspective: how else might the problem be described?

This does not look at how you locate material to answer the problem, but concentrates on how we perceive the problem itself. Try to apply this to any piece of research you have undertaken recently, or have been asked to undertake. Does it help to make the problem any clearer to you?

There are many ways to see a problem, as we have seen. If you would like to look into how we go about problem solving in more detail, there are many books you could look at. One of the most accessible is *Problem Solving* by Margot Costanzo, mentioned above. However, problem solving is only part of what we are attempting to address here. Research is not just problem solving. Research involves something more than that. Moreover, you are undertaking not just any research but, specifically, legal research. Attempting to solve legal problems may require different or particular skills. Legal problems often require a more analytical approach than many other types of problem.

In his useful book *Legal Research* (part of the Essential Legal Skills series), David Stott[6] provides a three stage model which looks at the conduct of legal research. The first stage looks at research planning. As part of your research planning, Stott suggests that you will (or should) consider all of the following:

- fact collection;
- legal knowledge;
- problem identification;
- legal analysis;
- fact analysis;
- further fact collection;
- identifying avenues of research;
- generation of key search words.

We should go through these in some detail, as it is imperative that you understand how to problem solve before you head for the library and start your research.

Fact collection is largely self-explanatory – what is the problem you are faced with? During the academic stage of your legal career, you will often be given the facts by a tutor; for example, in a seminar problem or a piece of coursework. In legal practice, fact collection may be rather more complicated; this is considered in depth in the next chapter.

Legal knowledge – you may already have an understanding of the relevant area of law, or it may be completely new to you. If you know the answer to the problem, this will be the end of your 'researches' and you will merely need to present the research in

---

6   Stott, D, *Legal Research*, 2nd edn, 1999, London: Cavendish Publishing.

the necessary form. However, it is a rare problem indeed which is so easily solved. Most will require substantially more input from the student to produce a sensible answer. Your existing legal knowledge may help to put you on the right lines to further your research, or you may need to go back to first principles: what area of law is this?

Problem identification is something we have already considered. You may need to analyse an unfocused problem to establish what the problem is about before you are able to start your research.

Once you have gathered the facts and identified the problem you are being asked to solve, you will need to progress to some legal and fact analysis. What legal issues are raised by the problem? Would your client have a legitimate claim in law based on the facts? If so, on what area of law is that claim based? To determine this, you may have to look at the facts you have been given and filter through them once again to determine what are the material facts to establish that claim. Fact analysis is an important skill to acquire and can save you much time when faced with a problem which seems very long and complicated. You should learn how to distinguish a relevant fact from the sum of the facts which you have been given, many of which will not help you to solve the problem.

To make this clearer, try the following exercise. Look at the following passages taken from the decision in the case of *Merritt v Merritt* [1970] 1 WLR 1211, CA. You should attempt to identify from the judgments the material facts of the case:

LORD DENNING MR. The husband and the wife were married as long ago as 1941. After the war, in 1949 they got a building plot and built a house. It was a freehold house, 133 Clayton Road, Hook, Chessington. It was in the husband's name, with a considerable sum on mortgage with a building society. There they lived and brought up their three children, two daughters, now aged 20 and 17, and a boy now 14. The wife went out to work and contributed to the household expenses.

Early in 1966 they came to an agreement whereby the house was to be put in joint names. That was done. It reflected the legal position when a house is acquired by a husband and wife by financial contributions of each. But, unfortunately, about that time the husband formed an attachment for another woman. He left the house and went to live with her. The wife then pressed the husband for some arrangement to be made for the future. On 25th May, they talked it over in the husband's car. The husband said that he would make the wife a monthly payment of £40 and told her that out of it she would have to make the outstanding payments to the building society. There was only £180 outstanding. He handed over the building society's mortgage book to the wife. She was herself going out to work, earning net £7 10s a week. Before she left the car she insisted that he put down in writing a further agreement. It forms the subject of the present action. He wrote these words on a piece of paper:

> In consideration of the fact that you will pay all charges in connection with the house at 133, Clayton Road, Chessington, Surrey, until such time as the mortgage repayment has been completed, when the mortgage has been completed I will agree to transfer the property into your sole ownership.

Signed John B Merritt: 25.5.66.

The wife took that paper away with her. She did, in fact, over the ensuing months pay off the balance of the mortgage, partly, maybe, out of the money the husband gave her, £40 a month, and partly out of her own earnings. When the mortgage had been paid off, he reduced the £40 a month to £25 a month.

The wife asked the husband to transfer the house into her sole ownership. He refused to do so. She brought an action in the Chancery Division for a declaration that the house should belong to her and for an order that he should make the conveyance. The judge, Stamp J, made the order; but the husband now appeals to this court.

The first point taken on his behalf by counsel for the husband was that the agreement was not intended to create legal relations. It was, he says, a family arrangement such as was considered by the court in *Balfour v Balfour* and in *Jones v Padavatton*. So the wife could not sue on it. I do not think that those cases have any application here. The parties there were living together in amity. In such cases their domestic arrangements are ordinarily not intended to create legal relations. It is altogether different when the parties are not living in amity but are separated, or about to separate. They then bargain keenly. They do not rely on honourable understandings. They want everything cut and dried. It may safely be presumed that they intend to create legal relations.

Counsel for the husband then relied on the recent case of *Gould v Gould*, when the parties had separated, and the husband agreed to pay the wife £12 a week 'so long as he could manage it'. The majority of the court thought that those words introduced such an element of uncertainty that the agreement was not intended to create legal relations. But for that element of uncertainty, I am sure that the majority would have held the agreement to be binding. They did not differ from the general proposition which I stated:

> When ... husband and wife, at arm's length, decide to separate and the husband promises to pay a sum as maintenance to the wife during the separation, the court does, as a rule, impute to them an intention to create legal relations.

In all these cases the court does not try to discover the intention by looking into the minds of the parties. It looks at the situation in which they were placed and asks itself: would reasonable people regard the agreement as intended to be binding?

Counsel for the husband sought to say that this agreement was uncertain because of the arrangement of £40 a month maintenance. That is obviously untenable. Next he said that there was no consideration for the agreement. That point is no good. The wife paid the outstanding amount to the building society. That was ample consideration. It is true that the husband paid her £40 a month which she may have used to pay the building society. But still her act in paying was good consideration. Counsel for the husband took a small point about rates. There was nothing in it. The rates were adjusted fairly between the parties afterwards. Finally, counsel for the husband said that, under s 17 of the Married Women's Property Act 1882, this house would be owned by the husband and the wife jointly; and that, even if this house were transferred to the wife, she should hold it on trust for them both jointly. There is nothing in this point either. The paper which the husband signed dealt with the beneficial ownership of the house. It was intended to belong entirely to the wife.

I find myself in entire agreement with the judgment of Stamp J. This appeal should be dismissed.

WIDGERY LJ. I agree with Lord Denning MR's judgment, feeling, as he does, that no criticism can be levelled at the finding of the learned judge below.

When a husband and wife are living together in amity it is natural enough to presume that their discussions about money matters are not intended to create legally binding contracts. As Atkin LJ said in *Balfour v Balfour*:

> The common law does not regulate the form of agreements between spouses. Their promises are not sealed with seals and sealing wax. The consideration that really obtains for them is that natural love and affection which counts for so little in these cold Courts.

But, of course, once that natural love and affection has gone, as it normally has when the marriage has broken up, there is no room at all for the application of such a presumption. Salmon LJ made this clear in *Jones v Padavatton*, to which reference has already been made, where he said:

> ... as a rule when arrangements are made between close relations, for example, between husband and wife, parent and child or uncle and nephew, in relation to an allowance, there is a presumption against an intention of creating any legal relationship. This is not a presumption of law, but of fact. It derives from experience of life and human nature which shows that in such circumstances men and women usually do not intend to create legal rights and obligations, but intend to rely solely on family ties of mutual trust and affection.

The experience of life and human nature which raises this presumption in the case of a husband and wife living together in amity does not support it when the affection which produces that relationship of confidence has gone.

I find it unnecessary to go so far as to say that there is a presumption in favour of the creation of legal relationships when the marriage is breaking up, but certainly there is no presumption against the creation of such legal relations as there is when the parties are living happily together.

I would dismiss this appeal.

KARMINSKI LJ. I agree, and only desire to add this. It is in my view of great importance, in considering whether or not an agreement of the kind which we have to consider here would create legal relations, to look at the surrounding facts. In the present case on 20 May 1966, the husband informed the wife that he was in love with another woman with whom he was living, and he added these words: 'When the house is paid for I will consider signing over the other half to you.' That was followed five days later by the meeting in the motor car which resulted, after full discussion, in the signing of the agreement to which reference has already been made by Lord Denning MR. I do not propose to read it again.

In deciding therefore whether or not an agreement is intended to establish legal relations, it seems to me essential to look at the surrounding circumstances. In *Balfour v Balfour* the relevant facts were that the husband, who was employed in government service in Ceylon, had to return there in 1916. The wife could not join him there at any rate for the time being because of her own ill-health and the husband agreed to pay her £30 a month for her support. At that time therefore the agreement was a perfectly friendly one occasioned by a separation which was not, at any rate at that time, the desire of either of them.

In the present case it is manifest that the husband had left the wife by his own choice, because he preferred the company of another woman. He was therefore not only presumably committing adultery with her, but was also in desertion. The wife therefore had several grounds for which she could have commenced divorce proceedings, or taken such proceedings as she might have been advised for maintenance, either in a magistrates' court or in the High Court, on the ground of desertion or wilful neglect to maintain. In fact no proceedings became necessary, because the husband arranged to pay £40 a month, and undertook that when she had discharged a small amount outstanding on the mortgage he would transfer the property to her sole ownership.

I have no doubt, therefore, that on the facts of this case Stamp J was perfectly correct in coming to the conclusion which he formed, and I agree that this appeal must be dismissed.

Appeal dismissed

You should have been able to narrow down the facts given in the judgments to focus on the material facts. This is often done for you in the case summary at the head of the case report.

Look now at the case summary for *Merritt v Merritt*:

The husband and wife were married in 1941 and had three children. In 1966, the husband became attached to another woman and left the matrimonial home to live with her. At that time, the matrimonial home, a freehold house, was in the joint names of the husband and wife, and was subject to an outstanding mortgage of some £180. The wife pressed the husband to make arrangements for the future, and on 25 May 1966, they met and talked the matter over in the husband's car. The husband said that he would pay the wife £40 a month out of which she must make the outstanding mortgage payments on the house and he gave her the building society mortgage book. Before leaving the car the wife insisted that the husband should put down in writing a further agreement, and on a piece of paper he wrote: 'In consideration of the fact that you will pay all charges in connection with the house … until such time as the mortgage repayment has been completed, when the mortgage has been completed I will agree to transfer the property in to your sole ownership.' The husband signed and dated that agreement, and the wife took the piece of paper away with her. In the following months she paid off the mortgage, partly out of the husband's monthly payment to her and partly out of her own earnings. When the mortgage was paid off the husband refused to transfer the house to the wife.

You should be able to narrow down the facts given in the case summary even further. This is often done for you in the case note at the head of the case report.

Look now at the headnote for *Merritt v Merritt*:

Contract – Intention to create legal relations – Presumption against intention – Inapplicable – Husband and wife not living in amity – Evidence disclosing intention to create legal relationship – Agreement after separation – Husband providing for wife – Wife paying off mortgage on matrimonial home – Husband to transfer home to wife after mortgage redeemed.

Did you identify the same material facts as in the headnote? Did you manage to reduce the facts given further than in the headnote?

Look now at the summary of the decision reached, to see what facts were deemed critical to the determination of the case:

Held – The written agreement of 25 May 1966, was intended to create legal relations between the parties because the presumption of fact against such an intention where arrangements were made by a husband and wife living in amity did not apply to arrangements made when they were not living in amity but were separated or about to separate, when (*per* Lord Denning MR at p 761) it might safely be presumed that they intended to create legal relations; the surrounding circumstances in the present case showed that the parties did so intend; accordingly, the wife was entitled to sue on the agreement, and it being sufficiently certain and there being good consideration by the wife paying off the mortgage, she was entitled to a declaration that she was the sole owner of the house and to an order that the husband join in transferring it to her (see p 761j to p 762a, p 762d to g and p 763b, d and h, *post*). *Balfour v Balfour* [1918–19] All ER Rep 845, *Jones v Padavatton* [1969] 2 All ER 616, and *Gould v Gould* [1969] 3 All ER 728 distinguished.

This exercise should have given you an indication of what is meant by fact analysis. There is a similar exercise in the next chapter if you would like more practice. What you should have learned by undertaking this exercise is that not all the facts you are given will be essential to understand the case and the legal points which may arise.

Once you have analysed the facts, you should consider whether you will require any further information to be able to solve the problem.

Now you should be in possession of all the relevant facts and have some idea of the relevant areas of law that you will be required to research. You can then start to formulate your plan of action – how will you research the problem? What source materials will you consult? What will be your starting point? What avenues of research will you follow? You will find that identifying certain key words will make that first step much easier. David Stott has the generation of key search words as the final step in research planning. You will have something to look up in the first source you consult to start your researches. This may put you immediately on the right path, or you may need to refine your search, but at least you will have made a start.

Try to apply this method of problem solving to any piece of research you have undertaken recently, or have been asked to undertake. This is probably slightly easier to relate to the research you have been carrying out than some of the other models considered above. You may well be able to see that you have worked through these stages in the course of your research. If not, would your research have been better or easier if you had done so?

If you would like more practice at this, you could look at *Legal Research* by Victor Tunkel,[7] which contains some useful exercises.

So far, we have concentrated on the nature of legal research and how you may approach problem solving. This should have suggested to you different ways of

---

7   Tunkel, V, *Legal Research: Law-Finding and Problem-Solving*, 1992, London: Blackstone.

approaching the problems you have been set and clarified the stages you would be expected to go through to prepare an answer to the problem.

Search and retrieval of information

You are now ready to start the second stage of the research process, which is research implementation. This is most probably what you would recognise as research – looking through texts, etc. However, that alone would not really constitute research: 'Lawyers describe looking up the law as research when what they do is more properly described as search.'[8] Merely finding the right legal material to answer the problem is not enough in itself.

Again, there are several steps you must go through to search and retrieve the information you need effectively. According to David Stott, this stage of the research process will require you first to undertake the identification of problems for resolution, which we have already considered above. Then, you may move to identifying and locating the relevant source materials and, importantly, learning to use these effectively. You may think that that is all there is to research implementation. However, there is more to it than that. At this stage you should also attempt to analyse your research findings. This may make you realise that there are further problems and you can research these before you move on from the search and retrieval process.

Even if all you are doing is looking up the law (for example, in attempting to answer a focused problem), there is a bewildering array of places in which to find it. If the problem posed requires you to answer a single question, you may only need to consult one source to find the relevant material. If, however, you are addressing a complex problem, which raises a number of issues, you may have to consider several different sources to provide an adequate answer to the problem.

Of course, the number of sources available will depend upon where and when you are doing your research. Most educational establishments offering law degrees or postgraduate legal qualifications will have some, if not all, of the sources considered below. Which source or sources you use will depend partly upon the nature of the problem you are seeking to answer, the sources available to you and also your own personal preferences. Some students will always go first to a computer-based source; others will prefer to consult paper-based sources as their first port of call.

The following is a suggestion of useful sources you may consult in attempting to answer legal problems. Remember that this book is not intended to inform you how to use a law library. There are many specialised and very informative books available which could give you more detailed guidance on the basics; for example, Clinch, *Using a Law Library* (2001, Blackstone) or Dane and Thomas, *How to Use a Law Library* (2001, Sweet & Maxwell). Nor is this list of useful sources a comprehensive list – you may well need to consult other sources to answer your particular problem. The list concentrates on the general sources which should be accessible to most students. As you progress with your course of study, you may find you need to use sources which do not appear on this list; for example, most specialised texts are excluded from the list. At the very least, the list should provide you with a possible starting point for your research. What

---

8   *Op cit*, Costanzo, fn 3.

the list should indicate is that you have available to you a very wide range of sources, which should enable each student to approach a problem in a way which best suits them. The list is divided into primary sources and secondary sources. You will usually find that the answer to most problems, particularly the simplest focused problems, can be located by using primary sources. Examples of primary sources listed below are the statutes and case reports. Where the problem poses more obscure points, these require the use of secondary sources, where the law is summarised. Examples of secondary sources given below include *Halsbury's Laws* and *Current Law*. The citators referred to below are basically indexes.

However, any discussion of available sources of information for those undertaking legal research, of whatever complexity, will usually start with textbooks.

Textbooks

For most students, trainee solicitors and barristers, 'The search for an answer will begin in a relevant textbook'.[9]

Clearly, however, you must first have identified the area of law relevant to your research to select a relevant textbook. Use textbooks sensibly – they may provide the complete answer to your problem, particularly if the problem is relatively straightforward and covers only one area of law. More often, textbooks will give you information on the subject area and provide a springboard to enable you to progress to other sources. Textbooks will often contain references to the relevant statutory provisions and case law. You then have the opportunity to take your researches further by going to those primary sources. If a textbook does not provide information on the subject area, go back – have you correctly identified the area you are researching? If so, are you sure the textbook covers that area of law?

Primary sources

You will at some point in your research almost always need to consult primary sources. Those set out below should provide you with a starting point when you go to a law library.

Legislation and Parliament

Most libraries will contain a number of sources of legislation. A common example is *Halsbury's Statutes* – a comprehensive annotated collection of UK legislation. This must be used in conjunction with an updating service such as *Is It In Force?* to ensure that the situation set out in *Halsbury's* is the most current. *Is It In Force?* gives details of the commencement of statutes passed since 1963.

Halsbury's Statutory Instruments provides a comprehensive collection of UK statutory instruments. Again, when using this source, you should also check an updating service.

---

9   Kenny, P, *Studying Law*, 5th edn, 2002, London: Butterworths.

As well as *Halsbury's Statutes* and *Statutory Instruments*, you could look at *Current Law Statutes Annotated* or such other sources of UK legislation. These will normally set out the legislation in full, without commentary.

If you are addressing a focused piece of research, for example, 'what are the provisions of s 15 of the Theft Act 1968?', a statute book may be your first port of call. You may have received an unfocused problem, but have analysed it to produce a focused problem which addresses the application of a particular piece of legislation; again, a statute book may be the quickest way to research the point. However, if your problem is unfocused, you might find it easier to consider a secondary source such as a textbook or *Halsbury's Laws* (see below, p 71) which provides some commentary on the application of the legislation.

If it is a question of interpretation of a statutory provision you are being asked to consider, following the House of Lords' decision in *Pepper v Hart* (1992), you could also look into *Hansard* or other parliamentary papers. This would enable you to look at the wording used in the debates on the legislation, which might make clear the intention behind a statutory provision.

Do not forget the internet as a useful source of information: there is a lot of free primary legal material on the internet. For example, all statutory instruments have been published in full on the internet since 1997 – see the HMSO (now the Stationery Office) site (at www.hmso.gov.uk). This site also enables you to search all UK legislation dating back to 1988 (acts prior to this date are not available on this site) and provides information about new legislation and legislation in progress. The House of Commons website (www.parliament.uk) will enable you to follow the status and text of bills before Parliament. *Hansard* is also available on the House of Commons website (www.parliament.uk).

Case reports

You may have been given the name of a case which you are being required to research, or you may have located the name of a relevant case as a result of your earlier researches. Either way, there are a number of case reports you can look at to read cases in full. You must learn how to use the case reports and how to read the cases you find; these are key skills for the study of law. Understand the case references and how to find the most important or relevant part of the case report. You may already have undertaken the exercise set out earlier based on the case of *Merritt v Merritt*. If so, you have had experience of reading a case report and identifying the important information. If you did not attempt the exercise, you may wish to go back and do so.

Amongst the law reports you could consult are the *Law Reports*, the *All England Reports* and the *Weekly Law Reports*. These are the most commonly used general law reports. There are also many other law reports which concentrate on cases relating to particular areas of law; for example, *Family Law Reports*, *Housing Law Reports*, *Road Traffic Reports* and *Tax Cases*. Most law libraries will include some, if not all of these sources. Some newspapers, most notably *The Times*, carry reports of some decided cases.

You could also look at the *Daily Law Reports Index* or UK law report CDs, but increasingly, you will find the internet is the most useful source of law reports. There are several internet subscription sites which offer daily law reports, but access to these will vary between libraries, etc. There are also some free internet sites giving case reports: for example, the House of Lords website or the Court Service home page.

The above are all primary sources – in many cases, these are unlikely to be your first ports of call when considering a piece of legal research and likely sources of information. These may well provide you with the answer to your problem; if so, you would obviously have to take your research no further, once you had established your sources were up to date. However, you may find that your research has taken you into an area of law with which you are unfamiliar or that it has uncovered an area of law which is not settled. In these cases, you may want to read further into the area before attempting to provide an answer to your problem. This is when secondary sources, such as commentaries on the law, may be helpful. Often, you will use these first to direct you to the relevant primary sources. There are numerous periodicals which could provide the commentaries to offer you guidance or an explanation of the law. Again, do not forget CDs and the internet.

Secondary sources

These will include general encyclopedias, digests and databases.

Halsbury's Laws of England

Halsbury's Laws will often provide either the answer in full or, at least, a source of sufficient basic information to direct your research elsewhere, possibly to a more specialised text or primary source. Most lawyers will use *Halsbury's Laws* as the starting point for their researches. You should learn how to use *Halsbury's Laws* and feel confident with it. It is authoritative, comprehensive and available in most libraries. Find the volume which deals with the subject of your problem, then check the index. Alternatively, you can first consult the consolidated index, which should guide you to the relevant volume and page number. If you cannot find an answer to your problem in *Halsbury's Laws*, you should usually be able to find an indication of where you should look to continue your research.

When using *Halsbury's Laws*, you must always check that the law set out in the volume represents the current position. A cumulative supplement is produced annually and a noter up monthly. Note that, in most libraries, there will also be copies of *Halsbury's Statutes* and *Halsbury's Statutory Instruments*; make sure you consult the relevant volume for the work you are undertaking.

Other digests, etc

There are several other sources you may want to consider, some paper-based and others IT-based. For example, *Current Legal Information* (whether on internet or CD), *Current Law Monthly Digest* and *Current Law Yearbook*. Again, do not forget to make use of internet sources; as well as subscription sites, there are free sites which may contain the information you need. Also, you may need to access some specialist digests, depending upon the area of law you are researching. The sources considered here are largely for UK law, but you may have to look into EU law and there are several EU law encyclopedias, digests, CDs or internet sites which you could use. One possible starting point could be the European Commission's website (www.europa.eu.int).

LEXIS-NEXIS

This is a subscription service and so not always available in every library. You need to be trained in the use of LEXIS as a research tool to frame your query in the most effective manner, as unguided research can prove very expensive (McKie has some good advice on formulating your query).[10] Once you have been suitably trained, LEXIS can be very useful. The LEXIS database includes reports in full of cases reported in England and Wales since 1945. It is possible, through LEXIS, to obtain the full transcripts of most cases. It also includes the text of most statutes and statutory instruments in force. These will probably be what you are most likely to use LEXIS to locate. However, it also includes some European Court of Justice decisions and some Scottish, Irish, Australian and New Zealand law reports, as well as a substantial body of US materials. You can locate these by inputting key words or words which identify the relevant material. LEXIS also offers details of unreported cases and transcripts can be printed off.

Internet

As mentioned above, the internet is a relatively new, but now invaluable source of up to date legal information. It is widely used as a research tool and its use as such is likely to increase, so you should ensure you are comfortable with using it and competent at doing so. However, do not become over-reliant on the internet as a research tool. It may not always be available to you, or its use may be restricted; for example, a particular research exercise may specify that you must use 'paper' sources. That said, the internet may often form the first research resource you address, and it is very useful for checking that your material is up to date.

There are internet charge-free sites open to all users of the internet and there are some internet subscription sites (for example, Lawtel, which is very useful). The internet subscription sites offer subscribers daily updated information on cases and statutes, etc. They are usually very accessible; a keyword can produce a list of relevant cases or current and proposed statutes, or inputting a case name can produce a case summary. Again, subscription services may not always be available.

One source which might be useful is *Researching the Legal Web* by Holmes and Venables.[11] This offers a guide to legal resources on the internet. *The Lawyer's Guide to Internet Legal Research* by Biehl and Calishain is another possible source of advice.[12]

As well as the secondary sources referred to above, there are other secondary sources which provide commentary on the law. These will include:

- *Legal Journals Index*;
- *Index to Legal Periodicals*;
- *Index to Foreign Legal Periodicals*;
- *Public International Law*;
- newspapers.

---

10   McKie, S, *Legal Research*, 1993, London: Cavendish Publishing.
11   Holmes, N and Venables, D, *Researching the Legal Web*, 1999, London: Butterworths and Carter, S, *Lawlinks*, as biblio.
12   Biehl, K and Calishain, T, *The Lawyer's Guide to Internet Legal Research*, 2001, London: Scarecrow Press.

Citators

These are basically indexes.

Current Law Case Citators – this is a valuable source, as it gives the full name of cases reported from 1947 and refers to law reports and journals where the cases can be found.

Current Law Statute Citators – this provides a list of statutes passed since 1947, including any statutes which have been repealed or amended since that date. Usefully, it also gives the names of reported cases since 1947 which have considered the various sections of the statutes. The *Current Law SI Citator* is included in the same volume as the *Statute Citator* and performs much the same role for statutory instruments.

Legal dictionaries – not a source as such, but very useful if your first analysis of the facts throws up some legal words or phrases which you do not recognise.

The sources listed above are, as previously stated, not a definitive list; all libraries will contain different sources and your access to the internet or other computer-based sources may vary. However, this should give you an indication of the many sources available to you to help you try to research an answer to any particular problem. With practice, you will find out which of these sources you feel most comfortable with. By doing so, you are developing the skills you will need to address problems you are set both in the academic stage of your legal training and thereafter. Becoming familiar with the methods of using the general sources referred to above should help you when you need to use more specialised sources, as your methodology should not need to be substantially different. If you think you need further assistance with how to use legal texts, you could consider Sharon Hanson's *Legal Method and Reasoning*.[13]

Remember Stott's analysis of research implementation – identifying, locating and using source materials is only part of the story. Search and retrieval of information will (or should) produce an answer to your problem after you have analysed your research findings. At this stage, you need to stop and assess your own research. Check: do you have all the information you need? Have you answered the problem? What if you have not answered the problem? This may not be the disaster you might at first imagine. Remember, many legal problems are not capable of a precise or complete answer. Identifying that it is an area of legal uncertainty may be what you are actually being required to do. However, you cannot use this as an acceptable answer unless you can show that you have done the necessary research to establish it. If you are concerned that your researches did not produce an answer, you could go back to the start. Did you identify the correct area for research? Could other sources be available? Could you approach the problem from a different angle? If you are certain that you have taken your research as far as you can, know when to stop.

Once you are sure you have completed the research implementation stage you will be able to move to the final stage – presentation of your research.

Presentation

Now you are capable of finding an answer to a problem, you must think about how you will present it. This is less important at this stage in your legal training than it may be

---

13   Hanson, S, *Legal Method and Reasoning*, 2nd edn, 2003, London: Cavendish Publishing.

later, for example, during your training contract if you are interested in becoming a solicitor, or pupillage if you want to become a barrister. However, remember that you are attempting now to acquire the skills you can carry into practice. If you try to concentrate on the presentation of your researches now, it may prove invaluable later.

An obvious point is that you must keep a written record of your research. This should not be merely a note of the results of your research, but should also record how you arrived at that answer. Note your sources, any relevant cases or statutes, etc, any journals upon which you relied (this is particularly important where you may have quoted a view set out in the article – this should be attributed, if only in a footnote to the research memo). It is surprising how many students fail to do this.

The research report may only be for your own benefit, for example, in the case of seminar preparation. However, it is still important. If your research is prepared for a third party, a supervisor or pupil master, for example, it is even more imperative that you make a clear record of your research for them to follow. When you finish your research, you must review it. You may complete your research and, when attempting to apply it to answer the problem, realise that you do not have sufficient information to provide an answer. You may even find that you have not researched the right legal points. Having a report of your research will allow you to retrace your steps to complete the research or to determine where you identified the wrong point to research.

To be effective in this role, your research report must contain certain information as a minimum. The textbooks or websites you consulted, any digests, case reports, statutes, etc, must be listed, but you should, if possible, include more information: page references, specific paragraphs of a case report, etc. Remember to check that your information is up to date and make a note of how you checked that, and to what date. It may help you to establish a standard form report that you follow whenever you undertake a piece of research. This need not be too complicated, but should help you ensure you have addressed all the necessary points. It should include:

- an identification of the problem you are trying to research;
- any key words which could help you start and refine your research;
- the results of your research;
- a note of the sources you used in your researches;
- a note of the steps you took to update your research.

This should be adequate to help you to keep a sensible useful record of your research.

David Stott's three stage outline of legal research concludes with some points on research presentation which you should bear in mind when producing your research report. He identifies as important: identification of recipient's needs or requirements; selection of appropriate format, for example, letter, memo, etc; use of clear and succinct language and the need to use appropriate language style, for example, informatory, advisory, recommendatory, demanding. This last point is often overlooked by students, but many educational institutions award marks in assessments for style and grammar. Not all of the points identified by Stott will be relevant to every piece of research you undertake. However, it may be useful to model your research record on this framework, deleting those parts which do not appear relevant to the type of research you are being asked to carry out.

The research may have been carried out for a dissertation. You will need an ongoing record of your researches to enable you to keep a track of your work to date and when you take a break from research, a record will enable you to pick up where you left off. Make your record as full as possible – it is for your benefit. It will even be helpful to make a note of those sources which turned out not to be useful, to avoid repeating fruitless research.

When you complete your research and are writing the dissertation, the research report will again be important. In this case, you must keep a very full record of your research, as you will be expected to produce a bibliography of your sources. Here, you must follow the accepted rules for citing sources. Most libraries will have a guide to correct citations.[14]

CONCLUSION

This chapter should have helped you understand more clearly what is meant by research. It should also have helped to identify the particular demands legal research will make upon you. Acquiring the skill of legal research will not be quick and can only come through actually undertaking pieces of research and getting practice at it. With each piece of legal research you undertake it should become easier. You will develop your own style. You will become familiar with the source materials and learn which best suits you. Each piece of legal research you undertake should help you to refine your skill until you are able to embark on a piece of research with confidence.

FURTHER READING

Biehl, K and Calishain, T, *The Lawyer's Guide to Internet Legal Research*, 2001, London: Scarecrow Press.

Clinch, P, *Teaching Legal Research*, 1999, Coventry: National Centre for Legal Education, University of Warwick.

Costanzo, M, *Legal Writing*, 1994, London: Cavendish Publishing.

Hanson, S, *Legal Method and Reasoning*, 2nd edn, 2003, London: Cavendish Publishing.

Holborn, G, *Butterworths Legal Research Guide*, 2nd edn, 2001, London: Butterworths.

Holmes, N and Venables, D, *Researching the Legal Web*, 2nd edn, 1999, London: Butterworths.

McKie, S, *Legal Research: How to Find and Understand the Law*, 1993, London: Cavendish Publishing.

Stott, D, *Legal Research*, 2nd edn, 1999, London: Cavendish Publishing.

Tunkel, V, *Legal Research: Law-Finding and Problem-Solving*, 1992, London: Blackstone.

---

14 Students should also be aware of the *Practice Note (Judgments: Neutral Citation)* [2001] 1 All ER 193, which introduces a form of neutral citation for cases.

CHAPTER 4

PRACTICAL LEGAL RESEARCH

INTRODUCTION

In the previous chapter, we considered the skill of legal research. This chapter is going to look at the application of the skill of legal research to practical situations. The need to be able to apply basic research skills can arise in many different contexts. If you are intending to take the study of law further and study for one of the professional courses, whether it is the Legal Practice Course (LPC) if you are intending to become a solicitor, or the Bar Vocational Course (BVC) if you are intending to become a barrister, you will be required to undertake legal research in a practical context.

This requires that you make an important change to your mental approach to research. You can no longer think like a student – you must now learn to think like a lawyer. You may argue that you cannot be expected to think like a lawyer when you may not even have set foot in a lawyer's office; you may think that you could not be expected to think like a lawyer until you had undertaken at least part of the final stage of your legal training, whether the training contract if you wish to qualify as a solicitor or pupillage if you wish to become a barrister. However, even before you start work it is possible to acquire the skills necessary to ensure you adopt a lawyer's approach to your research. Developing these skills is a vital part of making the transition from student to lawyer. The sooner you can demonstrate that you have made this transition, the more marketable you become to potential legal employers or the easier you will find it to meet the requirements of your employer. In almost every survey of legal employers about the skills they want their newly arrived trainees or pupils to possess and to excel at, legal research tops the list.

It is easy to see why this would be the case. Consider what you are likely to be doing when you first start your training contract or pupillage. It is unlikely that, on your first day at work, your supervisor or pupil master will send you off alone to court to represent a client; nor are you likely to be expected to negotiate a multimillion pound takeover alone or write a complex opinion without help. Being realistic, what you can do when you first start work is often fairly limited. Your supervisor or pupil master does not mind this – they know it and accept it. However, they do expect you to have acquired certain skills during your legal studies, especially the LPC or BVC, and to be able to use those skills effectively. This does not seem unreasonable. Supervisors or pupil masters know students have been taught the skills of legal research and practical legal research and find that this is very helpful to them, as they rarely have time to do their own research. Therefore, one of the skills you will almost certainly be using from day one of your legal career is that of legal research. What your employer expects you to be able to do is conduct legal research accurately and thoroughly. If you fail to do this competently, your supervisor or pupil master is entitled to be disappointed in you. If you have developed the skill of legal research and can think like a lawyer in conducting and presenting that research, you will stand out from the crowd – you increase your 'marketability'. Therefore, if you want to impress your supervisor or pupil master, to confirm their impression of you as being brighter and better than the other candidates for your job, you can demonstrate your ability to think like a lawyer when asked to conduct legal research. The LPC or BVC represents your opportunity to learn to think like a lawyer and acquire and practise the skill of legal research before entering practice.

Because the skill of legal research is so important in practice, the professional courses stress the importance of students acquiring that skill which is a transferable skill. Clearly, therefore, it is a vital skill for you to acquire at any stage in your legal education. If you learn how to carry out legal research effectively as a student and understand how this can be applied in practice, you are equipped with a skill which you will use throughout your professional career. So important is legal research that it is a required part of both the LPC and the BVC.

The BVC outcome specification for legal research requires that:

> The student should approach legal research in a practical rather than academic manner and be selective, precise and efficient in the identification and utilisation of resources.

To accomplish this students should be able to:

- analyse the issues raised by the case and identify which questions of law have to be answered;
- develop relevant keywords;
- demonstrate an understanding of the structure of legal literature and the media through which it is made available;
- locate and use a law library and the catalogues and indexes it contains;
- use IT skills to locate and retrieve relevant information;
- select relevant original material, commentary, opinion and guidance;
- use indexes within legal materials to find relevant information;
- use and interpret legal citations and abbreviations;
- check the currency of information;
- keep up to date with legal developments generally;
- organise the written response into a logical structure;
- concisely and accurately summarise or paraphrase relevant material;
- apply the law to the facts of the problem so as to produce satisfactory answers to the problem posed;
- provide clear advice;
- acknowledge the use of all sources and materials cited;
- devise a research trail to show how the answers have been reached;
- use IT skills to present the results of research.[1]

For the LPC, the specification for legal research is as follows.

> The student should understand the need for thorough investigation of factual and legal issues involved in a client's matter, the need for preparation and the best way to undertake it.

---

1   General Council of the Bar, *BVC Specification and Guidelines*, 2004/5, London: General Council of the Bar, p 33 (available at www.legaleducation.org.uk/downloads/bvcspec04.doc).

The student should be able to:

- identify the objectives of the employer or client;
- identify and analyse factual material;
- identify the legal context in which the factual issues arise;
- identify appropriate sources for investigating relevant facts;
- determine when further facts are required;
- identify and analyse legal issues;
- apply the relevant legal provisions to the facts;
- relate the central legal and factual issues to each other;
- identify the legal, factual and other issues presented by the documents;
- analyse the client's instructions and be able to identify the legal, factual and other issues presented by them;
- record and present the results of research in a clear, useful and reliable form.

The student should be able to demonstrate an understanding of:

- the use of primary and secondary texts;
- the methods of locating cases and statutes;
- the use of periodicals, digests and standard practitioner texts;
- the use of indices and citators;
- the use of electronic research tools.[2]

It will be seen from both the BVC and LPC specifications for research that students are required to tailor their research to meet particular objectives. This will also be relevant to students at other stages of their legal education. This approach looks beyond the academic legal research considered in the previous chapter and towards the skills of legal research you will need when practising as a lawyer. You will often find this described as practical legal research (PLR).

The underlying requirement of both the BVC and LPC specifications is that the context of your legal research should be focused to the needs of the client or to the facts of the particular situation you are being required to research. This is the 'practical' element of PLR, the 'thinking like a lawyer' referred to above. You are, therefore, being required to move away from legal research in a purely academic context. PLR requires you to apply your research skills in a different way. It is not research only to acquire knowledge: it is research to offer a solution to a client's problem.

In fact, PLR is not too different from pure legal research. The techniques required are often the same or very similar: what is different is the focus and often the presentation of your research. When undertaking pure legal research, it is likely that you would be the person who would derive most use from the results of your work. For example, you may have researched cases to enable you to find an answer to a problem that you were required to discuss in a seminar. This would possibly involve you in discovering what the law was in a particular area, whether statute- or case-based. Often, there would not

2   Law Society, *Legal Practice Course Board Written Standards*, Version 10, September 2004, London: Law Society (available at www.lawsociety.org.uk, under 'Becoming a Solicitor').

be a single identifiable answer to the problem posed by the tutor, but it would raise many issues that could be discussed further, again maybe without reaching any conclusions.

In PLR, you are not undertaking the research for your own benefit or to aid discussion in a seminar, but for a particular end-user. The person seeking the results of your legal research might be a tutor or examiner, or it might be a client, your supervisor or pupil master. Whoever has presented you with the problem to research does not want a discursive answer – they do not want to read everything you could find out about the law of negligence, for example. The client, supervisor or pupil master has presented you with the problem you are researching because they need an answer in an accessible and relevant format.

Learn to approach research problems like a lawyer. Your practical legal research skills must be brought to bear on the client's problem to offer a sensible solution. The client does not want to know what the law is in a particular area, or whether there have been any interesting developments in a particular line of cases. Your research has a practical aim: to answer the problem posed. The answer to your research will often be directly relevant to the recipient's next course of action: for example, the results of your research might determine whether a client should proceed with litigation or whether they would have little chance of winning; whether they were likely to receive a prison sentence after committing a particular offence; whether they could successfully bring a claim for unfair dismissal.

Obviously, researching these matters requires a different approach to that used for pure legal research. Your research must be precise; focused on the client's particular needs. The problem you are attempting to solve, being real, needs an answer. Your research must lead to some form of effective solution. Different factors will be relevant depending on whether you are considering a contentious or a non-contentious matter. You may need to refer to different source materials. We will consider these differences in this chapter. However, many of the skills of legal research that you possess already will also be relevant when you undertake PLR. Consequently, much of the previous chapter will also be relevant to PLR. Look again at the BVC and LPC specifications: how many of those criteria do you already meet in your usual legal research? You should be able quite easily to adapt your existing legal research skills to meet the requirements of PLR.

This chapter will concentrate on PLR: what it is, how to do it and how to present it to the end-user.

WHAT DOES PLR INVOLVE?

Essentially, PLR involves thinking like a lawyer. You should not approach PLR as you have legal problems in the past, because then you were most probably thinking like a student. As noted above, PLR will bear many similarities to pure legal research, but you must learn to approach problems differently. A lawyer will not approach problems in the same way as a student, and you must now learn to think like a lawyer.

When faced with a piece of PLR, you are still being asked to research the problem to reach a conclusion, as with pure legal research. However, there are several important differences between pure legal research and PLR. This chapter will consider the skills of PLR and methods of approaching PLR.

As you will see, the techniques that will make you an effective practical legal researcher are not mysterious. It is not so much a question of acquiring new skills as adopting a new approach to legal research. This approach is predicated on the purpose of PLR: you are not simply researching a point, but seeking to apply your research to a given set of facts of a case to produce a practical, useful outcome.

It is important throughout PLR to maintain your focus. Think: why am I being asked to research this matter? What is the point of this research? Only by reminding yourself that you are not engaged on a purely academic exercise will you develop the mindset necessary to approach PLR problems like a lawyer.

It will be seen from both the BVC and LPC specifications for research that students are required to develop three generic skills of PLR:

- problem identification and analysis;
- information search and retrieval (using both paper and computerised sources); and
- presentation of the results in an appropriate manner.

We have encountered these before, in the previous chapter; as noted earlier, much of the previous chapter will also be relevant to PLR. These skills will be considered again, in the context of PLR.

Problem identification and analysis

In the last chapter we considered problem solving skills. If you think you need to refresh your memory (or if you have turned directly to this chapter and think a brief refresher of problem solving skills would be beneficial to you), please turn back and read the chapter again.

All your basic skills of problem solving can be applied to PLR. However, the problems you may be required to research in practice will be based on real life and may be much more complicated than any matters you have attempted to research so far. They will almost always be unfocused problems. This may require you to further develop your problem solving skills. It may also require you to analyse the facts in a slightly different way.

Pure legal research in an academic context is subject to certain constraints; for example, you may be subject to time constraints if your legal research is being carried out as preparation for a seminar or in connection with a piece of coursework or a dissertation. You will also experience constraints when carrying out PLR. However, with PLR, there may be constraints on your research that you may not have encountered before. The nature of these constraints will, of course, depend on the particular facts of the matter with which you are dealing; however, it is possible to give some very general examples.

When in practice, you might find that your firm, supervisor or chambers may have a particular policy that you have to follow and ethical constraints may affect your research. Many firms or sets of chambers may have restrictions on the type of work which can be undertaken. There may be conflicts of interest between potential clients and/or existing clients. Before commencing your research, you may have to establish whether you are even able to act for the client.

There may be time constraints on you: you may have to reach some form of answer within a very short time. These may be imposed by the needs of your supervisor, pupil master or the person asking you to conduct the research. Alternatively, the time restrictions may arise from the nature of the matter with which you are dealing. You may be looking into matters which could be raised at a hearing to be held at very short notice – at a bail application, or an application for an injunction, for example.

There may also be cost or resource constraints: the time you have to devote to your research or the sources you could consult may be limited by the cost to your firm or chambers. Given unlimited time and resources, most problems would be capable of solution. However, you may be constrained by the resources you or your firm or chambers has available, or the resources you can access in the time available. You might be unable to use certain sources of information because of cost implications: for example, many firms limit the use of LEXIS, as it can prove expensive.

The problem you have been asked to research may not be one you can deal with in its entirety: it may raise issues that could only properly be addressed by another adviser, an accountant or doctor, for example.

These matters outlined above are all factors that you may have to take into account before you even start your research. In *Problem Solving*, Margot Costanzo[3] calls these 'threshold issues' and they form part of 'situation appraisal', which she describes as the first step in a four phase approach to problem solving. If you would like to read more about problem solving techniques, please refer back to the previous chapter or, for more detail, see Costanzo's book.

For whatever reason, you may find that you have to limit your research. The most sensible method of doing this is by identifying the key issues raised by the problem you are looking into. This is an important part of problem identification. Prioritise your research by focusing on the most important factors. This need to concentrate on an initial determination of what it is you are trying to answer will require you to analyse the problem before starting any research. When analysing the problem, endeavour to keep the requirements of the client or other recipient of the research foremost in your mind. Approach it not as a piece of pure legal research (where you might consider 'what issues are being raised here?') but rather as a practical question that must be solved (think: 'what is the question I am being asked to answer?'). This is a matter of problem identification and analysis.

Problem identification and analysis may well be wider than you would imagine. So far, we have considered problem identification. However, there is clearly more to it than that. We must also analyse the problem. In David Stott's book *Legal Research*,[4] he provides a useful three stage model for the conducting of legal research. Again, this was considered in the previous chapter; however, it is equally relevant to PLR. He identifies the first stage in any piece of legal research as research planning, and identifies the following areas as important parts of the problem identification and analysis process:

• fact collection;
• problem identification;

---

3   Costanzo, M, *Problem Solving*, 1994, London: Cavendish Publishing.
4   Stott, D, *Legal Research*, 2nd edn, 1999, London: Cavendish Publishing.

- legal analysis;
- fact analysis;
- further fact collection;
- identifying avenues of research;
- generation of key search words.

When approaching any problem, you must ensure that you go through most, if not all of these steps. Some are reasonably clear, but others require further consideration.

Problem identification

Example

David Adams was involved in a fight outside his local pub. It appears likely that he will be prosecuted for his part in the fight and the injuries he inflicted on several other persons. David Adams has also heard that the owner of a car damaged in the fight intends to sue him to recover the costs of repairing the car, although he denies he went anywhere near the car. During the fight, David Adams was kicked repeatedly in the legs. He went to the Accident and Emergency department of his local hospital, but was told that he had only minor cuts and bruising to his legs. The day after the fight he returned to the hospital as the pain had not decreased, but again was told there was nothing seriously wrong with his legs. When the pain increased, David Adams returned to the hospital for a third time. On this visit to the hospital, his legs were X-rayed and it appears that one of his legs was broken in two places. As a result of the delay in diagnosing the fractures to his leg, David Adams has now been told it is likely that his leg will not heal completely straight and that he will be left with a slight limp that could be permanent. He has also had to have an operation to insert metal plates and pins into his leg. His leg will now be in plaster for a minimum of three weeks. As David Adams is a self-employed roofing contractor, his incapacity is having a severe impact upon his financial position. He wants your advice.

Can you identify the problems here?

Faced with these facts, you must filter the information you have been given to identify the problem you are being asked to address. The problem is not a simple, single-issue question that can be easily answered. The problem raises questions of criminal law and tort, civil litigation, medical or clinical negligence and economic loss. You would be expected to identify the areas on which David Adams requires advice: the criminal prosecution against him; potential civil liability in relation to the damaged car; and his claim against the hospital. You would have to research each problem to be able to offer complete advice.

Legal analysis

This clearly shows the role of analysis in the early stages of PLR. Legal analysis is largely self-explanatory. It is also probably what you are used to from the academic stage of your legal training. You will already be familiar with the concept of considering a given set of facts from a legal viewpoint to establish what area of law is involved, etc. This will require you to demonstrate a level of legal knowledge. If the area of law you are being required to consider is unfamiliar to you, your problem solving may have to begin with some preliminary reading to acquire a basic level of legal knowledge. You will need the skills of legal analysis in PLR; in fact, if anything, it is more important than in pure legal research. As noted previously, problems requiring PLR skills to produce an answer will tend to be unfocused. Unlike seminar problems, etc, PLR problems may involve consideration of several areas of law to solve one query. In the very basic example above, the misdiagnosis or mistreatment of an injury sustained in a fight may require you to look into the areas of criminal law, tort and medical negligence. To be able to offer sensible advice on such a problem, you must have established what areas of law would be relevant before you could start to research the client's actual position. A failure to conduct a thorough legal analysis at this early stage could mean that your answer addresses some, but not all of the points raised by your client's problem. This advice would not be sufficient and may even be negligent (see below, p 96, for common student problems).

Fact analysis

You will have been given the facts, by your tutor, or possibly by your supervisor or pupil master, or you may have had to interview a client to elicit the facts. But you cannot stop there – to be able to answer any problems raised by the facts, you must engage in what is known as fact analysis or fact management. Again, to a certain extent, this may be something with which you are already familiar. When given a seminar problem, you may have been expected to reach some conclusion on the likely legal position based on the particular facts. A very simple example would be in tort: when studying negligence, you will have looked at the issue of causation and you may have had to draw conclusions on whether a particular set of facts and actions led to the commission of a tort, or whether an intervening act broke the chain of causation. This would require you to analyse the facts of each person's actions.

In PLR, fact analysis is very important. When faced with a typical unfocused problem, whether presented by a tutor or by a client, supervisor or pupil master, you must establish the relevant facts. A tutor may deliberately give you an unfocused problem to encourage you to develop your skills of fact analysis. In practice, you may find that much of the information you are given by a client, whilst important to the client, will not be relevant to his or her legal position. To carry out PLR effectively, it is vital that you learn to filter the information you are given and concentrate only on the relevant facts. This may be a skill you have acquired without necessarily recognising it as fact analysis. From the start of your legal education, you will have been required to read case reports. These can be very long and not all of the information contained within a case report would be necessary to your understanding of the case or the decision reached on the facts. In reading and understanding these reports, you will have engaged in fact analysis by concentrating only on those facts necessary to facilitate your understanding. This fact analysis is required in PLR and is something you should practise if you feel unsure about your abilities in this area.

In the previous chapter, there was an exercise involving the analysis of a case report and identification of material facts. If you would like practice at this, please turn back and attempt it now.

That was basic fact analysis. PLR will require you to go even further. Your problem will have a particular outcome, whether it is that your client decides to proceed with a civil case or decides not to do so, or whether you can advise a client what defences might be available to him or her in relation to the charge they face. The desired outcome will depend upon whether you are dealing with a contentious matter or a non-contentious matter. The nature of the matter will also affect your fact analysis. You must apply these skills of analysis to your problem. Most PLR problems will require both legal and fact analysis. It is important that you master the necessary analytical skills; many legal research assessments are designed specifically to draw on students' ability to analyse a case.

Consider the basic case analysis you must do when faced with a contentious matter requiring PLR. Look at the following set of facts. Imagine that you are the trainee solicitor or pupil dealing with this matter. You should attempt a legal and factual analysis of the facts given.

Example

You have been asked to look into the matter of James Brown, who has been involved in some trouble and wants to know what might happen to him. Last Tuesday, he went out with a group of 10 or 12 friends, not all of them well known to him, but some were his good friends with whom he went out often. They had gone out because it was James's friend Sue Green's 21st birthday party. The evening had started at about 9.30 pm, when they all met up in the local pub and had several drinks. James could not remember how many rounds of drinks were bought in the pub or by whom, but he thinks it must have been quite a few as they did not leave the pub until 10.45 pm. They had intended to leave the pub earlier, but had to wait for some of the group to arrive and they had been held up waiting for a bus which arrived about 20 minutes late. After everyone had arrived, they left the pub and went to a club which they go to often, not every week, but James and his friends had been to that club quite a few times before. They stayed in the club for the rest of the night, leaving at about 2.30 am. They had all had a few more drinks in the club, but not too many, as the drinks were very expensive and neither James nor any of his friends had much money that night. They also knew they would need to save some money to get taxis home as there was no night bus and it was too far to walk. When they left the club, James and his friends joined a queue at a taxi rank outside the club. While they were standing in the queue, James was aware of some pushing and shoving in the queue behind him, but did not think much about it. James then became aware of someone pushing him in his back. He turned and faced a man in a blue shirt and black jeans who put his face very close to James's face and shouted that James had pushed his way into the queue and taken the man's place. The man swore at James. James told the man that he had not pushed into the queue but that he had joined the queue before the man had arrived. He thinks he may have sworn at the man. James thinks he remembers the man pushing him and James fell backwards onto someone else. This was one of his friends, Katie Lee, who, when James fell on her, fell in turn onto the ground. James turned to face the man behind him and shouted 'look what you've done'. The man shouted that it had nothing to do with him and that James had started it. James thinks he might have pushed the man. He remembers that there was a scuffle between James and a couple of his friends and the man and some of his friends. James was left with a bleeding nose and a cut eye. The man had a split lip and Katie Lee had cuts and bruises to her arm where she had landed on the ground. James remembers the man with the split lip shouted he would 'get' James and make him pay. James cannot really remember things very clearly, as he had drunk quite a lot and it all seemed to happen very quickly. James has now received a letter from a firm of solicitors stating that the man, a Tom White, is seeking damages for his injuries from James. He wants advice: what can he do?

Consider the above. You need to identify the problem James Brown faces. First, therefore, there will be some legal analysis: what is the charge or the allegation facing your client? Here, it appears to include the tort of battery and, possibly, assault. Next, you must consider: what are the elements of that charge or allegation? Battery is defined as the intentional and direct application of force to another person. Assault is where a claimant apprehended contact. Who has to prove each element? In civil actions, usually the person bringing the action. What is the standard of proof required? In a civil action, it will be on a balance of probabilities.

Once you have carried out this basic legal analysis, you must consider the facts as your client has presented them to you. His version of events is rather long and rambling. You need to filter down what your client has told you to establish the facts. What does your client say happened? What are the facts as he recalls them? You can safely discard quite a lot of your client's story which consists of irrelevant facts. What facts are relevant to the allegation of battery or assault?

Once you have established the relevant facts, you need to take the matter to the next stage. Remember, in PLR problems dealing with contentious matters, you cannot just consider your client's recollection – you must also consider other versions of the events. Have the police been involved? Does anyone challenge your client's version of events? What would the other side say happened? Where are the conflicts between the two accounts? Really, all that is relevant is the account of the events in the taxi queue. If you do find that there are conflicting views of the events, which is likely in the circumstances, consider who proves your client's version. Would anyone else in the taxi queue be able to support your client's version of events? Would their evidence be reliable? Who could prove the other side's version? What facts from your client's account of events will be important in any forthcoming action and which would be irrelevant or undisputed?

If the matter is likely to go to court, further considerations apply. Some facts will be 'good' facts, which would appear to support your client's version of events. However, some facts can be 'bad' facts, which look as though they may disprove your client's story. Wherever possible, you should attempt to identify facts as such. This may aid in preparation of your client's case. You can attempt to address any 'bad' facts only if you have identified them as such and researched into what likely use the opposition may make of the facts. However, do not accept the categorisation of facts as either good or bad without further consideration. What might initially appear as a 'good' fact which could support your client's story may well, under further analysis, collapse or be of doubtful value. Similarly, a 'bad' fact may not remain as potentially damaging to your client's case as it initially appeared when analysed further or your research could uncover a good counter-argument. Do not be afraid to face 'bad facts' – it is better to face them at the case analysis stage rather than in court, unprepared.

That was an example based on a contentious case. However, similar analysis is equally important in non-contentious cases. Consider the following example.

Example

Scott and Sons Ltd is a national chain of estate agents, with over 500 branches. It has been in talks with Trevor Elliott and Tricia Hines to acquire their local chain of estate agents, Elliott Hines, which has 15 branches. Elliott Hines is a partnership: the partners are Trevor Elliott, Tricia Hines and Tricia's ex-husband, Tony. Recently, Tony has not been working as hard as Trevor and Tricia would like and they would be keen to remove him from the partnership, preferably before the sale if possible. You have been asked to advise Trevor Elliott and Tricia Hines on the purchase. Tony Hines has not yet contacted you. Scott and Sons has indicated that it might be prepared to pay up to £2 million, but Trevor Elliott, who has been carrying on most of the negotiations, anticipates that it might be prepared to offer more. Trevor Elliott and Tricia Hines have indicated that sums in the region of £2 million would not be acceptable, but Tony Hines apparently would be keen to accept an offer at such a level. Scott and Sons would like to retain the senior management of Elliott Hines, but would not want to retain all junior staff. Trevor Elliott and Tricia Hines are not too keen on this, as they would like all staff to be kept on; however, they would not be prepared to lose the deal for this. Scott and Sons would, of course, expect the name 'Elliott Hines' to be changed to Scott and Sons, but there has been some resistance to this in the talks from Trevor Elliott; Tricia tells you that she and Tony Hines are indifferent to this. However, Tricia tells you that she and Tony are very concerned that Scott and Sons would impose restrictive covenants to prevent them setting up another estate agency in the area for five years. Trevor Elliott is nearing retirement age and so would be quite happy to agree to any such restriction.

You would be expected to analyse the facts to answer questions like: what does Scott and Sons want? What does Trevor Elliott want? What does Tricia Hines want? What does Tony Hines want? What are the conflicts between them? What is Tony Hines's position? What matters could be negotiated? What would be non-negotiable? Could Trevor Elliott and Tricia Hines remove Tony Hines from the partnership? If so, when? How? What would Tony Hines be entitled to if the sale went ahead? Could Tricia and Tony Hines resist the restrictive covenants? Would it be possible for them to accept the restrictive covenants?

This should give you an indication of the necessary steps involved in problem identification and analysis. As you start to undertake PLR, you may want to follow an outline, such as David Stott's, quite strictly, to ensure you are addressing all the aspects of problem identification and analysis. However, as you become more experienced in PLR, you should find that several of these steps become more natural – you would not undertake PLR without addressing these points.

Problem identification and analysis must be your first step in any piece of PLR. It is an important preliminary step which can save you a lot of time at a later stage of your PLR:

> From a mass of raw information (including documents and clients' assertions of purported fact) the lawyer has to recognise and select the significant facts in order to arrive at the legal issue. Faulty analysis will lead to a mis-formulation and thence to an answer, perhaps correct, to the wrong question. Sound analysis of the raw material, identifying the legal issues, brings the problem into focus so that it is then susceptible to sound research technique.[5]

---

5   Tunkel, V, *Legal Research: Law-Finding and Problem-Solving*, 1992, London: Blackstone.

This is what you must aim for in your PLR. You can see from this how important the legal and factual analysis is.

Key words

At this stage, you might think that, having identified the problem and having analysed both the law and the facts, you are ready to start your research. However, there is still one more important step to address. Before you plunge headlong into a library, stop and think: what are you going to look up? Many students, having completed their problem identification and attempted to refine their search by analysing what it is they are being asked to research, will then undo all their good work by launching an unfocused assault on the source materials available. A far more sensible approach involves the student in the determination of a suitable starting point for their research. Indeed, David Stott includes the generation of key search words in the initial stage of legal research as part of the research planning, and the development of relevant key words is a key factor of the *BVC Outcome Specification* for legal research.

Clearly, the use of key words is important in PLR. In simple or focused problems, it is usually fairly clear which area of law you should be addressing. However, PLR problems can be multi-faceted and unfocused. They may involve several different areas of law. Or, they may involve very specific points in an area of law with which you are unfamiliar. The use of key words could give you a point of entry into the source material. Indeed, with some sources like LEXIS, the internet or other computer-based sources, like Lawtel, the use of key words can be vital. Part of your problem identification, therefore, involves you identifying suitable words or legal phrases which you can use as the starting point for your search through the texts, etc.

Example

Consider the case of a company director who is concerned that he may have broken 'some law or another' by selling some of his shares in the company three days before it made an announcement that it had not won an important contract that would have secured its future profitability. When the company made the public announcement its share price dropped sharply. What advice could you give him?

Where would you start? This is unlikely to be an area of law with which you are familiar, so will need all of your skills of legal research to tackle it. The problem is clearly identified for you; you do not have to do much, if anything, to filter the facts given to define the problem you have to address. The difficulty is more in knowing how or where to begin your research. This is where key words are important. If you think about the key search words in connection with this problem, it will give you a place to start your research. So, think: what key search words would you identify in connection with this problem?

Some of the key words you could have considered are: company; director; shares; sale; public announcement. Researching these key words would produce information about companies legislation and, hopefully, eventually, insider dealing legislation.

There is no right or wrong way to approach this question, but if you identified some or all of the suggested key words, you would at least be able to start researching this problem in a logical fashion. If you found that researching one of the key areas did not appear to produce an answer to the problem, you should not panic; merely regroup and search against another of the key words you had identified. Approaching the problem from a different angle may produce the answer you were looking for.

As should now be clear, before you attempt to look at any source materials, you must make sure you have sufficiently analysed the problem to understand what it is you are being required to answer. With many students, there is a great temptation to run off to a library and to start perusing *Halsbury's Statutes* before you have really understood what it is you have been asked to do. Think through the problem before even attempting to start researching the answer. Only once you have successfully identified your problem and analysed your facts to determine what it is you are being required to research, will you be ready to move to the next stage in PLR: information search and retrieval.

Information search and retrieval

Once you have assembled all the relevant facts, the second step in conducting legal research will involve a search for the principles and rules of law applicable to the facts of the case you have been asked to consider.

You should now be aware of the precise nature of the problem you are attempting to answer, following your problem identification and analysis. What you must now do is to determine what sources you must use to reach that answer.

In David Stott's three stage research process, this second step is known as 'research implementation' and involves the following steps:

- identifying problems for resolution (which we have considered above);
- identifying relevant source materials;
- locating source materials;
- effective use of source materials;
- analysis of research findings;
- identifying further problems.

Sources

Clearly, we should therefore look at the sources you may use. In the previous chapter, we considered some of the most useful sources you may consult when carrying out legal research. You may want to refresh your memory of these, although most should already be familiar to you. PLR will often draw upon the same sources of information as other legal research. There are some sources which are so widely used that it would be safe to assume they would offer a sensible starting point for most PLR exercises. You may have to consult more specialist sources which could be relevant to your research when carrying out PLR, for example, where you are required to consider European law or particular areas of criminal law. What sources you should use to research your problem will often depend upon the nature of the problem you are being required to consider, your personal preferences and also upon the facilities to which you have access, but certain general sources can be a useful starting point. However, before looking in detail at some sources of information or legal research, there may be factors which influence the choice of source material which are peculiar to PLR.

As considered briefly earlier, there may be constraints upon you when you are undertaking your PLR and these could impact upon the sources you use. These could be time or financial restraints. A vital question identified by Guy Holborn[6] that you must ask yourself is 'how comprehensive must I be and how much time do I have?' The time constraints under which you are likely to have operated so far will have been fairly slight; preparation for next week's seminar, for example, or a submission date for a piece of coursework. A piece of PLR may have to be completed by a tight deadline determined by the client's next visit or the need to serve or file papers within the set time periods. This will obviously have a bearing upon how comprehensive you could be in attempting to answer your PLR problem and how many sources you can consult and to what level of detail. You may have to do some form of cost/benefit analysis, weighing up the cost involved of using a particular source of information against the benefits of achieving a result relatively quickly. For example, should you use an on-line service like LEXIS, which is quick, but which costs money, or do a manual search, which is more time consuming, but which is free?

This may not be your decision; a supervisor or pupil master may make it for you. Your supervisor may already have carried out a form of cost/benefit analysis in deciding to give you the PLR to do, rather than doing it him or herself. However, when it is left for you to decide, you must take certain factors into account in attempting to strike the right balance: 'The variables are the quality of information required, the value of that information to you, the speed with which it is required and the cost (or value) of your time.'[7]

Something else you will have to consider is how comprehensive your answer to the problem should be. 'One of the techniques of legal research is striking a balance between over-retrieval and under-retrieval.'[8] You need sufficient information to be able to answer the problem thoroughly (and under-retrieval is often a common problem with students – see below, p 96, for common student problems) but not so over the top that the answer is unusable or ceases to be practical. Remember that you may need to be able to present your research in a form that is accessible to a client. Students lacking confidence often over-retrieve information and include all of it in their answer, afraid to discard any for fear of missing something relevant. This approach is unlikely to produce a competent assessment or a memorandum satisfactory to a supervisor or pupil master. You are required to be selective, accurate and relevant.

Information search

This is an area where your previous experience of legal research will be useful and can be applied to PLR. You will already have used a law library when you undertook pure legal research, so you should be able to locate and use a law library (you will note, for example, that this is a specific BVC requirement). This will, obviously, be as important to your information search and retrieval in the context of PLR as it was during the other

---

6   Holborn, G, *Butterworths Legal Research Guide*, 2nd edn, 2001, London: Butterworths.
7   *Ibid*.
8   *Ibid*.

academic stages of your legal education. You may find that the facilities to which you have access in practice are not quite as extensive as you may have been used to during the academic stage of your legal training and so this may curtail some avenues of research with which you were already familiar, but the legal research skills you have developed should be able to adapt to these circumstances.

However, a great many of the skills you have developed during the academic stage of your legal education will still be relevant. Such skills would include the ability to select only the relevant information from all that is available, to use indices within legal materials to refine your search and to use citations and accepted abbreviations, etc. Please turn back to the previous chapter if you think you need to be reminded of the most general source materials, for example, *Halsbury's, Current Law,* case reports, LEXIS, Lawtel, etc. You should also be aware of the steps you would need to take to ensure your material was up to date. In PLR it is especially important that you are considering only the current state of the law, and so the use of materials to ensure you are relying only upon up to date sources is vital. Increasingly, people are turning to the internet as a valuable source of information and this is no less important to PLR than it is to other areas of research. The internet is a particularly useful aid in checking whether information is up to date. You should, therefore, develop your IT skills to enable you to use the internet or other IT-based sources to locate relevant information.

So far, all the sources suggested above are likely to be familiar to you from the more academic stage of your legal education. However, we are mainly concerned here with PLR. Because PLR is different from pure legal research, the sources you may need to consult may differ. You are attempting to solve a real problem in a practical way. Often, these problems will not be capable of being answered merely by consulting the usual textbooks or digests. This is not to say that such sources will not be useful for PLR – they will. Such sources will be very useful for providing you with basic information or a springboard for the rest of your research. However, they may not be able to provide you with the full answer or offer you guidance on how the law would be applied in practical circumstances. For this, you may have to refer to more specialised texts – these are most often referred to as practitioners' sources. These will be the sources most frequently used by those in legal practice, whether as solicitors or barristers. You should, as far as possible, make yourself familiar with practitioners' sources, as they will be useful to you in PLR at any stage in your legal career.

For example, you will often have to refer to practitioner texts to obtain detailed information. An example of such practitioner texts would be the *Civil Procedure Rules* (1998, Sweet & Maxwell), *County Court Practice* (1997, Butterworths) or *Stone's Justices' Manual* (1997, Butterworths). The texts might not be so specific, but might be textbooks established as authorities in particular subjects; for example, Kemp and Kemp on *Quantum of Damages* (1975, Sweet & Maxwell). You may have to refer to journals which deal with particular areas of law, for example, construction law or patent law. The internet is also a source of specialist materials; for example, Medical Law On-Line, the reports of the Immigration Services Tribunal or the Employment Tribunals. Such specialist sites are often subscription sites, so your ability to access them may be limited.

Another example of the specialised materials you may encounter in PLR might be the *Encyclopaedia of Forms and Precedents* (Butterworths), or other similar precedent packages. Precedents are specimen agreements, etc, which lawyers can adapt to fit the circumstances of their client's case. These are not something you would have needed to use before, but are very popular with lawyers. The use of prescribed forms is quite common in practice and it is possible that the answer to your PLR may be as simple as finding the correct form to use in a particular case. Other sources of forms include *Atkin's Court Forms* (Butterworths) or packages available on PCs (for example, Laserforms or Oyez). Forms and precedents are also available on the internet; for example, at www.infolaw.co.uk.

A valuable source for lawyers is LEXIS, which has been referred to previously and was considered in the previous chapter. It is clearly useful in PLR, too; an analysis of existing and up to date case law could show whether your client's case has any chance of success on the facts. However, as mentioned in the previous chapter, LEXIS cannot be the starting point for your legal research. You must first have considered the problem and identified the essential questions to be answered and the relevant facts and key words before you could consider using LEXIS. As suggested above, you may find that access to LEXIS is restricted; many firms make surprisingly little use of LEXIS, possibly because the commercial charges for the use of LEXIS are considerably higher than academic rates. The cost to the firm of your finding an answer on LEXIS might not be recoverable from the client. You may have to rely on alternative sources. This is another reason why it is advisable to have an awareness of the wide range of sources available for PLR before you enter legal practice.

Another difference from the sources you may have used in your pure legal research is that PLR may involve you in a consideration of non-law sources. You are attempting to answer a practical problem. As mentioned previously, practical problems do not come neatly packaged like seminar problems or dissertations to address only one area of law. Practical problems can be unfocused, addressing many different points, and there is nothing which requires all those points to be purely legal points. Obviously, this is too wide an area to be dealt with easily, but it is possible to give certain examples. If you are considering a question of medical negligence, as well as looking at legal texts on negligence, you may also have to consider medical texts. There will be medical textbooks and also specialised sources, like Medline. If it is a business matter, you may need information about company finance and economics. There are several good internet sites which could be useful, like the Companies House website (www.companieshouse.co.uk). A matter concerning land may require you to get data from the Land Registry. There are many websites offering information about various government agencies: these are usually free and can offer some useful information, for example, about the Office of Fair Trading or the Patent Office. Again, the sources you will need to consider will depend upon the problem you are attempting to answer, but it is as well to be aware that it is not legal sources alone which will lead you to the necessary material for your answer.

That is an overview of the possible sources you may wish to consult. There are, of course, many more. Useful research tools mentioned in the previous chapter include *Legal Research: Law-Finding and Problem-Solving* by Victor Tunkel and, if you are looking more to the internet to provide your source material, *Researching the Legal Web* by Nick Holmes and Delia Venables.

Analysis of research findings

At this stage, you should sit back and reflect: have you answered the question or questions you identified at the start of your researches? Make sure all of the points have been addressed (see below, p 97). Did your research throw up more questions or raise further problems? If so, now is the time to attempt to research an answer to those matters before you deal with the presentation of your research. If you are confident that you have finished your research, you are ready to move to the next stage.

Presentation of research findings

Again, PLR is not merely about retrieving information. This is research with a practical aim. You are intending to offer the client an answer to their problem. Part of the skill of PLR will involve being able to present the results of your research in an accessible fashion. You want the tutor, client, supervisor or pupil master to be able to understand clearly how your research answers their problem.

Look back again at the LPC and BVC standards at the start of this chapter. Both identify presentation of the research as an important factor in PLR. Under the BVC Outcome Specification, students are expected to be able to come to a satisfactory answer to each of the questions posed and to give brief reasons for the answer arrived at, showing how those answers have been reached. The LPC written standards require that students should present the results of research in a clear, useful and reliable form. To meet the standards required of the professional bodies, the presentation of your research findings is obviously important. You need to be clear in your report about what questions you are answering, and reach a conclusion. The report needs to be in a 'useful' form, showing how you reached your answers. This will apply equally to any PLR you are required to do in practice, whether as a trainee solicitor, pupil or otherwise.

You also want the research to continue to work for you; if you are asked a follow-up question or if the results of your research are queried, you want to be able to answer any queries without having to go through the whole research process again. You might think it is unlikely that you would forget where or how you found a piece of information or a case reference, but it could be the case that your research is not read by the tutor, client, supervisor or pupil master for some time after you complete it. You may well have researched several other problems on different areas in the meantime. You want your research to include a record of how you obtained the information necessary to answer the initial question. That way, you can deal with any follow-up query, merely by referring back to your initial research report and taking it a step further. Your research report should make clear your research methodology, which is the methods and rules applied in conducting a systematic investigation into some matter.

David Stott's three stage model for the conducting of legal research identifies the following as important in research presentation:

- identification of recipient's needs or requirements;
- selection of appropriate format, for example, letter, memo, etc;
- use of clear and succinct language;
- use of appropriate language style, for example, informatory, advisory, recommendatory, demanding.

It is possible to expand upon these points and form a set of minimum criteria a research report should meet.

How are you to present your research? In what format? Does the client want you to send him or her a letter? (For more on this, you should refer to the chapters on legal writing.) Does your supervisor or pupil master want a memorandum? Although there is no one layout which would be correct in all circumstances, there may be a particular outline which you are expected to follow; for example, that adopted by your firm, chambers, organisation or teaching institution. Obviously one cannot address each potential formation here, but it is possible to identify certain key factors which will aid the presentation of your research findings.

The layout should aid logical organisation of your material. It should encourage you to order your thoughts and findings into a logical structure which is easy to follow for those reading your report. You should look, for example, at David Stott's outline, or the sub-headings here to offer a framework upon which to hang your research findings. As well as having a logical structure, your report must be grammatically correct. It is an obvious point, but think about your spelling, grammar, sentence construction, etc. The report should inspire the tutor, client, supervisor or pupil master to have confidence in you. Where relevant, do not be afraid to summarise or paraphrase; the person reading your report will be glad to have to focus only on the relevant information. The recipient of your research findings will not want to plough through every piece of information you uncovered; part of presenting your memorandum or letter is selecting which information to include. Let your guiding rule be – keep it relevant. Concise, but thorough, is the best approach.

In all cases, your research report should clearly apply the law to the facts presented by the tutor, client, supervisor or pupil master. This will allow whoever is reading your report to understand how you have approached the problem set and demonstrate the relevance of the findings of your research. Your report should provide clear advice to the client or reach a specific conclusion based upon the facts.

An example may help to illustrate this point:

Example

Consider the following:

INTERNAL MEMORANDUM   **STRICTLY CONFIDENTIAL**

FROM: *Supervisor*

TO: *Trainee*

Please could you find out whether Salomon v Salomon (date unknown) is still good law?

A straightforward question. In fact, so straightforward that it is not even a problem that requires any filtering or defining; however, it will serve to demonstrate a point about presentation.

Consider the following possible answers that a supervisor could receive in response to such a query:

INTERNAL MEMORANDUM   *STRICTLY CONFIDENTIAL*

FROM: *Trainee*

TO: *Supervisor*

Yes.

Although undoubtedly to the point, and correct, this is clearly inappropriate presentation for a research memorandum. There is no indication from the memorandum what sources were consulted, that those sources have been considered to determine whether the case has been overruled, or, indeed, that the point has been researched at all.

What about the following:

INTERNAL MEMORANDUM   *STRICTLY CONFIDENTIAL*

FROM: *Trainee*

TO: *Supervisor*

Regarding your enquiry on whether Salomon v Salomon is good law, it would appear that it is.

Although more wordy and less direct, it says no more than the previous example. A supervisor would be unlikely to place any reliance on a memorandum that did not refer to its sources.

Consider a third possibility:

INTERNAL MEMORANDUM   *STRICTLY CONFIDENTIAL*

FROM: *Trainee*

TO: *Supervisor*

Salomon v A Salomon & Co Ltd [1897] AC 22 is still good law.

This is better than the previous examples, as it at least indicates a case reference. However, the supervisor is still unlikely to be satisfied. What is the authority for stating that the case remains good law?

A final example should give an indication of a more comprehensive approach to presentation.

INTERNAL MEMORANDUM   *STRICTLY CONFIDENTIAL*

FROM: *Trainee*

TO: *Supervisor*

Question: *Is Salomon v Salomon still good law?*

Answer: *Although decided in 1897, Salomon v A Salomon & Co Ltd is still good law as the leading authority for a company having a separate legal personality distinct from its members. It has not been overruled.*

Source: *Salomon v A Salomon & Co Ltd [1897] AC 22*

Updating: *Current Legal Information, Current Law Case Citator*

Although personal tastes on presentation will differ between each supervisor, pupil master or tutor, and you will have to tailor your style accordingly, the recipient of such a memorandum could feel confident that the point had been researched and the up to date position stated. The answer is clear, thorough and fairly succinct. If you were asked a follow-up question on the same subject, you would have a note of where your previous research led you and so could easily pick it up from there, without having to retrace your research which, in the case of a complicated research memorandum, could save you considerable time.

Ensure you have a logical structure to your research reports – it will be easier for you to structure your research and easier for the end-user to read. For examples, have a look at the exercises and suggested answers at the end of this chapter.

You should include a list of your sources in the report. This 'research trail' is a vital part of your research, showing how you reached the answer to your research. It could comprise a list of textbooks consulted, with appropriate page references, cases read or internet sites searched (including the date of any such search). This provides a useful record for you, enabling you to retrace the research easily, or for a tutor, supervisor or pupil master to follow where you obtained your material. It is often helpful, for yourself if not for the person the report was produced for, to note whether your sources were primary or secondary sources. You should always acknowledge any materials cited by you in the report. If you have not already done so, make sure you can correctly cite cases, statutes, etc. (This point is also addressed above, at p 75.)

When presenting the results of your research, point out how the case law or statute is relevant; equally, you should note differences that could serve to distinguish your problem from the facts of the decided case or make it fall outside the ambit of the statutory provision. Do not be afraid of 'negative' results – if your research indicates that a particular line of inquiry is futile or does not represent current law, do not be afraid to say so. This 'negative' result may in fact be what your supervisor or pupil master, or tutor, was actually looking for, to eliminate a line of inquiry or to ensure you carried out the research effectively.

COMMON STUDENT PROBLEMS

Legal problems and PLR in particular are often not as simple to solve as we would like to make them. A cursory approach may produce an answer, but it might not necessarily be the right answer.

A problem commonly faced by students undertaking PLR exercises is an unwillingness to answer the question set, or, to put it another way, to answer the question they think they have been set, rather than the question as it actually exists. There is always a reason why the problem you are facing has been phrased in a particular way. A supervisor or pupil master, or tutor, is attempting to get an answer to a specific question, whether to answer a client's query or to determine your abilities at PLR. Therefore, failing to address that exact question, as it was set, is likely to mean that you will fail that PLR assessment or be required to redo the research, having made an unfavourable impression of your PLR skills. So, consider: what question am I being asked to research an answer to? Define the question first, filter the problem set to determine the relevant points and only then research those points. Do not be tempted into answering a question that, to you, appears to be easier than or roughly the same point as the question that your supervisor or pupil master, or tutor raised. Answer the question set.

Students will often do badly at PLR exercises by failing to apply the results of their research to the facts of the question they were required to research. Merely producing a list of cases or statutory provisions, although they may be relevant to the facts of the problem, is insufficient. You must demonstrate the relevance of your PLR by applying it to the problem you were addressing. A memorandum of the results of your research that does not relate the answer to the problem is likely to fail a PLR assessment or be returned to you by your supervisor or pupil master, or tutor, for further work. A short memorandum recording research competently executed and demonstrating its relevance to the problem posed is always preferable to a long, rambling, discursive memorandum. A supervisor or pupil master is likely to ask you to research a point because they do not have time to do so – obviously, therefore, they do not have the time to plough through a memorandum of research that lacks application. Demonstrate the relevance of your research as succinctly as you can. (This also raises questions about the presentation of your research findings – see above, p 93.)

Another common student shortcoming in addressing PLR exercises is failing to find the most up to date material relevant to the problem. This is clearly a product of inadequate research. Students may find what they think is the 'answer' to a problem and settle for that, without undertaking further research to determine whether that 'answer' does, in fact, represent the current state of the law. If this failure to complete the research properly occurs during the professional courses, whether LPC or BVC, the student is likely to fail that particular assessment. This in itself should be sufficiently serious to ensure that you always carry out the necessary checks to ensure you have correctly identified the most up to date position. However, if you fail to do so during a training contract or pupillage the consequences could be much more far-reaching – the inadequate research could lead to a supervisor or pupil master relying on out of date case law or statute and therefore being unable to represent the client's interests properly, which could be tantamount to negligence. So, it is vital that you make sure that the final stage of any PLR you undertake is always to ensure that the case or statute law on which you are relying represents the current state of the law.

Some students find their research works well and produces a sensible answer, but that they receive poor marks for it if it is done as part of a professional course, or that their supervisor/pupil master is not pleased with the answer if it is produced in practice. It may be that you have started your research from too narrow a focus. Whilst, from your point of view, the research may have been successful, in that it produced an answer, the answer may not be sufficient to satisfy the person posing the research problem. Your initial answer, although correct as far as it goes, may not address all of the complexities of the issue. You may only have addressed the main point posed by the problem, leaving secondary points unanswered. This will not be adequate. You might not have appreciated what an important bearing some of the minor points may have on the overall answer. Make sure you have sufficiently analysed the problem to understand what it is you are being required to answer. Explore all aspects of the problem.

It may be that you cannot reach a definite answer on the basis of the facts given. This is not a reason to panic. Remember that this is PLR, not pure legal research. There may not be an exact answer on the facts given. You may have to offer a series of alternative solutions for the client to consider. This is one of the cornerstones of PLR: the giving of advice. Your advice might lead the client to a particular course of action, but it may be one that the client has chosen from several possible courses of action suggested by your research. Another reason why you might be unable to reach a form of conclusion is that you may not have sufficient information to do so. This can happen even if you were given a full briefing before you started your research. It may be that your research uncovers several possible options, any one of which might apply, but you do not know enough about your client's circumstances to determine which definitely would apply. You may have to go back to the client for further information to be able to suggest one course above any other or for further information to be able to refine your search parameters before you could start your research again to provide a solution to the problem.

A common student problem is under-retrieval or settling for the first answer which seems to provide a reasonable solution to the problem. This answer may not be sufficient, or it may even be wrong. A frequently encountered example of under-retrieval is a failure to ensure that the first solution you encounter accurately reflects the most up to date state of the law. Make sure you have sufficiently analysed the problem to understand what it is you are being required to answer. Then make sure that the answer you have come up with does actually address the problem and does not stop short of offering a full solution or fails to present a complete picture of the relevant law because you stopped your research too soon. Be prepared to look further into the problem. The client will not be impressed by advice that encourages them to take a particular course of action, for example, taking the first steps towards litigation, if further research could have established that a recent case overruled the authority on which you had based your advice. It may well be that you have come across a particular problem before and are aware of matters which, whilst not raised specifically by the client's problem, could have a bearing on the advice you could give. Although, strictly speaking, this might be outside your brief from the client, you are attempting to give practical advice. Drawing upon your prior knowledge and investigating it further in the context of the client's problem would be PLR too. Consider this example:

Example

You are asked to consider the position where an elderly lady has recently changed her will to appoint her bank as executor, instead of her two nieces, aged 28 and 31, who are also the sole beneficiaries under the will. The nieces would prefer that they remain as joint executors, but do not want to upset their aunt by objecting. What you have been asked to determine is whether, after their aunt dies, the nieces could challenge the bank's appointment as executor and have themselves appointed instead.

Again, a reasonably focused problem. Think about how you could answer this query. The approach adopted to answer this query shows the difference between pure legal research, where finding the 'answer' would be sufficient, and practical legal research, where you are expected to apply the law to the facts.

The basic answer is that the aunt's choice of executor cannot be challenged. You could merely answer the query with this information and it would be correct, but not particularly helpful to the people raising the query. Stopping your research once you had uncovered this position would be an example of 'under-retrieval'. If you continued your researches beyond this point, you might uncover information that would be of interest to those raising the query. Merely answering the question would mean the nieces would be unable to do anything about a situation with which they are clearly unhappy. However, remember that it is important to strike a balance between 'under-retrieval' and 'over-retrieval' of information. A treatise on probate law would not be helpful. But, although the appointment of the bank as executor cannot be challenged, your answer need not stop there. You could offer some practical advice – that after the death of their aunt the nieces could ask the bank to renounce probate, although it could not be obliged to do so. You could also attempt to find out why the nieces are concerned about the bank acting as executor; you might be able to set their minds at rest by explaining how the bank should act, that it would have to consider the interests of the beneficiaries under the will, for example. Whilst this information was not specifically requested, providing it offers a better, more practical, answer to the query than a bald statement of the legal position. This is a clear example of the difference between pure legal research and PLR.

Another problem which students tend to have arises out of the initial fact analysis and concerns 'bad' facts. As mentioned above, it is important, in contentious matters, to identify facts as 'good' or 'bad' facts. Some students can have a tendency to ignore 'bad' facts, by not including them in the relevant facts requiring analysis. This is a fairly understandable approach, arising from the fact that you probably want to help your client. However, 'bad' facts cannot simply be ignored. If you fail to address them, you may be sure that the other side will not. By ignoring the 'bad' fact, you are denying your client an opportunity to have further research carried out into the point. In an assessment, a tutor may have included 'bad' facts specifically to determine how you deal with such a problem: failure to tackle the 'bad' facts will not impress, and this may be reflected in the marks you receive for any such assignment. Where you have identified bad facts, this should be looked upon as an opportunity to prepare your client's case to meet the point which is likely to be raised by the other side or to be important to the assessor. To be forewarned is to be forearmed.

EXERCISES

That is PLR in theory. You should now try to put your understanding of PLR into practice. Try some, or all, of the following exercises. Some are written as if set by a supervisor, some as if set by a pupil master. Whichever, all will be equally relevant, so you could attempt all the problems, regardless of whether you are intending to train as a solicitor or as a barrister. In any event, the need for research and the way in which you approach it would be very similar. What you are trying to develop is your skill as a legal researcher; once you have acquired that skill, you should be able to adapt it to address almost any piece of research you are asked to carry out during your legal career.

Remember the importance of layout in PLR. You may adopt any layout you wish for the answers to the following problems. When devising your own layout, remember the factors which must be included and how important it is that the structure of your answer is logical.

Exercise 1

You have received the following information and have been asked to produce a note of advice:

INTERNAL MEMORANDUM   **STRICTLY CONFIDENTIAL**

FROM: Edwina Halpern (Supervisor)

TO: Les Standford (Trainee)

RE: Allegra srl

Gianni Di Angelo is the sales director of Allegra srl, a very successful company registered in Italy. It has over 50 retail outlets in Italy and another 50 throughout mainland Europe. The company has decided to expand into the UK. A suitable site for the first UK retail outlet has been found, but we need to ensure that Allegra complies with UK registration requirements.

Please could you research this for me and prepare a report setting out the initial registration requirements for a company in this position.

Thank you.

Exercise 2

You have received the following information and have been asked to produce a note of advice:

INTERNAL MEMORANDUM   **STRICTLY CONFIDENTIAL**

FROM:	Edwina Halpern (Supervisor)
TO:	Les Standford (Trainee)
RE:	Jeremy Stocksfield/Beds & Co
OFFENCE:	Trades Descriptions Offences
DATE(S) OF OFFENCE:	January XXXX
PROSECUTOR:	Exborough Council
COURT:	Exborough Magistrates' Court

The background

This is a Trading Standards prosecution against Beds & Co. You don't really need to know all the details of the case: what is primarily in issue is whether the clothing supplied in their Pharaoh range was 100% Egyptian cotton as advertised – or whether it contained a substantial proportion of lower grade cotton.

We commissioned an expert's report from Dr Mary Taylor, who is head of Life Sciences at a local university. She has conducted chemical analysis of the cloth and her report indicates that although there is some limited 'contamination' by lesser grade cotton, the cloth is primarily made from premium grade Egyptian cotton. However, the council has instructed The Forensic Services Group, which has provided a report stating that electro-microscopic analysis of fibre samples shows the cloth is at least 60% lower grade American cotton.

The issue

The case was listed for trial at Exborough magistrates' court yesterday. The case rests almost entirely on the expert reports. Both experts gave live testimony and were cross-examined. When our expert, Mary Taylor, gave her testimony I was surprised because she was asked a number of very aggressive questions by the chair of the Bench, Norman Shawcroft. Up until that point, none of the Bench had said very much. The chair's questions to Mary were very hostile: he asked whether she had any qualifications from a 'proper' university; he interrupted her evidence at a number of points to challenge what she was saying and at one point he muttered to another member of the Bench something along the lines of 'Another so-called expert. Anything for a big fee'.

The case was only part-heard, and has been relisted for the rest of the defence evidence in four weeks' time.

This morning, however, Mary Taylor telephoned me. She said that she had been thinking about things overnight and she had suddenly realised that she had in fact come across Norman Shawcroft before. Mary lives next door to a golf club which last year made an unsuccessful application for extensions to the clubhouse. At the planning inquiry, Mary was one of the most vocal protestors against the application, and she addressed the planning inquiry on behalf of the local residents. Mary now recalls seeing Shawcroft at the planning inquiry and thinks he must be involved with the golf club. As far as she can remember, Shawcroft did not address the inquiry, but he was present with the other representatives from the golf club. I have rung the club and they confirm that Shawcroft is indeed one of the committee members.

Obviously I am concerned about this – perhaps it may explain why we received such harsh treatment yesterday. I would like to raise this matter when we are next in front of the Bench, but I need to know exactly where we stand legally. I'm pretty sure that there have been a number of cases during the last couple of years which could be relevant.

Please could you do some urgent research into the issues that arise – I need to know what the up to date legal position is.

Thank you.

Exercise 3

You have received the following information and have been asked to produce a note of advice:

INTERNAL MEMORANDUM   **STRICTLY CONFIDENTIAL**

FROM: Edwin Halpern (Pupil master)

TO: Lisa Standford (Pupil)

RE: TDP Smith Ltd

NOTE OF CONFERENCE WITH MR ANDERSON, INSTRUCTING SOLICITOR

Mr Anderson instructed me that he has just met with Mr Smith, managing director of TDP Smith Ltd. TDP Smith Ltd have, over the years, acquired several industrial units on the local industrial estate. Mr Smith told Mr Anderson that, due to changes in their business, they have let one of these units, which has become surplus to their requirements, to Steel plc (the tenant). The lease (which was not drafted by Mr Anderson's firm) is for a term of 15 years and commenced four years ago. It contains an option for the tenant to determine (break clause) on the fifth anniversary of the lease.

According to Mr Smith, when the lease commenced four years ago there was a shortage of industrial units in the area and this was reflected in the rent payable under the lease. However, since then the situation has reversed and there is now an oversupply of industrial units, leading to a general decrease in the levels of rent payable. Under the terms of the lease, the rent is reviewed every five years, but in an upwards only direction.

Mr Smith informed Mr Anderson that notice (break notice) has now been served purporting to exercise the option to determine the lease. The notice has been served by Metal Formations Ltd (who are in occupation of the unit), who are a subsidiary company of the tenant's, as they have found alternative accommodation at a substantially reduced rent. TDP Smith Ltd is keen to keep the tenant if at all possible. Although there have been several occasions when the rent was late in being paid and there have been some breaches of the repairing covenants, the rent TDP Smith Ltd can expect on a re-letting will be substantially less than they are currently receiving.

Attached are copies of the relevant clauses in the lease. Mr Anderson has another meeting with Mr Smith next week.

Please can you look at the attached documentation and let me know by way of a memorandum if there are any grounds on which TDP Smith can resist the break notice and if there is anything Mr Anderson should raise with Mr Smith at their meeting next week.

Thank you.

RELEVANT LEASE CLAUSES

7.2.1   In every fifth year of the Term and also in the last six months thereof whether determined by effluxion of time or otherwise in a proper and workmanlike manner to prepare and paint with two coats of good quality paint all the internal parts of the Premises usually or requiring to be painted and in like manner to prepare and repolish or revarnish with best quality material all the internal parts of the premises usually or requiring to be polished or varnished.

7.2.2 From time to time and at all times during the Term to well and substantially repair cleanse and keep in good and substantial repair and condition the Premises.

7.2.3 To clean the Premises and keep them in clean condition.

15.7 If the Tenant wishes to determine this Lease on the fifth anniversary of the Term commencement date and shall give to the Landlord not less than six months' notice in writing and shall up to the time of such determination pay the rent reserved by and reasonably perform and observe the covenants contained in this Lease then upon expiry of such notice this Lease shall cease and determine but without prejudice to the respective rights of either party in respect of any antecedent claim or breach of covenant.

Exercise 4

You have received the following information and have been asked to produce a note of advice:

INTERNAL MEMORANDUM   **STRICTLY CONFIDENTIAL**

FROM: Edwina Halpern (Supervisor)

TO: Les Standford (Trainee)

RE: *London Train Construction Ltd v Genocom*

MATTER: Breach of contract

I have a query regarding the conduct of one of our civil litigation files, *London Train Construction Ltd v Genocom*. A solicitor who has left the firm ran this file and it seems that it was not run well.

We began proceedings on behalf of the claimant against the defendant two years ago. The case concerns the breach of a commercial contract for the supply and delivery of materials for the construction of the Jubilee Line extension to the London Underground. Our case is pretty strong and if we win, very high damages could be awarded. There have been some considerable delays on this file including one of nine months when we should have been following the standard directions and preparing evidence. The defendant has just put in an application for the case to be struck out.

Please will you look into this matter. Are there any case precedents that we can refer to, to argue that the case should not be struck out?

Thank you.

SUGGESTED POINTS OF ANSWER TO EXERCISES

Suggested points of answer to Exercise 1

Identification of areas for research

From the information you have been given, it would appear that the areas you have been required to consider are:

- registration regime for overseas companies establishing a branch in the UK;
- requirements for registration.

Key words

The key words you could focus on might be 'overseas companies', 'branch' and 'registration'.

Where would you look to find this information? If it is an area with which you are unfamiliar, it may be best to go back to some general sources. Look in *Halsbury's Laws*, or a company law textbook, or the internet, using the key words as a starting point. These sources may give you the answer. If not, they should at least help you to identify the relevant legislation, the Companies Act 1985. Your research should direct you to the Companies Act 1989, which amended the 1985 Act to incorporate the 11th EC Directive on Company Law (89/666/EC). The 1985 Act provisions which are relevant are ss 690(A) and 691; Sched 21A–D. You should then be able to produce an answer to the problem posed.

Conclusion of research

Once you have found the necessary information, you need to present the findings of your research. Remember, this must be in a form suitable for use by supervisor/pupil master/client (for example, stand alone memo; accessible language, etc).

If you have carried out this research, what you should find is that there are two sets of rules applying to companies not originally registered in the UK but which set up business here.

If the establishment in the UK is a 'branch', then it must be registered under regulations implementing the 11th EC Directive on Company Law and not under the original Companies Act 1985 rules for an overseas company. This requires a Form BR1 to be delivered to the Registrar of Companies within one month of the branch opening in the UK, including the information required by para 2A of Sched 21A to the Companies Act 1985.

(You might have to set out information required, if that level of detail was required in the memo.)

If the company establishes a place of business in the UK which does not amount to a branch, it must be registered under the original Companies Act 1985 rules as an overseas company (and not as a branch). This requires delivery of a Form 691 to the Companies Registrar within one month of the place of business being established, including the details required by s 691 of the Companies Act 1985.

(You might have to set out information required, if that level of detail was required in the memo.)

Clearly, the question of whether the retail outlet being opened by Allegra srl is a 'branch' or not is the key question. However, as your research should have established, there is no statutory definition of 'branch'. It is largely a question of European law (*Establishments Somafer SA v Saar-Ferngas AG* [1978] ECR 2183). The key question is whether it is possible to enter into business with the company at that place, or whether such matters must be referred overseas. If it is possible to contract or enter into business with the company through the UK office, it must be a branch. This would appear to be the case, provided there is someone authorised to represent the company in trading matters at the UK office.

Answers to the supervisor's query

Applying the facts

- You would need further information from the client to determine whether a 'branch' is being established.
- It might be worthwhile pointing out to the client that there are certain advantages in establishing a 'branch'; for example, the ability to file accounts prepared according to the laws of the country of incorporation (Italy).
- If a branch is established, we should ensure we have from the client sufficient information to complete a Form BR1. This should be filed at Companies House within one month of the branch opening in the UK. A filing fee of £20 is required.

Research report

Do not forget that you should keep a research report (or 'research trail'), setting out the methodology of your research, what sources were used, etc. Also, to ensure material is up to date, use *Halsbury's Noter Up* or some other service, or the internet (in which case, make a careful note of the date of your search).

Primary source(s)

Sections 690(A), 691 and Sched 21A to the Companies Act 1985, as amended by the Companies Act 1989 – found via *Halsbury's Laws*.

References

Establishments Somafer SA v Saar-Ferngas AG [1978] ECR 2183.

www.companieshouse.gov.uk

Updating

Check there have been no further cases affecting the authorities you relied upon and that any statutes or texts relied upon are up to date.

You could check this via the internet or, for example, *Halsbury's Noter Up* service (again, it is important to make a note of the date on which you checked your sources were up to date).

Suggested points of answer to Exercise 2

Identification of areas for research

This is primarily a question to do with judicial bias.

In addition to this, you would probably be expected to deal with issues under Art 6 of the European Convention on Human Rights and Fundamental Freedoms (ECHR) (the right to a fair trial) – and, in particular, the right to 'a fair hearing ... before an independent and impartial tribunal', following the incorporation of the ECHR into UK domestic law in October 2000.

Key words/phrases

You should focus on key words such as 'bias' and 'impartiality'. Be careful not to get sidetracked into 'golf clubs' and 'planning applications'.

Conclusion of research

The long-established test for judicial bias is that in *Gough* [1993] AC 646: is there a real danger of prejudice? *Gough* will be found via any of the practitioner texts, or via *Halsbury's*.

In 1999, this was revisited by the Court of Appeal in five linked cases: *Locabail (UK) v Bay Field Properties and Other Applications* [2000] 1 All ER 65. However, the law relating to judicial bias was changed in *Director General of Fair Trading v Proprietary Association of Great Britain* (also known as *Re Medicaments and Related Classes of Goods (No 2)*) [2001] 1 WLR 700. This brought the traditional test in *Gough* into line with Art 6. The *DG of Fair Trading* case adjusted the test in *Gough* so that the test is not of actual bias but an objective appraisal of whether the circumstances of the case give rise to a reasonable apprehension of bias.

The facts

Director General of Fair Trading v Proprietary Association of Great Britain involved an appeal from the Restrictive Practices Court. That court sits with a judge and two lay assessors. One lay assessor is an expert on economic issues. Each of the parties in the case called their own experts. The lay assessor, some days into the trial, rang the experts for one party to ask if there was any possibility of her getting a job with them in the future! She then told the judge that she had done this. Both parties asked the court to recuse itself. The court declined, holding that there was no real danger of bias. The Court of Appeal considered the Convention jurisprudence and made a 'modest adjustment' to the test in *Gough* so that the test is not of actual bias but of the objective appraisal of whether the circumstances give rise to a reasonable apprehension of bias.

Answers to supervisor's query

Applying the facts

There are some striking similarities between the facts of the cases – but, arguably, the judge's comments here are couched very widely, and are not academic writings on an area of judicial specialism. It is certainly arguable that they do not, of themselves, amount to bias.

If the client wishes to go ahead and appeal against the decision, appeal routes will be to the Court of Appeal (Criminal Division). An initial application for leave to appeal against conviction will need to be made within 28 days of the date of conviction.

Research report

Primary source(s)

The case of *Gough* will be found via any of the practitioner texts, or via *Halsbury's*.

You could find the *Director General of Fair Trading* case via a number of sources; for example, *Current Law*. It could also be found by doing a search under the keyword 'bias' in Lawtel and in Criminal Law Week.

References

Gough [1993] AC 646.

Locabail [2000] 1 All ER 65.

Re Medicaments, etc (No 2) [2001] 1 WLR 700.

Updating

Check there have been no further cases overturning the decision in the *Director General of Fair Trading* case and that any texts referred to are up to date.

Use of internet sources should ensure the material is up to date, but it is worthwhile checking this point. A search on a database will produce many cases where the new test was applied, which may help you to answer your research question. An internet or database search may also show cases where the Director General of Fair Trading case was distinguished (as in *Kjell Tore Skjevesland v Geveran Trading Co Ltd* [2002], [2003] 1 WLR 912, for example), which again may be helpful when you attempt to apply the law to the facts of your problem. If you use traditional paper-based sources, you must make sure they state the current position.

Suggested points of answer to Exercise 3

Identification of areas for research

The question is mainly about the validity of the break notice. You could start your research by referring to *Halsbury's Laws* or go straight to a specialised textbook: Woodfall, *Landlord and Tenant* (Sweet & Maxwell), for example.

Key words

'Break notice'.

Conclusion of research

There are several main points to consider:

(a) The tenant (that is, Steel plc) hasn't given the notice.

Your research should establish that a notice specifying the wrong party as tenant may be ineffective: authority *Lemmerbell Ltd v Britannia LAS Direct Ltd* [1998] 3 EGLR 67.

Could the *Mannai* principle (from *Mannai Investment Co Ltd v Eagle Star Life Assurance Co Ltd* [1997] AC 749 (HL), and referred to in the textbooks) operate to validate the break notice? Would the reasonable recipient dismiss the possibility of assignment to an associated company?

Speedwell Estates Ltd v Dalziel [2001] EWCA Civ 1277.

Burman v Mount Cook Land Ltd [2001] EWCA Civ 1712.

Ravensoft Properties Ltd v Hall [2001] EWCA Civ 2034.

Havant International Holdings Ltd v Lionsgate (H) Investment Ltd [1999] EGCS 144.

Although these are key questions, it is hard to provide an answer on the information given: see further information required below.

(b) The date to determine the lease in the break notice is incorrect, as it is only four years since the commencement of the term.

Would it be obvious to a reasonable recipient with knowledge of the lease and the fifth anniversary date that the tenant wished to determine the lease on that date?

An answer to these points can be found in *Mannai Investment Co Ltd v Eagle Star Life Assurance Co Ltd* [1997] AC 749 (HL) and *Carradine Properties Ltd v Aslam* [1976] 1 All ER 573. These would suggest that it would be obvious to a reasonable recipient with knowledge of the lease and the fifth anniversary date that the tenant wished to determine the lease on that date.

(c) Late payment of rent and breaches of repairing covenants.

The break clause requires reasonable compliance with the covenants in the lease. To establish what counts as reasonable compliance, consider *Reed Personnel Services plc v American Express Ltd* [1997] 1 EGLR 229; *Gardner v Blaxill* [1960] 1 WLR 762; and *Bassett v Whiteley and Another* (1983) 45 P & CR 87. Again, further information would be needed from the client to establish whether there has been reasonable compliance with the covenants (see below).

Answers to queries

Applying the facts

What needs to be raised with Mr Smith at next week's meeting?

We need to know the details of breaches of covenant and late payment of rent to decide whether there has been reasonable compliance with the tenant's covenants under the lease.

We need more information of the relationship between Steel plc and Metal Formations Ltd before it would be possible to give an opinion on whether the break notice is ineffective (note: this is an objective test, so what must be considered is not how the client TDP Smith Ltd understood the notices, but how a reasonable recipient would have understood them).

Research report

Primary source(s)

Woodfall, *Landlord and Tenant* (or you could use a computer-based source).

References

Lemmerbell Ltd v Britannia LAS Direct Ltd [1998] 3 EGLR 67.

Havant International Holdings Ltd v Lionsgate (H) Investment Ltd [1999] EGCS 144.

Mannai Investment Co Ltd v Eagle Star Life Assurance Co Ltd [1997] AC 749 (HL).

Speedwell Estates Ltd v Dalziel [2001] EWCA Civ 1277.

Burman v Mount Cook Land Ltd [2001] EWCA Civ 1712.

Ravensoft Properties Ltd v Hall [2001] EWCA Civ 2034.

Carradine Properties Ltd v Aslam [1976] 1 All ER 573.

Reed Personnel Services plc v American Express Ltd [1997] 1 EGLR 229.

Gardner v Blaxill [1960] 1 WLR 762.

Bassett v Whiteley and Another (1983) 45 P & CR 87.

Updating

Check there have been no further cases and that Woodfall, *Landlord and Tenant* is up to date.

Suggested answer outline to Exercise 4

Identification of areas for research

This case is about the procedure to be adopted when an application to strike out a case is made due to delay on the part of the claimant: in particular, whether sanctions other than striking out might be available and proportionate in some cases.

We need to make sure that the case can continue. If it is struck out, an appeal would still be possible, but would waste more time and money for the client.

Because the problem is one of procedure, the first place to look will be the Civil Procedure Rules 1998 (CPR). Then look to see if there are any helpful cases.

Additional information required, if any

It would be useful to know about the conduct of the defendants in the case. The claimants have not pursued the case as they should have, but if there has been any delay or difficulty caused by the defendant this could be used in the client's favour.

Key words/phrases

'Civil procedure'; 'Strike out'; 'Delay'.

Conclusion of research

CPR, r 1.1.2 says that any sanction invoked by the court to deal with delay must be proportionate.

Biguzzi v Rank Leisure plc [1999] 4 All ER 934.

This case confirmed that no case law from before the implementation of the CPR in 1999 was generally of any relevance.

Annodeus Entertainment Ltd v Gibson [2000] All ER (D) 115.

In this case, the claimant's case was struck out due to a 10 month delay. However, it was reinstated because the court said that, under the CPR, a flexible approach to striking out should be taken and other sanctions such as payments into court or costs penalties could be used. (Applied in *Biguzzi*.)

Further searches will disclose cases where the judicial approach in *Annodeus* was applied or doubted. For example:

Neo Investments Inc v Cargill International SA [2001] 2 Lloyds Rep 33.

This applied the *Annodeus* case, though it was concluded that the circumstances were such that the length of the delay (11 years since the cause of action arose) meant justice required the case to be struck out.

Audergon v La Baguette Ltd [2002] EWCA Civ 10.

This case allowed strike out where the length of the delay made a fair trial extremely difficult and doubted the use of the judicial checklist from *Annodeus*.

Padfield v Harlowbury [2003] WL 21162338.

The court suggested that where valid and live questions between the parties remained which could be dealt with through the claim, a delay in bringing that claim before a judge would not make resolution of those issues impossible. (Applied in *Neo Investments*.)

Hateley v Morris & Others [2004] EWHC 252 (Ch).

In this case it was decided that a 30 month delay in bringing a petition would not make it fair or proportionate to strike out the petition.

Advice for client

It seems that there is a good argument to say that strike out would be disproportionate in this case as the delay is not as long as in those cases where strike out has recently been ordered. The client would have a good chance of winning and it is a high value case. Following the *Annodeus* case above, it should be possible to argue that other sanctions would be more appropriate though general principles under the CPR should be used in preference to the judicial checklist set out in that case.

Note: the firm should also review procedures for ensuring that files are not left for such long periods again to avoid similar problems and possible client complaints.

Research report

Primary source(s)

You should be looking at the CPR, whether on paper or computer. The Department for Constitutional Affairs website (www.dca.gov.uk) includes the up to date CPR and also offers links to websites offering useful commentaries on the CPR; these include Delia Venables: Legal Resources (at www.venables.co.uk), LawOnLine and Infolaw (www.infolaw.co.uk).

Look at the All England Law Reports; you could also look at an internet-based source, for example, Butterworths Direct, Westlaw or Lawtel.

References

Biguzzi v Rank Leisure plc [1999] 4 All ER 934.

Annodeus Entertainment Ltd v Gibson [2000] All ER (D) 115.

Neo Investments Inc v Cargill International SA [2001] 2 Lloyds Rep 33.

Audergon v La Baguette Ltd [2002] EWCA Civ 10.

Padfield v Harlowbury [2003] WL 21162338.

Hateley v Morris & Others [2004] EWHC 252 (Ch).

Updating

Check there have been no further cases overturning the authorities you have based your answer on and that any texts relied upon are up to date.

CPR – updates and changes are published first on the Department for Constitutional Affairs website (www.dca.gov.uk). Check that this shows no changes.

FURTHER READING

Biehl, K and Calishian, T, *The Lawyer's Guide to Internet Legal Research*, 2001, London: Scarecrow Press.

Clinch, P, *Teaching Legal Research*, 1999, Coventry: National Centre for Legal Education, University of Warwick.

Costanzo, M, *Problem Solving*, 1994, London: Cavendish Publishing.

General Council of the Bar, *BVC Specification and Guidelines*, 2004/5, London: General Council of the Bar, p 33 (available at www.legaleducation.org.uk/downloads/bvcspec04.doc).

Hanson, S, *Legal Method and Reasoning*, 2nd edn, 2003, London: Cavendish Publishing.

Holborn, G, *Butterworths Legal Research Guide*, 2nd edn, 2001, London: Butterworths.

Holmes, N and Venables, D, *Researching the Legal Web*, 2nd edn, 1999, London: Butterworths.

Kenny, PH, *Studying Law*, 5th edn, 2002, London: Butterworths.

Kolb, DA, Rubin, IM and McIntyre, J, *Organisational Psychology: An Experiential Approach to Organisational Behaviour*, 1984, Englewood Cliffs, NJ: Prentice Hall.

Law Society, *Legal Practice Course Board Written Standards*, Version 10, September 2004, London: Law Society (available at www.lawsociety.org.uk, under 'Qualifying as a Solicitor').

Stott, D, *Legal Research*, 2nd edn, 1999, London: Cavendish Publishing.

Tunkel, V, *Legal Research: Law-Finding and Problem-Solving*, 1992, London: Blackstone.

CHAPTER 5

OPINION WRITING

INTRODUCTION

It may come as a surprise to many students, but there is more to being a barrister than being a good advocate. A barrister's work can be separated into two main areas: advocacy, otherwise known as 'court work', and 'paperwork', which encompasses the skill of opinion writing.[1] Many civil barristers actually do very little court work and specialise almost totally in paperwork. In fact those who have large 'paper practices' may only go to court once or twice a year and spend the rest of their time drafting court documents and writing opinions. Whatever area of law the barrister eventually specialises in, be it criminal or civil, a proportion of his or her work (and therefore income) will come from writing opinions.

Opinion writing as a skill is assessed on the Bar Vocational Course (BVC) as a compulsory subject. However, it is also being used more and more in ordinary undergraduate law degrees as a method of assessing legal skills. Therefore, although what is contained in this chapter will be most relevant to BVC students, it may be that undergraduate law students will be required to write an opinion at some point during their legal studies, regardless of their choice of career.

WHAT IS AN OPINION?

An opinion[2] is the term used to describe a document prepared by a barrister that states his or her opinion (advice) on various issues arising from a case. Such issues commonly include liability, contributory negligence, evidential issues and quantum. However, this list is not exclusive and the opinion could be an advice on every issue in a case, which may, therefore, lead to quite a detailed and lengthy document.

There are various types of opinion that a barrister could be asked to write, and each requires a slightly different layout. The format for a civil opinion differs from that of a criminal advice and the format differs again if the barrister is drafting an advice on appeal (a document sent to the appellate courts to persuade them to hear an appeal). All three types will be examined in the following pages. However, the majority of this chapter will be devoted to civil opinion writing, as the principles of clear writing apply to opinion writing generally. At the end of the chapter you will find a few words on how a criminal opinion and an advice on appeal should be written.

---

1   The other main aspect of paperwork is drafting.
2   It should be pointed out that the word 'opinion' and the word 'advice' can be used synonymously. The term 'opinion' tends to be used for civil matters, eg, opinion on nuisance, and 'advice' for criminal matters, for example, advice on evidence.

What an opinion is not

Students often confuse opinion writing with normal academic essay writing. Occasionally students who are asked to write an opinion end up submitting a piece of work that, although displaying an excellent understanding of the finer points of academic law, fails to provide any practical advice. What starts as an opinion soon becomes what students are most familiar with: an academic essay. An opinion *is not* and *should never be* an essay. An opinion is a document providing practical advice; it is not a discussion of academic principles.

Know your audience: who is the opinion for?

One of the first questions that students ask when they start to learn about opinion writing is: who is the opinion actually for? A barrister is instructed by a solicitor – who is known as the professional client – on behalf of the individual with the legal problem – who is known as the lay client. But to whom is the opinion addressed?

To be completely correct, you should address the opinion to both the solicitor and the lay client. Lay clients can request to see all papers regarding their case and, depending upon their interest, they may wish to read any opinion that has been written. This being said, it is rare for a lay client to see an opinion and, normally, a solicitor will merely repeat the salient points of the advice to the client. This has a major benefit, in that the barrister can dispense with rudimentary explanations of the law. The solicitor will have undertaken similar exams to the barrister and should be well aware of any basic legal principles. A solicitor will not take kindly to having to read an opinion that includes the lines:

> There are three main requirements for a successful negligence action: establishing a duty of care owed by the tortfeasor to the victim; that this duty has been breached; and that damage caused to the victim results more or less directly from this breach.

Such a statement is far too basic and could be deemed insulting to a solicitor.

Why does the solicitor want an opinion?

Solicitors[3] will request opinions for one or more of the following reasons:

(a) they are not fully aware of the law and require specialist advice on the legal problem at hand;

(b) they do not have the time to find the answers to the questions themselves and it may be cheaper for solicitors to pay a barrister to conduct the research;

(c) they feel that a barrister's opinion would help them to conduct negotiations with the opposing side;

(d) a barrister's opinion may help convince a client as to the weakness of their case, or indeed that they have no case at all.

---

3   Other professionals are able to instruct barristers, eg, accountants. However, most instructions will come from solicitors.

WRITING THE OPINION

The set of papers delivered to a barrister requesting an opinion can be divided into two parts:

(a) the instructions to counsel – prepared by the solicitor;

(b) the documents that form the basis of the case.

Instructions to counsel

The document that sets out for the barrister what the solicitor wants to know is called the 'instructions to counsel'. Often the information required by the solicitor can be identified from the title of the instructions; for example, the title may be, 'Instructions to counsel to advise on merit', or 'Instructions to counsel to advise on evidence, plea and procedure'. Instructions often comprise of the following:

(a) a chronological list of the various papers included with the instructions;

(b) a summary of the case;

(c) a statement on the current stage of the proceedings, for example, 'no proceedings have been issued';

(d) particular problems with the case;

(e) what the solicitor wants to know.[4]

The instructions should, as a matter of course, contain all the essential facts and circumstances upon which the advice sought will be based and it is essential that the instructing solicitor has drafted instructions in a straightforward manner without including any irrelevant material. Instructions to counsel may also contain the solicitor's own opinion if he or she deems this to be helpful. It is often stated that counsel's opinion can only be as good as the instructions upon which it is based.

The drafting of instructions by a solicitor requires a high degree of skill and judgement. It is both rude and unprofessional for a solicitor to throw at counsel an unsorted file of papers or an unconsidered set of facts. In such circumstances, a barrister is perfectly entitled to refuse to accept such ill-prepared instructions. Such refusal will almost always occur with senior members of the Bar, whereas it has been known for a junior barrister to wade through an unsorted set of papers and provide advice on everything rather than run the risk of offending the solicitor and thereby prevent further work from materialising. The decision of course rests with the barrister concerned. Sometimes, the matter can be cleared up simply with a telephone call or an email. However, the general understanding is that a brief without complete instructions represents an incomplete brief and incomplete briefs should be returned. Nevertheless, a barrister should not be so selective as to only accept the most perfect instructions and reject those that fail to reach his or her own exacting standards. If this occurs, the barrister may find that he or she is a great deal poorer than he or she deserves and also, possibly, in breach of the cab rank rule.

---

4   An example of some instructions to counsel can be found in Exercise 1 at the end of this chapter.

The documents that form the basis of the case

The remaining part of the brief[5] consists of documents (also referred to as papers) that are relevant to the case. These should have been selected carefully from the case file by the solicitor and itemised in the contents of the instructions to counsel. These papers may include witness statements – dated and signed by the parties – expert reports, police reports, photographs, memoranda and items of correspondence. It is also perfectly possible for the papers to include audio or video tapes and even physical items of evidence.

It should be noted that although the documents should be complete, it is not uncommon for certain papers to be missing and therefore the barrister should check the brief's content at the earliest opportunity.

Preparing to write the opinion

It is important that the barrister takes time to plan the opinion carefully, as this can save a great deal of time in the long run. Planning the opinion can be broken down into three distinct stages:

(a) reading the brief and analysing the case;

(b) undertaking relevant legal research;

(c) drafting an opinion plan.

Only once all three stages have been completed should the barrister actually set about the task of writing. With experience, less time will need to be spent on each stage, but do bear in mind that even the most experienced barrister will still spend some time planning the opinion. These stages will be examined further.

Reading the papers and analysing the case

Analysing the case and noting the important facts within the case is the first stage of preparing to write an opinion. It is worthwhile taking this 'fact management/case analysis' process seriously. Barristers may be instructed on a particular case more than once, and time spent managing the facts well early on can save time if the papers return and the barrister is asked to conduct further work. If the barrister manages the facts well the first time, then this stage need not be repeated on subsequent occasions.

There are various methods of fact management/case analysis that can be used, although they all involve the same elements. These include:

---

5   In order to be correct, a distinction should be drawn between 'instructions to counsel' and 'brief to counsel' – or 'brief'. 'Instructions to counsel' refer to requests for advice on a case before trial, eg, an opinion, whereas a 'brief to counsel' refers to a request for the barrister to attend for trial, ie, in their role as advocate. However, the term 'brief' is often loosely used between barristers to refer to any work that they have been instructed to do.

Who is involved in the case?	You will need to identify the main characters in the case and their roles within it.
The important dates in the case	When did the legal cause of action arise? Who did what, with whom and when?
The important factual details in the case	These depend upon the type of case you are dealing with, but in a sense this should be who did what to whom and who saw it?
The legal issues in the case	It is important that you are able to discern from the papers the points on which the case may turn from a legal point of view. The cause(s) of action should also be identified.
The evidence supporting these legal issues	Few legal actions will be successful without evidence. It is essential, therefore, that when reading the papers, you look for evidence to support the case.

Therefore, what is required is noting the facts; identifying those facts that are both for and against the client; cross-referencing the stories of witnesses; and building up a chronology of what happened.

Undertaking relevant legal research

Students who approach opinion writing for the first time must be prepared to conduct some legal research (or even revision of the law) before attempting to write an opinion. Research must be conducted logically and thoroughly, and it is advisable that students consult one or more of the various texts on the particular subject. As an opinion is a practical document, it is important to highlight that practitioner texts should be used in preference to the student orientated texts. Practitioner texts[6] tend to state the law as it is and, although student texts will state the current position, they tend only to do so after a few pages of academic argument and legal history, coupled with the analysis of relevant case law.[7] Practitioner texts are also usually more up to date than student texts, and no one wants to deliver an opinion based on incorrect and out of date law. Also, when looking at an area of law for an opinion, either as revision or for the first time, it is vital to make a good set of notes and a research report. Notes can be used later on in your course or even as a pupil/tenant and the research report created so that you know where you found each piece of information in case you need to check again.

---

6   Titles of practitioner texts include *Chitty on Contracts*, 28th edn, 2000, London: Sweet & Maxwell and *Clerk & Lindsell on Tort*, 18th edn, 2001, London: Sweet & Maxwell.
7   It is worth noting that the use of academic texts also has the detrimental effect of subconsciously encouraging a student to write a discursive document as opposed to a practical one.

In time, knowledge of the law will increase and the level of legal research required for each opinion will diminish. This is one of the major benefits of specialisation.

The opinion plan

Although, by managing the facts of the problem and undertaking the legal research, you have done the groundwork for the opinion, it is not advisable to start to write an opinion until you have drafted an opinion plan.

The opinion plan should be as detailed as possible. The more detailed the plan, the easier the task of writing the opinion will be. When planning to write the opinion, it is important that the student thinks about its content, for example, what the solicitor wants to know, what the solicitor needs to know and what is the best way of communicating this information to the client. The easiest way to ensure that often complex information is communicated effectively is to adopt a clear structure. A failure to plan an opinion may lead to relevant issues being dealt with illogically, causing the reader to lose the threads of an argument. Consequently, the solicitor will find the opinion difficult to read. At the very least, the opinion plan should consist of a set of sub-headings and notes about the information that will be contained under each one.

Using the English language

One of the most important aspects of an opinion is the way that the opinion is written. By the time that students write opinions, they should have mastered the English language and be able to demonstrate the correct use of grammar, spelling and punctuation. English can be an inspiring language and words, when used effectively, make the text a pleasure to read. Although the opinions that you will write are not expected to be works of art, it is worth spending some time ensuring that the standard of English used is the highest that you can achieve.

Professionalism should ensure that, before any piece of work is submitted, it is checked for errors and you would be wise to submit the best work that can be done. Students – for some reason – often wish to delay starting work on opinions until the day before the submission deadline. Tutors for all subjects will advise against this, with good reason. For opinion writing, this is especially important. The best way to avoid missing errors is to prepare the opinion well in advance of the submission date and then forget about the piece of work for a few days. When looking at the piece of work after a short break – and, therefore, effectively through fresh eyes – it is quite surprising the number of errors that will be picked up this time round.

To make things easier for students these days, grammar and spell checkers are available on most word processing packages and it seems a shame to go to the trouble of word processing an opinion without making use of these functions. However, these functions are designed to help the correct writing of everyday English and they may question names, legal words and legal phrases. Therefore, if you decide to use one, check to see that the suggested alternative is actually better than the one that is written, before allowing any changes to be made.

Avoiding pomposity

A further problem that occurs when students write opinions is that they have a tendency to emulate the style of what is perceived to be the stereotypical barrister, that is, arrogant and pompous. These are bad traits. A number of student opinions overindulge in the use of sophisticated language that is often wrapped up in long and complex sentences. A good opinion will only use a sufficient number of words to convey precisely what is meant. Do not make the mistake of holding the view that the more words you use indicates greater knowledge and experience. Do not use 50 words to explain a point when the same point could be made in 20. Simple sentences will prevent ambiguity creeping in and will ensure that the finished opinion provides clear and concise advice.

On this point, it may be useful to point out another common student trait. Student barristers seem to enjoy referring to themselves as counsel. Do not start an opinion with the words 'Counsel is instructed' or later on, when some advice is given, use the words 'in counsel's opinion'. This practice is now outdated and pompous, and you should avoid it at all costs.

Use of case law

Cases should be used sparingly in an opinion. Remember that an opinion is not supposed to be an academic essay with every point made backed up with legal precedent. There is no need to refer to cases unless it is absolutely necessary. An opinion should only refer to case law when:

(a) the case at hand bears striking similarity to a previously reported case;

(b) the opinion is giving advice on levels of quantum for personal injury. If this is so, then two cases should be mentioned: one indicating the upper bracket of damages (a more serious situation than the lay client's) and another indicating damages on the lower end of the scale (a less serious case than the lay client's);

(c) the opinion is a criminal advice where sentence is in issue, in which case there should be an indication of possible sentence by reference to a case more serious and also a case which is less serious, thereby indicating the top and bottom bracket;

(d) the opinion is an advice on appeal and it is necessary to cite relevant authorities to show that a judge has made a procedural error;

(e) the law is complex and it is likely that the solicitor will be unaware of the case law on the matter;

(f) there is a very recent case relating to the law of which the solicitor will be unaware.

If a case is used, then there should be a full citation. There is nothing worse than mentioning an important case without telling the solicitor where to find it. Some barristers include a photocopy of the cases referred to at the end of their opinion, which seems to be good practice.

Use of legislation

Similar points can be made when the opinion refers to statutes or pieces of delegated legislation as have been made for the use of cases. There is no need, for instance, to state in an opinion on exclusion clauses that 'the leading statute in this area is the Unfair Contract Terms Act 1977'. This would, under normal circumstances, be unnecessary when dealing with a solicitor. However, if the opinion does need to make reference to statute, then it should be made in general terms, for example: '... in my opinion, the exclusion clause contained in the contract of sale would be unlikely to satisfy the test of reasonableness laid down by the Unfair Contract Terms Act 1977.'

The use of legislation by students raises an interesting point regarding abbreviations. Some Acts give rise to well known abbreviations, for example, UCTA – Unfair Contract Terms Act 1977 – or SOGA – Sale of Goods Act 1979. However, other Acts do not give rise to such well known abbreviations. Therefore, if the opinion will make reference to legislation on numerous occasions and if abbreviations are going to be used, ensure that the Act is stated in its complete form initially and then the abbreviation is made clear. There is little worse than a student using an abbreviation without informing the reader what it stands for.

How should the opinion be written? Using the first and third person?

An opinion, as already stated, is a document that gives a barrister's advice on a case. Throughout academic life, undergraduates are taught that they should avoid writing in the first person. With opinion writing, however, the professional client wants the barrister's view on a case and, therefore, writing in the first person is actively encouraged. For example, opinions often start with the line, 'I am asked to advise'. Also, as the opinion is the barrister's opinion, the barrister should feel free to state his or her opinion – 'in *my* opinion ...'.

When writing in the first person and referring to the addressee (normally the solicitor), the rules of English language would suggest that the addressee is referred to as 'you'. This does not follow with opinion writing, where convention dictates that the addressee is referred to in the third person. Therefore, when writing, the barrister should refer to the solicitor in a more polite form, for example, 'those instructing may wish to note ...' or 'perhaps instructing solicitors could find out ...'.

The structure of the opinion

No matter what anyone says, there is no right or wrong way to write an opinion. The aim is to provide clear practical advice on the matter at hand, and provided this is accomplished, then the opinion will have succeeded. One of the easiest ways to achieve clarity and practicality is to use a good structure.

Structure will make the opinion readable, and also ensure that the issues are dealt with logically. For example, it would be a strange opinion that would deal with quantum of damages before liability has been determined.

The following issues are important when looking at the structure of the opinion.

Ensure that you make full use of sub-headings

The use of sub-headings to break up the text of an opinion will assist the reader by indicating the information contained in a particular paragraph. Sub-headings should be used where appropriate. However, the use of sub-headings can cause problems and should not be used excessively. Only use as many sub-headings as are required, and no more. Try to think whether a sub-heading is necessary. Are you changing tack? Are you answering a query on a new area? Does the reader need to know where you are going? An example would be useful here. Read the following extract (from fictitious instructions to counsel):

> Counsel is instructed on behalf of James Bailey aged 14, the claimant in this action. James was injured whilst at the pleasure park 'Fun City' when the bumper car he was driving short circuited and the vehicle was given a sudden burst of speed. Due to the sudden increase in speed James' bumper car hit the side barrier with such force that he was thrown from the car onto the concrete. James sustained a broken wrist and ankle and reports a fear of driving in bumper cars.
>
> Counsel is instructed to advise on liability, quantum and procedure in the above matter.

It may seem difficult to imagine the sub-headings that may arise in an opinion on the above matter. However, careful thought should lead you somewhere near to the following possible structure for an opinion:

- introduction;
- conclusion;[8]
- liability of 'Fun City' in negligence;
- quantum;
- procedure;
- further information required;
- next steps.

You can see from the above list that the headings seem to be easily related to the problem. In essence this is because the sub-headings relate to the legal issues raised by the case and are not really about the individual facts of the case itself.

One important fact to remember when dealing with sub-headings is to make them useful and meaningful. Students often limit sub-headings to just one word. There is no reason for this, as sub-headings should be suitably descriptive. Always think when planning the opinion whether the sub-headings that are chosen adequately describe the content of the paragraphs to which they relate.

---

8   The reasons for the position of the conclusion being at the start of the opinion can be seen later in this chapter.

Ensure that you have numbered paragraphs

It seems to be standard these days to number the paragraphs of your opinion, although there is no definite set way to do it. Some barristers adopt a simple system where they number the paragraphs starting from 1 and increasing upwards in integers, that is, 1, 2, 3, 4 … 10, etc. Other barristers opt for the above system, but add decimals to help tie the numbered paragraphs with their sub-heading. This would mean that you would start with 1 and then, when at para 4, you begin to advise on liability, you start with 4.1, 4.2, 4.3, etc.

Essentially, the choice is yours. Note that having too many paragraphs has the disadvantage of being unsightly and confusing, whereas having too few paragraphs may look as though you haven't done enough work! Students should consider using the ordinary integer numbered system for relatively short opinions and the decimalised system for longer opinions.

Numbered paragraphs are present to help the reader find his way around the opinion and also to allow the barrister to refer the reader to a particular part of the opinion if necessary, for example 'see para 4'. The same rules apply to lists in opinions. Opinions should not contain bullet points. All points within an opinion should be numbered in a numerical form. This is illustrated below with a list of items that could be claimed for special damages:

Bullet point list		**Numerical list**
• Clothing	(i)	Clothing
• Broken watch	(ii)	Broken watch
• Bicycle repairs	(iii)	Bicycle repairs
• Travelling expenses	(iv)	Travelling expenses
• Entertainment	(v)	Entertainment
• Prescription charges	(vi)	Prescription charges
• Lost income from employment	(vii)	Lost income from employment

The reason behind this is that the constituents of the list are far easier to refer to when listed in roman numerals. For example, it is easier to question point (v) as a head of special damage than the fifth bullet point down.

Now that all the main aspects of the opinion have been examined, we can now turn to the actual content of the opinion.

The heading

All opinions should begin with a heading. Often, a barrister will simply copy the heading that the solicitor has used in the instructions. However, if there is no heading on the instructions to counsel, then the following examples could be used.

Non-contentious matters

Non-contentious matters are those where there will not be any opposed litigation. They can therefore simply be stated as:

> Re Carole Jones
>
> _____
>
> OPINION
>
> _____

Contentious matters

For contentious matters in their early stages, it is perfectly permissible to use the same heading as for non-contentious matters. However, the following heading is probably more appropriate.

> Carole Jones
>
> v
>
> Joanne Peterson
>
> _____
>
> OPINION
>
> _____

Once the action has begun, the heading for an opinion would be along the same lines as before, only with the case details inserted. The heading would therefore appear as:

> In the Newcastle County Court   Case Number 9382/06
>
> Between
>
> Carole Jones   Claimant
>
> and
>
> Joanne Peterson   Defendant
>
> _____
>
> OPINION
>
> _____

Getting the tramlines to appear in the heading

Students often have difficulty inserting the tramlines into the heading when word processing an opinion. There are two ways of doing this.

(a) The easy method

An easy way to create the tramlines is to use the underline or underscore key on the computer keyboard.[9] This will give a '_'. Therefore, when in front of a word processor,

---

9 An underscore can be achieved by pressing the shift key and the hyphen key at the same time.

press return or enter on the keyboard a few times to give yourself some space. Type the word OPINION. Move the cursor up two lines, hold down the shift key and press about 15 times (more or less if you wish). Then move to the line below the word OPINION and repeat the process, ensuring that you press the underline key the same number of times as before. If it makes the process easier, you can cut and paste the underline from the previous time, which will ensure that the line is the same both above and below the word OPINION. Then simply centre all the lines and the result will be the same. The following picture shows the line numbers and also the effect.

1	Re Carole Jones
2	
3	_____
4	
5	OPINION
6	_____

Line 1 has the title. Line 2 is blank. Line 3 has the first repeated underscore. Line 4 is blank. Line 5 is the word 'OPINION' and line 6 has the second repeated underscore.

(b) Using the table function to achieve perfection

	Re Carole Jones	
	OPINION	

To get a more accurate result for the above opinion heading, you can use a 3 x 3 table. Once this is created and the information entered, you can remove the lines on the table apart from the lines that will form the tramlines. Therefore, the table will start like the one above.

And then, once the unwanted lines have been removed, it will look like this:

Re Carole Jones
_____
OPINION
_____

A table can also be used to create the more complex opinion heading that was referred to in the previous section. Although setting up a table to create an opinion heading akin to the heading for a statement of case is complicated, it has the benefit of getting the words to appear precisely where they should be – some centred, some flush against the right margin and others against the left margin. This is far better than the inexact results achieved by repeated use of the space bar, which students normally use to achieve the heading for statements of case. Also, once one table has been created, it can be saved as a document template and thereafter used repeatedly.

With all the table lines in place, the heading would look like this:

In the Newcastle County Court			Case Number 9382/06
Between			
	Carole Jones		Claimant
	and		
	Joanne Peterson		Defendant
	OPINION		

This table started off as a 4 x 10 table. After merging a few cells together to give extra typing space and widening the cells on either side of the opinion cell, the completed heading looks as depicted below:

In the Newcastle County Court	Case Number 9382/04
Between	
Carole Jones	Claimant
and	
Joanne Peterson	Defendant
————	
OPINION	
————	

The introduction of an opinion

The introduction of an opinion contains two main pieces of information:

(a) the clarification of the instructions from the professional client;

(b) the material facts of the case.

Clarifying the instructions

It is good practice for the opinion to start with a clarification of the instructions that you have received. This does not mean that the opinion should reiterate the instructions in full. All that is needed is a brief paragraph confirming what you have been asked to advise upon, which will indicate what the opinion is about. It is possible that you may write a number of opinions on the same case and, therefore, confirming the instructions in this way helps prevent any confusion arising at a later date. On this point, it is also worth inserting the date that the instructions were received from the solicitor. It should be noted that there is no need for a sub-heading above the introduction.

I am asked to advise James Bailey on liability, quantum and procedure in a personal injury matter arising from an accident involving a bumper car at 'Fun City', Whitley Bay. I received these instructions from Tim Beaumont of Beaumont and Black on 31st March 2005.

Setting out the material facts

It is also good practice for the barrister to set out the material facts of the case. Please note the use of the word *material*. Not every fact is important to determine legal liability. It is the barrister's job to sort out those facts that are relevant to the client's case and only these facts should be repeated. A simple way of deciding what is and what is not a material fact is first to look at the legal issues in a case. Once you have done this, you can simply examine the facts that raise the legal issues. For example, if the legal issues lie in breach of contract, then the material facts would be the parties to the contract, the terms of the contract, the actual breach of the contract and the losses that have resulted from the breach. The sub-heading used for these material facts should either be 'Material Facts', 'The Facts' or 'Background'. Any of these would be appropriate, although either of the latter two appear to be good practice.

Ensure that the conclusion of the problem is clearly laid out

The conclusion is, arguably, the most important part of the opinion as it contains the advice that the solicitor needs. It is the conclusion of the opinion that provides the answers to the questions that the solicitor has asked and may conclude on whether, for example, the barrister thinks that the lay client has a good prospect of success at trial or not. Under normal circumstances, a conclusion would appear at the end of a piece of work. However, because the conclusion is so important, it should actually be at the beginning of an opinion. This way the solicitor can find the information that he or she wants quickly and easily. The advantages of each method are laid out in the table below:

At the beginning	At the end
The reader can easily locate your advice.	The reader can easily locate your advice.
The reader is then in a good position to follow your patterns of thought when reading the opinion.	Logic.
You should have already come to a conclusion before you write the opinion and this helps prevent the opinion becoming a discussion of the situation.	

The main body of the opinion

Once the introduction and conclusion has been completed, the main body of the opinion needs to be written. This will contain the barrister's comments on each of the issues within the case, and therefore the actual content of the opinion will vary depending upon the facts of the case. This is the part of the opinion that seems to cause students the most problems, as they are often unsure of what should be included and what should be ignored. Unfortunately, given the huge variety of scenarios that exist, there is no easy way to deal with these problems. The best advice that can be given is to separate the issues and deal with each of them logically and effectively. Which issues are relevant depend upon each case and the related area of law.

Some books on opinion writing include precedents (previous opinions) and, although these are excellent when available, and provide good examples of style, structure and layout, students may misuse them. They can lead to students being unable to think for themselves and, rather than take the route towards actually learning the skill, the student will take the easy route and blindly copy as much of the precedent as they can without much thought as to its application. Unfortunately, this often means that the student will copy parts of the precedent that are irrelevant, as well as those which are indeed relevant. No precedents are used in this chapter. Instead, a few sample opinion plans/templates have been included.

Giving practical advice

When writing the opinion, remember to keep asking yourself: what does the client want to know and why? In most cases the client wants to know whether they will be successful if they sue and how much compensation they can get. However, in some cases, there may be some other issues that need to be addressed and the barrister should be prepared to give purely practical advice if a non-legal remedy will provide the same degree of success as a legal remedy.

For example, if a young boy was injured whilst playing in an unoccupied council house, the mother will certainly want some compensation for the boy's injuries. However, what if she also wants some advice on how to compel the council to ensure that unoccupied council houses are made safe and boarded up? In certain circumstances, the law may provide a remedy – possibly judicial review – but these actions are complicated and expensive. It may be useful to point out that the purely practical answer of a community campaign (demonstrations and petitions, etc), designed to attract media attention and put pressure on the council, may prove more successful than litigation.

Further information required

When a barrister provides advice, it is likely that there will be some information that has not been included with the papers that the barrister believes would have some impact on the case. If this is the case, then the barrister must request that 'those instructing' should take steps to find this information. The best way to approach requests for further information is to deal with the missing information at the appropriate time when the lack of the information arises. Then, at the end of the opinion, include a paragraph summarising all the information that is required to further the case. In practice, barristers often emphasise the requests for further information within the opinion by making the request bold.

> ... Determining whether the precontractual statement would actually amount to a misrepresentation given the delay between the statement and the creation of the contract is difficult. **It would be helpful if those instructing could discover the reason for the 2 month delay.** ...

Examples of the types of further information requested include:

(a) CCTV recordings of the scene of an accident (to determine liability for a car accident);

(b) manufacturer's installation guidelines of a product (to determine negligence);

(c) valuation reports of a house (checking the decrease in value of a property after nuisance);

(d) whether a defendant is actually insured (personal injury action);

(e) a photocopy of an insurance cover note (personal injury action);

(f) that the taped copy of the telephone conversation is requested (in a telesales contract);

(g) a photocopy of the client's last three months' bank statements (for a contract case).

When requesting further information, you must think carefully about what you ask for. You should consider the limitations of the solicitor, the costs of finding out the further information, and also whether the solicitor is the best person to discover the information. It is good practice to note in brackets at the end of the line that repeats the information required which paragraph you requested the further information. This will allow the solicitor to see your reasoning for requesting this piece of information. As a result, it is usual to repeat the further information required in the order in which the information was requested. NB: an opinion should not list in the 'further information required' section information which has not been requested previously in the opinion.

A further information paragraph may therefore look as follows:

Further information required

22 It would be helpful if those instructing could find out the following:

(i) Whether there are any CCTV recordings of the accident (para 7).

(ii) Proof of a recent service carried out on the vehicle (para 8).

Next steps

One of the last paragraphs that should be contained in an opinion states what steps should be taken to further the lay client's case. This should not be used as a conclusion; it should be used as a gentle reminder to the solicitor to take action. It may be, for example, that a limitation date is fast approaching; or a witness is about to emigrate and a witness statement has not yet been obtained. Anyone making use of a next steps paragraph must ensure that it is polite and as such care must be taken not to insult the solicitor and inform them of next steps that are blatantly obvious. Such a reminder is insulting.

Ending the opinion

Ending the opinion can be difficult if you have decided to have the conclusion at the start, and it can appear that simply ending the opinion with a 'next steps' paragraph is a little too abrupt. Some barristers write what is known as a general advert – which is a short sentence stating that you, the barrister, will be happy to assist with drafting particulars of claim (or whatever is the next stage of proceedings after the opinion) if required.

Signing the opinion

Once the opinion has been finalised, all that remains to be done is for the barrister to sign the opinion. This normally consists of the barrister's name, date and the barrister's chambers being included.

Driftwood Chambers   Barry Star

Northumberland Road

Newcastle upon Tyne

31 March 2006

Now the opinion is complete; all that remains to be done is to print it out and ensure that you retain a copy for your own use.

CRIMINAL OPINION WRITING

Criminal opinion writing bears strong similarities to civil opinion writing. The opinion is addressed to the solicitor and also the lay client, and the guidelines for civil opinion writing stand also for criminal opinion writing.

Differences do, however, lie, first in the heading of the opinion. A criminal opinion is known as an advice, for example, 'advice on evidence', 'advice on plea', or general pre-trial advice called 'advice on evidence, plea and procedure'. As the title of the written work changes, so will the heading of the opinion:

THE CROWN

v

JOHN SMITH

ADVICE ON EVIDENCE, PLEA AND PROCEDURE

The second difference lies with the way that the case is introduced. Instead of simply stating the facts of the case, it is generally good practice to state first what the prosecution case is against the client, and then what the defence case appears to be. Therefore, there would be sub-headings under the introduction with prosecution case and defence case. If writing an advice from the prosecution perspective, it may be that the prosecution is unaware of what the defence case will be. If this is the case then, of course, the barrister will be unable to deal with this issue in the advice.

The third difference lies with the content. Criminal actions are proved by evidence to the standard that the judge(s) of fact[10] are sure of the defendant's guilt. Therefore, a large part of a criminal advice will deal with either the presence or absence of evidence. When dealing with a criminal advice, ensure that you have a sound knowledge of the case, the charge, and what is required to prove the case.

Below is a template for a criminal advice for the defence advising on evidence, plea and procedure. No papers have been included, as they are unnecessary to illustrate the point. Do not follow this template for all aspects of criminal advice. It may be that a particular case requires a different format.

---

10   The judges of fact could be either the jury, magistrates or a stipendiary magistrate.

THE QUEEN

v

PETER VINCENT

ADVICE ON EVIDENCE, PLEA AND PROCEDURE

(1) Confirmation of instructions.

(2) Identification of the charge and explain circumstances to set the scene.

Prosecution case

(3) Identify the case against Peter Vincent.

Defence case

(4) Identify the defence case, for example, alibi.

Evidence

(5) You should deal with each item of the prosecution case, for example, identification issues, corroborative evidence, witnesses, co-accused giving evidence against accused, etc. Each separate issue should be given a separate sub-heading to allow ease of navigation.

(6) Some of the evidential issues may give rise to particular procedural points. If they do, then they should be dealt with under the sub-heading procedure, for example, severing an indictment.

Sentence if found guilty

(7) You should deal with the sentence that the defendant would receive if found guilty. You should highlight aggravating and also mitigating factors. Guideline cases should also be mentioned.

(8) Give examples of previous cases to indicate the possible sentence. You should also identify the discount for a guilty plea at an early stage.

Plea

(9) In essence, advice on plea is the conclusion of the advice. When advising on plea, it is important to note that the professional codes of conduct for the Bar state that a lay client should not be advised in specific terms. Therefore, you must ensure that advice as to plea is given in general terms and that you point out that the final decision rests with the client.

Further information required

(10) List all items of further information required previously referred to in your opinion. NB: do not use bullet points.

Next steps

(11) Identify the next stage of the process and state whether a client/barrister conference should be held.

Driftwood Chambers   Barry Star

Northumberland Road

Newcastle upon Tyne

31 March 2006

CRIMINAL ADVICE ON APPEAL

A 'Criminal Advice on Appeal' is a court document that is used to obtain an appeal for a defendant on either conviction or sentence or both. It is sent in conjunction with criminal grounds of appeal – which is drafted alongside the advice – to the next appellate court for consideration. An advice on appeal is technically not an opinion at all; it is a court document and, therefore, falls within the realm of drafting. However, it shall be covered here.

The audience for an advice on appeal is not the same as for the opinions dealt with previously. For an advice on appeal, a further reader needs to be considered, namely, the single judge who will use the advice to decide whether the appeal should be heard. As such, the aim of the advice on appeal is different from normal opinions. Instead of performing the role of an adviser, the barrister becomes a persuader, that is, trying to persuade the judge that the conviction was unsafe, or the sentence passed was manifestly excessive. As the barrister is not playing the part of the adviser, the advice on appeal should significantly limit the use of the words 'in my opinion'. The judge wants to know what went wrong at the previous hearing, and not what the barrister thinks. Therefore, the tone of an advice is much more formal. Stating this, the format of an advice is not significantly different from an ordinary criminal advice. However, for an advice on appeal it is permitted to cite relevant authorities to back up arguments when a judge has erred.

When you write an advice on appeal, there are normally three things to look for in the papers before you:

(a) Wrong decisions in the course of the trial.

Judges are only human, and they can make mistakes when doing their job! Common areas falling into this category are when the judge fails to exclude evidence at trial, or refuses to allow a particular line of questioning of a witness.

(b) Misdirections in the course of summing up.

When all the evidence has been put before the court, the judge will sum up the case to the jury. When the judge sums up, he should inform the jury of certain things: for example, explaining the role of the jury as the judges of fact, not of law, explaining the offence and each part of it, and reminding the jury of the salient points of each witness's testimony. It may be that, in summing up, the judge has appeared to be biased in favour of the prosecution, for example, or has made improper comments on certain pieces of evidence. If the judge has acted in this way, this may form the basis of an appeal.

(c) The sentence is manifestly excessive.

It is possible that a defendant found guilty at trial will be given a sentence by the judge that is too harsh under the circumstances. If this occurs, then the barrister can appeal against the sentence. In this situation, the barrister will need to include example cases that illustrate the harshness of the client's sentence. These cases can be found in the *Criminal Appeal Reports*.

A template for an advice on appeal is given below. As an advice on appeal is a more formal document, additional information has been included:

REGINA

v

PETER VINCENT

ADVICE ON APPEAL AGAINST
CONVICTION AND SENTENCE

---

(1) Between [*insert dates*], the defendant was tried before [*insert judge's name*] and a jury at [*insert court*]. Mr Vincent was convicted of [*insert offence*] contrary to [*insert Act*]. On [*insert date*] Mr Vincent received a sentence of [*insert sentence*].

(2) I am asked to advise Mr Vincent as to whether there exist any grounds upon which he could properly appeal against his conviction and the sentence imposed. In accordance with the reasons that I have set out below, I advise that there are properly arguable grounds of appeal against both conviction and sentence.

THE FACTS

Prosecution case

(3) [*Insert details of the prosecution case.*]

Defence case

(4) [*Insert details of the defence case.*]

GROUNDS OF APPEAL AGAINST CONVICTION

Wrong decisions in the course of the trial

(5) [*Insert details of the wrong decisions given in the course of the trial. Use a separate sub-heading for each point.*]

Misdirections in the course of summing up

(6) [*Insert details of the misdirections in the course of summing up. Use a separate sub-heading for each point.*]

APPEAL AGAINST SENTENCE

Sentence was manifestly excessive

(7) [*Insert details of the sentence followed by details of a more serious case and a less serious case to show where the sentence should fall.*]

Driftwood Chambers   Barry Star

Northumberland Road

Newcastle upon Tyne

31 March 2006

(Grounds of appeal should be attached)

EXERCISES

Now that you have read over the preceding materials, it will be a good time to test your skills. Therefore, you should complete the following two exercises.

Exercise 1 requires you to draft an opinion plan on a misrepresentation problem that was once used as an undergraduate examination question.

Exercise 2 requires you to draft an opinion plan on a nuisance problem.

For the purposes of these exercises, you need to imagine that today's date is 1 December 2006.

Exercise 1

3 years ago Charles Laidlaw bought a bureau from a shop called Old & Ancient Antiques for £8,000. During the negotiations for the bureau, the owner of the antiques shop – Sebastian Emmett – told Charles that the bureau was made by a lesser known cabinet maker called Harry Shambles who was one of Henry VIII's personal carpenters. Sebastian also told Charles that Harry Shambles' work was beginning to attract a great deal of attention in the auction houses across the world and that consequently the bureau would be a very good investment. Sebastian said that the provenance for the bureau was at his other shop and that he would get it for Charles if he wished to see it. Charles, who was very impressed with the quality of workmanship, bought the bureau and said that Sebastian should send it to him when he found it. Two months later Sebastian posted the provenance to Charles, who did not look at the document and merely filed it in his safety deposit box at his bank.

Two months ago Charles' house burnt down and all of his belongings were destroyed. When assessing his sizeable claim, the insurers questioned the value of the bureau and Charles passed on the provenance document. The document actually said that the bureau was late eighteenth century and was a reproduction of a Henry VIII bureau by Harry Shambles made 300 years ago. The insurers have refused to pay the full value of the bureau and instead offered Charles £2,000 for this item of furniture.

Advise Charles.

Now, prepare an opinion plan for the above case. To remind you, an opinion plan is a document that contains the sub-headings that you will use in the opinion, together with some notes as to the content of the information contained under each heading.

On the following page is a suggested plan for this case. Please note that the comments made are in note form and are not intended to be a complete answer and, therefore, the content under each of the sub-headings below should be expanded upon in order to give a professional result. If your opinion plan doesn't match the one included below, then this doesn't mean that the one you have written is wrong. Provided that the advice that you would have given in opinion is broadly the same, then this should be sufficient.

Charles Laidlaw

v

Sebastian Emmett

SUGGESTED OPINION PLAN

Confirmation of instructions

Background

Summarise the material facts that have led to this contentious matter. Bureau bought, precontractual statement that is untrue, losses.

Conclusion

Insert a summary of all of the conclusions you have come to about the matter. NB: this should at least include answers to all of the questions that you have been asked to advise upon.

The contract for the Bureau

Identify the terms of the contract.

The misrepresentation

Identify the misrepresentation and the likely type of misrepresentation. Be wary of any temptation to insert case law and turn this opinion into an academic essay.

Remedies

Identify the remedies that are available for Charles, eg rescission and damages. Possible difficulties due to lapse of time and Charles' failure to check provenance documents at the time.

Further information required

Identify any necessary further information.

Next steps

Identify next steps.

Insert advert.

Sign.

Exercise 2

Imagine that you have received the following case concerning a possible claim in nuisance. Read the papers, undertake relevant fact management and legal research and prepare an opinion plan for the case. A suggested opinion plan is provided at the end of the exercise.

RE MARY COOPER AND
THE BLACKSMITH'S ARMS

INSTRUCTIONS TO COUNSEL
TO ADVISE IN WRITING

£250

Roger Hooper and Co,
12 Tinker St,
Smithfield

RE MARY COOPER AND

THE BLACKSMITH'S ARMS

INSTRUCTIONS TO COUNSEL
TO ADVISE IN WRITING

Counsel has herewith:

(1) Witness statement of Mary Cooper

(2) Sketch map of 73 and 75 Bargewright Street

(3) Promotional leaflet

(4) Witness statement of Gina Miller

Mrs Mary Cooper lives at 73 Bargewright Street, Smithfield, West Yorkshire, which is a private house owned by herself. Her two children, William, aged 14, and Angela, aged 10, also occupy the house.

Last month, a new business was opened at 75 Bargewright Street. Number 75 had once been a public house on the local coach route, but had been used as a private dwelling for as long as Mrs Cooper had lived at number 73. However, in 2000, it was purchased by National Breweries to be used as a public house. This opened on 15 June 2001 as the Blacksmith's Arms.

At the time that the conversion of the premises at 75 Bargewright Street was first proposed and an application made to the local planning authority for planning permission, a number of local residents, including Mrs Cooper, made objections. However, the local authority approved the change of use and subsequently also allowed the Blacksmith's Arms a licence to sell alcohol during the usual hours.

At first, although there was an increase of traffic on the road outside the pub and there was more litter, the change was tolerable. However, with the improvement in the weather, the public house has allowed its patrons to go into its gardens at the back. This has led to an increase in the noise and disruption to Mrs Cooper's enjoyment of her back garden. Furthermore, the public house has managed to gain a number of late night licence extensions that has increased the time for which the noise disruption has to be tolerated.

The public house has been extended at the back and Mrs Cooper feels that this will increase the chances of noise disrupting her enjoyment of the garden. She would like steps to be taken as soon as possible. The landlord of the pub is not inclined to stop the use of the back garden. They have offered to build a large wall at the back, but she feels this would restrict the access of light to her garden.

Mrs Cooper wants the noise stopped. Either as an alternative or in addition, she would like to be reimbursed for the disruption the noise has caused. Counsel is accordingly instructed to advise as to prospects of preventing the continuation of such noise in the near, and for the indefinite, future and further as to any damages award she might expect.

1 December 2006

I, MARY COOPER, of 73 Bargewright Street, Smithfield, West Yorkshire WILL SAY AS FOLLOWS:

1   I have lived at 73 Bargewright Street with my two children William, aged 14, and Angela, aged 10, for the past 8 years. I moved there with my husband, from whom I was divorced in 1998. As part of that divorce settlement, ownership of the house was passed to me to hold on trust until Angela reaches the age of 18, when the house will be sold and the proceeds divided between my husband and me.

2   The house is located in a quiet neighbourhood on the outskirts of Smithfield, a market town in West Yorkshire. Bargewright Street is not a main street, so there is little disruption from traffic. My house backs on to the River Miller and has a sizeable garden leading down to it. I have never before had any trouble from my neighbours on either side or from any other source.

3   Number 75 Bargewright Street is an old and historical building. It used to be a coaching house on the road between Liverpool and York. When I first moved into number 73 Bargewright St, number 75 was used as a private dwelling. Two families lived there over the years from 1992 to 2000. However, in November 2000, National Breweries Ltd bought the property.

4   Some time after they had purchased the house, a notice appeared on the front of the building stating that they intended to apply for planning permission to develop it into a public house.

5   There were a number of people living in the area who objected to this development. The area is residential and quiet. Other than a few small shops of the general grocery variety and a single fish and chip shop, there are no significant businesses in the area. Our closest public house, other than the Blacksmith's Arms, is about a quarter of a mile away on a main road.

6   Ultimately, planning permission was obtained despite our protests. Development work was carried out and the new pub opened in June 2001. Initially, there was no real problem with the pub. There were more cars parked on the road outside on some of the busiest nights but we residents thought our fears might be unjustified.

7   Over the following months, however, I began to become aware of new difficulties. More people began attending the public house and it became clear that the management had targeted the younger drinkers. Rather than a quiet country pub, the decor was new and garish and there were many features designed to attract young adults. Music would be played loudly and a number of patrons would gather in the street outside and drop litter. There has therefore been an increase in the amount of litter on the street in this time, particularly broken bottles. Furthermore, there has been an increase in fish and chip wrappings lying on the street. As the place caught on, it became obvious that the car parking built at the front was inadequate. As a result, more cars are parking on the street, which is not particularly wide, and even occasionally block access to the driveways of residents.

8   The public house also started obtaining extensions to their licence for the purposes of various events, all of which involved loud music. Very often, the place has music inside so loud that we can hear it in the bedrooms of my house into the small hours of the morning. I complained to Mr Hopkiss, the manager of the place, but he said that as he had a lawful extension to the licence, he was not prepared to change his policy of holding late night entertainment. He did say that they were going to extend the building at the back of the house away from my house so that noise would not reach my upstairs rooms.

9   As summer set in, more problems became apparent. On the days of good weather, more patrons would use the garden at the back of the pub. The hedge between the two properties, for which I am responsible, has become worn thin and now a lot of litter is spilling over between the pub and my garden. On weekends, it is not possible to gain any privacy in the back garden.

10   On 22 November, I complained to Mr Hopkiss about this problem and also the continuing noise. I noticed whilst at the Blacksmith's Arms that there were a lot of building materials at the back of the pub. Mr Hopkiss told me that the noise problems would be solved as soon as the building work was completed. He said that they were building an extension along the edge of my property, so that my privacy would be ensured. I was somewhat alarmed. This would be worse than what was already happening. Although long, my garden is narrow and it would lose significant amounts of sunlight if an extension of the type proposed were built. I told him this, at which point he became dismissive. He accused me of being unreasonable by wanting the 'best of both worlds'. This is not true. I simply want to enjoy my garden as I had before. The meeting did not achieve anything.

11   A couple of days after that conversation, the building work on the extension started. The work took place early in the morning so that the public house did not lose custom in the evening. This means that, since that date, I have been woken at 6 am by drilling or other building noises and then cannot get to sleep until after 11 pm because of the noises of the patrons. On a couple of occasions, 24 November and 27 November, there have been late night extensions so that the noise would continue until 4 am in the morning.

12   On 29 November, I happened to notice a billboard poster that advertised a band appearing in the gardens of the public house. They are due to appear on 15 December in the garden of the public house to commemorate the opening of the extension. The poster boasts a late licence (continuing until 4 am). While I think the continuing noise is bad in any event, that date is particularly bad as I have a job interview for an accounting position the following day at 10.30 am. Because of the financial circumstances following my divorce, it is particularly important that I am on my best form for that occasion. If there is noise in the garden of the Blacksmith's Arms for that long, I feel I shall almost certainly not get the job. Given the bad feeling between the manager of the Blacksmith's Arms and myself, I do not feel able to ask him to stop the event.

13   My fears in connection with the extension have been confirmed. There is a patio at the back of my house and since the walls of the extension have been built it almost never gets any sunlight now. In addition, the noise is no better. In fact, the bedrooms at the back of the house suffer more from the noise rather than less.

14   I would estimate that the public house had a late licence on at least 10 occasions during the time that they have been open. I cannot be sure of dates, except for the two that I have mentioned already.

15   The littering has not stopped. The extension does not reach the end of the garden and there is in fact an area at the end where some tables are located. Due to the building work and some other causes, my hedge has been damaged and there is a large gap there.

16 Due to the trouble there has been with the public house, I have suffered considerable stress. Also, my daughter, Angela, has suffered from the lack of sleep and her marks have dropped at school. I consider this to be caused by the noise and the resulting lack of sleep. I also fear that such a public house and the noise and dirt has caused my house to be less valuable. Given that it is worth less than when I bought it in any event, I cannot afford to sell it and meet the shortfall in value so as to pay off the mortgage.

Signed   *Mary Cooper*

Dated   29 November 2006

Figure 5.1: sketch plan

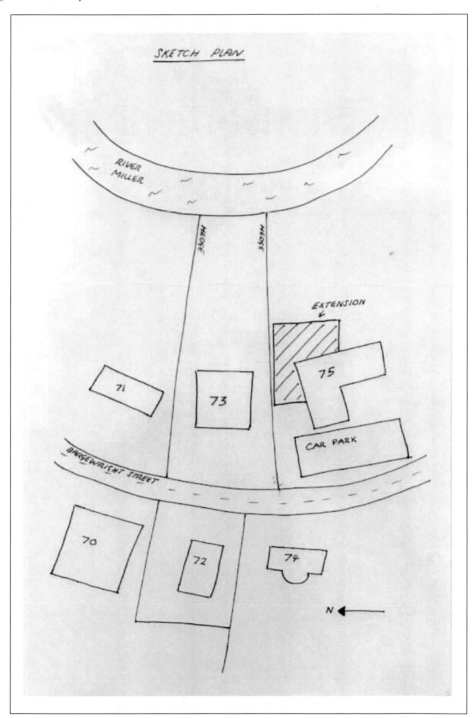

Figure 5.2: poster

The Battleship Welders

Are playing at
The Blacksmith's Arms

On 15 December

(Late licence available)

9.00 pm until 4.00 am

Be prepared for the wildest rock band in Yorkshire

I, GINA MILLER, of 74 Bargewright Street, Smithfield, West Yorkshire WILL SAY AS FOLLOWS:

1   I live on the same street as Mary Cooper, who is a friend of mine. My house is located over the road from her and the Blacksmith's Arms.

2   When we learned of the proposed development, we, along with a few other residents on the street, attempted to have the change stopped. However, it would seem that the company have a good relationship with the members of the local planning council and, therefore, were allowed to change the house at 75 Bargewright Street into a public house.

3   Since the pub has opened, there has been regular noise and trouble on the street. Previously, it was a quiet residential area. Now, there are a lot of youths on the street, especially when the pub has just closed. Sometimes, they do not hurry home, but stand about talking loudly and sometimes shouting and screeching. I have complained to the manager, but he says that what the patrons do after he has closed is not his business and suggested I contact the police if there was a long term problem. The police have told me that they cannot intervene unless I can identify people who are causing the trouble or there is clear evidence of a crime being committed.

4   The noise of the pub, when it has a late licence, is very loud. Sometimes I can hear it quite clearly from across the road. I can understand that it must be very deafening on the side of the street where the pub is located.

5   There has been a terrible increase in the litter on the street. Mary Cooper's front garden is often full of litter and broken glass. Before the Blacksmith's Arms opened, it was very tidy and well maintained.

Signed   *Gina Miller*

Dated   29 November 2006

[END OF PAPERS]

Now, prepare an opinion plan for the above case. To remind you, an opinion plan is a document that contains the sub-headings that you will use in the opinion, together with some notes as to the content of the information contained under each heading.

On the following page is a suggested plan for this case. Please note that the comments made are in note form and are not intended to be a complete answer and, therefore, the content under each of the sub-headings below should be expanded upon in order to give a professional result. If your opinion plan doesn't match the one included below, then this doesn't mean that the one you have written is wrong. Provided that the advice that you would have given in opinion is broadly the same, then this should be sufficient.

Re: MARY COOPER AND THE BLACKSMITH'S ARMS

SUGGESTED OPINION PLAN

Clarify the solicitor's instructions. You have been asked to give advice on stopping the noise and obtaining damages for disruption. You have been instructed by Roger Hooper and Company on 1st December 2006.

The Facts

State the material facts (these are the ones that give rise to the legal issues).

Conclusion

You should write your conclusion in prose and avoid listing. You should mention the following points:

A claim for nuisance is possible and the chances of success are good.

An injunction would be possible to delay the start of the building work until 8.30 am, that is, normal working hours. Instructing solicitors should apply for an urgent interim injunction, as the work is due to finish soon. Mrs Cooper would have to issue proceedings immediately afterwards.

An injunction to prevent the late bar extensions would have to be made with notice to the other side as there is time to do so. They may have to give an undertaking in damages which may be substantial.

Damages should be available for the damaged hedge.

The nuisance caused by the Blacksmith's Arms

It is evident that there is an unreasonable interference with Mrs Cooper's reasonable enjoyment of her property. This would fall under the broad heading of nuisance. The nuisance appears to be arising from three causes:

noise from the public house, in general and also with the late licences;

noise of the building work that is being undertaken;

the litter.

Noise of the pub in general terms

This issue would probably have been examined when planning permission was sought circa November 2000 to turn the property back into a pub. It will be unlikely that the noise can be stopped unless the pub can be shut down for breaches of the licence agreement or unless the noise is completely unreasonable. Have environmental health been informed?

Noise of the pub from the late licences

It is likely that the noise from the late licences would be deemed unreasonable in this residential area. It should be checked that there is in fact a late licence in existence. It would seem strange that one has been granted under the circumstances? Have environmental health been informed?

Noise of the building work

Starting at 6.00 am would certainly appear to be unreasonable. It is probable that the builders could be forced to start work a bit later. It may be that the actual building work itself is unreasonable – dust, etc, although it would appear unlikely, as Mrs Cooper fails to mention any harm suffered other than the noise. Those instructing should check this point.

Environmental health should be informed about all the noise issues. They may take urgent steps and this may save costs. However, environmental health may not act as quickly as Mrs Cooper requires.

The litter

Under the circumstances, proving that the litter is caused by the public house will be difficult. The fish and chip packets may be the responsibility of the fish and chip shop. The broken bottles and the crisp packets are more likely to be the responsibility of the pub. Investigations should be made on what the landlord has done to remedy the situation. This may be a breach of the landlord's licensing agreement.

An action in public nuisance

There is a possibility of public nuisance. Solicitors should get further information on this, including reports on parked cars (well established case law on this), also noise. There will need to be a class type action. I recommend informing the police.

Remedies for nuisance

Urgent interim injunction

An urgent interim injunction could be applied for. Although the case represents circumstances when notice would normally be given to the other side, delay would result in increased harm to the claimant as there would be a delay of an extra four days of noise and by then, the builders may have finished their job. The urgent application should only be made for the building work.

Instructing solicitors should be ready to issue immediately upon this injunction being granted.

Late licence interim injunction

The next scheduled late licence is for 15 December 2000. There is plenty of time to issue proceedings and make an application for an interim injunction with notice. If an injunction is obtained, then the claimant may have to give an undertaking in damages and this may be too much of a burden on Mrs Cooper. This downside should be investigated.

Damages for nuisance

Normal method of establishing damages for tort here. Broad estimate required.

Damage to the hedge

It is likely that the costs of a new hedge would be recoverable as damages under the nuisance. The cost of a new hedge should be investigated by instructing solicitors.

Damages for stress

Unless deemed to be a medical condition, the stress of the situation is unlikely to bring much in the way of compensation.

Damages for poor schoolwork

Unlikely to be recoverable.

Associated issues

Right to light

Right to light applies only to blocking of windows, not general blockage. No rule for open spaces.

Claim for the devaluation in the value of the property

This may be worth some investigation, although it is hard to sustain. It would require a valuation report (chartered surveyor). Devaluation would need to be attributable to the pub being very noisy. One would be unable to claim for the mere fact it is a pub.

Judicial review

It may be worth instructing solicitors investigating the decision making process for the agreement of the planning permission and also the granting of the late licences. There could be a possible claim for judicial review. This may not be feasible given the time delays, and may also prove very expensive.

Further information required

(a) Details of the planning permission granting the extension.

(b) Was Mrs Cooper warned of the extension to the back of the property?

(c) Are there any other residents of the locality who believe that the pub is a nuisance?

(d) Valuation report of decrease in house price.

(e) Cost of new hedge.

(f) Evidence regarding possible public nuisance.

NB: remember not to list with bullet points.

Next steps

Check with the client about the advice provided. A conference with the client is recommended. Possibly initiate proceedings for the urgent interim injunction. Insert a general advert.

Driftwood Chambers   Barry Star

Northumberland Road

Newcastle upon Tyne

7 December 2006

FURTHER READING

Blake, S, *A Practical Approach to Legal Advice and Drafting*, 6th edn, 2003, Oxford: OUP.

Inns of Court School of Law, *Opinion Writing* (published annually), London: OUP.

Rose, W, *Pleadings Without Tears: A Guide to Legal Drafting under the Civil Procedure Rules*, 6th edn, 2002, Oxford: OUP.

CHAPTER 6

LEGAL DRAFTING:
PLANNING, STRUCTURE AND
CONTENT OF FORMAL DOCUMENTS

INTRODUCTION

In previous chapters, we have looked at legal writing: how to do it well and, specifically, how to write letters, memoranda, briefs, attendance notes and reports. Many of the general principles of writing apply to drafting too. After all, drafting is just writing at the most formal end of the scale.

What is drafting?

Although most drafted documents will be pretty lengthy, length isn't the distinguishing factor between writing and drafting. The formal use of the document is. Drafting leaves less room for personal style; there are more rules to follow. Finally, drafted documents are likely to be used over a period of time (possibly many years) by a number of different people, so there is absolutely no room for ambiguity. You should never produce an unclear letter or memo, but if you do, a telephone call can often sort out any problem. If the will, lease or defence you have drafted is not clear, a telephone call will never be enough.

When considering drafting here, we will look at the composition of legal documents such as contracts, wills and statements of case. As we have said, although these documents can sometimes be fairly short and simple, they will generally be longer and more complex than letters. They will also, generally, have particularly important functions and very serious consequences may result in their being drafted wrongly.

However, the main principles of good drafting are the same as those for writing because they are both methods of communication. Clarity, accuracy and simplicity are still vital. You can never know what will happen to your document in the future. This means that you should always draft it so that even someone trying to cause trouble could not misinterpret it.

Drafting, like any other form of communication, is changing all the time. Many of the books on drafting spend a lot of time explaining why the old ways of doing things are out of date. On the other hand, there are some well established practices which remain relevant. We shouldn't throw the baby out with the bath water. So in this chapter, we will try to identify the things that should and should not be retained from established practice.

Two of the big criticisms of 'old style' legal drafting are that documents using it are too long and use too many old fashioned terms. Both of these problems are historical. In the past, more words earned lawyers higher fees. English, French and Latin were, at one time, used as legal languages. Some French words have remained, such as marriage, covenant and infant. Sometimes, both English and French words were used, giving phrases such as *goods and chattels* or *will and testament*.

So lots of words, some hard to understand, were seen as necessary to legal documents, and this is definitely a bad thing. Even the judges are keen to drop this complicated language, and will criticise lawyers who use ideas dressed up in Latin which are not easily understandable to the people they are supposed to help.[1] But we shouldn't forget that many of the rules about drafting have developed over a number of years. As cases come before the courts to clarify the meaning of certain words or phrases, the results are built into future documents. This is important to remember because there will occasionally be a good reason for expressing things in a certain, tried and tested way. Overall, however, the guiding principles have to be accuracy and clarity because in drafting, as in any kind of communication, if you get those right you're 90% of the way there.

What do lawyers draft?

The drafting of legal documents can be divided into two main areas: non-contentious and contentious. Contentious documents are those prepared as a part of litigation. Non-contentious documents are all other documents.

Non-contentious documents

Non-contentious documents are used to define relationships and set out procedures. They are often drafted with the aim of avoiding disputes so by looking at a written contract of employment, employer and employee can see clearly that 25 days' holiday are allowed. The employee can't take more, and the employer can't allow less. Wills, leases and partnership agreements also aim to set out clearly what should happen in the future, so that there is less room for conflict.

Some non-contentious documents have as their main aim the recording of an agreement. Leases and partnership agreements do this as well as setting out future obligations. Other kinds of written contract also aim to provide evidence of an agreement and may set out the complicated details of who has agreed to do what. Where agreements are recorded, the final document will often reflect a compromise agreement reached after negotiations between all those involved. So the fact that the rent on a shop unit in a big shopping centre is expressed in the lease as a percentage of the annual turnover of the shop could be the result of weeks of negotiation which started with the shopping centre demanding a high fixed rate and the prospective tenant refusing to agree to pay it.

Contentious documents

Contentious documents are those prepared as part of litigation. So when a dispute arises because two parties to a contract can't agree on what their obligations are and one thinks she's lost out, or when A drives into the back of B's car, giving B whiplash and a £900 repair bill, if they can't sort it out between them, they may be forced to take legal action. To bring and defend a claim, certain documents are needed. The documents that

---

1 *Fryer v Pearson and Another* (2000) *The Times*, 4 April.

we will consider are statements of case. Statements of case is the term used to describe the formal documents in civil litigation which set out the essential elements of each side's case. So the claimant's claim, and the defendant's defence, are set out in statements of case. There are strict rules about how these documents should be drafted and what information they should contain. These rules will be considered in detail towards the end of this chapter.

How is drafting used within law courses?

You might be introduced to the skill of drafting as part of your degree or a vocational course. The extent to which it might be part of a degree course will depend completely on which course you are on and where. You might look at drafting as part of a legal skills option or in the context of a particular subject like contract. Even if you don't do any drafting at all, knowing about the basic rules is useful when you read documents or statutes drafted by other people.

On the Legal Practice Course (LPC), drafting is one of the five skills which must be taught and assessed. On the Bar Vocational Course (BVC), drafting is almost as important as advocacy. We have aimed in this chapter to look at issues affecting the drafting of contentious and non-contentious documents. Most of what we say can be applied to both, but there are separate sections on contentious and non-contentious drafting.

GOOD DRAFTING – WHY IS IT IMPORTANT?

The problem with a badly drafted document is that it can often be worse than no document at all. If a contract for the sale of widgets is drawn up so badly that it doesn't actually reflect what has been agreed by the buyer and seller, all sorts of problems can result. The widgets aren't delivered on time because the delivery date was unclear in the contract. The buyer has to get some from another supplier and so doesn't need the original batch and rejects them, refusing to pay. The seller sues the buyer for non-payment and a complicated and expensive litigation process begins. If it turns out that the contract is just not clear enough, it could be held by a court that the whole contract is void for uncertainty.

In relation to statements of case, for example, the claim and defence in a civil case, a well drafted document can have a real impact on the litigation. If all the elements of your case are made clear from the outset, it is much more likely that you will be able to negotiate a settlement with the other side and avoid an expensive trial. If your drafting is razor sharp, this will impress the other side, whereas if it is sloppy and unclear your opponent will probably assume that your client's case is poor and you will be easy to beat. Worse still, other lawyers and judges will see your drafting and if it's consistently not up to scratch, your reputation will suffer.

Problems of bad drafting for lawyers

If it is your job to consider a draft document prepared by another lawyer, you will soon form an opinion as to whether they have good or bad drafting skills. A clearly drafted contract can be read and understood quickly and easily. If the draft is good, you still need to check it carefully, but you will probably not need to suggest too many amendments. It should be easy to follow and simple to make the changes you need.

If a document is badly drafted, it can be a real battle. The aims of the document will be less clear, and you will struggle to understand what is being said. You will have to read it again and again and will be forced to refer to your legal dictionary. If you are considering the document for your client, you will have to argue tactfully for the inclusion of any items you think have been left out and suggest the rewording of ambiguous phrases. This all takes much more time and effort.

If something does go wrong and two people start arguing over what a document actually means, the words used are even more important, because often the courts won't look at other evidence of the intention of the parties. For example, what went on in the negotiations before an agreement might be completely irrelevant in deciding what a document says, if the document itself seems clear and unambiguous. The parties will often be presumed to have wanted to say what was said even if one of them swears otherwise.[2] (This is referred to as the *parol evidence rule*.) This means you need to get it right in the document.

Problems of bad drafting for clients

Good drafting is always unambiguous, clear and concise and in accordance with instructions. A badly drafted contract can lead to problems if the people who entered the contract can't agree on what it actually says. This is quite possible if a contract was drafted some years ago and has been pulled out of a dusty drawer only to be found to be full of complicated terms and ambiguous words. It will mean, at best, wasted time trying to resolve the problem and, at worst, the people who entered the contract will fall out and one will sue the other for not complying with its terms. Time and money will be used up trying to sort out the mess. If litigation results, scarce court time will be taken up by a problem that was entirely avoidable. Again, when a judge comes to consider the contract, she may decide that the words in it are clear and therefore prevail over any intention of either party. Nobody wins.

Different, but important, problems occur if a contentious document like a statement of case is drafted badly. Failing to mention in a defence that your client had been drinking orange juice all night, rather than the 10 pints of beer alleged, is going to have important consequences. If your defence document doesn't deny everything your client has told you to, the best thing that can happen is that you have to get permission to amend it, and that takes time and money.

But the cost to clients is not just financial. What if Mr Brown's will is not drafted properly and doesn't do what he wanted? By the time the mistake is discovered, it will be too late to ask Mr Brown. His wife, devastated by his death, will face the additional worry of trying to sort out the financial problems, at a time when she is least able to cope.[3]

---

2   Though see the decision in *Investors Compensation Scheme Ltd v West Bromwich Building Society and Others* [1998] 1 All ER 98, which is indicative of a judicial trend towards consideration of intention and business efficacy.

3   The solicitor responsible for the will may also face a negligence action.

USE OF PRECEDENTS

Because there is so much law around these days and because pretty much everything you do has been done in a similar (though never exactly the same) way before, when you are drafting a document you will very rarely start completely from scratch. Generally, you will be able to use someone else's similar document, or precedent, as a basis for your own. Precedents come in two main types:

- published precedents;
- your own/colleagues' precedents.

There are lots of specialist publications which provide precedents for all sorts of documents. Some of the more common sources of these precedents are listed below. If you need to draft a lease of a plot of land for the erection of advertising boards, you can look up 'advertisement', then 'outdoor – site' in the index to one of these books and you will find a standard precedent with useful explanations of all the clauses in the document. Nearly all of the texts come in CD form, which makes it very easy to transfer the standard document on to your own disk and amend it.

Where can I find precedents?

Below is a list of some of the more commonly encountered and used published precedents, with a short description of what they contain:

- *Encyclopaedia of Forms and Precedents* (CD or 42 volumes of books, or on-line through the Butterworths website) – this is an excellent source of non-contentious document precedents which includes anything from an application for a licence to keep a pet shop to a warning notice of breach of boat regulation bylaws.
- *Practical Matrimonial Precedents* (Sweet & Maxwell) – here you can find drafts of documents like divorce petitions and applications for injunctions.
- *Practical Conveyancing Precedents* (Sweet & Maxwell) – this contains a number of conveyancing and land sale related precedents.
- *Practical Lease Precedents* (Sweet & Maxwell) – this gives examples of residential, business and agricultural leases.
- *Practical Commercial Precedents* (Sweet & Maxwell) – similar to those above, you can find precedents relating to anything from management buyouts through licences of copyright to sales of shares in this text.
- *Practical Civil Court Precedents* (Sweet & Maxwell) – this contains civil litigation precedents.
- *Butterworths Civil Court Precedents* – this gives a wide range of draft statements of case in detail. It includes, as an example, a particulars of claim for negligence to be used against a solicitor who missed a limitation period. These precedents are available on-line through Butterworths Civil Procedure On-line service at www.butterworths.co.uk.

If you don't have access to a published book or CD of precedents, you might have a similar document that you drafted yourself or that one of your colleagues drafted which you can use. For example, many firms of solicitors will keep a database of precedents of documents drafted by members of the firm.

Why use precedents?

Precedents can be helpful because they save time. It is nearly always easier to adapt what someone else has done than to do it yourself, and there is no merit in re-inventing the wheel. If you are not familiar with the kind of document you're drafting, a precedent will show you what should go into it and suggest a logical order. You can also use the precedent as a checklist for contents. Even if there isn't one particular precedent that fits your needs, you may be able to put two or more together to produce the document you want.

Problems with precedents

So precedents are the answer to all your problems? Not quite. There are some problems that can occur when using precedents. Generally, this won't mean that you shouldn't use one, just that you should be careful when you do.

Using your own style

It is harder to build up your own style if you always follow precedents and if you do have to draft something from scratch, you might then find it particularly difficult.

Bending the facts to fit the precedent

A very tempting aspect of using a precedent is to convince yourself that the precedent you have found is exactly what you need. This is quite natural: you are happy to use the precedent because it's easy to copy out and you don't need to worry about your own drafting being wrong. Because it is already there in black and white, it seems to have authority. You decide it is perfect for your client's situation. But do you know the case well enough to be sure that this is the right one? If you do, is it really likely that the publisher of a book of standard precedents predicted exactly the case that you have to deal with? There is almost certainly going to be something about the precedent that isn't quite right. Something that is there that doesn't need to be, something that should be there and is missing or something that just needs to be a little bit different. Be careful to accommodate your client's needs instead of slavishly following precedents.

How should precedents be used?

Exactly how you use a precedent will depend on your preference. The essence of effective precedent use is not to be good at using an index and finding the right precedent. That will get you off the starting line, but you need to do a lot more to produce a well drafted document. Two common ways to use precedents are to take a copy of the precedent and mark alterations on the copy, or to write out the whole thing again. Using and altering a precedent on disk is also common.

It is useful to refer to more than one precedent for the same document if you can. No two precedents will be exactly the same, so you can use the one that you prefer. If you use more than one precedent for your drafting, be very careful. It is easy to find that you have used different terms, repeated yourself or been inconsistent in style if you have taken some items from one and some from another.

If you are using a precedent, make sure you check that:

- you are clear which one you need;
- you don't follow it slavishly;
- the precedent reflects the up to date legal position;
- you don't bend the facts to fit the precedent;
- you don't include superfluous clauses;
- you make sure your client's instructions are fully reflected;
- you don't miss anything out;
- you understand what you are writing.

Build up your own supply of precedents for the documents that you have looked at on your course. If you might be asked to draft a document under supervision or in an exam and you are able to use precedents, you will find it easier if you already have copies of precedents which you are familiar with.

Drafting from scratch

If there really is no precedent that you can use and you have to draft a document completely on your own, how will you start? Assuming that you are on top of the relevant law and clear about your instructions,[4] the best way is to list the outline contents, then begin to flesh them out in stages. Start with a list of headings for the main things you need to cover, and get them into an order you are happy with, then add any sub-headings you need. After this, draft the clauses under your headings and sub-headings.

WHAT KIND OF CASE IS THIS?

Mr Brown comes in and says he wants you to arrange the sale of one of his fields. OK, you think, a transfer of land. But he wants to make sure the buyer can't build on the field or do certain other things, and he wants it done quickly and cheaply. So you think maybe a lease. It's quite likely that, after discussing it with him, he might decide that he would actually rather rent the field because it can be arranged more quickly and it gives him more control.

The client, subject matter and context of a case will all have significant effects on how and what you draft. Consideration should be given to the exact needs of the client, the legal context and any kind of general practice that might apply to certain kinds of cases before deciding on the document you will draft.

---

4   This is a huge assumption to make. You might need to spend a lot of time sorting these things out before you are ready to sit down and begin drafting.

What does your client want?

Before you draft anything, you need to be clear what it is that your client wants. You might think this is obvious, but there are plenty of documents out there which contain a lot of legal detail that the signatories are ignoring in happy innocence, and why not? Often they would not be able to understand this detail if they did bother to read it. This is not because they are not intelligent enough; it is because the document is not clearly drafted and has not been explained. This is all fine, until something goes wrong.

One of the first things that you will need to consider is whether your drafting skills are required at all. Sometimes it will be obvious that a document is needed, for example, where your client is selling his house. Sometimes someone may just come to you with a problem and it will only become clear after getting all the details that a document is needed, or at least advisable.

Lawyers need to be careful about categorising their clients' needs too quickly. Some clients are experienced and do know exactly what it is they want. But just because Miss Jenkins tells you straight away that she wants a partnership agreement doesn't mean that is what she would choose once she understands the risks and consequences. You need to check that it is really a partnership that she wants rather than, for example, a limited company. It is your job to make sure that your client understands the implications of the relevant law. If, after discussing the options, she is clear that this is what she wants, you must then go on to find out the details of what she requires, so that you can draft the agreement needed. Remember that if a lawyer decides too early on in an interview what it is that a client wants or needs, the client will feel as if they are not being properly listened to as well as very annoyed when they discover they've been given a document which isn't right for them. Refer to Chapter 8 for a more detailed discussion of how to understand your client's real priorities.

Make sure you have all the information you need from your client. The more complex the issues, the more complex the document is likely to be, and it might take some time to get all the facts you need. It is of vital importance that you are clear about what your client wants and extra time spent making sure will always save more time later on. You will need to find out what your client wants to happen should anything covered by the document go wrong. What notice must be given to end the employment contract? Should the parties use arbitration if they fall out; if so, who will choose the arbitrator? These kinds of clauses will be included in a good precedent.

It is unavoidable that sometimes you will start to research or even draft and then realise that there is some information you need but don't have. With very complex documents you might need a number of meetings between which you will research and prepare, before you even start to draft the document required.

What approach should be taken?

The way you approach your drafting might be affected by a number of factors relating to the case. If the case is very complex and your client is a large company with lots of money, your approach will be different from a case involving an individual with a straightforward problem and scarce finances. BP will be prepared to spend more on a 10 year maintenance contract for an offshore oil rig than Mrs Smith on her claim against the council for compensation for her sprained ankle caused by uneven paving slabs in the high street.

Someone with a basic problem and a small budget won't thank you for a long document and a huge bill. Even big companies may sometimes want short and simple documents, perhaps when there isn't enough time for something more detailed or the extra expense just isn't worth it. In practice, these matters will need to be sorted out with your client before you begin your drafting.

You need to think about any time constraints you are under. Does the document need to be ready by a certain date? If it does, this will be a consideration in your planning.

You should also think about how the document will be used. Is it going to be a working document that will need to be referred to often in the course of business? If so, it is even more important that it is easy to understand.

Who will produce the first draft?

In non-contentious drafting, it is common for a document to be signed and used by more than one person. An issue that will sometimes be covered by general practice is who produces the first draft. Where a document is to be signed by Smith and Brown, will Smith's or Brown's lawyer draft it? Usually, it is the person conferring a right who is responsible for drafting. If, for example, a building is being let, convention says that the landlord's solicitor will be the one to produce the draft lease. It makes sense because the landlord will know more about the property than the tenant. The tenant's lawyer will still get to scrutinise and suggest amendments to the draft. In practice, this is something you should check.

PREPARING TO DRAFT

Your preparation and drafting will take variable lengths of time depending on the subject matter, but they will nearly always take longer than you anticipate when you first begin to practise the skill. Below, we have outlined the issues you should consider when preparing to draft a document.

Researching the facts

The initial element of research is usually talking to the client and getting their instructions if you are a solicitor, or being sent a bundle of documents and instructions if you are a barrister. It's quite likely that after thinking about the information you have and the document you will draft, you will find that there are gaps in your knowledge. Sometimes, these will be so important that you will need to get hold of the missing information before you can go any further. Sometimes, it will be easy enough to carry on and draft the document while leaving a gap to be filled in later.

One way to research the facts is to send your client a questionnaire. This is most useful with relatively simple drafting exercises. A straightforward will or the sale of a house will often involve the client filling out a standard questionnaire giving facts such as who the sellers and buyers are, the address of the house and what exactly is included in the sale.[5]

Sometimes, your research will include getting hold of other documents. It may be that you need these to make sure your drafting is accurate. If your client has been writing to the football club buying his star player, setting out prices and terms, you will need copies of those letters. If you are drafting the sub-lease on some office space in the millennium dome, you will need to check the main lease to make sure your sub-tenant doesn't breach any of the terms in the lease.

Researching the law

Research is discussed in detail in Chapters 3 and 4. It is a skill which you will always need to use when you are drafting. In fact, you will often spend a lot more time on research than on drafting the document. Your research will include finding a relevant precedent, researching the relevant case law or statute and checking that the precedent is up to date.

The precedent

We have talked about precedents in detail above (see pp 153–55). Be thorough in your search for the most appropriate precedent. Check all the publications you can find but in practice remember to ask colleagues or use any internal databases you have access to. If you find more than one, all the better.

The law

You are the legal expert, so you need to be sure that you understand the law relating to the document you plan to draft. This stage is similar to getting your instructions from your client clear, because extra time you spend now checking the law will save you more time later on in the process. This is particularly true if the law has recently changed, as the precedents you use might not have been revised.

You will need to find the statute relevant to the subject of your drafting. If it is an assignment of copyright, the Copyright, Designs and Patents Act 1988 will need checking out. Statutes might imply terms into a contract, set out how a document should be signed or render invalid clauses that your client has asked for. You'll have to make sure that you find the most up to date version of the statute and you might also have to look at statutory instruments or regulations.

Everyone knows that an ordinary contract needs an offer, acceptance and consideration, but sometimes people forget even basic law when they start to draft. In contracts, be aware of the difference between a condition and a warranty (breach of the first means the injured party can treat himself as discharged, but breach of the second will only entitle him to damages). Check to see if there are any presumptions that you

---

5   Elmer Doonan gives some examples of checklists, such as the sale of a house and a partnership agreement, that could be used as the basis for questionnaires, in Chapter 2 of Doonan, E and Foster, C, *Drafting*, 2nd edn, 2001, London: Cavendish Publishing.

need to deal with. You need to be up to date here too. There could be recent case law that gives guidance on forms of drafting or interpretation of documents.

Planning the structure

The planning stage is very important and is worth taking time over. If you get this right, the rest should follow much more easily. It is often recommended that you prepare an outline of the document you want to draft as part of your planning. An outline is really just a basic list of contents. It might have headings and sub-headings if the document is fairly complicated. This is most useful when you don't have a precedent to work with. However, even with a precedent, when you are not experienced at drafting, an outline is a useful way of planning a document and of making sure that nothing vital gets left out. It will also help you to consider whether, for example, a certain issue should be dealt with in one paragraph or two.

An outline can be used as a check later, to make sure you have covered everything you should have. It can also help you put things in a logical order. If you do this at the outline stage, the final document should make better sense.

When it comes to this stage, you should make sure you have a reasonable chunk of time and somewhere quiet. If you can't concentrate on the planning, then things could easily be missed out or mistakes made.

How to use drafts

Especially when a document is complicated, you will find that you will prepare a number of drafts before you are happy with what you have done. This is part of the process; no one can dash off a perfect document first time. It is valuable to consider what you have drafted and make improvements.

It is easier to concentrate on a document clause by clause. Think about them separately and make sure they say exactly what you want them to. Only then will you need to look at the document as a whole.

You should number all your drafts on the front and keep them all. If they are numbered, you shouldn't find that you're using the third rather than the fourth to make your final amendments on. All drafts should be kept together and should be easy to distinguish from the final document. To ensure this you can write 'draft' on them, or put them all on coloured paper.

When preparing drafts you will often need to leave a blank space to be filled in later. Alternatively, you may put some information in but not be 100% sure it's right. It can help if you mark the space by highlighting it in colour or putting square brackets around the space or the words you're not sure of. This means you are less likely to forget that you wanted to make a change and leave the blank or the unchecked information in the final document. Some people will do this with cross-references and definitions too. This helps to highlight them when it comes to the final checks, especially if you can use a word processor to search for each marker.

Sometimes you may need to send a draft to your client to look at and check, or you may go over the draft with them in person. This is more appropriate when the document is a one off that includes fairly complicated elements, directly reflecting what your client has asked for. For example, it would always be a good idea to get a will, a witness statement or a draft contract for the sale of a business checked. These are detailed documents which you will want to ensure follow your client's instructions. On the other hand, if your client is being sued and has already given you enough detail of the case, you may feel it unnecessary to get the actual defence document checked. You may instead explain the main elements of the defence and leave it at that.

Finally, you need to check your last draft very carefully. There could be mistakes in the law or in the drafting, or there might be spelling mistakes or errors in numbering. Everything should be checked. You will lose credibility with lecturers and, in practice, with clients, even if your only mistakes are in punctuation. It is much more effective to do this sort of final check when you are fresh and haven't been staring at the document for the last two hours. We think you should leave at least a clear day. Some textbooks suggest that the draft shouldn't be looked at for two days. In practice, solicitors in particular will ask colleagues to check over final drafts of especially important documents.

The stages of drafting

The drafting process can be broken down into distinct stages. After you have done your research and found your precedent and you actually put pen to paper, this is roughly how the process will work:

(1) First stage – the first outline and rough form is produced.

(2) Second stage – check the law, facts, instructions, precedent's effect and amend the first draft. This stage might include more than one draft.

(3) Third stage – polish the language, correct any errors.

(4) Fourth stage – make your own final checks. Mistakes always creep in, so checking drafting is vital to producing a good final document.

Here is a list of items to check:
- effectiveness of provisions;
- typing and spelling mistakes;
- figures, dates and names correct;
- punctuation;
- contains all necessary information;
- contains no unnecessary information;
- clear and logical order;
- consistency in style and content;
- no unnecessary repetition;
- defined words are used consistently;
- accurate cross-references.

(5) Fifth stage – consideration by your client. This won't always be appropriate. It's more common with non-contentious documents like leases, partnership agreements or employment contracts being drafted for the employer. You will have to explain the contents and it's usually much easier to do this face to face than by writing explanatory notes.

(6) Sixth stage – last check by another lawyer. This might be part of the process, as with a lease which will be sent to the tenant's lawyer for checking. If this is the case, the draft should be approved by your client first. If the document is a will or litigation document, although it won't always be possible, it is good practice to get a colleague to read it through before it is signed by the client.

How to check other people's drafts

In practice you may find that you need to consider another lawyer's draft document. If your client is entering a contract to build Titanic II in accordance with specifications and a predetermined timetable, you will need to consider the commissioning party's draft contract. You will want to check that your client is happy with the terms; for example, is she happy to give an absolute guarantee that it cannot sink? You will also need to check the drafting style: is it clear enough and does it do what it intends to?

If you are checking a draft, it is your duty to consider its effect with your client's interests in mind. If it is unfair to your client, you will need to suggest an amendment. But never change things that don't really need changing. It will only affect your relationship with the person who drafted the document.

If you are not absolutely clear about what the document is saying, you may need to go as far as trying to rewrite the relevant paragraph in your own words. This is the best way to really get to grips with the meaning of words.

Just because the person who produced the draft is more experienced than you, don't assume that the document will be free from errors. Mistakes will always creep in when drafting. It can often feel as if the more important the document the more mistakes appear. A small typing error can occasionally make all the difference. If the price of equipment is £400, increasing the price *by* £500 and increasing it *to* £500 will make the kind of difference that could get you into real trouble.

STRUCTURING THE DOCUMENT

As with all writing, layout can help a great deal to make a document easy to read. Even the quality of paper used will have an effect. Everything we have said about writing in short sentences and using paragraphs and numbered points will still apply to drafting. If a document has no real structure it will be harder to understand; if the layout is inconsistent or inappropriate it can make the document misleading.

There are a number of ways of structuring documents to make them clear. For example, schedules can be used to move less important or more complex detail out of the main part of a document. Some documents can be made clearer by dividing them into parts, for example, Part One – introduction, Part Two – definitions, and so on.

If your document is long, you might want to include a contents page. Most documents will also have what is called a 'front sheet'. This is a sheet giving details like the names of the parties, the date, the title of the document and the name of the solicitors' firm acting.

Using spacing, different fonts, indenting and other techniques can make reading much easier:

Long sentences in difficult fonts are hard to read, and if included in a drafted document they will make it difficult for the reader to concentrate on the meaning of the words and the document as a whole.

As with all legal writing, shorter sentences will improve the piece. Always remember that too much highlighting or underlining will be counterproductive. Bold words are easy to read, as are fonts like Times New Roman and Arial.

BUT A SENTENCE IN CAPITALS IS NOT SO EASY.

<u>Neither is a particularly long line of text that is in an acceptable font but which is, for some reason, underlined.</u>

Clauses and paragraphs

Using clauses and paragraphs rather than dense blocks of text will make a document easier to read. Their use means that you can clarify meaning and avoid repetition. The words 'clause' and 'paragraph' have a particular meaning in the context of non-contentious legal drafting. A legal drafting paragraph is not the same as a paragraph in an ordinary book. The system is as follows:

Documents can be divided into parts;

Parts can be divided into clauses;

Clauses can be divided into sub-clauses;

Sub-clauses can be divided into paragraphs;

Paragraphs can be divided into sub-paragraphs;

Sub-paragraphs can be divided into sub-sub-paragraphs.

So material with a common theme, such as the powers of investment in a trust deed, might be grouped in a clause.[6] Sub-division into paragraphs might still be needed to make the contents clear. It will be rare that you get as far as a sub-sub-paragraph. If you do get that far, you might need to think about whether you couldn't rearrange your writing and take out a few divisions to make it clearer.

There are some complex rules concerning the construction of clauses which date back to the mid-1800s.[7] We do not have the space to detail them here. The basic principles to remember are that each clause should deal with one concept, you should draft in the present tense, and what you write should make sense and follow the basic rules of grammar.

When you are writing the use of lists or enumeration helps a reader understand the information more quickly. With drafting too, splitting a sentence into a list makes it easier to see at a glance what is going on. This can be done in the context of a clause or paragraph so that:

4   The Defendant was negligent in that she

   (a) did not look where she was going;

---

6   As Elmer Doonan points out in *Drafting* (*op cit*, fn 5).
7   Doonan considers them in some depth (*op cit*, fn 5).

(b) did not manage her car with enough skill and care;

(c) did not use her brakes in time ...

is easier to read, and easier to respond to, than:

4   The Defendant was negligent in that she did not look where she was going and did not manage her car with enough skill and care and did not use her brakes in time ...

even though the words are the same.

Rules about using clauses and paragraphs

- Each paragraph should deal with only one concept. If there is more than one, clarity is lost.

- There must be introductory words that relate to everything in the rest of the paragraph, for example: 'The Defendant was negligent in that she ...' But don't go too far. This kind of paragraph is not helpful:

    The

    (a) banks;

    (b) building societies; and

    (c) insurance companies;

    must retain money ...

    The use of a list is not necessary here.

- Test the sense of the paragraph by reading the introductory words and each listed item with the resuming words at the end if there are any. Doing this with (c), below, you can see that the paragraph needs changing:

    1   A licensee is entitled,

    (a) unless his licence, or any licence through which his interest is derived, provides otherwise,

    (b) to call on the proprietor of the registered trade mark to take infringement proceedings in respect of any matter which affects his interests.

    (c) If the proprietor refuses to do so or fails to do so within two months after being called upon,

    the licensee may bring the proceedings in his own name as if he were the proprietor.

This should read:

    1   A licensee is entitled, unless his licence, or any licence through which his interest is derived, provides otherwise, to call on the proprietor of the registered trade mark to take infringement proceedings in respect of any matter which affects his interests.

    2   If the proprietor –

    (a) refuses to do so, or

    (b) fails to do so within two months after being called upon,

    the licensee may bring the proceedings in his own name as if he were the proprietor.

- Never go lower than a sub-sub-paragraph.

- Convention says that you only need to put 'and' or 'or' after the penultimate item on a list as below (although we don't see anything wrong in repeating it after every item if you really want to):

  Law students must study

  (a) obligations;

  (b) property;

  (c) European Union law;

  (d) criminal law; and

  (e) public law.

- Never use 'and' *and* 'or' in this kind of list. If you do, the meaning will not be clear:

  Law students must study

  (a) obligations; or

  (b) property; and

  (c) European Union law; or

  (d) criminal law; and

  (e) public law.

  Do students have to study European Union law or can they choose criminal law and public law instead? You can make things clearer by saying: 'Law students must study all of the following'; or 'Law students may study any one of the following', depending on your intended meaning.

- Don't use 'and/or', as this is also unclear. If you want to say:

  To gain entry on to the course, a student must have three 'A' levels at grade B or above and/or an equivalent qualification.

  You could try instead:

  To gain entry on to the course a student must have

  (a) three 'A' levels at grade B or above; or

  (b) an equivalent qualification,

  or both.

- Indenting in paragraphs helps clarity:

  1 Law students must study all of the following:

      (a) obligations, being:

          (i) contract; and

          (ii) tort;

      (b) property, being:

          (i) land; and

          (ii) trusts;

      (c) European law.

The indenting of the subjects followed by the further indenting of the components of obligations and property makes it easier to see at a glance what is going on.

Numbering

Each clause or paragraph should be consecutively numbered. There are different styles of numbering. Generally, it doesn't really matter which you use, as long as you are consistent. The two main styles are the legislative and the decimal. In the legislative system:

1   Clauses can be divided into sub-clauses;

    (1) Sub-clauses can be divided into paragraphs;

        (a) Paragraphs can be divided into sub-paragraphs;

            (i) Sub-paragraphs can be divided into sub-sub-paragraphs;

                (A) sub-sub-paragraphs shouldn't be divided.

In the decimal system:

    1.1   Sub-clauses can be divided into paragraphs;

        1.1.1 Paragraphs can be divided into sub-paragraphs;

            1.1.1.1 Sub-paragraphs can be divided into sub-sub-paragraphs;

                1.1.1.1.1 Sub-sub-paragraphs shouldn't be divided.

Sometimes, you will want to make a cross-reference in your document. You may want to refer to cl 3, sub-cl (a), in the text of cl 10. It is fine just to refer to cl 3(a) and there is no need to repeat any of its contents. Saying 'cl 3(a) *above*' is superfluous. However, be careful when you use cross-references, because if you add a new clause to a draft, not only will you need to change the numbering of all the clauses, you will need to check that the cross-references are still correct.

Schedules

Schedules can be used to group information that would clutter the main part of a document. A schedule can be used to set out detail such as all the tenant's covenants in a lease, to attach copies of other documents such as plans or maps, or even to give examples. If you can set information out more clearly in a table, rather than in text, this should go in a schedule too.

Headings

You might want to give a short heading to each clause. This will depend to some extent on the document and how long it is. Headings should be emphasised by using a different size or font or by using bold. If you think it will make things clearer then do it, but be aware that too many headings will destroy, rather than enhance, clarity.

Capital letters

Looking at some legal documents, you might be forgiven for thinking that the more capital letters in a document, the more important the contents and of course, the lawyer who drafted it. Use them at the beginning of sentences and for defined words and names only. Headings can be highlighted in bold instead of capitals. Use of capitals in an otherwise ordinary sentence is seen in some precedents to add emphasis, BUT it is not necessary.

Definitions

A definition can allow you to:

(a) use a more convenient and shorter word or phrase for words used more than once; and

(b) make your meaning clear.

There are two main ways to give a definition; neither are right or wrong, but they do have different effects. They are to say:

(a) 'Document' means a computer disk; or

(b) 'Document' includes a computer disk.

If you say '"Document" *means* a computer disk', it means *only that* – a paper document will not be included when you say 'Document'. The definition is closed. If you say '"Document" *includes* a computer disk', your definition is not closed and will include paper documents and anything else that might be covered by the word. The definition is open.

Make sure you have used the same term throughout the document and that it matches the definition you set out at the beginning of the document. Calling 'the Company' 'the Business' halfway through a contract is not hard to do. If you have defined 'the Company', but not 'the Business', your document can easily stop making sense. If a particular statute is relevant to your document, check the definitions in the statute are consistent with your use of them in your document. If you want to use a statutory definition, you should still include it in your draft, as it won't automatically apply otherwise.

In non-contentious documents, particularly where there are more than one or two definitions, there will be a definitions section listing all of them in alphabetical order. This could be at the start (which we prefer), or at the end of the document. This is not done in contentious documents, where a definition is given in brackets after the first use of the term to be defined. This kind of definition is of the 'means' rather than the 'includes' type, and is invariably to allow the use of a shorter word or phrase as in:

> The Defendant is the publican and owner of The Holly Tree public house, Brampton, Cumbria (the Pub).

Usually defined words are flagged up by making the first letter a capital. So, every use of the word Pub later in the document will have a capital P.

When not to use definitions

Do not use misleading definitions like:

> 'Accidental Damage' includes damage caused intentionally by persons other than the insured.

This is the kind of definition you might expect from an unscrupulous insurance company in relation to a clause which says:

> Accidental Damage is not covered by this policy.

Make sure that you don't use a definition only once; there is no point in a one-off definition. Don't define something that doesn't need it. Defining 'the relevant date' as '12 May 2002' just doesn't help at all. It serves neither of the two functions of a definition, to avoid a longer phrase or to clarify. You may as well use the actual date throughout.

Page breaks

Try to put in page breaks at appropriate points in the text. When you have your final document ready, make sure that as far as possible a clause or paragraph doesn't start on one page and end on another. Make sure also that you don't end up with a heading or the first line of a paragraph at the bottom of a page.

RULES AND CONVENTIONS

Over time, the courts have developed rules about how to interpret documents. All drafting must be done in the light of these rules, because if your document comes to be considered by a judge, you need to know how she is likely to read it.

As well as rules, there are conventions governing drafting practice. A convention is a rule that is generally followed. The important thing to remember about conventions is that, although you might follow most of them, most of the time, occasionally they will be completely obsolete or their use will not be appropriate. There are good reasons for following many conventions, but if it really isn't useful, you shouldn't hesitate to ignore a convention.

Rules of construction

Because lawyers have been drafting documents for so many hundreds of years, rules have built up governing the way certain methods of expressing things will be interpreted. It's useful to know what the main ones are, so that you won't be saying one thing and meaning another in your drafting.

Below are examples of some of the more important rules.

A document will be read as a whole

In deciding on the meaning of parts of a document, the meaning and context of the whole will be important. If you use a group of words together it will be presumed, if there is any doubt, that they should all be interpreted as being used in the same context.

If words are clear, they will be given their clear meaning

This is always true unless it is very clear that something different and identifiable was intended. Clients can be surprised by this rule: that it is not necessarily their intention that is the most important consideration, but the words written in the document.

Words will be given their reasonable construction

If there are two possible meanings for words, they will be given their reasonable meaning, as that will be presumed to have been the intention of the parties.

Words are presumed to have a particular meaning

It will be assumed that every word in a document is there for a reason and that none is superfluous. So if you say 'the said premises' or 'the aforementioned premises' when you haven't referred to any premises yet in a document, the use of these words could throw the whole meaning into confusion.

Words are presumed to be used consistently

If you've changed the word, you've changed the meaning. The same word will be given the same meaning throughout a document. If a different word is used (because of the effect of the rule above) it will be presumed to have a different meaning. So this is where suddenly talking about 'the Business' when previously you had used the term 'the Company' can cause problems.

You have deliberately left out what you didn't want included

If you give a lot of detail, or are very specific about something, it will be presumed that if you've left something out it was because you decided you didn't want it included. So, a list including my chairs, sofas, bookcases, chests of drawers and stools will probably be assumed to have left out the table on purpose, rather than by accident.

General words following specific ones are read in the light of the specific words

If you give specific examples and then follow them with more general words, it will be presumed that the general words mean things of the same type as the specific examples. So, for example, ants, beetles, flies and other animals might be held to mean other insects, but not animals like cows or elephants. This is referred to as the *ejusdem generis* rule.

Your preferred interpretation may not be used

If there is a dispute about words which are not clear and one party tries to give them an interpretation to his benefit, the opposite meaning will be presumed. So an exclusion clause in a contract will be interpreted against the party trying to rely on it. This is referred to as the *contra proferentem* rule.

How should time be expressed?

This is a difficult one. Even when you are trying hard, making clear what you mean by specific time periods can be difficult. With contentious documents, the Civil Procedure Rules (CPR) set out how time periods will be calculated.[8] But you will actually be referring to time much more often in the drafting of non-contentious documents, such as when a lease starts and ends, or the notice period for ending an employment contract.

Conventions relating to time

There are some ways of referring to time in legal documents which are better and clearer than others. There are conventions too, which set out, for example, that 'from the date of notice being given' generally means *excluding* that date rather than *including* that date. It is better to be as precise as you can so that reliance on this sort of convention is kept to a minimum. It is impossible to avoid these conventions, however, so it is important to know what they are. Below are some of the more common ones:

From the date of ... (an act or event)	the date of the act or event is excluded
Within seven days after (an act or event)	the date of the act or event is excluded
Beginning on 25th	25th is included
Commencing on 25th	25th is included
Two weeks after 25th	25th is excluded
Between 21st and 25th	21st and 25th are excluded
Until 25th	25th could be either included or excluded
By 25th	25th is included

It is better to use clearer terms such as:

* within a period of two weeks commencing on ...
* until but not including ...
* on or before ...

If you try to be as precise and clear as you can, your reliance on the conventions can be kept to a minimum.

General terms for time

Sometimes, your client might prefer you to use terms such as 'immediately' or 'within a reasonable time', rather than referring to a specific time period or date. Such phrases can obviously be interpreted more flexibly than specific time periods. This has

---

8   These are the rules which govern the conduct of civil litigation. See, eg, *The Civil Procedure Rules*, 1998, London: Sweet & Maxwell. So r 2.8 explains that if a rule says 'notice is to be given at least three days before the hearing', this means at least three clear days must pass between the day the period begins and the day it ends. If a hearing is on Friday 20 October, the last day to give notice would be Monday 16 October.

advantages and disadvantages. There is a greater possibility of disagreement as to the exact meaning later, but when the parties are signing the document, they are more likely to be happy to agree, and it may never become a problem. Of course, you can always do both by using a general term followed by a specific limit as in:

> The seller must deliver the goods within a reasonable time but not later than 7 May 2002.

'Now'

Don't use the word 'now' in your drafting. It could be now, as you write, now when the document is signed or even now when it is read later. Be precise, so if you mean the date of the agreement, say that.

Write dates in numerals

> 27 December 2023

is clearer than:

> The Twenty-seventh day of December Two Thousand and Twenty-three.

It means the same thing, and everyone knows the 27th is a day. Sometimes, lawyers worry about numerically written dates being changed more easily. If, but only if, it really is possible that someone will benefit from changing this date to say, 28 December 2828, then by all means, write it in words.

Joint tenants or tenants in common

If a document gives an interest in something to more than one person, it should be clear whether the interest is to be held as joint tenants (with the consequent right of survivorship) or as tenants in common. When drafting wills and transfers of interests in land in particular, you should take care to use the appropriate words, otherwise either one or the other will be implied and it may not accord with the wishes of your client. The words below are used on the standard forms for a land transfer:

For joint tenants:

> The transferees are to hold the property on trust for themselves as joint tenants.

For tenants in common:

> The transferees are to hold the property on trust for themselves as tenants in common in equal shares.

THE LANGUAGE OF DRAFTING

Much of what we have said in the chapters on writing is also relevant here. Drafting should be in plain English, using ordinary words wherever possible. You should always try to keep your sentences short and use appropriate punctuation. We have explained in previous sections that the way you draft will be affected not just by using plain

English. There are established rules and conventions of legal drafting, which can also affect the way you word a document.

Historically, punctuation was used less in legal documents, as the rules governing it were neither commonly understood nor practised. This is no longer true and punctuation, correctly used, obviously adds to the clarity of the document. Don't be reluctant to use brackets (as opposed to commas) as they too can add clarity to your meaning.

There are a lot of legal terms you will see used which don't add to a document at all. Archaic and complicated language is still used by some lawyers, but there is rarely a need for it and it can be easily avoided as long as you really understand what it is you are trying to say. Be careful about using phrases like 'Last Will and Testament'. If you understand what you are writing, you will know that 'will' is enough. It is still quite common in legal documents to use more words than are needed. Never use three words when one will do.

Archaic and complex language

It is not necessary to use terms like 'hereinbefore', 'witnesseth', 'situate at' or 'wheresoever'. They all have much more modern equivalents which are easier to understand. It is always better to say 'above', 'witnesses', 'situated at' and 'wherever'.

We have given some of the more common examples of the kind of words which can be replaced by more modern equivalents below:[9]

Archaic words	Modern equivalents
bequeath	give
devise	give
provided that	if
endeavour	try
for and on behalf of	for
forthwith	immediately
give devise and bequeath	give
grant	give
howsoever	no matter how (or omit)
in the event of	if
Last Will and Testament	will
monies	money
provided that	but if
pursuant to	under
save	except
shall	will or must
until such time as	until

---

9   In Chapter 5 of *Drafting*, Doonan also provides lists of many words which can be replaced by more modern, simple equivalents (see *op cit*, fn 5).

upon the expiration	at the end
wheresoever	no matter where
whosoever	no matter who

Complex words	*Simpler equivalents*
cease	stop
consequence	result
expiration	end
possess	have
purchaser	buyer
retain	keep
vendor	seller

Use of the word 'shall'

Shall is a word that is worthy of particular attention. It has been used a lot by lawyers in the past, but is not commonly used in ordinary speech. This means that most people aren't sure of its exact meaning.

> The seller shall give notice …

This can mean the seller *may* give notice in the future or the seller *must* give notice.

So, if you mean, at some future point, the seller can give notice, use 'may'. If you mean that it is imperative that the seller does give notice, use 'must'.

Using too many words

In the past lawyers would often use two or three words where one would do. This has been referred to as killing one bird with three stones, as in 'to give, devise and bequeath', 'terminate, cancel and revoke' or 'legal, valid and binding'. This practice should not be followed.

Some precedents may overuse words which, by themselves, are perfectly acceptable. Saying 'each partner must vote' or 'all partners must vote' is fine to emphasise that no partner can decline to vote. But 'each and every partner must vote' is going too far. In some cases 'partners must vote' will do perfectly well.

In drafting clearly, you will be aiming to be as concise as possible. Always consider whether the words you have used add to the meaning of your draft. What you are not doing, however, is aiming to win the prize for the shortest document ever written. Sometimes in order to make yourself clear, you will opt to keep words that you might have considered dropping. Remember that being concise is very important, but being clear comes first. Some examples of superfluous word use are set out below:

at the time	when
during such time as	while
for the duration of	during
in the event that	if
the sum of £100	£100

'The said'

You should never need to use this phrase, as in:

> The Defendant was driving a VW Golf car registration number DFO 375F. On turning the corner, the Defendant lost control of the said car.

There is no doubt that we are talking about the Defendant's car, so we can simply cut out 'said' and use either 'the car', or, possibly better, 'his car'. Alternatively, if the document makes numerous references to this car, we could use a definition, as in:

> The Defendant was driving a VW Golf car registration number DFO 375F (the Car). On turning the corner, the Defendant lost control of the Car.

Using the active voice

The use of the active voice has already been discussed in the chapters on legal writing. Your clarity of drafting will be helped if you use what is called the active rather than the passive voice. That means you should say things like 'the seller must give notice' and 'the owner waives the right' rather than 'notice must be given' or 'the right will be waived'. As you can see, you are putting extra information into the first forms by stating *who* as well as *what*.

Consistency

It is very important that you are consistent in your style and use of words and phrases. If you start with 'the tenants and sub-tenants' and then move to 'the lessee and successors in title' out of carelessness, it might be assumed that you intentionally used different words to imply a different meaning. This is because the rule that words are presumed to be used consistently will apply.

Gender neutral language

The legal rule that the masculine includes the feminine is certainly still relied on to a much greater extent in drafting formal documents than in letter writing. However, there is no real need for this, and for the same reasons as apply to ordinary writing, non-sexist language should be used in drafting.

The language you use will depend on:

- your client's preference;
- the context and clarity of the drafting;
- the actual sexes of the parties referred to in the document.

Your client may prefer certain language to be used and, because you are acting under your client's instructions, this could be the deciding factor. You should use gender neutral language as the norm and be prepared to alter it, rather than only using it when specifically asked to. You can often reword a sentence to avoid the need for a reference to 'he/she' or 'he or she' if you think that is cumbersome. You can replace many masculine words with neutral ones so that postman and foreman can become postal worker and supervisor without any loss of meaning or clarity.[10]

If you are drafting a document which refers to other documents, or if you are merely amending a document, it may be confusing and unnecessary to use different language. Decide whether a change will cause confusion. If it will, keep your style consistent with previous drafting unless your client wants you to change.

Of course, if you are drafting a conveyance and the seller and buyer are both men, you should use the masculine only. If you're referring to maternity leave in an employment contract, the employee is going to be female.

Vague words

Words which could be interpreted in different ways or have more than one meaning should generally be avoided. They only make disagreements more likely. They can even make a document void for uncertainty. If a will says 'my record collection to be divided equally amongst my friends', who does that mean? No one will know unless 'friends' is defined elsewhere, or the ability to define the term is given to someone else and their word is final. The only time when vague words can be useful is when they represent a compromise between parties so that in fact 'in a reasonable time' is understood to be slightly different by each party. This is only acceptable if the term is unlikely to be relevant to the working of the document unless something goes wrong.

Avoid repetition

If your document is repetitious, it will be longer and less clear. Reading a repetitious document can be difficult. You lose track and have to go back and compare the repeated parts to check whether they are exactly the same or whether there is some important small difference. If such a difference has crept in by mistake, it will be very confusing.

Generally, you can easily cut out repetition in your documents by rewording or by using appropriate clauses and sub-clauses.

CONTENTIOUS DOCUMENTS

We have already explained that we will consider the detailed drafting of two categories of documents, contentious and non-contentious. The contentious documents we will look at are civil statements of case. These documents play a vital role in civil litigation, and all lawyers who might be involved in litigation should know how to draft them. The criminal equivalent of statements of case play a less important role in criminal actions. We will consider only civil documents.

---

10   As pointed out by Doonan in *Drafting* (*op cit*, fn 5).

Statements of case

Statements of case are the formal documents in which those involved in a civil action, the claimant and defendant, set out the facts they want to rely on to support their arguments. By exchanging these documents, they let each other know exactly what the main points of their arguments are. These documents also stop either side being surprised at the trial by defining what is disputed. There are specific rules that govern the way statements of case are drafted. There are also certain practices and tactics that are optional. We will consider these, but first we should explain more precisely what the term 'statements of case' includes.

The following are the most important statements of case:

- the claim form   drafted by the claimant;
- the particulars of claim   drafted by the claimant;
- the defence   drafted by the defendant.

There are others, but because they are much less commonly used, we will not be dealing with them in this book.

The claim form

The claimant in a case must set out the claim they are making against the defendant. They must first do this on a court form which will have the effect of starting the litigation. This form gives the basic details of those involved and the facts of the case. The form is straightforward and its completion is not strictly a drafting matter, so we will concentrate on the other statements of case below.

The particulars of claim

If a case is very simple, the details or particulars of claim will fit into the claim form. In most cases, there will be too much detail to do this and a separate document called the particulars of claim will be drafted to accompany the claim form.

The defence

When a defendant has seen the claim against him, he will want to respond with his version of what happened. This is done in the defence. In a defence, a defendant will respond to each of the allegations made in the claimant's claim.

General rules

The rules about drafting statements of case are set out in the CPR. These are the rules that govern all aspects of how civil litigation should be conducted. The rules are broken down into parts and practice directions. We will refer to particularly relevant parts or practice directions where necessary in this section, and we recommend that when you are drafting, you refer to a copy of the rules which are well written and fairly easy to follow.

There are some general rules which can be said to apply to the drafting of all particulars of claim and defences. When drafting these documents you *must* do the following:

- Follow your client's instructions.

  Make sure that everything in your document reflects completely and only what your client has told you.

- Use the correct heading (CPR Practice Direction 7A, para 4.1–2).

  The heading of a statement of case must include:

  (a) the claim number: this is the number given by the court to identify each action. It will be the same on every document in a case;

  (b) the court the case is proceeding in, for example, the county court or high court, and which one;

  (c) the full names of all parties and their status, that is, claimant or defendant; if there is more than one claimant or defendant, they should be listed. When you write a party's name, give as much detail as possible. If it is a company, you will need to write either limited or plc after the name, whichever is appropriate. If it is a partnership, put 'a firm', and if a sole trader, put the person's name, then 'trading as', and then the business name;

  (d) the title of the document, for example, particulars of claim.

So the heading of all statements of case will look like this:

In the Carlisle County Court   Case No CA 3471

Between

Adam James Thompson

Claimant

and

Superior Roofing Limited

Defendant

PARTICULARS OF CLAIM

- Be clear and concise.

  This means using the same principles as in any other kind of writing or drafting.

- Use plain English.

  Again, this means using the same kind of English as you use for other kinds of writing and avoiding unnecessary legal terms.

- Include a concise statement of the facts relied on (CPR, r 16.4(1)(a)).

  Your statement of case will obviously depend on the case you are dealing with, but some broad principles can be used as guidance. Remember, your main aim is to get the main facts of your story across as clearly and concisely as possible. This should be, as far as possible, point by point, in chronological order. We discuss how to set out the facts in more detail below.

- Use numbered paragraphs (CPR Practice Direction 5, para 2.2).

  By paragraphs here we mean that each issue should be dealt with in one paragraph, much as it might be in a letter or memorandum, except that each paragraph must be numbered. Paragraphs in contentious documents are not drafted in the same way as in non-contentious documents following particular rules about clauses and sub-clauses. You might still split a list of items to aid clarity, but whether you use (i), (ii), (iii) or (a), (b), (c) doesn't really matter as long as you are consistent within the document.

- Write all numbers including dates in figures (CPR Practice Direction 5, para 2.2).

  This means items like amounts and reference numbers, not just dates.

- Include a statement of truth (CPR, r 22.1).

  Every statement of case must be verified by a statement of truth. The statement of truth has a standard format:

  > [I believe] [the claimant/defendant believes] that the facts stated in this [claim form/particulars of claim/defence/defence and counterclaim] are true.

  It should be inserted at the end of the statement of case and the relevant parts deleted. It's best to get the claimant or defendant to sign it, but their legal representative can sign it for them.

When drafting your statement of case you *may*:

- Refer to a point of law (CPR Practice Direction 16, para 13.3).

  You need to make it clear in your statement of case what you consider the relevant law to be. When an employee sneaks off with a top secret recipe for chicken breadcrumb coating, are you claiming breach of confidence or breach of contract or both?

  What you should not do is go on to put in details of the law which will always apply, such as:

  > the defendant must put the claimant in the position she would have been in but for the breach.

  Everyone knows that; you don't need to repeat it.

- Give the name of any witness you intend to use law (CPR Practice Direction 16, para 13.3).

  You don't have to do this, but if it makes your explanation easier or supports the case you are making, you can do it.

- Attach a copy of any document you consider necessary to the case law (CPR Practice Direction 16, para 13.3).

  So, for example, if the claim is for breach of contract, you should attach any written contract.

- Include details of evidence.

  Although you can include evidence in your statement of case, you should only do so if you feel it is really necessary to explain your case. The main evidence will be detailed in the statements of witnesses, so you should avoid unnecessary repetition which might make your statements of case overly long and less clear. Sometimes the only difference between fact and evidence is the way something is expressed. It's better to say:

> ... the defendant's car collided with the claimant's bicycle,

which is expressed as fact, than

> ... the claimant felt the defendant's car collide with his bicycle,

which is expressed as evidence.

So, in summary, in all statements of case you *must*:

(a) follow your client's instructions;

(b) use the correct heading;

(c) be clear and concise;

(d) use plain English;

(e) include a concise statement of the facts relied on;

(f) use numbered paragraphs;

(g) write all numbers including dates in figures;

(h) verify with a statement of truth;

and you *may*:

(a) refer to a point of law;

(b) give the name of a witness you intend to use;

(c) attach a copy of any document you consider necessary to the case;

(d) include details of evidence.

Particulars of claim

The particulars of claim is the claimant's statement of case which sets out the claim being made against the defendant. The essence of a particulars of claim is to say to the defendant:

> These people were involved ... this happened ... as a result I have suffered ... so this is what I want from you.

As well as following the general rules which apply to all statements of case, there are certain issues that must be dealt with in a particulars of claim. We will look at some of the more common issues that need to be dealt with in a particulars of claim here, but the CPR contain much more detail about specific items that need to go into particulars of claim in certain cases. You should check the CPR, particularly r 16 and Practice Direction 16, when you come to draft a particulars of claim yourself.

All particulars of claim should contain:

(a) all those items (a)–(h) above, which must be in all statements of case;

(b) a statement of value (CPR, r 16.3), see below;

(c) a claim for interest (CPR, r 16.4), see below;

(d) such matters as are required in specific types of claim under CPR Practice Direction 16.

For example, if the claim relates to personal injuries details such as:

(i)   the claimant's date of birth must be stated;

(ii) brief details of the injuries must be included;

(iii) a schedule of past and future expenses and losses should be attached;

(iv) a medical report must be attached.

If the claim is based on an agreement:

(i)   if written, a copy must be attached;

(ii) if oral, details of the words used, by whom, to whom, when and where must be included.[11]

Statements of value

A claimant must include in a claim the specified amount being claimed or, if the case is one where it is impossible to give an exact figure, an indication of whether he expects to be awarded:

(a) not more than £5,000;

(b) between £5,000 and £15,000;

(c) more than £15,000.

If it is really impossible to say even this, the claimant can state that he cannot say how much he expects to recover.

In personal injury cases it is also necessary to state whether or not the amount claimed for pain, suffering and loss of amenity is more than £1000.

Claims for interest

If a claimant is suing for the non-payment of a debt, she will not just want the money, but interest on it from the date it should have been paid. There will always be a delay between a cause of action arising and the final judgment of the court, so this principle will apply whenever a claimant is asking for damages. If a claimant wants interest, this should be made clear in the particulars of claim. The rules about how to claim interest are in the CPR, r 16.4(2).

Defences

A defence is the document in which you will respond to a claim and put the defendant's side of the story. In the defence, a defendant is saying:

> In reply to your claim, I agree ... I deny ... because ... I'm not sure what you're talking about and I want you to prove it ... So I won't give you ...

All defences should contain:

(a) all those items (a)–(h) above which must be in all statements of case;

(b) an explanation of which allegations are admitted;

---

11   For full details of what must be included in specific types of claim see CPR Practice Direction 16 paras 4.1–9.3.

(c) an explanation of which allegations are denied;

(d) the reason for the denial and any different version of events;

(e) an explanation of which allegations it is not possible to admit or deny and which must be proved by the claimant.

So, every defence has to say whether each allegation in the particulars of claim is either:

(a) admitted – you say 'this is true', because you know it is or it makes no difference;

(b) denied – you say 'this is not true', because you know it is not and it is part of the defence case that it is not;

(c) neither admitted nor denied and required to be proved – you say, 'I don't know if this is true or not, so I can't admit it or deny it. I haven't got enough information so it's up to you to prove it'.

Deal with every allegation

There is an important rule that (subject to a few exceptions), if an allegation is not dealt with in the defence, it is taken to have been admitted. This means that when drafting a defence, you need to make sure you deal with everything clearly and set out your client's story as well as you can. To ensure you deal with everything, and to gain clarity, you should deal with the allegations in the same order as they are set out in the particulars of claim.

Note that there could easily be more than one allegation in each paragraph of the particulars of claim. Make sure you deal with all of them. If the claimant says:

> ... on 14 March the defendant negligently drove through a set of red traffic lights and collided with a car belonging to and driven by the claimant ...

she is alleging:

(a) the date was 14 March;

(b) the defendant was driving;

(c) the defendant was negligent;

(d) the lights were red;

(e) there was a collision;

(f) the collision was with her car;

(g) she was driving the car.

All of these issues need to be considered before drafting the defence response. It's likely that you will admit the date, the fact that the defendant was driving and that there was a collision. You will deny negligence, and you might deny that the lights were red. You may not have any evidence about who the other car belonged to, or who was driving.

Give reasons for denials

You cannot just deny what the claimant says without explaining why. You should always explain your alternative version. So, if the claimant says that the defendant didn't stop at the red traffic lights, the defendant can deny that, but will need to explain whether he denies it because the lights weren't on red, because he did stop, or for some other reason.

Make your main point first

With all statements of case it's better to put your main point first. This is particularly true when drafting defences where you are replying to an allegation made in a particulars of claim. It is better to say:

> Paragraph 2 is admitted except the claimant did not request a room with a sea view or an en suite bathroom ...

than to say:

> Save that the claimant did not at any time request a room with a sea view or request an en suite bathroom, paragraph 2 of the Particulars of Claim is admitted.

Your main point is to say that you admit paragraph 2 and it is clearer to put that first.

Do you have to respond to everything?

Actually, no. You don't need to respond to any claim for interest or the claim for remedies, most commonly damages. You will have denied the basis for these claims and that is enough. However, if the claimant has put forward any figures you may want to respond to these by either admitting, denying or saying that you can neither admit or deny them.

Tactics

As well as being important to inform the other side about the details of the case, there are tactical considerations relevant to the drafting of a statement of case. These must always come second to the rules relating to content, but as you gain experience in drafting, you might like to begin to think about the way you present your statement of case and what effect it might have on the other side.

Although you can include as many causes of action or defences as are relevant, it isn't a good idea to go overboard on either. It might look as if you are desperate for anything that you can throw in, some could be superfluous and your document might become confused. A better tactic is to stick to the ones that are stronger and ignore the weaker issues.

NON-CONTENTIOUS DOCUMENTS

Unlike contentious documents, there are an infinite number of non-contentious documents that might be drafted. Some of the most common are contracts for sale, leases and wills. But there are also secrecy agreements, recording contracts, shipping mortgages and many other documents.

Such documents are written to fulfil a number of functions.[12] These are as follows:

---

12 *Fryer v Pearson and Another* (2000) *The Times*, 4 April.

- To provide written evidence of transactions.

  With written evidence there is less chance that someone can say later on (either mistakenly or maliciously), 'this is not what we agreed'. In addition, some transactions like a sale of land have to be in writing to be valid.

- To prevent fraud.

  It's harder to go back on your word or argue about the terms of an agreement if the agreement is in writing and you have signed it.

- To set out future rights and obligations.

  If everything that might happen is discussed and recorded, when something does happen, the document will be used as a guide to how to deal with it.

- To record rights and obligations already conferred.

  So the document can be evidence that something has been done.

- To set out the details of complex transactions.

  Sometimes even if you wanted to you could not practically remember all the terms of an agreement without putting them in writing.

We will look at some general points about the structure of non-contentious documents.

Structure

Many documents will follow a general pattern:

- Title;
- Commencement, date and parties;
- Definitions and recitals;
- Operative part;
- Signatures;
- Schedules;
- Execution and attestation.

Title

The title of a document is usually just a description of the kind of document it is, such as 'Lease' or 'Contract'. It can be helpful to be more specific and give some indication of the subject matter of the lease or contract too, as in 'Lease of 12 Elm Street'.

There will often also be a front sheet. This is a plain sheet with the names of the parties, the title of the document and the name of the firm of solicitors on it.

Commencement, date and parties

The commencement of a document is just the introductory words. Longer commencements were more common in the past, but don't add anything to your drafting. Words like:

Now this deed witnesseth as follows ...

are completely unnecessary and can be left out with no effect.

All documents should record the date they are to come into effect. This will generally be the date the document is signed. The date can almost always be written in numerals, as in '16 June 2001' rather than 'The sixteenth day of June Two thousand and One', without any danger or loss of clarity.

The parties are the people involved and will generally be defined by their roles; for example, seller and buyer or lessor and tenant. There is a convention that the grantor of a right, that is, the seller or landlord, comes first.

Definitions and recitals

A definition section is often used at the beginning of longer documents to avoid repeating long words or phrases. In a lease you might see:

'The Flat' means the first floor flat at 45 Willow Court, Newcastle upon Tyne shown outlined in red on the attached plan.

You should use definitions if they replace a complex phrase with a simple and clear one. Don't use them if they are as long or ambiguous as the words you are defining or where a definition is not needed, as in '"The Contract" means this agreement'.

You will usually define the parties involved, often by using terms such as 'the Buyer' and 'the Seller'. Some drafting textbooks recommend that you avoid using terms that are very similar, like 'Employer' and 'Employee', to cut down the risk of mistakes and confusion. It's usually possible to find another descriptive word, like 'the Business' instead of 'Employer'. If not, you can always use short versions of the parties' names as definitions if you wish.

We think definitions are generally more useful at the beginning of a document. It is frustrating to read through a contract only to find at the end that some words have been given particular meanings. Use your discretion. If the definition section is very long, it might be inappropriate to put it at the beginning. On the other hand, it might just need some cutting down.

The recitals of a document will set out relevant background or the reasons for the document. They are not necessary, but can sometimes aid clarity. If they are included in a document, their content can still have an important effect when the document is interpreted. So just because they are not in the operative part, don't think that their drafting is less important.

You can use a heading for this section such as 'Background' or 'Introduction'. Some precedents will use 'Whereas', because it means the same in a legal document as background. But whereas lawyers use it in this way, the word has a different meaning in ordinary speech. We think it is better not to use it.

Operative part

This is the main part of the document which will follow your client's instructions. It might start with clauses saying that 'this or that will happen' or 'this or that will be done' and may go on to say 'if this goes wrong then … if that is not done then …'. So, a lease will start by stating that the lease of the property will be granted for a certain length of time and a certain amount of rent will be paid on certain dates. It may go on to deal with items such as what if the rent isn't paid or what if the house is damaged.

If there is a lot of detail, you might decide to put it in schedules, which are explained below. A schedule in a lease might include all the landlord's covenants or things the landlord is agreeing to. (A covenant is really just an agreement by deed, so you don't need to use the term 'the landlord covenants'; in a deed, 'the landlord agrees' is enough.)

Signatures

The way in which a document is signed will depend on what it is. In particular, a deed which is a particularly formal document required, for example, to transfer land, must be signed in a particular way. A will must also be signed by its maker and that signature witnessed by two other people. With wills, the identity of the witnesses can also have an effect on validity. You will need to check the relevant law to make sure you get this part right, as a mistake could invalidate the whole document.

This is another area where a lot of old fashioned words are sometimes still used. Words such as:

> In witness whereof the parties have hereunto set their hands on the day and year first hereinbefore written ...

can be replaced with:

> Signed on xxx.

> In witness whereof the parties have hereunto set their hands and affixed their seals ...

can be replaced with:

> Signed as a deed.

Schedules

If there is a lot of detail in your document, you might find it easier to group certain information in schedules rather than include it in the operative part of the document. You should make this decision based on which methods will produce the clearest and best structured draft.

It can be tempting, when you have a short and clearly drafted document and a blank sheet headed 'Schedule 1 – tenant's covenants', to go to town on all the possible permutations of what the tenant must do and how, when and why they must do it. Before you include too much detail in your schedules, make sure that you are not including unnecessary detail or going beyond your client's instructions. Remember also the *ejusdem generis* rule referred to above, which could catch you out if you forget an important detail.

Sale of land

A sale of land will need either a 'conveyance', if the land is not registered (this is now rare), or a 'transfer' if the land is registered. Nearly all kinds of land sales have to be by deed, so either document must be described as a deed and signed in a particular way. As mentioned in the section on precedents, there are plenty of examples available covering all sorts of variations in the kind of property that you might be transferring.

Section 1 of the Law of Property (Miscellaneous Provisions) Act 1989 sets out how a modern deed should be signed. When an individual will sign it, the document should be described as a deed and the signature must be witnessed by someone who also signs their name and then writes underneath their name, address and occupation.

Leases

Convention says that a lease will be drafted by the landowner's solicitor and checked by the tenant's solicitor. All leases have to be deeds unless they are for three years or less, so the commencement might refer to the document as a deed of lease. If not, the document must be referred to as a deed at the end.

The date of a lease is not the date the lease starts. It is the date the lease is effected (called the date of delivery). This might be the same as the start date, but it doesn't have to be. The lessor and lessee and the rent will be identified and the operative part will refer to the actual leasing of the property. The property, as with a conveyance, will have to be clearly identified and this part of a lease is called the parcels. The commencement and length of the lease are in a part called the *habendum* and the rent details (amount and times for payment) are in the *redendum*. All leases contain covenants by both parties, such as the tenant not making any alterations or sub-letting and the landlord insuring the property. A landlord will also want a right of re-entry or to forfeit the lease if the rent isn't paid or other covenants are broken by the tenant.

Wills

All wills will contain opening words such as 'I John Brown of ...' and a revocation clause stating that all former wills have been revoked. The date is vital if there are other wills, to see which was the last one. There will be an appointment of personal representatives, identifying them by name. Legacies of specific gifts generally come next, followed by a residue clause saying what will happen to everything left after any debts have been paid that does not form part of a specific gift. This clause is always the last gift. The attestation clause comes last. Wills must be signed by the testator and then by two people who have witnessed the testator signing. The shortest example can be used for most wills and reads as follows:

Signed by the above named John Brown in our joint presence and then by us in his.

A classic problem in will drafting is lack of clarity in a gift. When the will says:

To the children of Cameron and Mia ...

does it mean:

(a) Only to children whose father is Cameron and whose mother is Mia?

(b) To all children whose father is Cameron or whose mother is Mia?

(c) To Cameron's children and to Mia?

Draft to make the position clear, for example, by saying 'to the children of the joint union of Cameron and Mia'.

Another common problem in drafting wills is caused by the use of lists. Using:

My watches, rings, necklaces and bracelets to my daughter, Ann ...

is fine as long as this is all that was owned. But it might be better to say:

All my jewellery to my daughter, Ann ...

so that everyone will know what to do with the earrings when they are found at the back of the drawer.

CONCLUSION

We have looked at what drafting is and the work that needs to be done before you can sit down and begin to draft a document. We have also considered the kind of language you might use, and the way that you should structure your drafts. We have put a lot of emphasis on the importance of accuracy and clarity in drafting. You need to be accurate, to reflect your client's instructions, and clear, to make sure that your documents will be read and understood by other people.

If you take the time to research and plan what you are doing, the actual drafting will be much easier and you will probably need to go through fewer drafts before you get your final version.

Supporting skills

What are the main supporting skills needed to draft well?

Research

Because you need to know the relevant facts and law before you begin to draft, your research skills are an important support to your drafting. You will often also need to find a precedent to base your document on, and which precedent to use will require research too.

Interviewing

Your interviewing skills will be important in getting the right information on which to base your decisions about what kind of case you are dealing with and what kind of document is needed. You need to get the facts, and also your client's preferences about the way the case should be dealt with. In some cases, your client might be more concerned that the document is short and simple and less that it covers every possibility; whereas in others, a fully comprehensive and lengthy document might be needed.

Learning to draft

Knowing the rules is never enough, and practice is the only way to really improve your drafting. During your course, if drafting is taught as a skill, you will be given the chance to practise. This practice could be through the drafting of contentious or non-contentious documents. It is possible that you will also be assessed on your drafting competence. In this section, we will consider how you may be taught and assessed.

How will students be assessed?

If you are assessed on your drafting skills, you could be asked to produce any kind of document. It is likely that you will be given a variety of information and asked to draft a particular document based on that information. The assessment of drafting is more rarely done under exam conditions, as this is particularly unrealistic, and makes it difficult to use the precedents that might be needed. The assessment will almost always be based purely on the document produced, rather than on any additional supporting preparatory material.

What are lecturers assessing?

A typical assessment checklist might look something like this.

Did the student:

(a) Show evidence of a sound knowledge of the facts of the case?

(b) Show evidence of a sound knowledge of the relevant law and procedure?

(c) Avoid mistakes in spelling, punctuation and grammar?

(d) Use clear, concise and appropriate language?

(e) Structure the document in a logical way?

(f) Omit irrelevant or superfluous information?

(g) Use appropriate layout?

(h) Include all relevant detail?

(i) Demonstrate an understanding of the facts?

(j) Demonstrate an understanding of the law?

Points to watch out for

When you are producing a draft document for assessment, there are a number of particular points to keep in mind.

Use of precedents

You should definitely use precedents if they are relevant. Your lecturers will know which ones they expect you to use. Lecturers will be looking to see whether you have made effective use of precedents. That means you will be expected to show (a) that you have found and used a relevant precedent and (b) that you have not followed it slavishly. A common way to lose marks in drafting is to leave precedent details in a document which are either superficial or wrong.

Typing and spelling errors

Remember that using a spell check will give you the correct spelling, but not always the correct word.

Figures, dates and names

Check they are accurate. In particular, it won't go down well with lecturers if you make mistakes concerning details that you have been given in other documents.

Definitions

Are they consistent and useful?

Lack of clarity in lists

When you say the tenant cannot keep dogs, cats and rabbits, do you mean she can't keep all three together, or that she can't keep any of them? Could you say the tenant is prohibited from keeping any of the following: (a) dogs; (b) cats; (c) rabbits?

Lack of clarity in time

When you say within one month from the date of this contract, do you mean the same date next month, yesterday's date next month or tomorrow's date next month? Could you say 'within a period of 28 days, the date of this contract being day 1'?

Lack of clarity in obligation

We suggest that you use the word *must* if there is an obligation to do something and the word *may* if there is a choice. Using words like *shall* can be confusing.

FURTHER READING

Blake, S, *A Practical Approach to Effective Litigation* , 6th edn, 2005, Oxford: OUP.

Doonan, E and Foster, C, *Drafting*, 2nd edn, 2001, London: Cavendish Publishing.

Rose, W, *Pleadings Without Tears: A Guide to Legal Drafting under the Civil Procedure Rules*, 2002, Oxford: OUP. (This book is especially useful for drafting contentious documents.)

Rylance, P, *Legal Writing and Drafting*, 2004, London: Blackstone.

CHAPTER 7

ADVOCACY

INTRODUCTION

To the public, to writers for television and film, advocacy is what lawyers do. Standing up in court, arguing their client's case, fielding judicial interventions, beguiling the jury. Can you imagine a Hollywood film about a crusading lawyer (lawyers who are the heroes of films must always be crusading) who sits at his or her desk and drafts documents? The idea of advocacy as the skill that most closely relates to actual legal practice insidiously affects even law students. Writing and drafting documents, researching problems, finding cases – these are all skills that are developed within the academic stages of law degrees. But advocacy remains resolutely a practice-based skill. Yet, as this chapter will show, advocacy is often intrinsic in every aspect of law degrees. Advocacy develops the preparatory skills of interviewing, of drafting, of research and analysis and gives them focus: the argument in a courtroom setting.

In this chapter of the book, we consider the skill of advocacy as an integral element of learning about law. We look briefly at the relationship between advocacy and its near cousin, mooting, and between advocacy and its more distant relative, debating or oratory. We look at the preparation skills that are the foundation of all advocacy, and at how those apply in preparing to make the speeches and applications that make up the day to day work of the advocate. We consider the basic conventions of courtroom behaviour, before then turning to look at trial advocacy and, in particular, the requirements and techniques of witness-handling (examination-in-chief, cross-examination, re-examination).

Near relatives – mooting and debating

Both mooting and debating are often elements of law degrees, although normally on an optional basis. What is the relationship between these two oral skills and the skill of advocacy?

Mooting is the closer of the two to 'real' advocacy, but it has limits. In mooting, the argument is on points of law. Often, the mooting exercise will be set in an appellate court, so that the initial findings of fact have been made by the lower court and are, for the purposes of the exercise, not open to debate. In this way, the exercise has the same relationship with reality as tort exercises which tell you that Dave owns a ferret that escapes and ravages Ted's garden and asks you to consider the liabilities of all parties; where, in reality, Dave denies that the ferret is his, and Ted says he didn't see the animal clearly, but thinks it could have been a dog, and the court requires proof as to the extent of the damage in the garden. In mooting, the facts are established for you and are clear and unambiguous in a way that is rarely the case in reality. Mooting, as an exercise, comes closest to appearing in the real appellate courts, where facts (at least traditionally) are not in issue, and the argument is on matters of law alone. Accordingly, the focus of mooting is to develop your skills of legal analysis alongside your ability to stand up and to argue your point with reference to authority.

Mooting is a valuable preparation for advocacy, and in particular, the making of speeches and submissions, but it is not itself advocacy. In practice, in these days of more activist trial management by judges, you are likely to be told which matters the court wishes to be addressed on and which it does not, especially in the higher courts. Can you imagine a moot where the assessor presiding stopped you after 10 seconds and told you that your first three points were bad, and he or she only wished to hear your fourth point? Mooting teaches valuable skills, although paradoxically, it may be more valuable in teaching you how to analyse case law, so as to distinguish cases and identify the points of law that are in issue, than it is in developing your skills of oral presentation.

What, then, of debating? Debating is, again, a skill allied to advocacy. It requires you to marshal facts and to organise arguments, but it also requires you to develop your oratorical skills – the winning of an argument by winning over your audience's heart rather than its head. In this sense, you may feel that it comes close to genuine courtroom work – but this is a misleading view. The great oratorical flourishes which you will so often see set out in traditional advocacy texts belong to a different age, when oratory was still perceived as an essential element in the skills of the top flight advocate.

It is still your task to persuade, but you are more likely to be addressing a professional court (a district judge or a judge sitting without jury), and your advocacy must be more measured, more analytical. Your debating skills will always be of use in helping you to develop your presentation skills, and in giving you the confidence to stand up and seek to persuade a tribunal, but debating lacks the discipline of the law, and this ultimately separates it from true advocacy.

The range of advocacy

Even in a solely legal context, advocacy arises in a huge variety of different forums. The classic context for advocacy – and the one that we all envisage – is the criminal jury trial. But, as you may be aware, less than 4% of criminal cases are now heard before a jury, the overwhelming majority being dealt with in the magistrates' court. Even in the magistrates' court itself, you may be faced with two very different forums: the professional District Judge, legally qualified, sitting alone, and well able to direct you to issues on which he or she wishes to be addressed; and the Bench of lay magistrates, assisted by a legally qualified clerk, and more inclined to listen without interrupting (and hence a difficult forum in which to gauge the effect of your advocacy). Criminal advocacy will also include the different forms of the appellant courts – whether the splendours of the Court of Appeal, or the paradoxically more mundane setting of the House of Lords, sitting in a committee room in Parliament. Criminal appeals take in appeals to the Crown Court from the magistrates' court, where you will be addressing lay justices sitting with a Crown Court judge, as well as appeals to the Divisional Court by way of case stated, where you will be addressing a Bench of High Court judges on a point of law as stated by the lower courts. Even within the criminal context, there are many different settings for your advocacy, and many adjustments which you will have to make in moving from court to court.

Criminal advocacy is, of course, only a small element of the spectrum. Advocacy in a civil context has an even wider spread. It will include hearings in Family Courts of different kinds; mainstream hearings in the Queen's Bench Division of the High Court; and in the multitude of county courts; hearings in the specialist construction and

Admiralty Courts; judicial review hearings and other forms of administrative law challenges in the Administrative Court. The range of forums for civil advocacy is huge.

So far we have only considered the 'formal' courts. Yet, a vast number of matters, ranging from the trivial to the most serious, will start off in the system of tribunals and other administrative hearings. There are employment tribunals, mental health tribunals, social security tribunals, immigration tribunals, Lands Tribunals – to cite only a small number of the range of different tribunals – as well as countless numbers of local government tribunals and hearings run by professional or regulatory bodies. Often, there will be a right to legal representation, although this has historically tended to be the preserve of law centres, Citizens Advice Bureaux and other voluntary sector agencies, because of the lack of legal aid funding. Each of these forums brings with it different challenges, and different approaches to your advocacy.

In this chapter, we will consider advocacy primarily in the context of mainstream civil and criminal work, but you should not let yourself overlook the sheer range of contexts in which you may be called on to practise your skill.

A career as an advocate

Traditionally, advocacy was seen as the preserve of the Bar. This overlooked the fact that solicitors had rights of audience in both magistrates' and county courts, and that the advocacy (at least in the former, and to a considerable extent in the latter) was generally conducted by solicitors. For over a decade, it has been possible for solicitors to take extra qualifications in order to gain a 'higher rights' qualification and to gain access to the higher courts, such as the Crown Court and the High Court.

The Access to Justice Act 1999 sought to increase competition in legal services by breaking down the barriers between work which was traditionally reserved for solicitors (such as the conduct of litigation) and work which was reserved for barristers (such as advocacy). The rules from the Law Society now impose a far shorter training period for solicitors who wish to obtain a higher rights qualification, so that it should be possible to obtain the right to appear in all courts within six months of qualifying as a solicitor. This change has increased the number of solicitors with higher rights qualifications, but has not had a dramatic impact on the number of solicitors appearing as advocates in the higher courts. In theory the changes mean that your initial choice of profession (solicitor or barrister) is somewhat less restricting than it has been in the past. However, at present is still the case that the Bar remains the central provider of specialist advocacy services.

PREPARATION

Good advocacy is based on excellent preparation, but it must never show. This is not to say that advocacy is simply a matter of preparation. If it were, then you could just hand up your written notes and leave the court! Advocacy is the art of persuasion in a legal context, and you cannot be persuasive unless you have a thorough understanding of the issues in the case, a clear appreciation of the law, and you are able to present the material in a structured and persuasive way before the court or tribunal. In this section we look at the skill of preparation.

Case analysis – what is the case about?

Case analysis is not a term of art; it does not have a prescribed meaning. There are any number of different methods of approaching the mass of information, both factual and legal, which may make up even a simple case, and of then analysing the information for relevance, and organising it for accessibility. In this section, we will look at two contrasting methods of organising materials so that you can prepare your advocacy. We will use the criminal trial as the context for looking at case analysis. Unlike a civil case, where many of the issues in a civil matter will already be defined for you within the pleadings, in a criminal case you will often need to work out what the issues are.

Basic case analysis

This method of case analysis for a criminal case has three main stages:

(a) the identification of the elements of the charge;

(b) the identification of the facts that are disputed between prosecution and defence ('the facts in issue');

(c) analysis of how each side will seek to prove its version of the facts that are disputed.

Identification of the elements of the charge

It is always worth looking up the charge and identifying with precision the *actus reus* and *mens rea*. This may seem obvious when you are a law student and you are still studying the criminal law, but, in practice, it is easy to get complacent about your knowledge of the law, and to lose track of recent cases which may have a bearing on different elements of the offence. It is also easy to let your familiarity with a basic concept such as theft blind you to the need for the prosecution to prove, for example, an intention permanently to deprive. Checking the elements of the offence ensures that you do not overlook anything. A good starting point for this exercise is to use a practitioner text, such as *Archbold* (2005, Sweet & Maxwell) or *Blackstone's Criminal Practice* (2005, OUP). This will provide an outline of the offence, and a summary of the relevant case law on the elements of the offence, and on likely sentencing outcomes.

Thus, if we take an offence of 'going equipped' (s 25 of the Theft Act 1968), research shows that this comprises the following elements:

- a person
- having with him
- any article for the use in the course of or in connection with any burglary, theft or cheat
- when not at his place of abode.

There is case law on the meaning of 'not at his place of abode', 'has with him' and 'articles for use in course of or in connection with burglary, theft or cheat', as well as on the need for a *mens rea* of intention (the accused must have intended the item for use in the proscribed manner).

In looking at the prosecution case against your client, you will need to check that there is evidence in respect of each of these points. You will, of course, bear in mind that it is for the prosecution to prove *each element* of the offence beyond reasonable doubt; failing this, your client must be acquitted of the offence.

Identifying the facts in issue

In any case there may be a number of different elements which the prosecution must prove. However, your client's version of events may make clear that a number of the aspects of the prosecution case are not disputed. So your client may, for example, accept that he was present at the party, but deny that he hit the host. Or he may deny that he was present at the party at all. Or he may accept both that he was present and that he hit the host, but may wish to raise the general defence of self-defence, as the host was about to hit him. You therefore need to be able to compare the two 'stories' – that put forward by the prosecution, and that put forward by the defence – in order to see where the two versions are in conflict. Those points of conflict are the 'facts in issue'.

Let us take the example of an assault occasioning actual bodily harm (contrary to s 47 of the Offences Against the Person Act 1861):

Prosecution narrative:

James Smith was walking down the High Street, when he was stopped by a young man who was wearing an Arsenal shirt. The young man asked Mr Smith which team he supported. When Mr Smith said that he did not follow football, the young man said, 'You should,' and hit Mr Smith in the face with his closed fist. Mr Smith fell to the ground and the young man ran off, but was stopped outside a supermarket by two security guards who had witnessed the incident. Mr Smith suffered a broken nose. He attended an identification parade at the police station and identified Peter Roberts as the young man who had assaulted him. In interview, Mr Roberts refused to answer questions.

Defence narrative:

Peter Roberts will say that he was walking down the High Street wearing an Arsenal shirt when a man who was walking past him spat on him and said, 'Football scum'. Mr Roberts stopped to remonstrate with the man, who lifted his fist as if he was about to strike Mr Roberts. Mr Roberts punched him once in self-defence and then, scared of what he had done, attempted to run off but was stopped by the security guards. He said nothing in interview as his solicitor was not present.

In a real criminal case of this type, the prosecution materials are likely to take the form of (at a minimum):

* witness statement: Mr Smith;
* witness statement: first security guard;
* witness statement: second security guard;
* witness statement: arresting officer;
* witness statement: second officer;
* witness statement: identification parade officer;
* second witness statement: Mr Smith (confirming identification of the accused);
* witness statement from hospital consultant (confirming Mr Smith's injuries);
* copy transcript of tape-recorded interview;
* witness statement: photographer, to accompany;

- bundle of photographs of injuries;
- charge sheet;
- copy custody record;
- copy criminal record (if any) of Mr Roberts.

You will see, therefore, the extent to which the two short 'stories' set out above have summarised what occurred, reducing it to the bare facts that establish the elements of the offence, namely:

- a person   Peter Roberts
- assaulted   blow with fist to the nose
- another   James Smith
- causing actual bodily harm   broken nose
- intending or being reckless as to the assault.

It is a common error to fail to be sufficiently selective about which facts should be included in your two narratives. If you are not careful, you will end up with two long accounts, which are then very difficult to compare and contrast. Ideally, you should confine yourself (where possible) to one or two short paragraphs. It is then much easier to compare the two versions and to identify which facts are disputed.

What is in dispute in our example is:

- whether James Smith was simply walking along when Peter Roberts confronted him and asked him what team he supported;
- whether James Smith first spat on Peter Roberts and said 'Football scum';
- whether James Smith raised his fist in a threatening manner;
- whether Peter Roberts punched James Smith in self-defence.

Why do the facts in issue matter?

Identifying the facts in issue is essential in enabling you to see what the issues are in any given case. This, in turn, enables you to identify the areas where you will need to call evidence in support of your version, and where you will be seeking to challenge and to undermine the other party's version.

Equally, the identification of the facts that are in issue enables you to identify those facts which are not in issue. Thus, in our example, you will note that the following elements are not in dispute:

- It is not in dispute that James Smith was hit.
- It is not in dispute that it was Peter Roberts who hit James Smith.
- It is not in dispute that Peter Roberts intended to hit James Smith.
- It is not in dispute that Peter Roberts then ran away and was stopped by the security guards.

It is not clear whether there is any dispute about the extent of the injuries suffered by James Smith. Once the defence has considered the witness statement from the doctor, alongside the photographs of the injury, the defence may agree to this evidence being adduced in written form, hence avoiding the need to call witnesses on the point if it is not disputed.

Analysing the evidence

You are now in a position to take each of the facts in issue and to consider what evidence each party has available to it in order to prove its version.

Thus, if we consider the basic question of whether James Smith first spat on Peter Roberts, or whether it was Roberts who first approached Smith and asked him which team he supported, it is clear that the two primary witnesses are likely to be Smith, for the prosecution, and Roberts, for his own defence. We do not know if there are any other witnesses, such as passers-by. We will need to look at the statements of the security guards to see if they were watching at this point, and if so, whether they could see anything. We will need to see whether there is any record on closed-circuit television cameras along the High Street or in nearby shops.

If we then consider the evidence of Smith, whom the defence will be cross-examining, we can see already what the defence version of the facts is – which we must 'put' to Smith in our cross-examination. We can investigate whether Smith is of good character (in other words, whether he has any previous convictions which might help to undermine his credibility as a witness or to show him to have a history of previous violence)[1]. We can investigate what his motivation may have been for spitting on Roberts, and whether there is any additional material which might help us to establish this motivation.

In respect of the testimony of Roberts, the defence will be calling him to give evidence in his own defence.[2] In preparing the examination-in-chief, the defence will need to anticipate the challenges that are likely to arise from the prosecution. Some of the challenges will be legal; for example, in this case, Roberts did not put forward his defence when he was questioned under caution at the police station, so that an inference may be drawn under s 34 of the Criminal Justice and Public Order Act 1994. Other challenges may be designed to undermine Roberts' credibility; for example, that there was evidence that he had been drinking, or that he is not a credible witness as he has previous convictions.[3]

Thus, this basic case analysis technique provides a 'way in' to a case which can otherwise at first seem simply a muddled mass of papers.

---

1   The new character evidence rules contained in the Criminal Justice Act 2003 mean that there are restrictions on the use of evidence of 'bad character' in relation to a non-defendant: s 100. However, we still need to consider if Smith is of good character in order to decide whether to apply to the court to introduce evidence to show that, for example, he has a history of offences of violence.

2   Note that Roberts does not, as a matter of law, have to give evidence in his own defence, but if he fails to do so an 'inference' can be drawn by the jury that he didn't testify as he knew that his story would not stand up to cross-examination: Criminal Justice and Public Order Act 1994, s 35. In any event, in a case such as this, where Roberts is effectively the only defence witness, it would be very hard to win the case without his testimony.

3   There are also new rules, again from the Criminal Justice Act 2003, which govern the use of the defendant's bad character in criminal trials. One circumstance where the prosecution are likely to be given permission to introduce evidence of the defendant's previous criminal history is where the defendant (or his advocate) attacks the character of another. So in this example, if the defence allege that it was Smith who first spat on Roberts and called him 'Football scum', this is likely to permit the prosecution to call evidence of any previous criminal convictions of Roberts.

From hypothesis to narrative: another case analysis technique

In *Advocacy*, Andy Boon offers a different method for case analysis, which starts at a far earlier point – the obtaining of the initial information.

In this method, the case analysis starts with division of the witness information into categories of 'fact' and 'opinion'. You need to consider the extent to which witnesses are able to give relevant testimony on the facts, and whether the witnesses will fall into the narrow category of persons entitled to give opinion evidence to the court. However, having reviewed the facts in this way, it is necessary to come up with an initial 'working hypothesis'.

The working hypothesis

Boon suggests that you must make sure that your hypothesis is based on the available facts, including those facts which are disputed. He also takes the view that you need to draw in a wide range of fact – it is too early to decide which facts may or may not later turn out to be relevant:

> It is sensible not to reject facts as irrelevant too early in your preparation. Nor is it sensible to become wed to any one hypothesis at an early stage. As you collect evidence you may find yourself prematurely rejecting evidence which conflicts with your hypothesis. Try to remain open minded for as long as possible.[4]

In some cases, the facts may not be in dispute, and you will find yourself simply dealing with a dispute as to the interpretation of the relevant law – not unlike a mooting exercise. Such cases are relatively rare. In most cases, the factual background remains elusive and unclear and your hypothesis will enable you to draw together the facts into a coherent structure.

The 'theory of the case'

The next stage is to formulate a 'theory of the case', a view of how all the factual and legal issues can be combined to lead to the result which your client is seeking. (There will be cases where, after full analysis, you take the view that, even on your client's version of events, your client will not succeed at trial. In such cases, you will have to advise your client accordingly. The case may still have settlement value, and it is important to bear in mind that the other party may be equally concerned about matters that they see as being crucial weaknesses in their own case.)

With your theory of the case, you are trying to predict the evidence which will be accepted at trial. You may, therefore, end up with different theories, depending on which version of events is accepted in evidence. As Boon points out, this can lead to problems for you as an advocate, in seeking to keep a number of potential options open without appearing to present inconsistent or unreliable versions. It is, of course, essential that you also try to formulate the theory of the case which the other party will be seeking to promote. You need to anticipate their version of the case, as this will help you to identify their own weaknesses, many of which will later become the focus for your own cross-examination.

---

4   Boon, A, *Advocacy*, 2nd edn, 1999, London: Cavendish Publishing, para 3.4.

Organisation

Having formulated the theory of the case, you need to organise your materials. Organisation here includes not only the mental categorisation and organisation of the facts and the law into an accessible structure, but also the physical organisation of the myriad papers so that you are able to find material quickly and easily.[5]

The narrative transition

At this final stage you are now in a position to transform your bare 'theory of the case' into a narrative form. It is hard to overemphasise the importance of this stage. As listeners, our first exposure to the organisation of oral material is in the form of narratives. In assessing the likelihood of events and, in particular, in assessing individuals' motivation, we rely on stories almost without thinking about it: 'Would a person really act in this way?' 'Would this actually happen?'

> As Keith Evans points out:
>
> First: although they [the jury] are obliged to sit there, they are not obliged to listen to you.
>
> Second: since you have a captive audience you must regard yourself as obliged to make it as entertaining for them as you possibly can.[6]

There are limits to your duty of 'entertainment', but it remains a valuable reminder that you need to keep the court's attention. Ensuring that your version of events is accessible is a vital step in ensuring that it is interesting, and if it is interesting, you will help the court to pay attention to what you are saying. If they listen, then you may persuade them.

Other modes of case analysis

Case analysis is a huge topic, and there are many books written on fact management alone. One classical method of evidential analysis which you may encounter is Wigmorean analysis. This is based on the writings of John Henry Wigmore, who was Dean at Northwestern Law School and whose book *The Science of Judicial Proof* was published in the 1930s. Wigmore's view was that the normal courtroom approaches to evidential analysis were insufficiently rigorous and that a more overtly logical approach could be imposed which would enable the issue of 'proof' to be determined on sounder grounds. In order to achieve this, he borrowed the language (and accompanying diagrams) from formal logic, using charts with symbols for different types of evidence and a variety of linking symbols to indicate the relationship between the facts. The purpose is to achieve a single accurate and analytic overview of the differing weight of the elements of evidence and the relationships between them:

> To perform the logical (or psychological) process of a conscious juxtaposition of detailed ideas for the purpose of producing rationally a single final idea. Hence, to the extent that the mind is unable to juxtapose consciously a larger number of ideas, each

---

5   For a brief discussion of the American system of 'trial notebooks', see *op cit*, Boon, fn 4, para 3.7.
6   Evans, K, *The Golden Rules of Advocacy*, 1993, London: Blackstone, pp 36–37.

group of detailed constituent ideas must be reduced in consciousness to a single idea; until the mind can consciously juxtapose them with due attention to each, so as to produce its single final idea.[7]

Wigmorean analysis is not for the faint-hearted, with its complex hierarchies of classification ('testimonial evidence affirmatory', 'circumstantial evidence negatory') and its lengthy series of symbols and numbering systems. However, it seeks to introduce something of the rigour of a scientific process into the analysis of competing factual interpretations and it is a shame that more law students are not introduced to its methodology. As Terence Anderson and William Twining point out:

> ... application of the method compels a disciplined and patient approach to evidence. Adapting Marshall McLuhan, if Wigmorean analysis is the medium, the message is that analysis of evidence involves hard work.[8]

Other variants on case analysis exist. At the other end of the spectrum to Wigmore's careful terminologies is the 'good fact/bad fact' approach to case analysis which is often employed with the NITA/IATC schools of advocacy training.[9] Good fact/bad fact starts with the initial identification of a theory of the case, followed by a brainstorming approach to the evidence, dividing the material into facts which support the hypothesis (good facts) and facts which do not (bad facts). The approach can be extremely effective. Often, you will find that during the exercise of allocating facts, you will reclassify evidence from 'bad' to 'good' and vice versa as you refine and redevelop your theory of the case in the light of all the material. Moreover, the great merit of this form of analysis is that it forces advocates to recognise that 'good facts' may come from the other party's witnesses – so that any cross-examination will not simply seek to undermine the witness's credibility, but will also seek to adduce the 'good facts' which that witness can put forward.

All methods of case analysis, however, are only as good as the use to which you put them in court. We now turn, therefore, to consideration of the issue of how you use your materials in court.

Reading, reciting and other enemies of advocacy

Into every student's life falls a lecturer who comes to lectures with a sheaf of (often yellowing) handwritten notes, which they then read to the assembled student body for the allocated hour. The content may be outstanding – but few of those attending are able to concentrate for long enough to benefit from the experience. It takes considerable training to be able to read material in a way which sounds natural and interesting. The

---

7 Wigmore, JH, 'The problem of proof' (1913) 8 Ill L Rev 77, cited in Anderson, T and Twining, W, *Analysis of Evidence*, 1991, London: Weidenfeld & Nicolson, p 109. Anderson and Twining remain two of the foremost proponents of Wigmorean analysis, and their book is an essential introduction to this complex system.

8 *Ibid*, Anderson and Twining, p 119.

9 NITA: the National Institute of Trial Advocacy. IATC: the Inns Advocacy Training Committee. These are related forms of advocacy training which utilise a particular structure of giving feedback to trainees by clearly identifying a single crucial point of improvement, providing the student with an opportunity to see that aspect of the exercise correctly carried out, with the student then having an opportunity to re-do the element in focus.

normal tendency is for the voice to flatten, the pace to quicken, the natural pauses and emphases of the speaking voice to be lost. Above all, from the perspective of the skill of advocacy, all persuasive impact is lost. The exercise is reduced to a mere oral presentation. The reader lacks conviction; the material can never be convincing.

It is strange that law students, who are so often the recipients of uninspired presentations of this type, should themselves so often make the same mistake in their own advocacy. The reason is obvious. Advocacy is going to require you to stand up in front of an audience and to argue your case. You do your preparation so that you won't look like a fool. You bring your notes with you to ensure that, if you lose the thread of your argument, you will have a reminder to hand. Then, when the point comes to actually stand up in front of your audience, you take refuge in reading from your notes, since these are carefully crafted products of your hours of preparation, and thus a safer bet than trying to speak to the court without notes. It is the obvious thing to do, and it is fatal to good advocacy. Even in a moot, where you may be arguing only a point of legal interpretation, you will always be more convincing where you can talk to the court, where you can make eye contact, respond to the court's concerns, and where you can actively work on persuading the court that your version of the facts or the law is the one that the court should follow. This cannot be achieved when you are reading.

(Nor should you assume that the problems of reading can be 'cured' by simply learning your set speech. A learnt speech is no more than a recitation, and, unless you are a very effective actor, your recitation will contain exactly the same problems as your reading. Your voice will lose its tonal range; your pace will speed up; you will lose the natural emphases. Of course, since you will not be hiding behind your notes, you will (at least in theory) be able to maintain some form of eye contact with the court, although you will often find that your eyes unconsciously drift off (generally to the right) when you are trying to recall what you had written. However, you will, of course, lack any flexibility in your approach. If the court asks you questions, or asks you to deal with matters in a different order, you will (if anything) be in an even worse position that someone who is reading, since you will not be able to shuffle the pages of memorised script.)

How, then, can you use all the material which you have so conscientiously prepared from your case analysis?

Notes, plans and other support materials

You may have sufficient confidence, not only in your advocacy skills but in your memory, to feel that you can work to a large extent without notes. Most advocates, while avoiding the dangers of a 'script', still feel the need for some form of written reminder which will direct them to the key stages in their application, their cross-examination or whatever other element of advocacy they are conducting.

How you prepare your notes is largely a matter of finding the method that best suits you. Some advocates find that, rather than using notes, it is easier to use some form of mind map or chart, so that the different categories of issue can all be seen in a single glance, and it becomes easier to keep in mind a sense of the case as a whole.[10]

---

10   You will find an example of a mind map, and a brief discussion of its use, in *op cit*, Boon, fn 4, para 1.3.

Alternatively, you may find it useful to get in the habit of drafting short skeleton plans of the points which you intend to make.

You need to organise these in such a way that the hierarchy of importance of the information is immediately apparent. You will generally put the central points in large type, with subsidiary points in a smaller typeface and set in from the margin, with these then broken down into their constituent elements in smaller type and so on. Thus your cross-examination of James Smith might look like this:

Facts to be challenged

JS was simply walking along before confrontation

- where did JS come from?
- what was JS doing on the High St?
- speed?
- bags in hands?
  - if so, which hands?
  - how heavy?
  - what in the bags?

JS spat on PR

- where JS when first saw PR?
- relative position of two men?
- 'what football team ... etc'?
  - challenge?
  - had JS stopped?
    - if so, why?
  - how loudly was it said?
  - much traffic?
  - how did JS hear?
  - etc.

JS said 'Football scum'

- etc.

JS raised his fist in a threatening manner

- etc.

PR punched JS in self-defence

- etc.

JS's bad character

- etc.

Evidence of bias

- etc.

The advantage of such a plan is that it maintains your freedom to move from point to point, in any order that your cross-examination of the witness requires, but, at the same time, it gives you a clear structure and an *aide memoire* to ensure that you properly cover all the issues. By not 'scripting' your questions, you also maintain your flexibility and your ability to phrase your questions in a persuasive or insinuating manner, basing your questions on the actual answers from the witness rather than on the answers you had expected to get when you first did your preparation.

So your preparation will always be integral to your advocacy, but you must find a way to use your preparation to support the advocacy, or you may find that it actively obstructs you.

Skeleton arguments

It is becoming increasingly common for all courts to look to advocates to supply skeleton arguments. A skeleton argument sets out the core points which will be addressed by the advocate. A good skeleton argument helps the court to prepare for the hearing by setting out the central argument. It helps the advocate by showing the court the way in which the argument is developed. It helps to ensure a fair hearing by ensuring that even under tight time constraints, all relevant matters can be put before the court.

Often formal rules and practice directions will provide how a skeleton argument should be prepared. The Civil Procedure Rules (CPR) even dictate the way in which a skeleton argument should be set out. The following is taken from the Practice Direction to R52, which deals with appeals, and it contains a useful summary of not only the purpose of a skeleton argument, but also the key principles in formatting a skeleton argument.

(1) A skeleton argument must contain a numbered list of the points which the party wishes to make. These should both define and confine the areas of controversy. Each point should be stated as concisely as the nature of the case allows.

(2) A numbered point must be followed by a reference to any document on which the party wishes to rely.

(3) A skeleton argument must state, in respect of each authority cited –

(a) the proposition of law that the authority demonstrates; and

(b) the parts of the authority (identified by page or paragraph references) that support the proposition.

(4) If more than one authority is cited in support of a given proposition, the skeleton argument must briefly state the reason for taking that course.

(5) The statement referred to in sub-paragraph (4) should not materially add to the length of the skeleton argument but should be sufficient to demonstrate, in the context of the argument –

(a) the relevance of the authority or authorities to that argument; and

(b) that the citation is necessary for a proper presentation of that argument.

(6) The cost of preparing a skeleton argument which –

(a) does not comply with the requirements set out in this paragraph; or

(b) was not filed within the time limits provided by this Practice Direction (or any further time granted by the court), will not be allowed on assessment except to the extent that the court otherwise directs.

5.11   The appellant should consider what other information the appeal court will need. This may include a list of persons who feature in the case or glossaries of technical terms. A chronology of relevant events will be necessary in most appeals.[11]

There are a number of general principles which you must take into account in preparing a skeleton argument. The first is to recognise the importance of the skeleton as an intrinsic part of your application: this means that you must include all significant points which you wish to raise. There is no point in providing a skeleton and then seeking to raise fresh points at the hearing; the judge may well not permit you to do this.

However, the other side of the coin is that you must keep your skeleton as brief as possible, or the material will become inaccessible. Your skeleton is not a written speech; it is a very concise summary of your points. It must cite the relevant cases on which you are going to rely, and you must ensure that it cross-refers, where appropriate, to any documents in support.

In addition to your skeleton argument, it is increasingly regarded as good practice to prepare a short chronology of the events in the case – both the facts that are the subject matter of the dispute, and the procedural steps (such as the service of the claim or of the defence). In more complex cases, the court will also appreciate a *dramatis personae* to explain who the various participants are.

Skeleton arguments can be very valuable adjuncts to almost all advocacy. They help to clarify your oral argument by giving it a clear structure; they keep your argument in front of the court; they are available to the court when it is writing its judgment.

Personal preparation

As an advocate, you must know your case. There are few shortcuts in this process. Case analysis will help you to identify what is in issue. Planning your speeches and your witness handling will help to ensure that you cover the ground which you intended to. However, nothing can replace the need for complete familiarity with the details of the case so that you have the confidence to deal with the unanticipated issues which will inevitably arise.

However, in addition to your case preparation, you must also ensure that you, yourself, are prepared for advocacy. You need to consider your presentation skills and, in particular, your use of your voice. As an advocate, all the information which you convey will be relayed by way of your voice. Even where you may seek to put paper evidence before the court, or evidence on video, you will be introducing it, and seeking to persuade the court as to its significance. You need, therefore, to be conscious of the effect of your voice, and to be able to modulate your voice so as to ensure that it makes a positive contribution to your advocacy.

---

11   CPR PD 52, paras 5.9–5.11.

Voice

The keystone to effective use of your voice is posture. Voice is the product of breath, and bad posture will mean that you are not able to breathe properly, and subsequently to project your voice. The ideal posture is upright, and with your feet slightly apart. This will assist in supporting the spine, which anchors your diaphragm and, thus, your breathing ability. (It is worth noting that the upright posture will, of course, cause you problems if you are unduly reliant on any kind of written script: you will either have to lean forward and look down to use the script, or you will have to lift the script up to your face, partially obscuring your mouth and your visual contact with the court.)

There are a number of books on the use of voice, and many of them are written with actors in mind. However, this does not mean that the only effective use of your voice is the rounded, sonorous tones of some classically trained thespians; you are not being asked to abandon your natural voice, but rather to develop a technique of breathing and projection which will ensure that your voice reaches its intended audience. All the books are clear that, allied with correct posture, relaxation is a key element in effective use of your voice. This is because, when you are tense, you will not be able to breathe effectively, using your stomach, and breathing right down into the lungs, rather than simply taking short, superficial breaths. A deep breath will give you the power to project your voice without straining your voice by shouting. However, it is only too likely that at first, at any rate, you will find that getting to your feet in court is not conducive to relaxation at all. You will, therefore, need to consciously relax your body, particularly concentrating on relaxing your neck and shoulders so as to free up your chest so that you can breathe properly. You should also remember to try to relax your face by smiling and by blowing out your cheeks and releasing the air slowly, although these may be exercises which are best conducted before going into the courtroom. By relaxing your face, you will be making it easier to articulate clearly, and thus to ensure that you speak clearly and audibly.

Manner and mannerisms

In advocacy the appearance of confidence is essential. If you look as if you have no faith in your words, you cannot expect your audience to have any faith in you. You need to persuade your audience that what you are saying can (and should) be relied upon. This cannot be done if you clearly do not feel that you can rely on yourself.

For some students, lack of confidence can become a vicious circle; they lose confidence precisely because they do not feel confident. Such students are not, perhaps, being realistic. Few advocates – and even fewer student advocates – start off by feeling confident; the most that you can hope for is that you can hide how nervous you are feeling. It is your job to look confident. Provided you look confident, no one will know how worried you are, unless you tell them. Which is why you should never admit your nerves to any other person. Nervousness is your secret. Keep it secret, and you will find that you are better able to put forward a façade of confidence. There will then come a point where you no longer need to work at putting forward that façade – not because you are now so confident in your performance, but perhaps simply because the façade is simply part of your normal courtroom manner.

Each advocate will have his or her own courtroom manner. Some advocates are aggressive; others are quiet and very calm; some rely upon humour to win over a tribunal, while others present the facts carefully and painstakingly, building up an apparently unshakeable case. All of them, however, will appear confident in the work that they are doing, whatever other mannerisms accompany their presentation. You will find the style of advocacy that best suits you, and if you are fortunate, you will be able to develop as an advocate so that you are able to deploy a range of different approaches to suit the demands of different situations.

As part of this process, you will inevitably develop your own repertoire of mannerisms. Many mannerisms are harmless. They make up part of the general character of the advocate. However, it is worth reviewing your performance, especially in the early stages in the classroom, to make sure that you eradicate any mannerism that detracts from your advocacy. There may be a particular phrase which you use every time you get an answer from a witness, such as 'I see', or 'Right'. These can become very distracting for your audience if overused, and you may be entirely unaware that you are using them at all! Get a friend to watch you, or (even better) video yourself, and look out for such phrases. Be aware that you are using them. Ask yourself why you are using them. (The most common reason is to give yourself time to digest the information while you formulate your next question.) And once you are aware of the habit, work to eradicate it.

Similar mannerisms may include clicking your pen, sighing, rocking backwards and forwards, standing with your hands in your pockets, tugging at your face: the list is endless. Review yourself and ask whether you are doing anything that might distract your audience. (Be aware of your body language, as part of this process of review. If you have properly considered your posture, you will be in the habit of standing up straight in court, and while this will enable you to use your voice effectively, it also has the great benefit of projecting a message that you are confident and in control of your case.)

Readiness

Readiness includes all the preparation which we have considered above. Of course, it includes your case analysis and your preparation of whichever piece of advocacy you are being called upon to perform. It also includes your review of your voice and your posture, your manner and your mannerisms. It must also include such simple matters as ensuring that you have the correct clothing, and that you know where you have to go, and how to get there. Ask any advocate in practice and they will have at least one horror story about going to the wrong court, or getting lost en route. It is hard to maintain an appearance of relaxed competence when you have run all the way from the station and you are already 15 minutes late.

In your early days as an advocate, you may find that you spend at least as much time worrying about whether you are sitting in the correct bench as you do on worrying about your advocacy itself. It is impossible to generalise about where you should sit in court. Each court has its own peculiarities. You will rarely go wrong if you consult the usher. As to appearance, bear in mind that you must not distract your audience from what you are saying. You are seeking to persuade the court, not to dazzle them. Dark clothing is the norm (and generally the rule) in courts and tribunals, and in most courts you may also have to appear robed (and, if you are a barrister, wigged). As the Code of Conduct of the Bar of England and Wales puts it: 'In court a barrister's personal appearance should be decorous ...'

THE BASIC CONVENTIONS OF ADVOCACY

In this section, we will look at the basic professional conduct rules which underpin your advocacy, and the rules of courtroom conduct which you will need to bear in mind.

An advocate, not a witness

You must never forget that you are in court as an advocate, and not as a witness. It is your job to argue your client's case – it is the court's job to make any decision as to its merits. For this reason you may find that you will be interrupted if you get into the habit of saying things such as 'I think' or 'I believe', as it is not what you think or believe that is relevant; it is what the court thinks or believes. Advocates avoid this by rephrasing the proposition: 'Your Honour may think that ...' 'In the light of the evidence, Sir, you may take the view that ...'

Even in interlocutory applications (that is to say, applications which are made during the pre-trial process), you need to be careful to avoid giving evidence to the court. For this reason, you will often support your application with witness statements.

Misleading the court

The proposition that you must never, as an advocate, mislead the court may seem straightforward enough. However, it is easier to end up misleading the court than you might think. The most common reason why advocates fall foul of this basic rule is because they are unwilling to admit that they may not know the answer to a question which has been asked. Let us take the example of a personal injury action. The court, without warning, asks whether the client has a clean driving licence. The advocate does not know the answer, is reluctant to admit that he or she is not sure, considers the question to be wholly unimportant and irrelevant and so guesses that the client does have a clean licence. Inevitably, it is these off the cuff responses to apparently insignificant questions which later turn out to be central to an issue in the case. It is very easy to fall into this trap, and from the beginning of your advocacy career you must be in the habit of only answering questions that you know the answer to. If you are unsure, you should check your papers, or ask for a minute to take instructions.

The other reason why the proposition that you must never mislead the court can be less than straightforward is that you have differing duties to inform the court of issues which have been overlooked, depending on whether the issue is one of fact or law. Both barristers and solicitors are subject to the same basic principle: you are under a duty to draw the court's attention to any relevant legal provision *even if it does not support your case.* In contrast, you are not under a duty to correct a factual omission, although you (and your client) must do nothing to suggest to the court that the situation is a correct statement of the position.

Thus, in a sentencing case, you become aware that the prosecutor has overlooked a recent sentencing authority from the Court of Appeal which suggests that the normal entry point for sentencing will be a custodial sentence rather than a community sentence. The prosecutor also fails to mention the fact that your client has a very recent conviction for a similar offence. You are under a duty to draw the authority to the attention of the court, although you may then go on to seek to distinguish the authority, by arguing that it is not on all fours with the facts in your client's case or that your client has particular personal mitigation which means that the entry point sentence is inappropriate. In relation to the recent conviction, however, you are under no duty to raise this with the court, although, in your mitigation, you must do nothing to suggest that the convictions that have been put before the court comprise a full list, or to suggest (for example) that your client is a reformed character who has not been in any trouble recently.

Additionally, in very many cases, you may not believe your client's account of events, and yet, as his or her advocate, you will still be under a duty to put forward that account to the court. This can also seem as if you are misleading the court. Again, the rules of professional conduct permit you to question your clients and to put to them any inconsistencies in their accounts. However, it is not for you to usurp the position of the court in deciding where the truth, or otherwise, of the matter lies. You must not invent an account for your client, but your duty is to put forward to the court the account that they have given. Only if you stray from this account will you be misleading the court.

Addressing the court

Modes of address

There are whole books that have been written on modes of address. We have drawn the following useful chart from *Civil Advocacy: A Practical Guide*:[12]

Officer	Direct address	Indirect address
High Court judges, any other judge in High Court, Court of Appeal or House of Lords, circuit judges in the Old Bailey	My Lord/Lady	Your Lordship/ Ladyship
Circuit judges in other courts, Recorders in Crown/county court	Your Honour	Your Honour
Masters	Master	You
District judges, magistrates, tribunal chairpersons, coroners	Sir/Madam	You (and your colleagues)
Justices' clerks	Sir/Madam clerk, You	Your learned

(It should be added that, in many parts of the country, lay magistrates will still expect to be addressed as Your Worship, and solicitors will do so.)

Barristers will often refer to one another as 'my learned friend', although traditionally solicitors are referred to only as 'my friend'. Perhaps for this reason, it is increasingly common for advocates to refer to one another by name.

---

12   Foster, C *et al*, *Civil Advocacy: A Practical Guide*, 2nd edn, 2001, London: Cavendish Publishing, p 12.

Courtroom etiquette

It is not only a question of remembering the correct modes of address; you must also comply with the basic conventions of courtroom behaviour. In particular, it is a basic convention that only one advocate should be on their feet at any one time (unless invited by the court to do otherwise), and that only the advocate who is on their feet may address the court. Thus, you stand when you are addressing the court; you sit when your opposite number rises to address the court. This reflects parliamentary procedure (or perhaps vice versa) and ensures that only one person should be speaking at any given time. It is an easy habit to get into.

You must also get into the habit of bowing whenever you enter or leave a court which is sitting in open court. The bow normally takes the form of an inclination of the head, but it is intended as a mark of respect to the court and you should be careful not to omit it. You will also rise and bow whenever the judge enters or leaves the courtroom. Especially in busy magistrates' courts, it can sometimes feel, amidst the hubbub, that these basic elements of legal courtesy have been lost; you should be careful to comply, however; the court will certainly notice. And while we are on the subject, you must never move or start taking instructions from your client or doing anything else while a witness is being sworn in. This is a solemn moment, and you should behave accordingly.

Finally, you should be aware of the basic convention that applies where you are the last advocate in a court where the judge is sitting in robes. Rather than abandoning the judge, you should remain 'dressing the court' until the judge gives you permission to go. It is another minor form of courtesy, and judges will invariably excuse you almost immediately.

We have now looked at preparing for your advocacy, and at the basic conventions of advocacy. In the next sections, we look at how to make applications to the court, and how you make speeches.

Applications

There are a vast number of different applications which you may find yourself making to the court. In the criminal context, you may be applying for legal aid, for bail or appearing at a pre-trial review.[13] In mainstream civil actions, you may nonetheless find yourself at an allocation hearing, at an application for summary judgment or for strike out, at applications for interim payments (to keep your client going until the trial itself) or for some form of injunctive relief. It is possible for many applications to be made without notice to the other side (what used to be known as *ex parte*) if the matter is urgent or there is some very good reason why the other side should not be informed. However, under the CPR, without notice applications should be exceptional, and the court will normally expect the other party to be given some degree of notice. The

---

13   In this section, we have focused mainly on civil applications. For an account of advocacy in criminal applications – such as applications for bail – see Plowden, P, *Criminal Litigation in Practice*, 2005, Newcastle upon Tyne: Northumbria Law Press.

majority of applications will be on notice, and the two sides will attend the court for a district judge or High Court Master to rule on a matter which is in dispute.

What almost all applications will have in common is that no witnesses will be called to give evidence. You may be supporting your application with witness statements which set out the factual basis for your case, but you will not be calling those witnesses. This means that, in your applications, you will be focusing on the legal remedy that you seek, and attempting to show the court why certain steps should be taken in the case.

Presentation and research

The first step in any application is to research the relevant law. There is no point asking the court to make a certain order for your client if the court has no power to make the order. In the case of an application for summary judgment – the process by which the court may dispose of a case without proceeding to trial – you will need to read Part 24 of the CPR, and the accompanying Practice Direction. You will also need to read through Part 25 of the CPR, as this lays down the basic requirements for applications for interim remedies. This will tell you when you are able to make the application. It will also remind you of the particular notice requirements (14 clear days – substantially longer than the three clear days which are required in most interim applications). Faithful compliance with notice requirements is essential in civil applications, and your application may well be rejected if you have failed to give the other party the notice to which they are entitled.

Having ensured that you are up to date with rules governing the application, you need to start marshalling your arguments. What is the test that the court must apply in deciding whether to grant the application? In the case of an application for summary judgment for a claimant, you must show that the defendant has no real prospect of successfully defending the claim or issue, and that there is no other reason why the case or issue should be disposed of at trial.[14] Your application will be by means of an application notice, supported by evidence, often in the form of witness statements. You will, therefore, need to look at the witness statements which you have prepared at this stage and you may well need to prepare a fresh statement which addresses any issues raised by the defendant in the defence, so that you can persuade the court that there is no real prospect of a successful defence to the claim.

There is extensive case law on summary judgment, both under the CPR and under the earlier Rules, and you will need therefore to do some further research to satisfy yourself that you are not seeking an order in a situation where the courts have indicated that summary judgment is unlikely to be appropriate. For example, it has been held that summary judgment is inappropriate in cases which are likely to involve protracted argument.[15]

You should prepare a basic checklist, breaking down the requirements of the CPR, and noting down beside each one how that requirement is satisfied. You must try to step back from your application in order to consider how the other party is likely to respond. In the case of a claimant's application for summary judgment, the defendant

---

14   CPR, r 24.2.
15   *Home and Overseas Insurance Co Ltd v Mentor Insurance Co (UK) Ltd* [1990] 1 WLR 153.

will presumably argue that the defence is meritorious, and that it raises complex issues which can only properly be decided on the hearing of the evidence at trial. What are your arguments to the contrary? On what basis can you show that the elements of the defence cannot be sustained? What is the basis for your assertion that there is no other reason why the matter should proceed to trial?

Making the application

Applications may be made in open court – for example, an application for bail in the magistrates' court will be dealt with in open court. However, most civil interim applications are likely to be dealt with in chambers. You will make the application sitting down. You are likely to be before a district judge in the county court, a Master or district judge in the High Court.

The party making the application should begin by introducing himself or herself, and introducing the other party. You should then check that the court has copies of the relevant documents. (It is always a good idea to bring a number of copies with you, so that you have spares to hand up to the court.) You will also often need to hand up a chronology of events, so that the judge can follow your application without needing to work through all the papers.

Check whether the judge has had the opportunity to read the application notice and any attached witness statements. If the judge has not had the opportunity to do so, ask whether the judge would like you to go through the material. You will then present your arguments in favour of the application. Don't simply repeat the test for granting the order that you seek; show the court why the criteria laid down in the CPR are satisfied. Try to anticipate any contrary submissions, and show why they are not made out. The other side will then put forward its arguments as to why the application should be rejected. You will then have a brief opportunity to reply, and your opponent may then be given an opportunity to reply to you. The judge is likely to make a decision at this point, although it is possible in more complex cases for judgment to be reserved (that is, given on a later date). You must then be prepared to make submissions as to costs.

Costs and applications

Under the CPR, it will normally be the practice to have summary assessment of costs at the close of an application. The practice is for the parties to serve in advance of the hearing statements of their costs. This then enables the court to make an immediate award of costs, rather than waiting for costs to be dealt with after any later trial. The normal rule will be that the person who succeeds at the application will get their costs met by the other party. You will, therefore, need to be familiar with the costs rules, and ready to argue your point, whether you have won or lost the substantive application.

Advocacy in applications

In most civil applications, you will be required to state the time estimate for your application, and this will be used in listing the matter for a hearing. In your application, you must keep the time limits in mind, and must ensure that you do not exceed your allotted time without good cause. The onus is, therefore, on you to keep your submissions short and relevant – and not to waste time finding documents which you should have had to hand. Applications are a forum for advocacy where it pays to be concise. You are not trying to sway a jury; you are addressing a person who was almost certainly a professional advocate themselves before becoming a judge. Identify your legal arguments with clarity, and take the judge to the evidence or the case law which supports your case.

Skeleton arguments

Skeleton arguments are not yet required in every interim application, but a skeleton argument can be such a useful adjunct to your advocacy that you may find that the preparation of a skeleton argument is a habit which is worth getting into. Clearly, a concisely argued paper account of your points, to which you can refer the court as you deal with each point, is a hugely useful support. Under the very time-constrained conditions of a typical interim application, a skeleton argument will be essential in setting out your points, enabling you to focus on the key points, and to expand on any issues which are raised by the court.

Feed your judge: dealing with questions

The common reaction of inexperienced advocates to questions from the judge is to look alarmed. The advocate feels safe so long as they are able to present the material in the way that they have prepared and without interruption. But you should treat questions from the judge as a way of helping you. The judge is telling you that there is a point that concerns him or her. Don't ignore the question or brush it aside; think about it, and explain why you feel that your case is, nevertheless, a valid one. As one judge has put it:

> Questioning (rather than silence) is the hallmark of a fair hearing – questions are a plea for assistance in clarifying, understanding and enabling acceptance of submissions. They are a challenge to the advocate – to a good advocate they afford the opportunity to make good the vulnerable areas in his case. A judge may appear fierce when he is really only hungry for assistance. The trained advocate recognises the symptoms and sets out to feed and satisfy him.[16]

Even if the question suggests that the judge is wholly against you, you must take the opportunity to seek to persuade him or her of the merits of your position. For example, in an application for summary judgment for the claimant, which you are making, the Master interrupts you:

> Surely there is a defence here, Mr/Ms Smith. They have three witnesses who say that your client was driving too fast.

> Yes, Master. But you will have noticed, Master, that two of those statements are coming from the defendants to the action, who, on their own admission, were engaged in a furious disagreement as they drove in the opposite direction in their car. We would say that it is clear that even on their own account, they paid little heed to the any other road users and their impression of my client's speed is, as might be expected, hopelessly vague. The third statement is from a person who turns out to be an employee of the first defendant, and whose evidence was produced for the first

---

16 Lightman J, 'The case for judicial intervention', speech to the London Solicitors' Litigation Association, 9 November 1999.

time at the court door today. We say that the evidence from this mysterious new witness, who was not known to the police, and whose evidence has come forward at this late stage in the application, and who appears to have employment links with the defendant, is deeply questionable, and can be given little credence. On this basis, Master, we would say that there is nothing in this evidence which displaces our contention that this is not a matter where there is a sustainable defence.

You must use the judge's questions as a means of helping to strengthen your case.

SPEECHES

It is tempting to see speeches as a forum where, since you are less likely to be interrupted, you can give free rein to your oratorical skills. This is not the case. As an audience in the age of widespread literacy, and of film and television, we have lost the habit of listening. Research has shown that within a very few minutes of listening to a speaker, the audience begins to become distracted and to cease listening. In your speeches, therefore, you need to gain your audience's attention, and you need to work hard at keeping it.

Structuring a speech

Just as you will find that there are a myriad of different types of speech that you may be called upon to make, so there is no single method of structuring a speech. You may be making speeches at the opening or closing of a civil trial, in the appellate courts on a point of law only, in criminal trials, including speeches in mitigation, before administrative tribunals (such as the Social Security Commissioner). All speeches have two principles in common: your speech must be structured, and it must be clear.

Structure

John Munkman, in his famous book *The Technique of Advocacy*,[17] proposes that a speech must fall into two essential parts: the statement and the proof. The statement outlines the factual basis of the case and what is to be proved; the proof then sets out the arguments in support. Additionally, he suggests, speeches may contain an introduction, and may end with some form of 'peroration', or epilogue. You should use oratory carefully in a court of law, even where you are addressing a jury, but you will often find that some form of peroration or recapitulation at the end of your speech can be used to drive home your central argument and to finish on a strong, confident note.

Different forms of speeches will make different demands upon you. Even in the context of criminal work alone, you will find that your opening speech (if you are entitled to one)[18] is very different from your closing speech, and that a mitigation

---

17   Munkman, J, *The Technique of Advocacy*, 1991, London: Butterworths.

18   In the magistrates' court, the prosecution will normally get an opening speech, but will probably not get a closing speech. Conversely, the defence can have either an opening or closing speech, and so will normally elect to have a closing speech so as to get the advantage of having the final word. In the Crown Court, the defence may have an opening speech provided that they are calling witnesses of fact other than the defendant alone.

speech requires a wholly different level of organisation to a submission of no case to answer. (Indeed, you may well find that mitigation speeches are particularly challenging; certainly, they often seem to be remarkably poorly performed in practice. Sentencing law is often unclear, but advocates who try to avoid dealing with the legal principles tend to flounder in a swamp of clichés about the ability to reform, and how sending the defendant to prison will only punish his family. Always be prepared to use the legal framework as a means of structuring your speech.)

As a general rule, you will want to be brief in any speech, so as to ensure that you keep your audience's attention. In an opening speech, you will need to bear this in mind for two particular reasons. First, you will need to be accurate; you cannot afford to make any mistakes. Andy Boon quotes the Roman writer, Quintillian:

> To be confused in memory, or to lose our fluency of speech, has nowhere a worse effect than at the commencement. The pilot is surely one of the worst who runs his vessel aground as it is leaving the harbour.[19]

The other reason for brevity is that you must ensure that you do not give up any unnecessary hostages to fortune. You do not want to be in a position where you tell the jury that you will call a witness who will say x, y and z, but who, when the witness is called, in fact only says x and y. The other party may make a great deal of the fact that you said you would establish all three points, but have failed to do so.

In any speech, however, you must make sure that the structure is logical and that it enables you to present your material in a coherent manner. Try to find your central theme, about which you can organise all the materials which you wish to put in front of the jury, and avoid repetition if you can help it as, to your audience, it can seem that you are going round in circles. It is easy to concentrate on your opening and your closing, as these are the two points at which you can hope to have your audience's full attention; but work at presenting the material in such a clear and accessible manner that your audience willingly listens to the whole of your speech.

Clarity

It is all very well to say that your material must be presented in a clear and accessible manner, but for your meaning to be clear, you must know what you mean to say. The level of preparation required for a speech may be just as great as when you are preparing an application or a cross-examination. What is the aim of the speech? What is the central legal point on which you are relying? Is this a general 'standard of proof' speech – or are you arguing that some particular element of the offence has not been made out? You must ensure that your speech focuses on the issue which is central to your case. If you employ a scattergun approach, the impact of your speech will be diluted and your audience will be confused.

How you approach the issue of clarity will be determined by the tribunal that you are addressing. A speech to a jury will be very different from a speech to a judge. Where you are presenting a matter to a jury or any lay audience, remember the key role that narrative plays in getting and keeping people's attention. Thus, if you are prosecuting

---

19   Quintillian, *Institutes of Oratory*, quoted in *op cit*, Boon, fn 4, p 70.

a criminal matter and you start your speech with a long explanation of the legal elements of a charge, your audience will probably soon abandon you. If they wanted to sit through law lectures, they would have become lawyers. So, start with the story: tell them what happened in clear and accessible terms. Then explain why what happened amounts to an offence. Explain which witnesses you will be calling and what – in broad terms – they will establish (always bearing in mind the need to avoid giving hostages to fortune). So long as you are able to maintain your focus on your central theme, you should find that it is easier to develop a logical structure for the presentation of your material, and also to present that material in a clear and attractive manner.

Consider the following opening to a prosecution opening speech, and note the use of narrative as a means of ensuring an immediate engagement by the jury in the case that they have been asked to decide:[20]

Members of the jury, this is a case of robbery. It concerns a young man, who went out to celebrate the end of his exams, and was attacked by the two men who are on trial today. If you cast your minds back to the spring of last year, you remember that it was a warm start to the summer. Now, on the night of 18 May of last year, Michael Richards and his friend, Andrew Smith, had been out on the town in Westchurch. They were both then 18 years old. They had just finished their A levels. They were out on the town, celebrating. But, by about 11.00 that evening, Mr Richards had to get home. He lives outside Westchurch, and because he had been drinking, he decided to take the bus. And so he and his friend, Mr Smith, walked over to the bus stop on Westchurch High Street.

Now, and you may think this is typical, but no sooner did Mr Richards approach the bus stop than, to his horror, he saw the last bus home beginning to pull out. So he shouted a hasty goodbye to his friend and began to run for the bus. But as he did so, something strange happened. He heard a shout from behind him, telling him to stop. He looked back as he ran, but he saw only a man that he did not know. Seeing the bus pulling away from the kerb, he ignored the man and ran to catch the bus. However, the man who was shouting ran after him, along with a second man, and they caught Mr Richards just as the bus pulled away. The first man grabbed hold of Mr Richards' shoulder, and pulled him round. He and his accomplice shoved Mr Richards up against a wall, and then, as Mr Richards began to protest, hustled him into a narrow alley just past the bus stop. There, the first man told Mr Richards that he and his accomplice were police officers – and indeed, that they were employed by the CID. Mr Richards will tell you that he was so shocked that he did not know what to believe. But when they demanded identification from him, he was understandably anxious to provide it. He pulled out his wallet to show them his driving licence. When the first man attempted to take the wallet away, Mr Richards protested. And then, without warning, the first man hit Mr Richards in the face, once, with his closed fist, hard, and the second man pulled the wallet from his hand.

Mr Richards was knocked back against the wall by the force of the punch. Fortunately at this point Mr Smith arrived in the alley with another man, to come to their friend's assistance. The two attackers dropped Mr Richard's wallet on the ground. They turned. They walked away.

---

20 This opening speech is loosely based on the facts of the case reported as *Attorney General's References (Nos 24 and 25 of 2000)* [2001] 1 Cr App R(S) 237.

However, they did not get far. They had been seen by police from a nearby rooftop, and they were stopped in the next street and arrested. They were, of course, not police officers at all. When they were arrested one of the men claimed that the whole incident had been a joke that had gone wrong. The other man claimed that Mr Richards had shouted racial abuse at him. They have both been charged with robbery. And whether they are guilty, members of the jury, is the fact that you will decide during this trial.

Members of the jury, what is robbery? At its simplest, robbery is a theft accompanied by violence or the threat of violence ...

The great merit of using narrative as basis for an opening speech is the way that it can force you to be clear and organised in using your material. The material is presented to the jury in an immediately accessible way. When we listen to stories, immediately and without thinking about it, we begin to judge the story: does it makes sense; is the motivation clear; would a person really act in that way? If the story does hold up to scrutiny – if it makes sense to the listener – it takes on a form of reality, and it becomes hard to dislodge from the listener's mind.

You may think that this is a technique which is only appropriate for addressing lay tribunals. It is true that, where you are dealing with a professional court, such as a judge alone, you will need to temper any oratorical flourishes. But this does not mean that you should abandon the use of narrative as a technique of your advocacy. Even in a mitigation speech, it is useful to construct a narrative which sets out not simply what happened in the incident, but which explains why it happened. Try to use narrative to give the judge a sense of your client and his background, and how he came to offend. You can then use this to relate the narrative to the proposed sentencing option. Narrative can introduce a sense of coherence to your speech.

Speeches and applications are, however, only one aspect of advocacy. In both, you have an opportunity to prepare with the confidence that the majority of the material which you have prepared will be material which you will present to the court. In the case of witness-handling, however – the examination-in-chief, cross-examination and re-examination of witnesses at a trial – there is a far greater degree of unpredictability. In the case of your own witnesses, you may have a copy of their 'proof of evidence', but live oral testimony is fundamentally unpredictable. You can never be entirely sure what witnesses will say or do when they are in the witness box. In the following sections we look at the particular demands of witness-handling, and the rules that govern this aspect of advocacy.

WITNESS-HANDLING

Witness-handling may be a different aspect of advocacy from the making of speeches and submissions, but the same basic rules of advocacy apply. You, as the advocate, are not permitted to give evidence yourself; the evidence must come from the witnesses. You also remain an officer of the court, and have a duty not to mislead the court, or to permit anyone else to do so. However, there are a range of other principles which you need to consider in this context.

The basic principles

Leading and non-leading questions

Examination-in-chief is the process by which you will take your own witnesses through their testimony. It is essential that the witnesses are able to give their testimony to the court in their own words. For this reason, you are not permitted to ask 'leading questions' in your examination-in-chief. There are a number of different definitions of leading questions; none of them is entirely satisfactory. A leading question is a question which suggests the answer to the witness or which puts material into evidence which is in dispute and has not been given by the witness.

It is easy to see how a question such as, 'You hit the man, didn't you?' would be a leading question if your witness has not said anything about hitting anyone, or has not said that it was a man that they hit. Indeed, the question as phrased is the sort of question that is often used in cross-examination because it is 'closed'; it permits the witness only to say 'Yes', or 'No'. If you are trying to get the witness to give his or her account of the brawl in the pub in which they lashed out in self-defence, you will need to get the witness to give this evidence in their own way, without 'leading' the evidence yourself:

Q: Where were you on the night of the 21st?

A: I was in the public house.

Q: Which public house was that?

A: The Coach and Horses.

Q: And what happened while you were in the Coach and Horses that night?

A: There was a huge fight.

Q: And what happened during the fight?

A: John Rogers came up to me and threatened to hit me in the face with a beer glass.

Q: And what was your reaction?

A: I hit him first.

Q: What did you hit him with?

A: Just my fist.

In this very simple example, you can see that none of the questions 'leads' evidence which the witness has not already put before the court. In some cases, where the date is in issue, you may find that the other side would object to the first question – 'Where were you on the night of the 21st?' – on the basis that it indicates to the witness that this is the significant date. Otherwise, however, the questions all ask the witness to tell the court what happened. (In reality, you would, of course, wish to go into events in a much higher level of detail. You might also find that your witness was far less co-operative.)

Initially, at least, students find the avoidance of leading questions one of the most challenging aspects of witness-handling. It does get easier with practice, but it is rarely easy; you will often see even senior advocates asking leading questions, although, for some reason, they are somewhat less likely to get told off for it than you are. (In the section on examination-in-chief, below, p 218, we will look in more detail at ways of avoiding asking leading questions.)

In the context of civil litigation, it is now increasingly the norm for there to be no examination-in-chief. Instead, the witness statement of the witness is put before the court and this stands in for the examination-in-chief. However, you still need to be able to avoid asking leading questions, as there is a prohibition on such questions when you re-examine your witness after the other side's cross-examination. (Re-examination is discussed in more detail below, p 235).

Open and closed questions

An open question is one which leaves the witness free to give evidence in detail, and often to explain their motivation. 'Why did you hit the man?' is an open question. So is a question such as 'What happened next?' In contrast, a closed question is one to which the witness can only give a limited answer. 'You hit him with your fist, didn't you?' is a closed question. So, too, is a question such as 'Which side of the bar were you standing at this point?' Both questions limit the evidence that the witness can give.

Unlike the rule about leading questions in examination-in-chief, there is no rule about the use of open and closed questions. You may want to use both types of question in your examination-in-chief, using open questions to give the witness an opportunity to explain what was happening and how they were feeling, and then using closed questions to focus on the evidence that they have given and to concentrate on particular elements of their testimony. Because the use of closed questions is all about controlling the witness, it is likely that you will want to use predominantly closed questions when cross-examining the other side's witnesses. It will be rare that you ask an open question, as this will give the witness an opportunity to give their evidence in the way that they wish, rather than under your control.

Prompts and transitional questions

You will need to be able to move witnesses from one point in their testimony to another. This is easy in cross-examination, where you are permitted to ask leading questions. You can simply say to the witness: 'Mr Rogers, let us now move on to what you said to my client after he hit you. You said, "Don't think you'll get away with this," didn't you?' Where you are examining your own witness, however, you must be careful not to lead the witness while guiding them to the next point. You will generally want to do this by way of closed questions, so as to control the witness's response: 'Mr Smith, you have told the court about the fight in the bar. What did you do after the fight?' You may be able to close down the question even more by asking a question such as: 'After the fight did you stay in the bar, or did you go elsewhere?' A question such as this is not strictly a leading question, as it is clear that the witness must have done one or the other. It also has the advantage of prompting the witness to deal with exactly the point that you wish to start with – 'Oh, I stayed in the bar' – but because such questions prompt the witness to such a great extent, you must make sure that you do not overuse them.

Sometimes, you may find it very difficult to move your witness on without leading the witness. This is often the case at the start of the examination-in-chief, where you are trying to get the witness to move to the start of their relevant evidence. You can of course simply ask: 'Where were you on the night of the 21st?' But often, instead of getting the answer that you want – 'I was in the public house' – the witness may start at some earlier point:

> Well, I got home at about 6 and went to have a bath because in my job of course you get very sticky, and I thought to myself that maybe I could have a shower, but a bath

would be better. But before I could have a shower, I had to make a few telephone calls, and then I had to feed the dog, as he likes his food ...

You will need to interrupt at an early stage:

Q: And when you got home, did you stay at home that evening, or did you go out?

A: Oh, I went out to the Coach and Horses.

Similarly, if, having got Mr Smith to the pub, you ask: 'And what happened while you were in the Coach and Horses that night?' and Mr Smith starts telling you all about who he talked to, and what he drank, and where he sat, you may again need to prompt him:

Q: Mr Smith, while you were at the Coach and Horses that evening, did anything unusual occur?

A: There was a huge fight.

The principle of prompting the witness goes hand in hand with the need to help your witness. You must never simply abandon your witness; it is your job to help the witness to give relevant and concise testimony to the court. Don't be so directive that you prevent the witness from telling his or her own story, but use prompting questions to show the witness where you want more details, and where you would like the witness to move on to a more significant point.

Keep your questions short

Whether you are examining a witness in chief or cross-examining the witness, you must try to keep your questions short. A common problem for advocates is that they feel the need to keep talking while they are still formulating the question that they wish to ask. You can easily end up with questions such as: 'So, Mr Smith, could you please tell the court, in your own words, where, in so far as you are able to remember, but as precisely as you can please, you were standing in the public house, that is, the Coach and Horses, on the evening in question, at about the time that the fight started, which I think you have already told the court may have been at about 9.00.' Invariably if you ask a very long question – particularly in cross-examination – the witness will ask you to repeat it; invariably, if it is a very long question, you will not be able to do so! Try to keep your questions short and your language straightforward.

One question at a time

In the same way as some advocates find it hard to ask short questions, so, too, some advocates find it difficult to ask one question at a time. 'Where in the bar were you standing, Mr Smith, and could you hear exactly what Mr Rogers said?' Giving evidence is often a stressful experience, and you need to help the witness to concentrate on the question that you are asking. This is not simply a question of helping your own witness; it is a principle which applies equally in cross-examination, where you want to make sure that the points that you are putting to the witness are clear and unambiguous.

Don't ask: 'You weren't near the bar at that time, were you, because you were over by the fruit machine, which is why you couldn't hear anything that Mr Rogers said, so that when you hit him, you did so because of what Ms Jones had told you and not because Mr Rogers was issuing any kind of verbal threat. That's the case, isn't it?' Instead, break down your questions:

Q: You weren't near the bar at that time, were you?

Q: You were over by the fruit machine?

Q: And that is why you couldn't hear what Mr Rogers was saying, isn't it?

Q: And so you hit him, didn't you?

Q: You hit him because of what Ms Jones had told you, didn't you?

Q: You didn't hit him because he was issuing any kind of verbal threat, did you?

Often, inexperienced advocates like to wrap up all these questions into one big question because they know that the witness that they are cross-examining is simply going to say 'No' to each question, and they would rather get one 'No' than seven. However, this is not an effective strategy. Short, direct, single questions are a clear and effective way of putting your version of events to the witness. Even if the questions elicit a whole series of 'No's, the impact is more positive.

Know where you are going

The underlying cause of many long or multiple questions is simply that the advocate is trying to buy time to think of their next question. Rather than talking at length, in the hope that inspiration will strike, it is better to say nothing and to take a moment to formulate your next question. Of course, it is even better if your preparation is such that you are able to ask your next question without pausing to think. In order to do this, you must know what it is that you are trying to achieve with the witness.

If you are conducting an examination-in-chief, you will need to identify the key elements of the witness's testimony which are necessary for your case. You must make sure that the witness gives evidence on each of these points. Similarly, in your cross-examination, you will need to identify all the useful testimony that you can elicit from the witness, those points on which you are under a duty to put to the witness your version of events (known as 'putting your case'), and those areas where you feel you can undermine the witness's evidence. Inevitably, new matters will arise as you conduct your examination of the witness, but without earlier preparation to ensure that you have a clear idea of what you need to achieve with the witness, you will end up floundering. As in all forms of advocacy, the key is preparation.

Examination-in-chief

Examination-in-chief is the process by which your witnesses will give their testimony to the court. As was noted above, examination-in-chief is now rare in civil cases, where the witness statement will normally stand in for the witness's evidence. However, examination-in-chief is still the rule in all criminal cases, and it is the point where you will want your witnesses to give an account of events that is so clear and coherent that the court is left with an abiding impression of your version of the events in question.

The most common structure for your examination-in-chief will be a chronological one, so that the witness works through the events in question in the order in which they occurred. In some complex cases, however, you may need to divide up the evidence into subject-based chunks, so that, for example, you invite the witness first to deal with their own employment history, their position in the company, their responsibilities and the projects that they have been working on. Only then do you go back to review the history of the witness's contacts with your own client, and the context in which they know one another, both at work and socially. You might then move on to look at the facts of the case, having got the witness to give the court a full setting to which these facts can now be related. Whichever form of structure you choose to use, the key is to identify, at an early stage, which elements of your witness's testimony are essential to your case, which are useful, and which are merely scene-setting. You then need to make sure that your preparation is sufficiently clear to ensure that you are able to adduce the evidence that you are seeking on each point.

Avoiding leading questions

The key to avoiding leading questions is proper preparation. You do not need to write down in full your examination-in-chief before you go into the court. Indeed, if you do so, your questions may seem stilted and you will find it difficult to react to any unexpected points which your witness raises. However, if you have identified in your preparation the key points on which you wish to get the witness to give evidence, you should be able to work back from those points to create a series of non-leading questions.

Example: you need to get the witness to testify that she saw a red car at 6.00 am (the expected answers are taken from the witness statement):

Q: You have said that you left home on the day in question to go to work, at what time did you leave home?

(Expected answer: about 6 am.)

Q: Where is your home?

(Expected answer: 23 Donaldson Drive, Westchurch.)

Q: And is that address a house or a flat?

(Expected answer: a house.)

Q: How did you intend to travel to work on that day?

(Expected answer: by bus.)

Q: And when you leave your house, how do you get to the bus stop?

(Expected answer: you turn left up the street and ...)

Q: Pausing you there, when you reached the street on that morning, did you notice anything?

(Expected answer: yes, a car.)

Q: Where was this car?

(Expected answer: across the road.)

Q: Can you say how far away from you it was?

(Expected answer: about 20 yards.)

Q: Could you see the colour of the car?

(Expected answer: Yes. It was red.)

Q: And can you recall what time it was when you first saw the car?

(Expected answer: Yes. It was 6 am.)

And having done your preparation on this point, you can also consider how to insulate your witness against cross-examination. You are seeking to make their version watertight, and while you are still not permitted to ask leading questions, you can now use the evidence which they have given to formulate your questions:

(1) Maybe the witness has got the time wrong:

  Q: How can you be so sure that it was 6 o'clock?

  (I had just turned on my Walkman, and the 6 o'clock news had just started.)

(2) Maybe the witness has got the colour wrong:

  Q: You have said that the car was red: how certain are you of the colour?

  (I am sure it was red. I could see it clearly.)

  Q: What was the light like at 6 on the day in question?

  (It was summer and it was daylight by then.)

  Q: Were there any streetlights nearby?

  (Yes. But it was light already and I didn't need the streetlight to tell the colour.)

(3) Is it likely that the witness might be challenged on the date of the sighting?:

  Q: You have told the court you saw the car on the morning of the 19th. How can you be so certain?

  (It was my daughter's birthday.)

Drills for avoiding leading questions

It is sometimes said that questions which begin with words such as 'why', 'what', 'where', or 'how' are unlikely to be leading questions. In contrast, so it is said, sentences which start with words such as 'did' or 'have' are likely to be leading questions.

However, you need to be careful with such drills, and to remember that a question will be leading only if it is suggesting to the witness the answer to the question, and the witness has not given that evidence already. Questions such as 'Why did you hit the victim?', 'What did you hit the victim with?', 'Where were you standing when you hit the victim?' and 'How did you hit the victim?' may all be leading questions if the witness has not given evidence that they did hit the victim. Similarly, a question such as 'Did you hit the victim with a hammer?' or 'Have you hit the victim with a hammer recently?' may not be leading questions if the witness has already testified that they hit the victim with a hammer. It is not simply the phrasing of a question which will make it a leading question. However, if you are conducting an examination-in-chief, a question which starts with 'Did' should ring alarm bells, and you should mentally pause to check that the closed question is on a point where the witness has already given the evidence.

The trouble with the prohibition on leading questions in examination-in-chief is that it can become an obsessive concern, which prevents you from focusing on other issues which may affect your witness-handling. It is therefore worth practising your question formulation skills, to try to ensure that you get into a habit of not leading the witness. It is certainly useful to conduct short simple drills with other students to get into the habit of asking open and closed questions, and leading and non-leading questions. A good exercise is simply to challenge the other person to get an account of what you have been doing in the last 24 hours without asking any leading questions, or to find out where you purchased your clothes, but using primarily leading questions. Drills such as these can enhance your questioning skills, so that you can start to move on to more interesting aspects of presenting your case.

Different styles for different witnesses

You must bear in mind that there is no such thing as The Witness. Each witness will be different. Some witnesses will be confident, others will be timid. You may find that you need to rein back confident witnesses, so that you can ensure that they give a full account of each of the points that you have prepared. Conversely, you may need to prompt timid witnesses, encouraging them to expand on their testimony or indicating that they can move on to the next point: 'How did you feel at this point?' 'What happened next?'

One advantage of professional witnesses, such as police officers, who are used to giving evidence in court, is that they will often be able to give a clear, succinct account of events with minimal prompting.[21] With a witness of this type, you may decide to allow them to give their version of events with relatively few interruptions, and then to go back over the details in closer focus. This enables you to ask clearly pointed questions without leading, as the factual evidence has already been adduced:

> Officer, you have said that the car was parked on the far side of the street. Are you able to recall the colour of the vehicle?

> When you said earlier that the defendant, Mr Smith, appeared to you to be drunk, could you tell the court what made you come to that conclusion?

You should not assume that class, education or gender have any particular bearing on the likely behaviour of a witness. The challenge of witness-handling arises precisely because each witness is an individual and may react to questioning in any number of different ways. You need to ensure that your preparation is flexible enough to take this variety of response into account.

An aside: hostile witnesses

You may sometimes find that a witness whom you have called to give evidence in support of your case does not give the evidence that you expect when they are in the witness box. There is a common student belief that any such witness must be a 'hostile' witness. This is not the case. It is only too often the case that witnesses fail to give the evidence that you had expected; this may be for any number of reasons. It may be that the original statement which was taken from them was ambiguous or inaccurate; they may have changed their mind about what occurred; they may have forgotten what happened. None of this makes the witness 'hostile'; they are simply referred to as a witness who has failed to 'come up to proof'. You must simply consider whether you can salvage the point via a different witness.

A hostile witness is a witness who displays 'a hostile animus to the party calling him' – a witness who makes clear that he or she is not 'desirous of telling the truth'. The normal procedure, therefore, is to establish as clearly as you can that this is a witness who is now lying in order to damage your case. You will generally need to put their previous inconsistent statement to them, to ask if this earlier statement is one that they made, and to ask them to account for their change of story. If the witness persists in their

---

21 In criminal trials, police officers will often be permitted to use their notebooks to give evidence from, provided that the notes were written up substantially contemporaneously with the events.

changed version of events, and it is clear from their manner that they are doing so with hostile intent, you may ask the court for permission to have the witness treated as hostile. If the court gives leave, you may then cross-examine the witness just as you would any witness called by the other side. However, having a witness declared hostile is very much the last step; it rarely achieves much. At best, it may help you to salvage part of your case, but it is unlikely to enable you to advance your case in any way. The examination of a hostile witness is not, therefore, an exception to the rule that you cannot ask leading questions in examination-in-chief; you are permitted to ask leading questions of a hostile witness only because you are now cross-examining that witness.

Getting started

Often the hardest stage in your examination-in-chief is to get the witness started. It is customary to ask a few questions to 'settle' the witness in the witness box, such as their name, age, occupation and so on.[22] If the matters are not in issue between the parties, you may be permitted to lead the witness on introductory material:

> Now, Mrs Smith, it is not in issue that you were in the Coach and Horses on the evening of the 21st. That's right, isn't it?
>
> And I understand that you had arrived in the public house at about 6 o'clock that evening, is that the case?
>
> Did you have much to drink that evening?
>
> And can you tell the court in your own words what happened later that evening in the Coach and Horses?

The first two questions are clearly leading questions. The third question is leading only to the extent that it presupposes that Mrs Smith was drinking during the evening. In practice, it is unlikely to be objectionable. The final question is open and non-leading, as the advocate steers the witness towards the area where the facts are likely to be disputed. Note, however, that if you are leading your witness in this way, you may want to acknowledge the fact to the court:

> Your Honour, these matters are not in dispute.
>
> Your Honour, my learned friend has kindly indicated that I may lead on these matters.

Even if matters are not in dispute, however, you should consider whether you wish to lead the witness. Remember that the objection to leading the witness is that it makes it appear that the advocate is giving the evidence rather than the witness. You may do better to ask the witness open, non-leading questions in order to ensure that the evidence is seen as coming from them, and given greater weight by the court as a result.

There may be some cases, however, where you are told that you cannot lead the witness at all. In such a case, having settled the witness, one suggestion is to ask the witness why they are in court.

---

22 Guidance (unreported) suggested that witnesses in criminal cases should not normally be asked to give their addresses in open court. However, in many courts, this continues to be common practice.

Q: Mrs Smith, do you know why you have been asked to come to court today?

A: To give evidence.

Q: To give evidence about what?

A: About the fight at the Coach and Horses.

Q: And can you remember the date when this fight took place?

Q: I think it was 21 May.

Q: And who was involved in the fight?

A: John Rogers and Martin Smith.

Scene-setting

In this chapter, we have focused on the need to identify clearly exactly what evidence you need to adduce from the witness, and which issues are in dispute. However, you should not overlook the need to ensure that the witness is given an opportunity to set the scene. If you fail to do this, you will find that you need to deal with the issues later, and you may end up destroying the flow, and thus the impact, of your examination of the witness.

Consider the following extract from the middle of an examination-in-chief:

Q: And what happened next?

A: Martin came towards John Rogers. He had his fist raised and he was shouting something.

Q: And what happened then?

A: Well, John got up from the table and he shouted something at Martin Smith.

Q: And what did Mr Smith do?

A: He just lashed out.

Q: At whom did he lash out?

A: John.

Q: And did he make contact with Mr Rogers?

A: Yeah, John fell over. I think Martin got him in the face.

Q: Now where was Mr Smith standing in relation to you?

A: He was over by the table. I was by the bar.

Q: And where was the table in relation to the bar?

A: It was over the far side of the room.

Q: And how far away was that?

A: About 20 feet.

Q: And how many people were there in between yourself and Mr Smith?

A: Not many. Maybe five or six.

You can see how the advocate has to break off from the action that the witness is describing in order to establish the general layout of the bar and the position of the parties. This is necessary so that the advocate can then explore how much the witness could see from her position, and what she could have heard from there. It would have been better to establish this basic scene-setting information early in the examination-in-chief so that the later examination could then proceed uninterrupted, referring back to the earlier evidence where necessary:

Now you said earlier that you were about 20 feet away from Martin Smith. Could you hear what he said at this point?

You said earlier that there were no more than five or six people between you and Martin Smith. Was your view obstructed in any way at this point?

Scene-setting, of course, may also extend to establishing the wider background to events. You may want to establish the witness's relationship with the other participants at an early point:

Q: Can I ask you, what is your relationship with John Rogers?

A: We are friends.

Q: How long have you known Mr Rogers?

A: We were at school together.

Q: And were you friends at that point?

A: Yes.

Q: And what is your relationship with Martin Smith?

A: We work together.

Q: He is your colleague?

A: Not really. He's in a different department from me.

Q: And how would you describe your relationship?

A: It's OK. I know the man. Nothing special.

Guiding the witness: piggy-backing

Piggy-backing is a technique for guiding the witness without resorting to leading questions. It is a simple technique and must not be overused, as it is, of its nature, repetitive.

Piggy-backing involves taking the witness's previous reply and incorporating it into the next question. Thus:

Q: What happened next?

A: I answered the door.

Q: And when you answered the door, what did you see?

A: There was a man standing on the mat outside.

Q: And what did the man do?

A: He threatened to hit me in the face.

Q: And when he threatened to hit you in the face, how did you feel?

...

You can see why you would not want to conduct your whole examination-in-chief by way of piggy-backing, but it is a useful technique for controlling the witness and ensuring that the evidence is produced in the sequence which you wish.

Advocacy and witness statements

In criminal cases, there were until recently quite strict rules about the use of memory-refreshing documents. These have now been relaxed and a witness will be permitted to refresh his or her memory of the matter from a document made or verified by them at an earlier time if they confirm in their evidence that the document records their recollection at that earlier time when their recollection is likely to have been significantly better than it is now.[23]

In civil cases, witness statements will normally have been exchanged prior to trial and, indeed, your witness's statement will normally stand in for their examination-in-chief. Any material on which you wish to rely will need to be included in that statement. The issue of memory-refreshing does not, therefore, arise in the same way.

Professional conduct issues and examination-in-chief

Witnesses who give inconsistent evidence

The key professional conduct requirement is that you must not mislead the court. What, then, is the position if you believe, as an advocate, that your witness is misleading the court by putting forward a false account?

The starting point is that it is for the court to decide where the truth lies. Witnesses may change their accounts for any number of reasons, many of which may be entirely honest. If your client, or any other witness, changes their account in a significant manner, you will need to inquire into why they are making the changes. If your witness makes clear that they are changing their account in order to mislead the court, you cannot call that witness. If the witness is your client and they insist on testifying, you will have to withdraw from the case. However, in most cases, clients and other witnesses do not make clear that they are intending to lie to the court, and you are left uncertain as to whether their new account is true. You will need to put the changes to them, and to emphasise the duty of honesty to the court. Ultimately, however, the issue of their truth or otherwise is a matter for the court and you can continue to act, notwithstanding your suspicions.

Similarly, if your witness changes their account while they are giving evidence, you may need to ask for a short adjournment to talk to your witness about the reason for the change. Again, if they were to admit that they have misled the court, you would have to require them to put the correct facts to the court when they commenced their testimony. If they refused to do so, you would have to withdraw from the case.

Coaching the witness

Solicitors have always been able to take statements from witnesses, even when the solicitor would later be appearing as the advocate in the case. Traditionally, barristers would rely upon solicitors to take statements for them, and there was, therefore, a rule of conduct which made clear that barristers should not normally have contact with witnesses of fact, other than the client in the case. This rule has been changed, and barristers may now have contact with all witnesses in the case. However, whether it is a barrister or solicitor who is appearing as advocate in the case, the advocate must be careful to ensure that he or she is not coaching the witness in any way. Because of the particular pressures of criminal cases, the Bar conduct rules make clear that barristers should not discuss the testimony of any witness with that witness, with the exception of their lay client and any expert or character witnesses.

---

23 Section 139 of the Criminal Justice Act 2003.

Coaching a witness does not simply mean telling the witness what to say. It includes coaching the witness in how to present the material to the court. Finding the dividing line between legitimate clarification of evidence and coaching the witness can be difficult. Similarly, it can be hard to draw a firm line between preparing the witness by explaining what will happen in court, and coaching the witness as to how they should behave while giving their evidence.

Cross-examination

If cross-examination is to be effective, it must be purposeful. It is a common error to believe that you are obliged to cross-examine every witness. Always ask yourself if the witness has said anything that has damaged your case, or if there are any points that you are under a duty to 'put' to the witness. If there are not, what purpose does cross-examination serve? It is better by far to rise briefly to inform the court that you have no cross-examination; it can send out a powerful message that this is a witness whose testimony has been irrelevant to the issues in the case.

Marcus Stone makes the point forcefully:

> Aimless cross-examination wastes time, gains nothing, invites criticism, suggests the absence of a real case, emphasises challenged evidence, elicits harmful testimony, dilutes any gain achieved, or creates new rights to re-examine.
>
> ...
>
> The commonest type of futile cross-examination consists of going over the evidence-in-chief aimlessly, or, perhaps, with the vague hope that some defect will emerge or that it will be changed somehow in going over it again. An aggravation is to delve into pointless detail.[24]

As Stone points out, often the only effect of such aimless cross-examination is to emphasise the harmful evidence which the witness has to give. This is not simply because the witness has the opportunity to repeat the evidence, but also because it may give the witness a chance to adduce further evidence in support of his or her version, hence making a bad point even worse. It is essential, therefore, to have a clear aim in mind before you decide to stand up and to cross-examine the witness.

What, then, is the purpose of cross-examination? Cross-examination has a twofold purpose: it is your opportunity to undermine the evidence of a witness who has been called by the other side; and it is your opportunity to put your case to the witness. In this section, we will look at both aspects of this purpose, starting with the duty to put your case.

Putting your case

This is an aspect of cross-examination which is news to many students. You are under a duty as an advocate to put to any witness for the other side any points where their

---

24 Stone, M, *Cross-Examination in Criminal Trials*, 2nd edn, 1995, London: Butterworths, pp 112–13.

evidence conflicts with the evidence that your witnesses will give.[25] The purpose of this is to ensure that all witnesses have an opportunity to comment on any contradictory evidence that will be given by later witnesses. If you fail to put your case in this way, then, strictly, the court will refuse to permit you to lead the contradictory evidence at the later stage in the trial. Worse still, the court will assume that, since you are a competent advocate and would have put your case, the conflict between the accounts must arise because the later witness is now making up new evidence in the witness box.

Students dislike putting their case, knowing that they are likely to attract only a series of negative responses. They therefore tend to try to ask only one, very long, multiple question – and hence to attract only one 'No'. Or they take refuge by formally signalling that they are only doing their duty and putting their case:

Q: Mr Rogers, I put it to you that you hit my client, Mr Smith.

A: No.

Q: I put it to you that you were angry about his comments about your performance at work.

A: No.

Q: I put it to you that you came over to the table with the intention of hitting him.

A: No.

Q: I put it to you that you then lashed out at him.

A: No.

Q: I put it to you ...

However, it does not have to be done this way, and you do not need to feel that you are losing ground simply because you are faced with a series of negative responses. You must be careful not to descend into arguing with a witness, but you can still put your case in a clear, forceful way which indicates real confidence in the version of events that you are putting forward:

Q: Mr Rogers, you hit my client, didn't you?

A: No.

Q: You work together, don't you?

A: Yes.

Q: And you knew that he had been making comments about your poor performance at work.

A: No.

Q: Mr Rogers, you knew he had been making comments about your performance and you came over to the table with the intention of hitting him, didn't you?

A: No.

Q: You came over to the table and you lashed out at him.

A: No.

---

25 Strictly, the requirement to put your case does not arise in the magistrates' court: *O'Connell v Adams* [1973] Crim LR 113. This is because many defendants in the magistrates' court are unrepresented and are, therefore, unable to put their case. Where you appear as an advocate, however, it is good practice to put your case. It is in any event a tactically wise step, since it ensures that your version of events is in front of the court at an early stage in the proceedings.

You must make sure that you put your case, but you need not feel that you are losing ground while you do so.

Undermining the witness

Your only duty in your cross-examination is to put your case. If you put your case to the witness, you are fully entitled to sit down and to do no more. However, if you do this, you are losing the opportunity to try to undermine the testimony that the witness has given. You may have formally challenged aspects of its accuracy, but you have done nothing more than to make a bare denial.

The view of cross-examination which tends to be expressed in films and television shows is of the devastating sequence of questions which so clearly demonstrates that the witness is lying that the witness breaks down in the witness box and admits the untruth. You need to recognise that this is not going to happen in reality. You are rarely going to expose the witness unequivocally as a liar; instead, you are aiming to explore the limits of the witness's testimony, to identify inconsistencies, areas of uncertainty, errors and omissions. In short, you are gathering material for your closing speech, in which you will be able to tell the court and the jury why they should approach the witness's evidence with extreme caution, or should discount it altogether.

Just as there are different types of witness who you will have to guide through their evidence-in-chief, so, too, you will encounter many different kinds of witness in cross-examination. It is true that some witnesses will have come to court with a false account. With such witnesses, you will often find that profitable cross-examination explores the details of the account, since no fabricated version of events can ever be entirely internally consistent once the witness is moved away from their prepared account.

Equally, however, you may be cross-examining witnesses who are entirely honest, but who are mistaken. One of the most difficult areas in criminal evidence concerns the status of visual identification. Humans have a generally poor ability to recognise faces, but, more dangerously, many of us do not realise that we are limited in this ability. A number of miscarriage of justice cases arose where innocent people were convicted on the testimony of honest witnesses who were simply mistaken in their identification. Because the witnesses were honest, it was, of course, very difficult to shake their testimony in cross-examination. As a result, the Turnbull guidelines were laid down.[26] The guidelines require the judge in criminal cases to withdraw the case from the jury where it is a case which rests substantially on identification evidence, if it becomes clear that the quality of the identification is poor and there is little or no other evidence supporting the correctness of the identification. In every identification case the judge will, in any event, give the jury a direction, warning them of the dangers of honest but mistaken identification, and identifying for the jury those aspects of the identification which may make it more or less reliable. Thus, for example, the jury must consider the length of the original sighting by the witness, the distance, the lighting, whether there were any impediments and so on, as well as the circumstances of the subsequent identification. When you are conducting your cross-examination, you must bear in

---

26   *R v Turnbull* [1977] QB 224.

mind the possibility that the witness is honest but mistaken, and you will need to adjust your approach to explore how the mistake could have arisen.

Must cross-examination be cross?

It is a common misapprehension to think that your cross-examination must be aggressive. It is true that there may sometimes be tactical advantages in attacking a witness and seeking to intimidate them. However, you must consider what effect this behaviour is likely to have on the court; will the judge or jury simply conclude that you are bullying the witness, and will their sympathies switch to the witness as a result?

Aggression is a tactic, and it needs to be used with caution. You must always remember that even the other side's witnesses may have evidence which can help your case – 'good facts' – and you will often be able to lull a witness into a false sense of security by starting your cross-examination with a series of questions with which you know that the witness will agree, before you change tack and start to deal with those matters that are in dispute. Similarly, where you are dealing with an honest, but mistaken witness, there is nothing to be gained by attacking the witness's integrity. They are not giving false evidence – they are mistaken – and it is the basis for their error that you are seeking to expose.

Finally, unvarying aggression is tiring to listen to – as is any advocacy which is conducted at a single pitch. You must keep in mind that your cross-examination is directed not simply at the witness, but at the court as well. You must keep the attention of the court, and this will often call for a variety of different approaches to the witness, with appropriate variations in tone.

Formulating questions in cross-examination

It is sometimes said that, in contrast to examination-in-chief, in cross-examination you must lead the witness. This is not entirely the case: even in cross-examination, it is better that the witness gives the evidence themselves. However, it indicates the high level of control of the witness which should be employed in cross-examination. This is achieved by asking closed questions.

A closed question is one which permits only a limited answer. 'Why did you hit him?' is an open question, because it permits the witness freedom to give a full explanation in whatever terms they wish. 'You hit him because you hated him, didn't you?' is a closed question: the witness can only answer yes or no.

The easiest way to formulate a closed question is to phrase the question by way of a statement. If you want to put to the witness that they went to a certain place by car, you can simply say: 'You went by car?' Similarly, if you want to put the fact that they hit the victim because they were angry, you can again make an interrogative statement: 'You hit him because you were angry?' If you want to make clear that the statement is interrogative, you can turn it into a question by simply adding the words: '... didn't you?' Thus, 'You hit him because you were angry, didn't you?'

If you bear in mind Stone's comments (discussed above) on the danger that cross-examination can simply permit a witness to repeat and reinforce earlier testimony, you can see that you need to be able to limit the witness's replies. Indeed, you will sometimes hear advocates instructing witnesses that they are to answer all questions with a simple yes or no. This obviously ensures that the witness is kept on a very tight rein, but it can also look as if the advocate is worried about what the witness might say and is attempting to keep the truth from the court. (You must also remember that if you are taking this approach, you must phrase all your questions in such a way that they can be answered yes or no. It is no good directing the witness to answer yes or no, and then asking the witness what their date of birth is.)

However, although a series of closed direct questions will control the witness, it can become monotonous. It is an effective way of putting your case, but it is not always the most effective way of seeking to explore the witness's testimony. It is often said that you should not ask a question in cross-examination to which you do not know the answer, but this is a useful warning which you may have to disregard on occasion if you are to identify with precision what the witness could perceive. There may, therefore, come a point in your cross-examination where you need to be prepared to ask an open question. However, this is potentially dangerous. In the following example, the advocate wants to be able to put to the witness that he was too far away to see clearly what happened to the victim:

> **Q:** So how close were you to the fight, Mr Edwards?
>
> **A:** Close enough to get spattered with blood.

Before you ask the open question, you should try to approach the matter carefully to try to limit the damage that an unexpected answer could cause:

> **Q:** You have said that you were standing next to the table?
>
> **A:** Yes.
>
> **Q:** And this was the table that Mr Smith was sitting at?
>
> **A:** Yes.
>
> **Q:** And the bar was at this point relatively empty?
>
> **A:** No, it was quite full.
>
> **Q:** So there were a number of people standing around the table?
>
> **A:** Quite a few.
>
> **Q:** Roughly how many?
>
> **A:** I don't know.
>
> **Q:** Five?
>
> **A:** No. More.
>
> **Q:** As many as 10?
>
> **A:** Possibly.
>
> **Q:** And the table is a small circular pub table, is it?
>
> **A:** Yes.
>
> **Q:** You have said that Mr Smith was sitting next to where you were standing. Mr Rogers came from the bar, didn't he? On the far side of the table?
>
> **A:** Yes, but he came round to talk to Mr Smith.
>
> **Q:** And when Mr Smith stood up, was his back to you or was he facing you?
>
> **A:** His back was to me.

In this example, although the process has taken longer, the advocate has taken the cross-examination one point at a time to establish a setting. In reply to the penultimate question, the witness makes clear that, because Rogers came round the table, he must have been close to the witness. The advocate does not, therefore, need to ask an open question about what the witness could see. Instead, the advocate adjusts the line of attack and starts to explore the possibility that perhaps Smith himself might have been standing in between the witness and Rogers and, therefore, blocking his view. (It should also be noted that the advocate has still managed to obtain useful information for a closing speech. It may be possible to argue that the number of people standing around such a small table meant that there was inevitably some degree of confusion, and some interference with what the witness could see.)

It is important in your cross-examination to be able to judge when to be persistent and when to abandon a point which is going nowhere. In the preceding example, note that the advocate persists in trying to get an estimate of the number of people in the immediate vicinity of the fight. You will often find that witnesses are unco-operative and you will need to press them in order to obtain the information which you need.

Controlling the witness – never argue, never debate

If you start to argue with a witness, you surrender your position of control. You may wish to put facts to the witness, and sometimes you will need to put them forcefully, but you do not argue with the witness. One of the most common ways of getting drawn into an argument or debate is to react to a question from the witness:

> **Q:** When you got to the Coach and Horses you went over to my client, didn't you?
>
> **A:** Is that what he says?

or:

> **A:** Why shouldn't I?

Don't answer back. Persist with your question:

> **Q:** Could you please answer my question, Mr Edwards. Did you go over to my client?'

Keith Evans[27] makes the point that, if you are to have the court trust you, you must take on the role of the honest guide, leading the court towards the true version of events. If you argue with the witness, you abandon this role.

Listening to the answers

As with examination-in-chief, you can find yourself so wrapped up in formulating your next question for your cross-examination that you neglect to listen to the answers that the witness is giving you. This may not be so critical when you are simply focusing on putting your case to the witness. However, it is essential that you listen to the answers when you are asking questions that are testing the witness's perceptions in an attempt to weaken or undermine the testimony:

> **Q:** From your position beside the table, you must have found that when Mr Smith stood up, his body was between you and Mr Rogers.
>
> **A:** Yes. But I could see over his shoulder.

---

27   *Op cit*, Evans, fn 6, pp 109–10.

Q: But you accept that your view was obstructed?

A: I had a fairly good view.

Q: Fairly good?

A: I could see most of what was happening.

The advocate has listened to the answer 'I had a fairly good view' and has picked up on the qualifying adjective 'fairly'. When the answer is repeated back, the witness again qualifies the answer: 'I could see most of what was happening.' At this stage, the advocate can then take a decision to leave the matter alone and reserve the point for the closing speech ('Members of the jury, consider the evidence of Mr Edwards. What was it that he told you about what he could see? He said he had a "fairly" good view. And when I put this to him, he said that he could see "most" of what happened. But, of course, necessarily, he is accepting that he could not see everything. He cannot say that he may not have missed something of significance. This is not a criticism of Mr Edwards. He has, after all, come to court today to tell you what he could see. And inevitably, because of where Mr Smith and Mr Rogers were standing, Mr Smith's body was in the way; it partially blocked Mr Edwards' view'). Alternatively, you may decide, as the advocate, to pursue the point a little further, to see if you can get any further admission from the witness.

The extract is also a good example of the way that you need to listen and to think about what you have heard. You need to try to assess the probability of the version that the witness is putting forward – whether they are (in your estimation) an honest or dishonest witness – and you need to consider whether there are inconsistencies:

Q: Now, Mr Edwards, you told the court earlier that there were a number of people standing around the table?

A: Yes.

Q: Perhaps as many as 10 people?

A: Could be.

Q: It could be. And you also said that Mr Smith pushed Mr Rogers, didn't he?

A: Yes, he did.

Q: And he pushed him away from the table, didn't he?

A: Yes. Towards the bar.

Q: So the other people who were standing up, I suppose they had to get out of the way quickly?

A: Oh yes, they were all trying to get out of the way.

Q: What had happened was very unexpected?

A: Well, yes.

Q: It would be fair to say that there was some confusion then?

A: Some.

Q: And all these people were milling around as they attempted to get out of the way?

A: To some extent, yes. It all happened very quickly.

The advocate does not know the answer to many of these questions, and so breaks down the cross-examination into small steps, using fully the answers that he or she has obtained from the witness earlier. However, the advocate has tried to think about the implications of those answers, in this case by visualising the situation that the witness has described. There is a table with a number of people standing around it. A fight breaks out. It is likely that any bystander will find their view at least partially obstructed by either the participants or the other onlookers. The advocate's questions, therefore, explore this probability, with the intention of using the admissions as means of gently undermining the witness's credibility as a person who saw 'the whole thing'.

Going for the kill?

Perhaps because we are so used to thinking of cross-examination as a process which must lead to some dramatic breakdown by the witness in the witness box, there tends to be a belief that cross-examination must contain a 'killer punch' if it is to be adjudged a success. Often, however, it is the attempt to deliver a killer punch that will let the witness off the hook.

The question too far

Every advocate in practice will have tales of questions too far that they have heard. The 'question too far' arises where the advocate has, by fortune or hard work, manoeuvred the witness into a position where it looks as if the witness is going to have to admit some fact which is very damaging to the evidence that he or she has been giving. Thus, for example, the defendant has been charged with robbery. The case is that a man wearing a red boiler suit held up a post office using a sawn-off shotgun. The officer who conducted the search of the defendant's flat gives evidence that a boiler suit was found during the search. In cross-examination, the advocate takes issue with the point:

Q: Now officer, you say that you found this boiler suit in my client's wardrobe, is that correct?

A: Yes.

Q: And what did my client say when you found the boiler suit?

A: He said, 'Yes, that's mine'.

Q: And I believe that you told us that the boiler suit that was worn during the robbery was a red colour?

A: Yes, sir.

Q: And what was the colour of the boiler suit that you found in my client's flat when you conducted your search?

A: It was blue in colour, sir.

This is the point to terminate the cross-examination. The point is entirely clear. In the closing speech, the advocate will reiterate the point that the boiler suit that was found in the search is clearly not the boiler suit that was used in the robbery and, hence, weakens the prosecution case that it was this person who committed the crime.

However, for many advocates, the temptation to go further and to deliver the knock out punch is irresistible:

Q: So let us be clear about this please, officer, you did not find a red boiler suit when you searched my client's flat, did you?

A: No sir, we found the red boiler suit in his locker at work.

All the extra question has done is to give the witness an opportunity to salvage the point.

A similar form of the same mistake is to give the witness an opportunity to explain why he or she acted in an apparently unlikely way:

Q: You have said that your assailant was over six feet tall?

A: Yes.

Q: And that he had a weapon in his right hand?

A: Yes.

Q: A length of metal piping, I think you told this court?

A: Yes.

Q: And that he was waving this around over his head?

A: Yes.

Q: Understandably, you have said that this was very frightening?

A: Very.

Q: Because you felt that you were personally at risk?

A: Yes.

Q: Then why did you run towards this person? Wouldn't you wish to run away from him?

A: He was standing in front of the only exit.

It doesn't matter how much preparation you have done in trying to shut down all the possible answers that the witness could give. If you ask a 'why' question in this way, you will almost invariably give the witness the opportunity to explain away the apparent inconsistency that you have created.

Closing the gate

The exception to the 'don't ask the question too far' principle arises where you have evidence which clearly controverts the version of events which the witness is putting to the court. The starting point for this may arise from a relatively minor discrepancy, but by slowly closing the gate on the witness, you ask for more and more detail from the witness until it comes to a point where the only explanation for the witness's account is that he or she is lying.

Thus, in a case where you have a copy of the witness's criminal record, and this indicates that the witness was convicted of drink driving six months ago and disqualified from driving for one year, the witness lets drop that they had parked their car round the corner from work. Rather than immediately confronting the witness with this fact, the advocate works at getting more information from the witness with a series of apparently innocuous questions:

Q: And where do you work, Mr Edwards?

A: Bligh and Co.

Q: And they are civil engineers, is that correct?

A: Yes.

Q: And where are the offices where you work?

A: College Street.

Q: But you are unable to park in College Street?

A: No. It's normally absolutely full.

Q: And so you park around the corner, as you have told us?

A: Yes.

Q: And this is what you did last month, on the day in question?

A: Yes.

Q: Do you drive to work alone, or do you give anyone else a lift?

A: No. I drive to work alone.

Q: And you drive to work regularly, do you?

A: Yes.

Q: And that is why you are so sure that you drove to work on the day in question?

A: Yes.

Q: You have no doubts about that?

A: No.

The advocate has now painted the witness into a corner. There is no way that the witness can now turn around and suggest either that he did not drive to work on that particular day, or that he took the car to work and some other person drove. If the advocate wishes, he or she can now proceed with a line of questioning which establishes that the witness appreciates the importance of honesty in giving evidence, and that the witness regards himself as law-abiding and trustworthy, before proceeding to confirm that the witness was disqualified from driving at the time that he claims to have driven.

Re-examination

You are entitled to re-examine your own witnesses after they have been cross-examined. However, re-examination, whether in civil or criminal cases, is not a second opportunity to adduce evidence-in-chief. Re-examination is an opportunity to deal with matters which have been raised in cross-examination, where you may wish to see if you can clarify the evidence that your witness has given. Primarily, then, the purpose of re-examination is to repair any damage that has been done. For this reason, it is often said that you should avoid re-examination if at all possible, so as to send out the message that the cross-examination has achieved nothing of consequence.

There will, however, be times where there are matters from the cross-examination which you feel can effectively be neutralised. The opposing advocate may, for example, have produced an apparent inconsistency which you believe you can resolve:

Q: Mr Edwards, you told this court in cross-examination that your view was 'fairly' good?

A: Yes.

Q: And yet you also told the court that there were a large number of people standing around the table at the time of the fight?

A: There were.

Q: So could you explain how you had such a good view?

A: I stood on a chair.

Bear in mind that re-examination is subject to the same rules as examination-in-chief; in other words, you may not lead your witness, and that you are only permitted to raise matters in re-examination which have been dealt with in cross-examination. If you have simply forgotten to deal with something in your examination-in-chief, you will not be able to raise the issue in re-examination unless it is something that the other party has raised during its cross-examination of your witness.

It is worth noting that, in civil litigation, because of the tendency for witness statements to stand in for the examination-in-chief, re-examination is becoming increasingly significant. It is the only opportunity for you to ensure that your witness adduces the evidence that you wish by way of testimony, rather than on paper. However, the rule still remains that you may only re-examine on matters raised in cross-examination. You must also understand that the court will not appreciate your using your re-examination simply to reiterate matters that were already set out in the witness statement, and in these days of interventionist trial management, the judge will let you know this. Make sure, therefore, that you use the re-examination to achieve a limited number of clear objectives that arise from the cross-examination. And if you find, on reflection, that there are no matters that need clarification or repair, don't re-examine.

CONCLUSION

Advocacy can appear the most daunting of the legal skills. It leaves the student exposed in a way unlike any other skill. However, the skill of advocacy brings together all the other legal skills from this book. It is your initial interviewing of the client, your fact finding and your legal research which will determine the factual and legal basis for the case that you will be presenting in court. Your writing and drafting, whether of letters of advice or the formal pleadings (or, in criminal cases, the indictment or the defence statement), will determine the matters that the court is to consider. Your advocacy is then the key skill which brings together all your preceding preparation and presents your case to the court, whether by way of speeches and submissions, or through the controlled testimony of witnesses.

Preparation is at the heart of advocacy, and it is easy to become so obsessed by the rules that prohibit leading questions in examination-in-chief, or which propose that you should only ask closed questions in your cross-examination, that you overlook the role that preparation – and, in particular, good case analysis – must play in helping you to comply with these principles. A good advocate must have good presentation skills, but you must never forget that this most courtroom-based of skills is rooted in the work that you undertake outside the courtroom. If you prepare your case with your advocacy in mind, your preparation will benefit, and your advocacy will be immeasurably enhanced.

FURTHER READING

Boon, A, *Advocacy*, 2nd edn, 1999, London: Cavendish Publishing.

Foster, C *et al*, *Civil Advocacy: A Practical Guide*, 2nd edn, 2001, London: Cavendish Publishing.

Evans, K, *The Golden Rules of Advocacy*, 1993, London: Blackstone.

Evans, K, *Advocacy in Court*, 2nd edn, 1995, London: Blackstone.

Munkman, J, *The Technique of Advocacy*, 1991, London: Butterworths.

Shaw, N, *Effective Advocacy*, 1996, London: Sweet & Maxwell.

Stone, M, *Cross-Examination in Criminal Trials*, 2nd edn, 1995, London: Butterworths.

CHAPTER 8

INTERVIEWING/CONFERENCING SKILLS

INTRODUCTION

Every lawyer will conduct an interview at some point during his or her working life and, therefore, both the Law Society and the Bar Council require students studying the relevant vocational course to undertake some interviewing training. Even though there are certain differences between a solicitor's interview and a barrister's conference (the term used to describe a barrister's interview with a client) the basic skills required for a successful interview are the same and, therefore, they can both be dealt with together.

As a skill, interviewing is not something that can be learned completely from reading a textbook or cramming the day before an assessment takes place. The best way to learn the skill of interviewing is through practice. However, certain steps can be taken to improve an interviewer's performance and this chapter will aim to identify these steps.

Why hold an interview?

Interviews are held for three main reasons:

(a) so that the client can inform the lawyer about a legal problem and obtain advice;

(b) so that the lawyer can elicit the relevant information from the client about his or her case in order to assess the legal position;

(c) so that the lawyer can advise the client as to an appropriate course of action.

Where are the interviews held?

The location of a client interview often depends upon the type of work that a lawyer specialises in. Lawyers who specialise in criminal litigation may conduct the majority of their interviews in police stations, prisons, or in the cells attached to courts. Those who primarily deal with non-contentious matters, however, may find that they rarely conduct interviews outside their own office. Of course, whether lawyers are in the comfort of their own offices or in a prison, they must be flexible and able to adapt their interview technique to any given situation.

PREPARATION FOR THE INTERVIEW

The importance of interview preparation cannot be overemphasised. Although the level of preparation will differ, depending upon the experience of the lawyer and the stage of the legal proceedings, no lawyer should conduct an interview without performing some preparatory work. Without careful planning, the lawyer cannot hope to achieve a successful outcome to the interview.

When preparing for an interview, care should be taken to ensure that you create a good first impression with the client. If the interview is being conducted in your own office, some thought should be given to the way that the interview room is organised.

It is important to ensure that there is adequate seating available for those attending the interview and that sufficient time has been set aside for the meeting, which is free from interruption. You should also plan carefully to ensure that all the papers required for the interview are with you and within easy reach. In some situations, leaving the interview room will be unavoidable, but forgetting to take some key papers to an interview can leave a lasting impression on the client.[1] Finally, and most importantly of all, you should have spent some time before the interview drafting an interview plan.

The interview plan

There are a number of reasons why it is necessary to draft an interview plan. It will focus your mind on the forthcoming meeting and will assist you in adopting an appropriate structure for the interview. The plan should, at the very least, consist of a list of the areas for questioning, though not the questions themselves. Lawyers, especially those who have had limited interviewing experience, may find that an interview checklist can be helpful to jog the memory during an interview and, in the eyes of the client, you will seem efficient and well prepared. Sample interview plans can be found at the end of this chapter.

Structure

A well structured interview will always run a great deal more smoothly than one which is not and, although a good structure will not guarantee interviewing success, it will certainly put a student on the right track. When an interview is well structured, each party to the interview will benefit. The lawyer will benefit because he or she will find it easier to obtain the relevant information and an interview which deals with the issues in a sensible order will take less time than an interview which jumps from one point to another. The client will also feel more secure knowing that their legal concern is in the hands of an individual who is both organised and professional.

Preparation and planning should help a lawyer to determine what the structure of an interview will be, and although it will be helpful to know what the client's problem relates to, a lack of knowledge on this issue should not preclude a good structure being worked out beforehand.

Normally, an interview should start with an introduction, which will deal with the preliminaries to the interview; move on to the main body of the interview, where the lawyer will ask relevant questions about the client's legal concern and provide advice; and end with a conclusion. Each of these will be examined in greater detail.

THE INTRODUCTION

As previously stated, first impressions are lasting and, therefore, it is important that the lawyer makes a good impression with a client from the outset. You should make an

---

1   It is worth noting that a barrister will rarely conduct an interview without the client's solicitor being present. Therefore, poor preparation can leave an indelible mark on the instructing solicitor!

effort to greet the client by their name, introduce yourself and explain your role. When clients meet a lawyer for the first time, they are often nervous and, therefore, it is important to put them at ease at the earliest opportunity. Some lawyers choose to greet their client at the door and show them to their seat; others may find that offering a cigarette or some sweets may make a young offender feel comfortable. This will help the parties build a rapport, which can assist the interview process. Before actually getting down to the content of the interview it may be worthwhile engaging clients in some 'ice-breaking' conversation that is unrelated to their case, to help them settle. For example, asking the client if they found the office or chambers easily, or how they heard about your law firm.

During the introduction, you should take time to explain to the client the purpose of the interview and also set an agenda that explains its proposed structure. This will help to reassure the client and let them know what to expect from the meeting.

Questions from the client

It is common for a client to want to ask a number of questions at the start of the interview. Often, students will be told that they should control a client from the outset, which can lead to a student telling the client that all questions will be dealt with at the end of the interview. This can lead to problems. First, a client may forget to ask the question at the end of the interview. Secondly, by not asking the question, the client may be so preoccupied with trying to remember the question that they do not relax. Thirdly, and perhaps most importantly, it may give a client the impression that they should not ask the lawyer to clarify a point that they do not understand. This should never be allowed to happen.

A better formula to adopt would be to inform the client at the start of the interview that there will be an opportunity to ask questions at the end, but that if they wish to ask a question at any stage, they must feel free to do so. It may be that the question will be answered as the interview progresses or that the answer cannot be given until the client has provided some information on the issue. If either of these is the case, then the client should be told that the question will be answered a little later, or that more information is required before the answer is given. For example, it is common for criminal clients to ask at the beginning of an interview whether they should plead guilty. Until the lawyer has heard the client's version of events, it would be unwise to respond, as this may upset the structure of the interview and may lead to advice being given before the lawyer is in possession of all of the facts.

Personal details

Usually one of the first steps a lawyer takes in an interview is to record the client's personal details. Solicitors will spend a significant part of the first interview doing this, usually by completing a pre-printed form that can then be attached to the file or by typing the information into a case management system on a computer. Equally, a barrister, while in conference, will spend a few moments checking the client's personal information held on file. It is important that the lawyer has a record of the client's name, address, contact telephone number and, depending upon the situation, a client's employment details, family situation and relevant financial information. If the lawyer has not seen the client for a while, it may be wise to check that the information on file is up to date. The client may have recently moved, have a new job or be recently divorced.

Once these details have been either checked or taken, the lawyer can proceed with the main body of the interview.

THE MAIN BODY OF THE INTERVIEW

The main body of an interview presents an opportunity for the lawyer to question the client in detail about his or her legal concerns. When dealing with the issues that are raised by the client, the lawyer should try to deal with the various issues chronologically and deal fully with each area before moving on to another. This should prevent a client from becoming confused.

Questioning techniques

There are a variety of questioning techniques that can be used when trying to obtain information from your client. These are outlined below.

Yes/no questions

Asking what are known as yes/no questions can be the simplest way of eliciting information from a client, as the answers to the questions are either 'Yes' or 'No'. Some examples of yes/no questions are:

Is your name John Brown?

Do you live at St James' House, London?

Do you have a daughter called Elizabeth?

Have you seen Elizabeth recently?

These questions are designed so that only an affirmative or a negative can be given. They are sometimes used when the lawyer wishes to go through basic information quickly, such as the client's address or family situation. These questions can also be useful when the client is talking too much and the lawyer wishes to move on to deal with another issue. However, yes/no questions can lead to a client not telling the lawyer about some piece of information that is highly relevant to their case. For example:

Q: Did you see Mr Brown before you noticed the fire?

A: No.

This answer has concealed the fact that the client's partner saw Mr Brown before the fire broke out and he was acting suspiciously. Consequently, yes/no questions are best used when clarifying information, as opposed to obtaining it.

Closed questions

Closed questions significantly restrict the answer that a client can give. Examples include:

> What is your name?
>
> Where do you live?
>
> How many cars do you own?

Closed questions can be used in conjunction with yes/no questions to elicit either basic or personal information very quickly. Again, however, as they restrict what the client can say, they can have the disadvantage of preventing useful information from surfacing.

Open questions

Open questions give the client the widest possible choice of answers, because they do not limit the response. Examples include:

> Why were you walking the streets of Newcastle at 2.00 am in the morning?
>
> What was your relationship with Mrs Hutchinson like?
>
> Why do you think that Mr Cross took such a dislike to you?

The advantage of open questions is that they allow a client to talk, which can help them to settle into an interview more easily. Clients often need this opportunity to get a version of events off their chests and, in doing so, may mention something which is important to their case. Unfortunately, open questions have the disadvantage in that there is no way to control what the client says and the lawyer could be inundated with irrelevant information, leading to a more protracted interview where note taking is difficult.

Which type of questioning technique should be used?

No interviewer will ever use just one type of questioning technique, and the best interviews will often contain a combination of them all. The type of questions that a lawyer will adopt will often depend on the type of client being interviewed. A commercial client who is confident and has a good understanding of the law may be able to respond to an open question with a concise answer. On the other hand, a client held in custody for the first time may be so overwhelmed in an interview that the lawyer needs to use a series of closed questions to elicit the relevant information. Similarly, if a client has a tendency to talk a lot, then yes/no or closed questions could be used to prevent a client moving off the point.[2] Getting the balance right can be difficult, and often comes with experience.

One question at a time

Whichever type of questioning technique is used, it is important to ensure that the question is phrased in a clear and unambiguous way and appropriate language is used. With longer questions, the interviewer may fall into the trap of asking multiple questions that raise a series of issues at the same time within one question. For example,

---

2   On this particular issue, it is well worth noting that talking a lot can be a sign of nervousness and, therefore, putting the client at ease may help significantly.

are you currently divorced, and do you live with your mother in York? Such questions sometimes confuse a client, who tends either to lose the thread of the question completely or chooses to answer only one part of the question with the other points falling by the wayside. The result of this would be that the lawyer has an incomplete version of events with important details omitted. Asking multiple questions in this way is a common trait, and should be avoided. Often, the reason why interviewers ask multiple questions is because they have not thought carefully about the question before it is put to the client. As such, when one question is asked, the interviewer often thinks of a better question and puts it to the client at the same time. Also, multiple questions are often asked in order to fill silences during an interview. Some lawyers find it difficult to afford a client an opportunity to think before answering a question and feel it is necessary to attempt to rephrase the question to assist the client with an immediate response. Do not be tempted to do this – it is a practice that often frustrates and confuses clients. In fact, silences may be very useful in an interview and have the effect of slowing the pace of a meeting and of drawing out further information from clients by allowing both parties an opportunity to consider the information before them. Pausing for short periods in order to collect your thoughts will not mean that the client will think any less of you. In fact, a client is more likely to be impressed by an interviewer who obtains information from them clearly and steadily and who looks as though they are considering each answer that the client has given.

Planning the questions

It is very tempting, when planning an interview, to write out every question you feel you need to ask the client. Although, this is reassuring for those who are learning how to conduct an interview, it is a bad habit that should be avoided. Two main disadvantages stem from the scripting of interviews:

(1) Reading not listening.

It is vital that the lawyer listens to the client's answer to a question. The client's response to a particular question may be unexpected and may lead to a completely different avenue of questioning and new facts arising. If an interview has been scripted, the lawyer may be more interested in following the script and trying to see what the next question is, rather than listening carefully and analysing the client's responses.

(2) Following the script to your disadvantage.

If a student goes to the trouble of writing a script, it is likely that the script will be used, regardless of its relevance. Clients sometimes give information before they are asked, and scripted interviews run the risk of asking questions to elicit information that has already been given. This may lead to the interview becoming counter-productive and the client losing faith in the lawyer. On this point, it is also worth noting that clients may mention something during the interview that the lawyer did not expect or plan for. This may mean that the interviewer is thrown completely off track, as he or she has not prepared questions on the particular point raised. It may also mean that the lawyer is more interested in getting back on track than in pursuing what could be a worthwhile line of questioning.

A far better way to prepare for an interview is to examine and note down the areas that you wish to question the client upon. This way, the disadvantages mentioned above should not occur.

Listening

During the interview, you should listen and respond appropriately to what the client says. This will help build a rapport with the client. It is most disconcerting for clients to observe the lawyer silently making notes or staring distractedly at documents when they are recounting what they perceive to be important events. When the client is speaking, always ensure that you maintain eye contact and that you respond positively to what is being said. You should not lose sight of how important it is for the client that he or she has an opportunity to discuss a problem and that he or she feels that the problem is being taken seriously. Lawyers who do not give the impression of actually listening to clients may find that clients will soon lose faith in them.

There are various types of listening techniques.

Passive listening

Passive listening is where the lawyer allows the client to continue completely uninterrupted and makes no comment.

Responsive listening

Responsive listening is where the lawyer intersperses the client's answers with a nod or a 'Yes, I see', 'Right' or some other form of the affirmative.

Active listening

Here, the lawyer repeats the salient points of the client's answers either before or during the next question:

Q: What time did you go out that evening?

A: About 7.30 pm.

Q: You went out at 7.30 pm. Where did you go?

A: To the Blacksmith's Arms pub.

Q: You went to the Blacksmith's Arms. Who did you see there?

A: Peter and Elizabeth.

Which listening style should be adopted?

Whichever method of listening that you choose will ultimately depend upon your own personal style and your personality. However, anyone who is learning about conducting an interview should know that following one particular style all the way through may result in the interview becoming dull. A mixture of all three, ideally, should be the way forward. Therefore, when checking personal details, passive listening may be of use, and when dealing with the important details of the case, you may wish to adopt more active listening.

Giving advice

Legal advice is probably the main reason for a client going to see a lawyer and, although not every interview will result in advice being given, a client will probably feel cheated if they are expecting some advice and none is given. Sometimes, there will be reasons why you are not able to give full advice: for example, the client has raised a separate issue that you were not previously aware of, or it is the first interview, where the client is informing the lawyer about their problem for the first time. Under all other circumstances, especially where the lawyer knows the legal problem, there is little excuse for not providing some tentative advice. The advice given, of course, will depend upon the legal area being dealt with. For civil claims, the client will wish to know their chances of success, how much they could expect to receive in damages and also the cost of the litigation. For criminal matters, the client will want to know whether they are going to be found guilty and, if so, what the punishment is likely to be. Whatever the advice given, it is vital to ensure that it is correct, delivered clearly and in terms that the client is able to understand. It is also a very good idea to check that the client has understood your advice before you move on to deal with any other issues.

Taking instructions

Depending upon the area of law that is being dealt with, and the advice that is given, it may be necessary to take instructions from the client on how he or she would like to continue. It may simply be whether a client would like to plead either guilty or not guilty, or whether a person would like to issue proceedings against another. Whatever the instructions, the lawyer should note down the instructions given and confirm them back to the client.

THE CONCLUSION

No one should be under the misapprehension that the conclusion to an interview is any less important than the other parts of an interview merely because it comes at the end. The actual content of the conclusion will depend upon the questions of law being dealt with; however, it should at least contain a summary of all the major factors decided upon during the interview, the arrangements for a subsequent interview if required, and information on what will happen next. For example, it may be that the next time that the lawyer and the client meet will be at court, in which case the client may need to be told that he or she should surrender themselves to court staff when they arrive.

The farewell

Once the conclusion of the interview has been accomplished satisfactorily, the lawyer should make the farewells. Often students make the mistake of rushing at the end of an interview, either due to time constraints, or because they do not realise the importance of closing the interview in a professional manner. The last impression in an interview can be as important as a first impression. Therefore, when a client leaves, it is important that they leave as happy as can be expected under the circumstances. Giving the client a firm handshake and accompanying them to the door may ensure that what started off as a first time interview grows into a long standing professional relationship.

OTHER FACTORS TO CONSIDER WHEN CONDUCTING AN INTERVIEW

In addition to the points mentioned above, there are some other factors to be considered when conducting an interview.

Note taking

During the interview, you should make an accurate note of the meeting, bearing in mind that these notes may be the only record of what is said during the interview. The notes taken should be complete, and you should avoid the habit of taking one word notes to signify a whole statement, as this can lead to the difficulty of looking over the notes at a later date and being unable to remember what they actually mean. It is also worth remembering that you may not be the only person who uses the interview notes. It is possible that another lawyer may refer to them to progress the client's case and, therefore, you should ensure that the notes are legible and follow a reasonable structure.

Before you start writing anything, it is always polite to inform the client that you will be taking notes during the interview. In certain situations, especially sensitive ones, it is also worth pointing out to a client that whatever is said during the interview is confidential. This may put the client's mind at rest, especially when you are noting down what they say. Occasionally, clients will speak quickly and you may find that you are unable to take an accurate note of what is said. If this occurs, you must ask the client to slow down or even stop for a few moments.

Controlling the client

During an interview, the lawyer should remain in control at all times. This does not mean that the lawyer should only permit the client to speak at certain times, or that the client should be shouted down – a lawyer should never talk over the client unless it is absolutely necessary. Controlling a client means that the lawyer is the person who sets the structure and decides what issues are dealt with and when. A failure to control a client may lead to the lawyer failing to deal with important preliminary issues, or giving advice before all the important facts have been obtained.

Nervousness

Nervousness before or during an important interview is a common problem with lawyers, and it can only really be combated with experience and confidence in their own abilities. Although, at a student level, it is very difficult to obtain the experience to combat nervousness fully, it is possible to control the outward appearance of nerves to give a relaxed and professional impression. Nervousness often manifests itself in an exaggeration of mannerisms or the use of common phrases. Some students who are nervous will often portray this factor in the body language that they use. They may fiddle with pens, riffle through the papers or play with their hands or their hair. Other students may repeat a particular phrase or saying. For example, a student may say 'right' at the end of every sentence giving the effect:

Q: So you were walking down the road, right?

A: Yes.

Q: And you saw Paul Collins walking towards you, right?

A: Yes.

Q: And he had a crowbar in his hand, right?

If the word 'right' is used at the end of every statement, the client will soon tire of the term and, if this occurs during an assessment, the tutor will almost certainly deduct marks for it.

The best way to remove such mannerisms or prevent a repetitive phrase from appearing is to first recognise its existence. Often, such problems can be detected when watching a videoed performance. Once you are aware of any of these problems, you can take steps to remove them.

Practising your skills

The only real way to improve your interviewing technique is to practise. This can be done either in front of a mirror, which is useful for planning what to say for the introduction to an interview, or live, with the help of another person. Although a friend or a member of the family can help you practise your skills and provide a useful element of interactivity, a better choice would be another person on the particular programme that you are following. This person is more likely to know what is expected and be able to give you constructive criticism on where you are going wrong. When using this method, it is worthwhile considering trying to video record your performance, either by camcorder or by using facilities provided by the university for such purposes. This way, you will not only gain the benefit of another person's view, but you will also be able to undertake some form of self-assessment. Often, the people who are most critical about a performance are students themselves. Peer and self-assessment sheets are included at the end of this chapter.

Communicating with people from all walks of life

A lawyer will conduct an interview with a wide variety of people, the vast majority of whom will have no legal training. As such, legal jargon should be avoided – clients will probably have no idea what you are talking about if you mention the need for a 'Newton hearing', or that their father made a 'half-secret trust'. This, of course, does not mean that you should talk to the client in words of one syllable, as patronising a client can be equally as bad as using technical terms. It is also worth noting that some of the clients you encounter may only be using your services because they do not have the time to do the work themselves.

Body language

When dealing with interviews, it is worth giving some consideration to non-verbal communication, which is otherwise known as body language. Body language comprises the signals given off by movements of the body, which can illustrate what is being thought, as opposed to what is being said. Consideration of these signals can help a lawyer pick up on what the client is not saying, and can also improve the way that lawyers themselves come across.

The lawyer should try to give off positive signals. For example, sitting upright and squarely on a chair denotes confidence; giving a firm handshake shows sincerity. Lawyers should avoid leaning back in a chair, as this signals disbelief; or leaning back with your hands folded behind your head, which impresses superiority. Eye contact is also an important part of body language and it is important that the lawyer gets the balance right. Too much eye contact (staring) can give an impression of aggression. Too little shows a lack of confidence or untrustworthiness. There are numerous books available on body language, and those who wish to improve their body language may, at some stage, wish to refer to them.

INTERVIEW SELF-ASSESSMENT CHECKLIST

INTRODUCTION. Did you:

Put the client at ease? ☐

Explain the role and purpose of the interview? ☐

Explain that you'll be taking notes and mention client confidentiality? ☐

Define a clear agenda/structure of the interview? ☐

INTERVIEW CONDUCT. Did you:

Use a correct level of language for the client to ensure client understanding? ☐

Ask appropriate questions? ☐

Listen and react to what the client said? ☐

Use time effectively? ☐

Effectively answer queries raised by the client? ☐

ADVICE. Did you:

Outline the legal position and identify the legal issues? ☐

Set out the strengths and weaknesses of the case? ☐

Give realistic advice on further action and point out the consequences of such action? ☐

Obtain instructions from the client on how they wish to proceed? ☐

Ensure that the client understood what was discussed? ☐

GENERAL ISSUES. Did:

The interview follow a logical structure? ☐

You appear confident? ☐

You illustrate a grasp of all factual and evidential issues? ☐

You adequately plan the interview? ☐

You act professionally? ☐

INTERVIEW PEER ASSESSMENT CHECKLIST

INTRODUCTION. Did the student:

Put the client at ease?   ☐

Explain the role and purpose of the interview?   ☐

Explain that s/he would be taking notes and mention client confidentiality?   ☐

Define a clear agenda/structure of the interview?   ☐

INTERVIEW CONDUCT. Did the student:

Use a correct level of language for the client to ensure client understanding?   ☐

Ask appropriate questions?   ☐

Listen and react to what the client said?   ☐

Use time effectively?   ☐

Effectively answer queries raised by the client?   ☐

ADVICE. Did the student:

Outline the legal position and identify the legal issues?   ☐

Set out the strengths and weaknesses of the case?   ☐

Give realistic advice on further action and point out the consequences
of such action?   ☐

Obtain instructions from the client on how they wish to proceed?   ☐

Ensure that the client understood what was discussed?   ☐

GENERAL ISSUES. Did:

The interview follow a logical structure?   ☐

The student appear confident?   ☐

The student illustrate a grasp of all factual and evidential issues?   ☐

The interview show adequate planning?   ☐

The student act professionally?   ☐

SAMPLE INTERVIEW PLAN FOR A CIVIL MATTER – PERSONAL INJURY

(1) Introduction/opening of interview

Remember throughout the interview to keep your language simple and clear, and avoid formal legalistic terminology as much as you can. You do not need to write out a prepared script of what you plan to say, but ensure that you cover the following general areas:

- Welcome the client (and anyone else present). Introduce yourself.
- If the client appears nervous, then use an ice-breaker if necessary. (This is not always needed.)
- Explain the purpose of the interview. Explain your role.
- Emphasise the informal nature of the interview and the importance of the client being as open and frank as possible. Reassure the client that you are bound by strict codes relating to confidentiality.
- Identify the general structure of the interview.
- Tell the client that they should make the decisions on the case and that your role is strictly as adviser.
- Warn the client that you will be taking notes.
- Inform the client that there will be an opportunity to answer any questions at the end of the interview. However, if they do not understand anything that is said, they should say so.

(2) Take/check personal details

In any interview, these details should be either taken or checked at the very beginning. You should ensure that you have the client's right name, address and family details. NB: if there is information on file, it may not be up to date.

(3) Relevant areas for questioning

The basic structure and pattern of your questions will vary according to the type of case you are dealing with. Consult practitioner texts for guidance on individual matters.

Try to compartmentalise your questioning as much as possible in order to obtain the information that you require as efficiently as possible. Asking questions at random will mean that it will be very difficult to evaluate the information that you have been given and appear to the client that you have no real direction or control.

(4) Evaluate the case

It is essential that you do not advise the client on their case or express a general view until you have obtained all necessary information from questioning the client.

Proper preparation and research should allow you to give a broad outline of the strengths and weaknesses of the case in a relatively short time. You should avoid any temptation to treat a client interview as an opportunity to display your legal knowledge.

Make your evaluation hinge on the precise details that have been given to you by the client. List the main strengths and weaknesses of the client's case as comprehensively as possible with as much explanation as the client requires.

(5) Advice

The lawyer's advice on the case is likely to be the client's main concern. He or she will want to know whether the case will be successful and, if so, how much in compensation can be obtained. Ascertaining the general range of damages applicable is by no means an exact science and only through practice will you 'get a feel' for the likely range of compensation a type of injury or symptom falls under. Advise the client of the likely top and bottom ends of the scale and ensure that they understand that the figure is an estimate.

You should try to give full reasoned analysis of why you have come to your decision. Above all, be realistic. If, in your professional opinion, you think that the client has no case at all, then you are duty bound to inform him or her, as tactfully as possible, that this is the case.

- Explain what could happen next – depending upon the client's decision.
- Answer any questions that the client may have.

(6) Conclusion

- Take client instructions on how they wish to proceed.
- Explain what will happen next. It is important that the client is kept fully briefed as to the next steps.
- Make further arrangements if necessary.
- Say farewells.

SAMPLE INTERVIEW PLAN FOR A CRIMINAL MATTER – PLEA BEFORE VENUE HEARING

(1) Introductions/opening of the interview

Remember, throughout the interview, to keep your language simple and clear, and avoid formal legalistic terminology as much as you can. You do not need to write out a prepared script of what you plan to say, but ensure that you cover the following general areas:

- Welcome the client (and anyone else who is present). Introduce yourself.
- If the client appears nervous then use an ice-breaker if necessary. (This is not always needed.)
- Explain the purpose of the interview. Explain your role.
- Emphasise the informal nature of the interview and the importance of the client being as open and frank as possible. Reassure the client that you are bound by strict codes relating to confidentiality.
- Identify the general structure of the interview.
- Tell the client that they should make the decisions on the case and that your role is strictly as adviser.
- Warn the client that you will be taking notes.
- Inform the client that there will be an opportunity to answer any questions at the end of the interview. However, if they do not understand anything that is said, they should say so.

(2) Take/check personal details

In any interview, these details should be either taken or checked at the very beginning. You should ensure that you have the client's right name, address and family details. NB: if there is information on file, it may not be up to date.

(3) Relevant areas for questioning

The basic structure and pattern of your questions will vary according to the type of case you are dealing with. Try to compartmentalise your questioning as much as possible in order to obtain the information required as efficiently as possible.

With defence criminal matters, it is a good idea to identify the prosecution evidence and then try to get the defendant to comment on it. Asking questions at random will make it very difficult to evaluate the information that you have been given and appear to the client that you have no real direction or control.

(4) Evaluate the case

It is essential that you do not advise the client on their case or express a general view until you have obtained all necessary information from questioning the client.

Proper preparation and research should allow you to give a broad outline of the strengths and weaknesses of the case in a relatively short time. You should avoid any temptation to treat a client interview as an opportunity to display your legal knowledge.

Make your evaluation hinge on the precise details that have been given to you by the client. List the main strengths and weaknesses of the client's case as comprehensively as possible with as much explanation as the client requires.

Strengths

Identify the strengths for the defence, for example, alibi or grudge.

Weaknesses

Identify the weaknesses of the case: these are normally the prosecution strengths, for example, eye witnesses, co-accused testimony and fingerprints, etc.

(5) Advice on plea

- Emphasise that this decision is solely that of the client. NB: lawyers should only give general advice on plea; they should never give specific advice and tell clients how they should plead. They should point out the sentencing benefits of an early guilty plea.
- If the client pleads not guilty, then the mode of trial will need to be considered (outline the differences between the two modes of trial if necessary).

(6) Advice on sentence

Advice on sentence should be given. When dealing with sentence, *never* mention to a client the maximum sentence possible, for example, seven years for theft on indictment, unless there is a very strong likelihood that the client will get it. A client will expect some definite advice on sentence and, therefore, the lawyer should be in a position to give it. You can check the Magistrates' Sentencing Guidelines available in most law libraries or look in the Criminal Appeal reports which are available on Westlaw.

(7) Conclusion

- Confirm that the client fully understands the advice that has been provided. Provide a quick summary to ensure this is the case.
- Reiterate that the client himself must make the decision. Allow time for him to go away and think about his plea if unsure.
- Take clear instructions as to the plea and/or mode of trial.
- Explain the basic procedure about what will happen in court (the detail will depend upon the client's previous experience with the criminal courts).
- Reassure the client that advice is available via the solicitor's office.
- Arrange to meet again if appropriate.

FURTHER READING

Chapman, J, *Interviewing and Counselling*, 2nd edn, 2000, London: Cavendish Publishing.

Inns of Court School of Law, *Conference Skills* (published annually), Oxford: OUP.

King, AG, *Effective Communication*, 1992, London: Blackstone.

Mathews, R, *Body Language*, 1990, Hove: Wayland.

Pease, A, *Body Language: How to Read Others' Thoughts by Their Gestures*, 1997, London: Sheldon.

Sherr, A, *Client Care for Lawyers*, 2nd edn, 1998, London: Sweet & Maxwell.

Twist, H, *Effective Interviewing*, 1999, London: Blackstone.

Webb, J and Maughan, C, *Lawyering Skills and the Legal Process*, 2nd edn, 2003, London: Butterworths.

CHAPTER 9

NEGOTIATION

INTRODUCTION

What is negotiation?

You know what you mean by negotiation; you will know that we all do it, albeit at varying levels of sophistication and with varying success. Some people say it's an art, not a science. But what is it exactly? The term itself is not easy to define precisely. It has been defined as:

> A basic means of getting what you want from others. It is back and forth communication designed to reach an agreement when you and the other side have some interests that are shared and others that are opposed.[1]

If you want something less long winded you could describe it using the dictionary definition:

> To confer for the purpose of mutual agreement.[2]

So whenever you talk to someone with the aim of reaching an agreement, you are negotiating. It is common in all relationships, either personal or professional, to discuss issues and come to agreement about what should be done. With your friends and family, you will use an informal, more unstructured approach where the only rules will be not to offend or resort to violence (and even these rules might sometimes be changed); but in most professional discussions, the negotiations will be formal.

Formal negotiation has been likened to the game of chess. There is a framework of rules. Each move depends on the last, and you need to be thinking ahead to take full advantage of your position. You can't play without knowing the rules and you might study particular moves to help you decide what to do, but that knowledge on its own won't make you a good player.

Like all the skills we consider in this book, negotiation is really a process rather than one single skill. There is a whole range of discrete skills that are needed to handle the process of negotiation effectively. We will look at those skills in this chapter, as well as studying the process itself.

But first, let's go back to the definition of negotiation. The definitions above aimed to encapsulate the characteristics of negotiation in as short a phrase as possible. That's the point of a definition. But in being concise, they miss out information. There are, in fact, seven characteristics which have been identified as being common to all negotiations. We have outlined these characteristics below in the hope that they will add to the definitions above.

---

1   Menkel-Meadow, C, 'Toward another view of legal negotiation: the structure of problem solving' (1984) 31 UCLA L Rev 754, pp 754–842.
2   *Chambers English Dictionary*, 1994, Edinburgh: Chambers.

The seven characteristics of negotiation are:[3]

(1) negotiation involves two or more parties who need (or think they need) each other's involvement in achieving a desired outcome. There is a common interest that connects the parties;

(2) the parties start with different opinions or objectives. It is these differences that prevent agreement;

(3) the parties think that negotiation is the best way to resolve their differences (or at least, a possible way);

(4) the parties also think that they may be able to persuade the other party to modify their original position;

(5) even if they do not get their ideal outcome, both retain the hope of an acceptable outcome;

(6) each has some influence – real or assumed – over the other's actions. If one party is completely powerless, negotiation will have little point for the other;

(7) the negotiation process itself involves interaction between people. This interaction might be in person, by telephone, letter, etc, or it might use a combination. Because it is personal, emotions and attitudes will always be important.

Negotiating and lawyers

Legal negotiations are different from other kinds of negotiations, especially informal ones, in three important ways:

(a) as a lawyer you are speaking on behalf of your client, not yourself;

(b) thorough preparation is a vital stage in the negotiation process;

(c) you are bound by legal rules (professional conduct rules are one example).

Once lawyers have become involved in a problem when negotiations are needed it will nearly always be the lawyers who do the negotiating. So what sort of negotiation will lawyers conduct? Some experts on negotiation say there are really two forms of negotiation that occur in a legal context: those which aim to resolve disputes, and those which aim to prevent real disputes arising. This makes sense because it reflects the two kinds of work that lawyers do: contentious and non-contentious.

Most negotiation will occur in a civil, rather than a criminal context, though negotiation can take place in relation to criminal matters; for example, plea bargaining is a form of negotiation.[4]

Resolving disputes

When you are acting for a client, whether claimant or defendant, in a disputed case, your client won't have freely chosen to become involved with the law. They will have

---

3   From Fowler, A, *Negotiating: Skills and Strategies*, 1996, London: Chartered Institute of Personnel and Development.

4   However, we will look at negotiation from a civil perspective, because this is where it will generally arise both in practice and on law courses.

been forced to either take legal action to enforce their rights, or defend an action brought against them. The use of litigation and trial as a means of resolving legal problems is notoriously inefficient, lengthy and for clients shockingly expensive. This is why the use of negotiation is encouraged as an alternative right from the start of a case. When negotiations are successful, a case will be settled before it gets to trial, or even before litigation is started. Roughly 98% of civil cases are resolved in this way.

Preventing disputes

In this case, the parties have chosen to become involved with each other. The aim of this sort of negotiation is to clarify an agreement and prevent disputes arising later on. Sometimes, it is referred to as *transaction-based* negotiation. For example, when two people enter a contract for the sale of a business, they want the terms of their agreement to be clear so that there is less chance of disagreement later on if things don't turn out as planned. Negotiations will take place between them about issues such as the purchase price, which assets will be included and what warranties will be given.

So these two forms of negotiation are different. You will be involved in one before a problem arises in the hope of avoiding it completely, and the other after the problem has already appeared. In both, you will be using your knowledge and communication skills to achieve the best possible result for your client.

The lawyers

Obviously, both solicitors and barristers can be involved in negotiations. Their role in a case can have significant effects. A solicitor in a road traffic accident case will have been working on the case for weeks or months since her client first came into her office to ask for her advice. She might have been to the scene of the accident, seen photographs of the damaged cars, talked to her client's doctors and met his wife. In other words, she will know the case inside out and can take the opportunity to try to negotiate a settlement whenever she and her client want to. However, if a barrister who has been asked to appear at a trial finds himself negotiating a settlement an hour or less before the trial is due to begin, things might be quite different. He is under strict time pressure, is less familiar with all the background details and may have only met the client for the first time five minutes ago.

Neither of these is necessarily a better or worse scenario. They are just different, and the differences will have predictable effects on the way the negotiations are conducted. The first negotiations you practise in the context of a law course will be much more like the second example than the first.

Context – why negotiate?

There are a number of reasons why negotiation is perceived as a good thing. It can save time, money and trouble and it offers an infinite number of creative solutions.

Negotiation is particularly valuable in dealing with civil disputes. The Civil Procedure Rules 1998 (CPR), introduced in 1999, heavily emphasise the need to reach a negotiated settlement wherever possible. Taking a case to trial is notoriously expensive. It can take months or years before the trial actually happens, by which time the claimants and defendants have spent vastly more time and money than they wanted or expected, and have often either come to the brink of divorce, gone bankrupt or started their fifth course of Prozac. Even if they win, as an answer to a complex and multifaceted problem, they will often simply be handed a cheque for an amount determined by someone else and expected to go away and be grateful.

If a case can be settled through negotiation, time, money and anxiety can be saved and your clients might actually get what they really want rather than what the court gives them.

Clients will come to lawyers with problems; lawyers are problem solvers and when the problem involves others, then negotiation must be part of the problem solving process. You could say that a good lawyer will negotiate more than a bad one. Although, of course, some lawyers might be negotiating a lot, but still doing it very badly. Which brings us on to our next point.

Course demands

Lots of people, lawyers and even possibly some of your tutors, will tell you that reading books on negotiation skills is pretty much a waste of time. They will say that you need to watch others doing it and then just do it yourself. There is possibly more debate over the teaching of negotiation than any other legal skill. The obvious problem with the *just jump in and do it* approach is that, although with more practice you might start to feel confident about your negotiating, how will you know whether this confidence is justified? How will you know how to improve?

The truth is that, like any other skill, negotiation should be learnt by combining an understanding of the principles with practice and reflection.

Negotiation is taught as a skill in most professional courses here and overseas. It is also included in undergraduate courses, but is unlikely to be assessed on non-professional courses.

There is no requirement for you to be either taught or assessed in relation to negotiation on LLB courses. At some universities, you will get the chance to study negotiation, possibly as part of a course considering alternative dispute resolution, clinical legal studies or legal skills. You might get the chance to role play negotiations either while studying the skill itself or as part of another course.

Negotiation was, until the 1997–98 academic year, one of the skills taught and assessed on the Legal Practice Course (LPC). It was removed mainly to allow for more concentration on the skills of research and writing, which were identified as being of greater importance to trainee solicitors. Negotiation is therefore no longer assessed on the LPC but should still be included in the teaching.

It is recognised that, although barristers' primary role might be as advocates, they will spend a fair amount of their time negotiating. The teaching and assessment of negotiation therefore plays a large part in the Bar Vocational Course (BVC).

What form does a negotiation take?

When you read textbooks describing negotiation, you may form the impression that a negotiation is something that happens between two people, face to face at one meeting. Although this is the simplest form, it's definitely not the only one. A single negotiation might be spread over days or weeks and include meetings, telephone conversations, letters and emails. Each forum for negotiating has its own advantages and disadvantages. Letters are recorded, but take time; telephones and email are quicker, but don't enable you to read body language; meetings can get through a large number of issues, but require instant decision making. In practice, the case and the client's needs should govern your choice.

When considering the techniques of negotiation in this chapter we will be looking at the kind of negotiation where lawyers meet face to face with the aim of resolving an area of dispute. This might be described as negotiation in its purest form. If you study negotiation as a student, this is the kind of negotiation exercise you will use.

A LEGAL NEGOTIATION

In this section, we will look at the common ways of categorising legal negotiations. This should give you a clearer idea of what a legal negotiation is and how it can be used.

Although negotiation is something that you have done before, you have two problems with legal negotiation:

(a) You want to be sure that the way you've been doing it is correct. You probably haven't thought that much about what you were doing before. To enable you to think, you need to know the theory behind the practice.

(b) You know that particular rules will apply to legal negotiations. Agreeing where to go on holiday or compromising on a political problem may involve negotiation, but the processes and the outcomes are not governed by a strict set of rules as legal negotiations are. The law, and the way a court might look at your problem in the light of the law, is always of extreme importance in legal negotiations. Legal negotiations take place in the shadow of the law.

There has been a lot of research and writing regarding negotiations in commercial contexts and some that considers negotiation by lawyers. A list of some of these texts is given at the end of this chapter. The way that lawyers actually negotiate in practice and the way they approach simulated exercises has been analysed. We can use this research to help to understand what legal negotiation is about. You will see that your personality and experience will be relevant, but also that you can learn how to be an effective negotiator by practising the skill and applying your knowledge of what negotiation is. We should point out, however, that there are no rules to follow which guarantee that you will be a great negotiator. You just need to practise and to understand what it is you are doing.

Through the research that has been done in the area of negotiation, certain approaches have been seen and recorded. The approaches that can be taken have been categorised. Although there are some variations in the categorisation, all the descriptions you come across in other texts will be very similar to the ones set out below, in Figure 9.1.

Figure 9.1

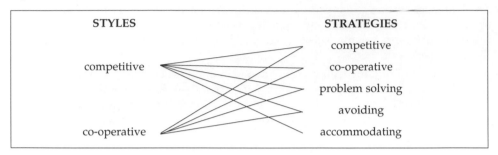

As you can see, negotiation is broken down into what we have termed styles and strategies, and no one style has to be used with one particular strategy. You can choose any combination. When you look at other texts on negotiation, you will find that the terms style and strategy are not used consistently. A negotiator's style is the manner in which he conducts himself; the style he uses can often be dictated by his personality. The strategy a negotiator uses is the approach taken to the negotiation and the way it is progressed.

Essentially:

- style – defines the kind of personality you portray, your own personal style;
- strategy – defines your underlying plan or tactics.

Negotiation styles

The style of your negotiation is defined by the way you react on a personal level with the other person. It governs the way you ask questions, the way you react, and how polite you are. It is more superficial than your strategy, though it can be just as important to the outcome.

The two main styles are easy to categorise. These two styles are competitive and co-operative. Although described as two distinct styles, they are really just the opposite ends of a spectrum of possible styles.

Competitive style – aggressive

Negotiators who use this style try to get the best deal by appearing aggressive, argumentative and very sure of themselves and their case. They aim to undermine their opponent and to intimidate them into submission.

Co-operative style – friendly

Negotiators using this style are seen to be polite, reasonable, friendly, fair, open and honest.

Negotiation strategies

The strategy you use in a negotiation is defined by your approach to the whole process. It will depend on how you see the negotiation, how you intend to get the best deal and what sort of offers and concessions you are prepared to make. It defines the tactics you will use to get the best result.

We have outlined five negotiating strategies – competitive, co-operative, problem solving, avoiding and accommodating – of which the first three are the most commonly used. Rather confusingly, the first two are given labels which are the same as those for the two styles outlined above. There are real similarities between the competitive style and the competitive strategy and the co-operative style and strategy. It is certainly easier to employ the corresponding style and strategy, but they are not the same thing. A competitive strategy could be used with a co-operative style to open a negotiation. A negotiator who appeared to be reasonable and open, who listened carefully to the other side, but who was making objectively very high opening demands and offering few concessions, would be doing this.

You need to be fairly competitive in your strategy when you seek answers to questions; you should be highly assertive and pursue a point until you get a satisfactory answer. At the same time, you must usually be particularly polite and less competitive in style when you do this, otherwise your relationship with the other side could break down.

A simple personality test

The graph below in Figure 9.2 shows the five possible strategies. Consider how competitive/assertive your personality is on a scale of 0 to 5 (0 meaning you would do almost anything to avoid an argument, and 5 being very competitive and assertive). Next, consider how co-operative you are. Again, use a scale of 0 to 5 (0 being very unhelpful and unco-operative to others). Then place a mark on the graph reflecting your scores: you will get a very rough idea of the strategy that might come most naturally to you. Someone with a naturally co-operative personality who is not at all competitive may naturally tend to an accommodating strategy; learning to be more assertive may help them to use a more problem solving strategy.

You can see that there are no absolute borders between these strategies, and that small alterations in your approach will take you from one to another. A good negotiator should switch from one to another throughout a negotiation as appropriate.

Figure 9.2

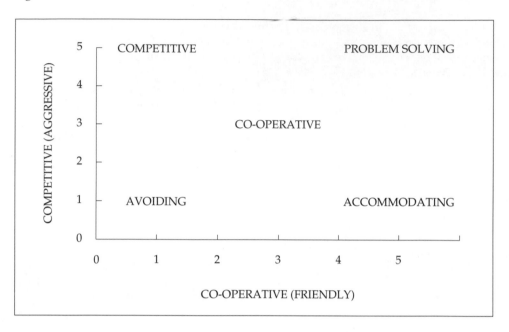

Consider this example:

Negotiator A I'm very pleased to meet you and to have this opportunity to talk about our clients' problems. I'm confident that we can have a fruitful discussion. The main problem as I see it is the lack of agreement over the purchase price of the new shampoo range. We think that we have offered a very fair price. Can you tell me why your clients find it unacceptable?

Negotiator B Well, really it's because it's so much higher than they expected. It's a substantial increase on our previous contract prices with your client. I'd like to propose a lower figure.

Negotiator A There are very good reasons for the increase which I can go over if you wish. I think, in fact, that the prices you have paid in the past have been generous. It would be very hard to lower the price we have offered unless you can offer some kind of collateral benefit. It does take account of the goodwill that exists between our clients.

Negotiator B What do you mean by collateral benefit?

Negotiator A Well let's say your clients increased their order size, we may be able to look again at the price. Although any adjustment could not be large and would obviously need to be expressly authorised ...

Negotiator A is using a co-operative style and a competitive strategy. The tone is polite and friendly, but a strong stance is taken and no concessions are made. B is being less assertive in style. Negotiator B's strategy seems at the moment to be co-operative, but this obviously isn't going to work. B might be better off moving towards a problem solving approach by using what seems to be A's underlying interest in increasing the order sizes to suggest a more creative solution involving a bigger order for a reduced price per unit.

The five negotiation strategies

Below, we have outlined the main characteristics of the strategies shown on the graph. Knowledge of the different strategies should help you to:

(a) know the strengths and weaknesses of your predominant strategy;

(b) spot and react to the other negotiator's strategy.

Competitive

If you use this strategy, you are taking the approach that, whatever the other side gains, you have lost, and vice versa. You want the whole cake; there is only so much to be shared and your aim is to get as much as possible. This means you will start with high demands and will not want to make concessions. It could be described as a 'tough' approach. Its most extreme result will be that one side does get the whole cake and the other side doesn't even get a crumb. In a relatively simple negotiation over, for example, one issue such as the price to be paid for goods, this strategy can be useful. This strategy is also referred to as adversarial. At its worst, it is a win at any cost strategy. For an inexperienced negotiator, it can be a dangerous strategy to encounter when combined with a deceptively co-operative style. Don't be lulled into a false sense of security by politeness. If it is combined with a strongly competitive strategy, you might find yourself walking away with very little of what you had hoped for, before you realise what has been going on.

Background

This approach aims to destroy the confidence of the opponent, making them more likely to give in. Some commentators and researchers think that this approach is less effective than others in achieving the best possible outcome.

Characteristics of a competitive approach

A competitive strategy may be characterised by:
- making very high demands;
- making few or very small concessions;
- a reluctance to give any concessions;
- giving little information;
- possibly giving misleading information;
- demanding information;
- taking control from the start;
- exaggerating own case;
- seeing non-competitive negotiators as weak;
- often being used with a competitive style.

Advantages

- Helpful in very simple cases – it can be useful when there really is only one issue to deal with.
- Intimidating – it can result in a beneficial outcome if there is a real power imbalance and one party is very easily intimidated.
- Effective – it can be effective when used sparingly, particularly at the beginning of a negotiation.

Disadvantages

- Non-creative – this strategy can lead to simple bargaining over one issue and does not encourage creative solutions.
- Stalemate is possible – if a level is reached below which you cannot go, being less creative can mean that the negotiation fails as the parties cannot come together. This can also result in long term relationships breaking down.
- Unrealistic – it is very unusual for there really to be only one issue in a negotiation. There may actually be more than one issue that is relevant, but this strategy forces concentration on a single item.
- Difficult to sustain – it can be very difficult to use this strategy if it goes against your personality type. If you are quiet and very accommodating by nature, you might find it very difficult to act in a competitive way.
- Unexpected reaction – your opponent might not react in the way you want them to. They might carry on being reasonable, or start being as competitive as you are rather than backing down. If this happens, you won't get the results you were hoping for.

Co-operative

Using this strategy, you will be looking for the best joint outcome. It is common using this strategy to make certain concessions in the hope that the other side will do the same. It could be described as a 'reasonable' approach, where the aim is that each side gets half of the cake. Part of its aim is to enable each party to trust the other and give something in order to reach a compromise. At its worst it is an 'agree at any cost' strategy.

Background

Unlike the competitive approach, there is an assumption here that you are looking for the overlap in your objectives and those of your opponent. Rather than seeking to win, your aim is to reach agreement.

Characteristics of a co-operative approach

A co-operative approach may be characterised by:

- an open approach;
- a conciliatory atmosphere;
- only reasonable suggestions;
- attempts to explain actions and proposals;

- attempts to gain trust by giving information;
- a willingness to give concessions;
- avoidance of conflict;
- perception of self as honest and ethical.

Advantages

- Stalemate is less likely – because concessions can be made, a deadlock is rarer.
- Continued relationship is likely – because this strategy is not aggressive, it is usual to be able to continue a relationship after the negotiation.
- Less stressful – this sort of encounter is less stressful and both parties will probably feel they have been fairly treated.

Disadvantages

- Needs an opponent with a common strategy – if the other side will not use this strategy and refuses to give concessions, the party using this strategy may give too much away.
- Finite amount of concessions – if concessions are given too easily, you could find that you're left with nothing else to give before the negotiation has ended.
- Weak – an opponent with another strategy might see this approach as weak. It could encourage competitive behaviour.
- Vulnerable – others may take advantage if you use this approach. It is vital to check to see if it is working and that you are getting as many concessions as you are giving. This problem can be mitigated by making your concession offers conditional, or first indicating a willingness to be flexible to gauge the reaction before making specific concessional offers.
- Can give too much – if you are too concerned with getting any form of agreement, you might find that you haven't got as good a deal for your client as you might have using a more competitive style.
- High risk – this strategy is very risky when used against a competitive opponent. It is likely that an effective settlement won't be obtained.

Problem solving

This strategy concentrates on finding a creative solution that serves both parties' interests. If it can be discovered that one side prefers the marzipan and the other side prefers the fruit, but doesn't want to be left with the washing up, the final decision about what happens to the cake can reflect this. This strategy aims to find out what is really important to each side and to find a solution that accommodates this. It is sometimes referred to as a principled approach. To some extent, it assumes that both sides can get what they want from the negotiation and will test the acceptability of the outcome by asking whether it is fair and reflects both sides' interests. It can require a great deal of effort to generate creative solutions and evaluate them thoroughly.

Background

The idea behind this approach is rather different from the two above. It is based on work done by two American researchers, Roger Fisher and William Ury, and on their book *Getting to Yes*.[5] The approach does not assume that each party moves from extreme positions on a straight line towards the middle, both losing and gaining something. Rather, they throw the line away and build an alternative compromise which satisfies them both. The negotiators are seen less as adversaries and more as collaborators, looking jointly for a solution. The approach is one that has been developed as much as a model for effective negotiation as an observation of how people actually negotiate.

The aim of this strategy is to consider the problem separately from the people and to come up with options for agreement.

A famous example of this approach is quoted by Fisher and Ury in their book. It concerned the peace treaty negotiations between Egypt and Israel in 1978 at Camp David. Egypt was demanding the return of the Sinai Peninsula which had been captured by Israel. Israel was refusing to release its possession. Egypt's underlying interest was in the principle at stake and its national pride. Israel's underlying interest was its fear of Egyptian forces being close enough to its borders to attack. The creative solution – the return of the Sinai Peninsula to Egypt, but with an undertaking that it would remain a largely de-militarised zone.

This strategy also emphasises the importance of identifying a BATNA (which stands for Best Alternative To a Negotiated Agreement, and is discussed in more detail below). This means you will think about what your alternatives to agreeing are. For example, if no negotiated agreement is reached, litigation might be the next step. When considering proposals, you will be able to compare them against this alternative to help you decide whether you should accept them or not.

Characteristics of a problem solving approach

A problem solving approach will be characterised by:

- attempts to understand the other side's point of view;
- recognition that emotions can get in the way;
- an emphasis on good communication;
- a concentration on each side's interests;
- creative and inventive solutions.

Advantages

- Stalemate is unlikely – because there are an infinite number of solutions and the parties don't take fixed positions, a deadlock is not common.
- Focus on main issues – this approach makes it much easier to focus on the important issues in a case.
- Creative – because both sides are encouraged to come up with creative options, it is more likely that a solution which is effective for both sides will be found.

---

5 Fisher, R and Ury, W, *Getting to Yes*, 2003, London: Random House. Certainly one of the most important books on this subject.

Disadvantages

- Requires more information – this approach can only work effectively when the negotiator has enough information on which to base proposals. This means it can be used more efficiently later in a negotiation.

- More difficult if the other side won't take the same approach – particularly where an opponent is using a competitive strategy, you may find it difficult to continue with this approach. Note, however, that it isn't impossible to continue with this approach, even if the other side refuses to. In this respect, therefore, it has the edge over the other approaches.

- Unrealistic – although presented in many texts as the best of the strategies, there may be points in a negotiation when this approach cannot be used. In the end, there may be no solution that keeps both sides happy. One may have to get more, while the other gets less. It is rare to find a negotiation where a creative solution completely satisfies all concerned. Generally, there will also need to be concessions on both sides.

Avoiding

This is a strategy which seeks to avoid any real progress. Those using this strategy will not really engage in the negotiation at all. At its most extreme, it would involve cancelling or postponing the negotiation. If this strategy is used for some time, of course, the cake might start to mould and become inedible.

Background

This strategy would rarely be used, but is found at the point where both assertiveness and co-operation in strategy are low. Because it is rarely used, it is often excluded from discussions of negotiation strategies.

Characteristics of an avoiding strategy

A negotiator using this strategy will be very unhelpful. She might be trying to buy time so that circumstances change.

Advantages

- Can put the other side under pressure.
- Forces the other side to take the initiative.
- Can buy time.

Disadvantages

- Can give control to the other side.
- May force the other side to start or take further steps in litigation.
- May be contrary to the CPR (which require that reasonable attempts to settle cases should be made).
- At its extreme, it may be unethical.

Accommodating

This strategy involves agreement to the other side's proposals and, at its extreme, is therefore useless as a strategy in negotiation. If the other side has any sense, it will mean they get the whole cake.

Background

In some ways, this strategy is the co-operative strategy taken to an extreme. It is not a strategy commonly considered or used.

Characteristics of an accommodating strategy

This strategy would probably only be used by an inexperienced negotiator following their own personality style, although any concession could be described as accommodating to some extent.

Advantages

• None.

Disadvantages

• Failure to achieve a good result for your own side is almost inevitable.

Which strategy to use?

There is no one strategy that is always better than the others and you can't really plan and use one strategy for a whole negotiation. The strategy you use will depend on the issue you are dealing with and the way you are reacting to the other side. It will also depend on your personality. There is nothing to say that you have to stick to one strategy. If you consider all the non-legal negotiations you have taken part in, you will probably see that you have used all sorts of approaches, some with more success than others. Your success as a negotiator will depend on an understanding of the styles and strategies open to you and on choosing the most effective approach to take throughout the negotiation. This will allow you to make flexible and appropriate use of them all.

The competitive strategy is often criticised and it is probably true to say that this strategy, especially used on its own, is the least likely of the main three (competitive, co-operative, problem solving) to get results. But that doesn't mean that it will never be appropriate to use. Certain competitive behaviour, such as withholding a piece of information, could be necessary as part of a creative problem solving process. The important thing is to understand these approaches. You can then adapt them to your needs with a full knowledge of what you are doing and what you are likely to achieve.

In the beginning, you may find it easier to consider the strategy you used *after* a negotiation rather than plan it before. You can then review whether the strategy or strategies you used at particular points in the negotiation helped or not, and you might decide to modify your approach next time.

Issues that might affect which strategy you choose

The approach used by the other side

This is very important to your choice. A problem solving approach, for example, will only work really well if both sides are willing to give it a try. You might already know the person you will negotiate with. If not, you will need to assess their approach when you meet.

Whether the parties want to continue their relationship

You will need to check and discuss this point with your client. You might be less inclined to adopt either a competitive style or strategy if you want to ensure that the parties can easily continue a relationship after the negotiation. For example, you would generally have failed miserably if you conducted a negotiation as part of divorce proceedings where, as a result of the antagonistic climate of the negotiations, the former couple were no longer on speaking terms. In transactional negotiations, in particular, an ongoing relationship will be vital.

How important is it to reach an agreement/avoid a trial?

If your client is happy to go to trial if necessary, you will be able to take more risks when deciding on your strategy. If your case is strong, and your client can afford to pay for the trial, you may be less inclined to make concessions and be more competitive in your strategy. Conversely, if it is of the utmost importance to avoid any breakdown in negotiation and an eventual trial, you will be more inclined to adopt a co-operative strategy.

What are the parties' goals?

If a case is decided by court trial, the range of outcomes is very restricted. A claimant might win and be awarded one of the remedies the court is able to order, such as damages or an injunction, or they might lose and get nothing except a very large bill. If you are really looking for a more creative solution, possibly involving things that a court cannot order, you will wish to maximise your chances of a negotiated settlement. Again, you will probably not want to risk failure by adopting too competitive an approach.

What are your instructions?

If your client has told you that £10,000 is the lowest figure she will accept, you could use this as part of a competitive approach. You might demand this figure from the outset, and make it clear that you will end the negotiation if it is not agreed. On the other hand, if you have been given full authority to come up with any solution you think might be acceptable, you will have the freedom you need to employ the problem solving strategy.

The stage of the negotiation

Most people will use a variety of approaches throughout a negotiation. A competitive approach might be used earlier in a negotiation, moving to a more co-operative and problem solving approach only in the later stages, when it has become clear that the competitive approach is no longer proving useful. Timing is essential to a good result.

The issue

Some issues may demand a particular strategy. As we mentioned earlier, a negotiation over a simple monetary value, such as how much you will pay me for this car, may be better suited to a competitive strategy, while issues concerning the performance of a detailed contract, with many more variables, will be better suited to a problem solving approach.

Particular actions will also be more or less acceptable in different negotiation situations. A threat to take court action would be seen as understandable, though competitive, in a personal injury case where one party had been run over by the other's two tonne truck. But it would be completely over the top in a negotiation over the terms of a lease where the parties were having difficulty agreeing on which day the rent should be paid.

The negotiator's preference

A negotiator may have a preferred approach. This is likely in relation to style, to reflect their personality. In addition, when responding to the other lawyer, a negotiator may feel a particular style or strategy is needed. For example, if the other side is particularly competitive and aggressive, there is little to be gained by sticking to a co-operative approach.

PREPARATION

We have already mentioned the fact that good preparation is essential to successful legal negotiations. No matter how much you know about the theories of negotiation, the strategies and the psychology, if you have no foundation of preparation to build these on you may as well give up and go home. Preparation is so important that, if you do not feel ready to negotiate, either because you are not prepared or simply don't have enough information, you should defer the negotiation if you can.

In this section, we will consider exactly what good preparation will involve, looking in detail at the steps you will need to follow before the negotiation. The steps we will consider are as follows:

- researching the facts;
- researching the law;
- identifying objectives;
- identifying strengths and weaknesses;
- preparing a written plan;
- considering contingency plans;
- getting authority.

Researching the facts

If you are going to negotiate in the light of what a judge is likely to decide about a case, you must know the facts of the case inside out. This means you need to conduct a preliminary analysis of the case and read carefully all the information you are given.

You can't make accurate predictions about what a court will say if you don't know what evidence the court will have heard. If you have missed something that gives your case a real advantage, the other side is not going to tell you, even if they know. If you overlook important details, you may expect less than you could get. If you expect less, you will almost certainly get it.

Researching facts is a bit like revising for an exam. For solicitors and employed lawyers, researching the facts will generally mean going through the whole case file. For barristers, it will mean reading over the papers sent by the solicitor. For a student, it will usually involve reading the instructions you have been given. It could also mean watching video evidence.

Some commentators recommend that you develop a notebook with all the necessary information for each case using dividers or page tabs to help quick and easy reference. You should include, for example, a list of the disputed issues and all the relevant facts and figures. You should also identify the information you want from the other side and the information that you are prepared to give to them. This will enable you to form a clear picture of the case and to access information quickly during the negotiation.

Researching the law

It is as important to know exactly what the law is as it is to know the facts of the case. What if a recent judgment has changed the law in your favour, but you aren't aware of the case? Your opponent is not going to say: 'By the way, have you seen this recent decision which confirms my client is wrong and yours is right?'

Research has shown that if you expect more in a negotiation, you are likely to get more. But if you aren't up to date, you will be negotiating on a false basis; possibly you may think you are likely to lose when you are not. It is almost inevitable that you will come out of the negotiation with less than you could have.

Researching the law can also help to give you objective criteria against which to argue and measure possible solutions.

Identify your client's objectives

The quality of the final agreement will depend on how well it serves your client's interests. This makes it necessary to set out exactly what your client wants and what you think the other side wants. In practice, you will need to sit down with your client and explore the options so that you are as clear as possible about what he or she really wants. You will not be looking only for basic objectives; you need to know your client's underlying interests. This is especially important if you want to use a problem solving approach. Your client's desires will usually be more complex than it first appears, and will reflect legal and non-legal motives, such as a hope for compensation, a fear of appearing at a trial and a concern about what other people might think.

Ordering objectives

Once you have identified your client's objectives, put them in order of priority: that is, your client's priority. It is not for you to decide that compensation is more important than an apology, or that a sale at the right price is more important than a sale to the right person. When you have done this, make a similar list for the other side. When you have an ordered list of your side's objectives and a list of what you think the other side's objectives are, check to see whether any of your client's objectives and the other side's objectives are the same. This can be very useful, as it will guide the approach you take to giving concessions later on. If you have identified the fact that one of your opponent's most important objectives is something which has little importance either way for your client, you will be able to use it to its full advantage, rather than conceding it as an irrelevance early on. For an example, see Figure 9.3.

Figure 9.3

Essential facts of the case

The claimant is suing the defendant hotel for food poisoning. The claimant wants to get as much compensation as he can, and an apology for a ruined weekend. However, he is very keen not to let the case go as far as a trial, as he would not want to appear in court. The hotel management denies that the problem was their fault. But they are planning a major expansion and publicity campaign later in the year, and they want to get this out of the way by then, as it will take up all the time they have. They are particularly keen to prevent any adverse publicity.

Ordered list of priorities

Claimant	Defendant
High damages	Fast settlement/no trial
No trial	No publicity
Apology	Low damages
Fast settlement	

It looks as if the claimant here could be able to put pressure on the hotel to give him more compensation if he agrees to it quickly and promises not to publicise the problem.

As well as considering how your client's main objectives might be modified, you should think about possible alternatives that might also satisfy each side's underlying interests. You might identify as many possibilities as you can with your client before critically evaluating each one. This kind of exercise can allow you to be more creative in the negotiation and to expand the agenda.

It is useful to identify the normal practice, if there is one, that applies to your situation. This gives you something to measure your objectives against, and can be used to persuade the other side to comply with your demands. When you've reached agreement on a compensation figure for your injured client, you can more easily argue that the defendant driver should also pay all her legal fees if you know that is standard practice.

Best and worst possible outcomes

So now you have a bunch of objectives, like a hand of cards in your grasp to be swapped or kept. But things aren't as simple at that. Each objective can be modified. The breach of contract compensation can be of a high or low value; the defamation apology can be worded and published in different ways. In relation to each objective, you can now identify the best and worst possible outcomes. Your client might want a complete and grovelling apology to be broadcast on prime time television, in person, with real tears. You might persuade him that, realistically, a full and complete apology in a letter might be the best he can expect, and at worst, a partial apology might suffice. Demands might be met permanently or temporarily, unconditionally or conditionally, wholly or partly. Again, remember that you are acting on your client's instructions, so it is his decision as to what is acceptable in the end. See Figure 9.4 for our hotel's best and worst possible outcomes. Note, the damages figure will be based on the awards given in previous similar cases.

Figure 9.4

	Best	**Worst**
Damages	£4,000	£9,000
Admission/apology	No admission or apology	A written apology
Speed of settlement	Within the week	In some months

Your detailed consideration of best and worst possible outcomes will guide you in your opening positions and in how much you can concede on each point. Opening positions will usually be at the top end of your best possible outcome: this gives you room to concede if you need to. Opening with demands in excess of your best possible outcome can be counter-productive. If you ask for £3,000 when all the cases say £2,000, you can appear unrealistic and will not be able to justify your position.

Very occasionally, there will be no best or worst possible outcomes; your client will have a clear and unalterable objective, with no room for manoeuvre. If this is the case, you should make it very clear to the other side, otherwise they are likely to assume that your refusal to move is just part of your negotiation tactics.

Best and particularly worst possible outcomes will need to be modified in response to each new piece of information. This means they may change during the course of a negotiation. They can also be changed by collateral issues which you might or might not have considered. Your client might take less money if an offer were made to pay the money within a shorter period, if, in future, a higher interest rate would apply to the contract or if free samples of a new product would be provided. The more creative the negotiation, the more likely it is that these kind of issues will be relevant. This means you must constantly reassess the best and worst outcomes for your client.

Settlement zones

When you have considered the best and worst possible outcomes from your client's point of view, you should do the same from the other side's point of view. What are their best and worst outcomes likely to be? This is an important step. Particularly in more straightforward cases, once you have done this, you can work out where your client's objectives overlap with the other side's. This will give you a settlement zone. See Figure 9.5.

Figure 9.5

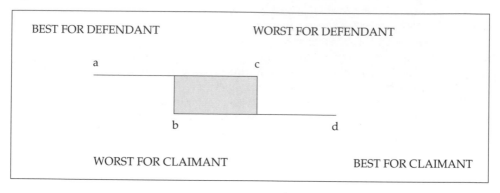

In this example, the settlement zone is between b and c. Settlement zones can be large, small or non-existent.

Identifying strengths and weaknesses

When you make your initial assessment of the facts and law, you should try to do it on a reasonably objective basis. However, in the negotiation, you will spin everything you can in your client's favour. You will want to utilise the strengths of your case and the weaknesses in the other side's case to be persuasive and to gain concessions.

To prepare effectively for this, you should identify all your client's strengths and weaknesses, and those of the other side. Identifying the other side's strengths and weaknesses will mean you are better prepared to respond to their arguments. These strengths and weaknesses will relate to the facts and the law.

You should prepare questions that will expose and probe the other side's weaknesses. But be prepared – they will be planning to do the same to you.

Prepare a written plan

Although you can't predict exactly how the negotiation will go, or draw up a script as you might for advocacy, you can set out a plan. One aspect of this is to identify all the issues that have to be discussed, so that you don't miss anything out. There may be certain information that you need from the other side in order to get a clearer picture of the case, or issues that you want to probe them on. Note these items.

As well as having a good understanding of the issues, you will need to think about your strategy for the negotiation. An important part of this is deciding on your opening offer. It is useful to identify the areas where it might be easy to make concessions should they be needed, as well as the areas where there is no, or very little, flexibility. Identify what you can afford to give. You might also think about when you would give it: early on or as a last resort?

You will also need to consider the order in which you would prefer to deal with the issues. Set out an agenda for the negotiation. We have discussed negotiation agendas in more detail below.

Consider contingency plans

As part of your planning, you might want to consider your client's *bottom line(s)*. A bottom line is the point after which you must say *this is not acceptable*, where further concession is not possible. How far will you go in relation to each issue in dispute? Some negotiators use a chart to identify their best result, acceptable levels and bottom line. Others say that this approach is unhelpful, too simplistic and restricts flexibility and creativity. There is a danger that a bottom line set before the negotiation will be based on incomplete information and might inhibit a problem solving approach.

Whether you identify a bottom line or not, you always need to know what your BATNA is. Fisher and Ury first considered the need to identify a BATNA in their book *Getting to Yes*.[6] It is extremely useful as part of your preparation to be clear what your BATNA is. It means that you can compare any proposed solution with your BATNA and decide which is better. This should stop you ever agreeing to anything that is actually worse than letting the negotiation break down. It will also let you see when something is better than just walking away. In civil disputes, your BATNA will often be to litigate to trial. This a bit tricky because, of course, you don't actually know what the trial judge will decide. You have to rely on your knowledge of the law and facts to predict the chances of certain outcomes. This involves some risk, and that risk should be included in any calculations you make. In transactional negotiations, your BATNA could be to call off the deal and approach someone else. Sometimes letting the other side know what your BATNA is, and that you won't hesitate to pursue it if forced to, will encourage them to be realistic and constructive.

Get your client's authority

In practice, because you are providing a service to your client and because your client is in control, you need your client's authority before you can make any agreement. If your client is trusting, your authority might be unlimited. More likely, it will be limited to a certain range, or open, but subject to final confirmation. If your authority is not unlimited, you cannot come to any final agreement without checking with your client. This issue will affect the strategy you use. It's probably easier to be creative with unlimited options, but limitations can be used tactically to force concessions.

LOGISTICS

A small but essential part of your planning for face to face negotiations is to decide where the negotiation will take place and how much time will be available. There are some conventions about meetings taking place at the offices of the seller or claimant or their lawyers, but there are no hard rules. Below are some of the issues you might take into account regarding venue.

6   *Op cit*, Fisher and Ury, fn 5.

Your offices

- Saves time, as you have no travelling.
- Comfortably familiar; you are likely to be less nervous.
- Easy access to information.
- You feel more in control; you have a 'home ground' advantage.
- It is rather hard to walk out.

Their offices

- You get some travelling time to prepare and focus your mind.
- It is hard for them to be difficult by saying they can't get access to information.
- You can mitigate their sense of control if you know how.[7]

Other venues

- It is neutral territory.
- Interruptions are less likely.

Venue isn't the only logistical factor to think about. You should agree how much time each side has available for the meeting. Timing can sometimes be crucial. Certain times of day are better or worse for some people. A time deadline will often help negotiators move towards an agreement.

In practice, it will also be useful to check who will be present, as it's generally better not to let yourself be outnumbered. How many lawyers are there; will clients be present or not? It's usually easier to negotiate without clients, but you should be able to contact them easily if necessary.

Seating arrangements should be considered too. If you don't like them, ask for them to be changed.

STRUCTURE

As we have explained above, if you have a good understanding of what is happening during a negotiation, you will be better able to perform well yourself. We will now therefore consider how a negotiation might be structured. You can use this knowledge in planning your own negotiations.

Like an interview or advocacy, to be effective, a negotiation must have a structure; broadly a beginning, middle and end. From the research on negotiation a common and useful structure can be reproduced. In practice the stages of a negotiation won't be as clear cut as this. Information gathering, for example, though discussed in stage two, will continue throughout a negotiation. So this isn't the structure that is *always* used or the one that *should always* be used; it just shows a general pattern and is useful to know when planning a negotiation:

---

7   Detailed negotiation texts might go into this level of detail; one way of mitigating their sense of control might be by requiring a smoker not to smoke.

(1) *Set the agenda.* Before you begin the negotiation, you will need to agree an agenda for discussion with the other side. This is always useful, even if it is subsequently altered during the negotiation.

You might already have prepared your own preferred agenda, or you may wait until you meet for the negotiation. Some negotiators will place more important or contentious issues at the top to reflect their significance and in the hope that early success will make it easier to deal with the other issues. Others will place them further down the agenda, to give the parties a chance to get a feel for things first. You might feel that you need to consider a number of issues at the same time. A simultaneous consideration is complicated, but does have the advantage of allowing constructive analysis of the whole situation.

From the very beginning you can set the tone of the negotiation. This is easier to do if you take the initiative, as long as you don't completely take control. Alternatively, you might want to wait to see how your opponent deals with the meeting.

Within this period it is also useful to clarify items such as the purpose of the meeting, its status and its length.

(2) *Consider the facts.* As a first stage in the negotiation you may both identify the facts you consider to be relevant. If you identify those that are disputed and those that are agreed by both parties, you can narrow the issues you must deal with. Generally, each party will set out their case in some detail, taking a few minutes each. This summary should not anticipate the other side's reactions or priorities. It is important that you listen carefully to the other side's case and note specific issues. You can start to evaluate their experience and approach, but should not react too obviously to what is said.

During this stage, there will be some exchanging of information about each side's case. The co-operative or problem solving negotiator will share information at an early stage to develop trust in the hope that information will also come from the other side. The problem solving negotiator will search for underlying interests. A negotiator using a competitive strategy is likely to request more information than she reveals.

You can use your interviewing skills to question and to make sure you have understood the information you are given. Direct questions such as 'do you think this case is relevant?' might elicit the facts you need, but if not, indirect questions such as 'what do you think the court's view of this point is likely to be?' are worth a try. It is very important that you actively listen, check your understanding and ask for clarification of anything that seems unclear. You might feel embarrassed to admit to a lack of understanding at an early stage, but misunderstandings will only make things worse later on.

(3) *Opening positions.* You will let the other side know what your client's objectives are and they will respond. In practice, you might have already done this, at least in part, before your meeting. In addition, an opening bid might be made. Making the first bid allows you to take control, but of course there is some risk because you don't know the other side's position. Making a specific offer when you have no idea of the other side's range is very risky and should be avoided. You could be way out. The approach taken to your opening bid will depend on the strategy you are using. If you are taking a competitive approach, you might make a high

offer; if you are taking a co-operative approach you might make a more 'reasonable' offer. Some research has shown that higher opening offers will result in higher settlements. It gives you more room to make concessions. So you might want to make your first offer around the top of your range. Of course, if it is so high as to be completely unrealistic, then this is going to be counter-productive.

Note that some negotiators might make false demands, which will be conceded later. This sort of practice is unethical if it involves the making of a false statement and it can damage credibility. Good negotiators are firm and justify their positions either subjectively, or by reference to objective criteria. Making an offer within a range, such as saying 'I think my client will accept anything from £8,000 to £10,000' is usually pointless; you may as well save your breath and just say £8,000.

Taking a problem solving approach will make this stage more complicated and will not generally involve a simple offer. You should demonstrate an understanding of the other side's position before you make any creative proposals. This may mean setting out your client's most important objectives and interests and finding out what the other side's reaction is to them. If the other side give you a list of objectives, make sure they have included all of them. This avoids being surprised later by an unexpected demand.

(4) *Repositioning*. You will need to make counter-proposals or offer alternative solutions in an effort to work towards a solution. This discussion forms the middle part of the negotiation. This part of the negotiation is very dependent on strategy and may involve both sides making concessions, discussing creative solutions or attacking the other side's position. You will put your own interpretation on the facts and law to justify your demands and to try to persuade your opponent to see things from your point of view. Point out their weaknesses firmly and politely. You may also be able to identify common interests. If you can work out their underlying interests, you should be able to come up with some creative solutions. This is vital to a problem solving approach.

Concessions will be made during this stage. Concessions relate purely to what each side will get from any agreement. It is better not to agree to give something without being clear what you will get in return. You can do this by making conditional offers: '... if my client does this, will yours do that?'

Listening and questioning skills will be very important at this stage. You now know what the other side's objectives are, but do you know why? You know what they think the facts and law are, but why? What evidence do they have, what research have they done? 'Why' is also important if you are to discover their underlying interests. You need to be firm and assertive to get the answers you want. Don't let the other side avoid your questions. If you need to, put the question again, possibly in a slightly different way, until you get an answer.

(5) *Convergence*. This stage involves the narrowing of differences. It tends to be more open and less guarded than the previous stages. There might be a feeling that time is starting to run out and something has to be done if an agreement is going to be reached. Positions will be clarified and the areas and extent of dispute will be narrowed. A competitive approach at this point would involve strong argument and threats to force concessions. This is, however, where some

competitive negotiations break down. Co-operative negotiators might use promises instead of threats. Creative negotiators may use this period to jointly decide which of the proposals identified is best and to make final adjustments to those proposals or bring collateral items into the final agreement.

Try always to keep in mind the whole case rather than each separate point.

(6) *Closing.* At this stage you may reach a final agreement. This can be because you have come naturally to this point, or because a deadline is almost on top of you and you know there's no chance of getting a better deal.

Alternatively, you might need to take proposals back to your client for consideration or, if no agreement seems likely at this point, you may arrange to meet again later when more information is available, or just leave the door open without making any specific plans to negotiate again. If you want to bring the meeting to a close, you could make it clear you have reached your final position, suggest splitting the final differences or leave an outstanding point to be decided by an agreed third party.

(7) *Recording.* Although you might be dazed and relieved to have got an agreement, you have not completed the process until you have properly recorded the outcome (you will be negligent if you don't).

If possible, you should note all important points during the meeting. If agreement was reached, you will also need to confirm and record the agreement and set a timetable for carrying out its requirements.

The drafting of the agreement is very important. It is generally better to be the one to write up the agreement. Obviously, not so that you can squeeze in a couple of extra goodies for your side, but because it will give you more control over the language used and over any small ambiguities. Unless it was specifically agreed (which will be rare), never say that you have *won*. This will only cause bad feeling. You might even consider drafting the agreement in terms that allow both sides to save face and argue that they won.

THE PSYCHOLOGY OF NEGOTIATION

It is well recognised that there are two sets of issues to deal with in a negotiation. The first set relate to the matter being discussed; these are relatively easy to identify:

(a) the details of the catering contract for the wedding;

(b) the wilted state of the salad;

(c) the food poisoning;

(d) the unhappy guests;

(e) the refusal to pay.

The second set relate to the relationship between the two negotiators:

(a) friendly;

(b) suspicious;

(c) unco-operative;

(d) patronising.

Some of these issues can be much harder to recognise. Nevertheless, this second set of issues is as important as the first to the outcome of the negotiation. If you are intimidated by a more experienced and aggressive opponent, you are likely to give more weight to what he has to say and might give more concessions than you would to a more co-operative negotiator. Preparation is the only way to offset this kind of problem: that is, to know that this will be your likely reaction and to consciously stop yourself being intimidated. To prepare in this way, you need to know something about the way opponents react to each other psychologically in a negotiation.

You need to know the detail of the facts and law. Did your client really disclose confidential information without permission? Who owned the information? Did your client know it was confidential? But, if you are to succeed in your bid to strike a victory for the forces of free speech, you also need to know about the subtleties of the personal interaction between you and your opponent.

Methods of persuasion

As part of your negotiation, you will need to use techniques of persuasion to convince the other side, as far as you can, of the strength of your arguments. The most common categories of argument that you will use are probably legal and factual. You might seek to persuade the other side that your interpretation of a case is right and theirs is not. You might also try to convince them of your interpretation of the facts of the case. If you put your arguments strongly and argue well, you should be able to persuade the other side, to some degree at least, of the merits of your view. You are very unlikely to be able to get them to change their minds completely, but you can move the focus of the negotiation in your favour. To do this, you must make sure that your argument is well prepared, accurate and concise. You should also remember to use argument only when it is really necessary, not to put the other side down or because you are frustrated by the way the negotiation is progressing.

How might your personality type affect your approach?

Researchers have found that personality traits can affect the way in which someone will perform as a negotiator. This is not to say that certain types of people will definitely react in certain ways; just that there are patterns, awareness of which can be useful. It has been found that the more anxious a negotiator is, whether generally or in relation to the particular situation, the less co-operative he is likely to be. If a negotiator tends to be rather authoritarian, then it is likely that she will be less co-operative than other less authoritarian individuals. If an individual is not a risk taker, they are likely to behave in a more co-operative manner: this is exaggerated if the negotiator has low self-esteem.

This sort of knowledge can be used when planning a negotiation. If you know that the other party is very self-confident, you can predict that they are more likely to use less co-operative behaviour.

Emotional significance

Emotion can play an important role in a negotiation. Whether you feel particularly confident or intimidated will have an effect on your performance. Issues such as your feelings about the negotiation and your opponent are often referred to as cognitive influences. What you feel about the negotiation will depend on your expectations. Your expectations will be based on what you know about the case and about the other side. Of course, the more accurate your knowledge, the more accurate your expectations should be, so thorough preparation is important here to avoid unrealistic expectations, either positive or negative.

Below we have listed some of the psychological responses that can occur during a negotiation, often without either negotiator being fully aware of what is going on.

Mirroring

Most people want to be accepted. That means it is natural in many situations to modify your language, accent, posture and attitude to match someone else's.

It is common in a negotiation to find yourself reacting to the other party in the same way that they are acting towards you. If they are friendly, you are more likely to be friendly, and if they are aggressive, you are likely to react to them in an aggressive way. You need to be aware of this so that you can stay in control of your behaviour and not let the other party dictate it. There are dangers in escalating friendly behaviour as well as the obvious problems of escalating aggressive behaviour. You may find yourself being more co-operative and giving more concessions than you had planned if your opponent is very friendly, or in a deadlock or walk out situation if you mirror your opponent's aggressive behaviour.

Lack of concentration/stress

In a long meeting, concentration is bound to wane due to tiredness. Alternatively, stress may build, also affecting concentration. Recognise what is happening if you feel like this. If you were well prepared, there will be a good reason why you are feeling this way. It is quite likely that your opponent is feeling the same. Suggest a review of what has been achieved so far, or stop to draw up a list of the issues still to be dealt with. Take a short break if you have been negotiating for some time.

Power imbalance

There are many reasons why in a negotiation there might be a power imbalance that relates to issues other than the facts or law. One of you might be less experienced, badly prepared or under time pressure. If it's you, you will feel at a disadvantage. Do whatever you can to avoid this kind of problem. If it's too late for that, don't let this one point get out of proportion and let your assumptions about your shortcomings become self-fulfilling prophecies. If you are the inexperienced one, remember that experience can bring over-confidence, which comes with its own set of disadvantages.

Formality

Things like your surroundings can also have an effect on your performance in a negotiation. When face to face negotiations take place in a more formal context, you are likely to find it easier to concentrate on what is being said. This should be considered when deciding where and when to have a negotiation. Try to use a setting in which you are not likely to be distracted. You could also think about what you wear. If you are involved in a simulated exercise, you are likely to find it easier to get into your role if you dress as you would if in practice.

PROBLEMS IN NEGOTIATIONS

As you have now seen, negotiating is a fairly complicated process. This means that there is plenty of potential for problems to arise. There are certain ethical issues that might come up; for example, when you don't want the other side to know some damaging information. Problems can also arise if the relationship between the two negotiators breaks down. Below we consider some of the more common problems you might encounter and how you might deal with them.

The ethics of negotiating

Should I always tell the truth?

Of course; you should not lie in a negotiation. It could be an offence, and for barristers and solicitors the professional codes of conduct specifically identify it as unacceptable. Lying will include deliberately misleading, concealing something you know should be disclosed or denying that you agreed to something when you did – even if it was a mistake. Subject to this, it is obvious that some lawyers will be more ready than others to divert attention from some points and exaggerate others. Research has shown that exaggeration of your case and minimisation of the other side's can poison the atmosphere of a negotiation. So we think that even this kind of manipulation, which falls short of lying, should be avoided.

Having said all this, we must make it clear that you are under no duty in the negotiation itself to disclose things that are adverse to your case. If you know about a court decision that shoots a hole in one of your main arguments, you don't have to point it out to the other side in the negotiation.[8]

Honesty to your clients

Honesty is as important in your relationship with the client as with other lawyers.[9] In particular, you must make sure your client knows as well as you do the strengths and weaknesses of the case and the realistic range for success. If your client has unrealistic expectations, you must tell them that they are likely to be disappointed.

---

8   If you are negotiating as part of a civil or criminal litigation process, however, you might be under a duty to disclose certain information, including information that is adverse to your case, at some stage in the process. You should make sure that you fulfil any such duty. If you think that a lawyer on the other side has lied, you should report them to the Law Society or the Bar Council.

9   Solicitors' Practice Rules, r 1, says that 'a solicitor shall not do anything in the course of practising as a solicitor, or permit another person to do anything on his or her behalf, which compromises or impairs or is likely to compromise or impair any of the following: (a) the solicitor's independence or integrity; (b) a person's freedom to instruct a solicitor of his or her choice; (c) the solicitor's duty to act in the best interests of the client; (d) the good repute of the solicitor or of the solicitors' profession; (e) the solicitor's proper standard of work; (f) the solicitor's duty to the court'.

Use of threats

The most obvious threat is 'if you don't give me ... I will end the negotiation'. But any situation where one party says they will act in a way that is damaging to the other is a threat. It is sometimes hard to know when someone is just pointing out what will happen if a certain course of action is taken and when a threat is being made.[10]

The client is in charge

Remember that you are acting on behalf of your client. Make sure that you never agree to something that you don't have your client's authority to agree to. You should always keep your client informed of progress, and advise him honestly on the benefits of any offers made. Never try to make the client do what you want them to.

Remember, you can only act on your client's instructions. If you have not discussed with your client the exact terms which she would be happy to settle on, you will not be able to enter any final agreement without first checking. If you do not have express authority to settle a case, you should make it clear to the other side that any agreement you reach is subject to your client's final approval.

Check that the other side have authority so that they don't try to re-open the discussion later.

Without prejudice negotiations

All negotiations to settle a case should be 'without prejudice'.[11] If they are, what is said in the negotiation is protected by privilege and can't be used later as evidence to help win the case. Although, in theory, any negotiation which aims to reach a compromise is a 'without prejudice' negotiation, it is safer to make the position clear by saying so or by putting the words at the top of a letter.

Problems of confidence

Being inexperienced

Just because the person you are negotiating with has more experience than you doesn't mean they will be any better. If you have thoroughly prepared the matter, you are more than halfway there. It could be that they will underestimate you.

The competitive or aggressive negotiator

If a negotiator tries to take advantage of your lack of confidence with a competitive or unco-operative approach, you may need to fight fire with fire and show that you can

---

10 This point is particularly important for barristers, who are barred from making unethical threats as a matter of professional conduct.

11 When information is given without prejudice, it cannot be used later as evidence. All legal negotiations aimed at settlement of a litigated case will be without prejudice, but it is a good idea to always make this clear.

deal with a competitive meeting before suggesting that a more co-operative tone might be beneficial.

If you are confronted by anger in a negotiation, remember it could be real or feigned. Probably the best response is to expressly acknowledge the anger and the reason for it, but do not give concessions.

Last minute changes

What if you are well prepared, but just before your negotiation over damages for severe back injury caused by negligent driving you find out that, in fact, your client isn't as badly disabled as was first thought? What if when you get into the negotiation, the other side tell you they have video of your client playing football?

The key here is to take time to think before reacting. It would be unwise to assume things are as bad as you first suspect without checking. Maybe it's not your client at all. You could take a break to reassess the position. If you were caught by something as serious as this, it would be advisable to postpone the negotiation until after you have seen the video and discussed the matter with your client and his medical advisers.

Stalemate

Sometimes a negotiation might come to a dead end. One party might threaten to leave or you might just find that, although you are still talking, you aren't getting anywhere. Not all negotiations will end in agreement, and it could be that it is time to end the meeting. But this isn't necessarily the case when you get to stalemate; sometimes you might just need a change in approach to get things moving again.

What can you do?

- Move the problem item to the end of the agenda.
- Have a break – this could be five minutes or it may mean coming back another day after you have discussed the issue with your client or obtained further evidence.
- Make a concession – this might change the other side's attitude.
- Discuss the disadvantages of giving up – this can give the parties' motivation to carry on a boost.
- Discuss the advantages of an agreement – this will have a similar effect.
- Go over what has been achieved.
- Search for alternative, creative solutions.
- Discuss the reasons for the stalemate.

Forcing yourself into a corner

If you find yourself in a difficult position in a negotiation, it may sometimes be because you have put yourself there. Obviously, you should try to avoid this.

If you are particularly adamant that you cannot give way on an issue, to do so later may well be seen as evidence of weakness. You might feel that any concessions given show a weakness on your part, but this is particularly true if they involve an apparent change of mind. What can you do to avoid this? Of course, giving concessions itself is not weak; it is part of the process. To stop the feeling that you may be losing face, you can try to make sure that you generally only make conditional offers when discussing concessions. For example, 'if you were to drop your demand for compensation for X, then I think I could accept less for Y'. In addition, take care not to state that you will not move your position in relation to a certain issue unless you are absolutely sure that this is the case and will remain so.

Surprise attacks

Some negotiators might use surprise tactics, such as abrupt changes in approach or unforeseen demands, to try to throw you off balance. The answer here is to stay calm.

You should try to ignore any personality-led issues and focus on the facts of the case.

Misleading information

You might be given information that, although not untrue, is misleading. It could relate to the importance of an objective, a deadline or a willingness to concede. Don't necessarily take things at face value. Listen carefully to exactly what is said, the words used can conceal subtle differences:

My client will absolutely not provide more than £20,000 …

I'm not authorised to go over £20,000 …

and:

I'm not authorised to go over £20,000 at the moment …

are not the same. If you're not absolutely clear what is being said, you can sometimes test it by pushing. Ask:

Is x your final offer?

or:

Is there anything we could do to make x more acceptable?

CONCLUSION

We have considered what exactly negotiation is and how different approaches to a negotiation can be classified. We have also considered how to prepare for a negotiation and how to enhance your performance through a knowledge of the psychology of negotiating. We hope you can see that, in fact, negotiation itself is not one skill. It is a combination of skills which together enable a negotiator to perform well. In this concluding section we will look at the main supporting skills needed by a good negotiator after making a few general points.

Giving clients what they want

In the end, a negotiation is about getting the best results for your client. It is important not to lose sight of this at any stage. You, as a lawyer, are acting for your client on her instructions and everything you do should be in her best interests.

Remaining objective

Although it is sometimes hard not to become personally and emotionally involved in a negotiation, you should try to remain as objective as you can. By doing this you will be able to perform better and deal more calmly with any problems that might arise. It will also allow you to keep in mind the needs of your client.

Supporting skills

What are the skills you will need to develop your expertise as a negotiator? Below are listed some of the most important skills which will form the foundations of your negotiation.

Listening

If you are going to respond effectively in a negotiation, you need to understand what the other side is saying. This might seem obvious, but if you are not careful in your listening you can easily misunderstand or miss a vital piece of information that could be used to your advantage. Listening takes real concentration. You need to think about what is said and the way it is said. There is a danger that you will be so busy thinking about your next move that you won't pay attention to your opponent. You might also have a feeling that it is more important to talk than to listen, but of course communication is about both. Be aware that external distractions, worries about other issues, time pressures and tiredness will all make concentration and, therefore, listening more difficult.

Active listening

This term is used to describe a method of checking you have understood what your opponent is saying. When you are actively listening you will repeat your opponent's position to their satisfaction before putting your own view. In fact, active listening goes much further than just checking. It forces you to state things from your opponent's point of view. This helps you to understand their viewpoint and it helps them to see that you recognise their position, even though you dispute it. Ultimately, this makes it easier for both parties to step back, deal with the problem itself and be creative rather than being controlled by the emotions of conflict.

Understanding body language

There are certain forms of body language that might reveal what you or your opponent is really feeling, and it is very useful to have some knowledge of these.

Changes in the tone of someone's voice, their facial expression or their posture can say a lot about what they are thinking. If your opponent hesitates or seems embarrassed, it may be that they are not really convinced of what they are saying. Although they are telling you they are being conciliatory and co-operative, someone who sits with their arms folded and fists clenched will not be as convincing, or get the same response, as someone who sits back with their hands open.

Here are a few other examples of body language and their likely meanings that you may already be familiar with:

Body language	Meaning
Leaning forward	Interested
Face touching/mouth touching	Uncertain/doubtful, possibly deceitful
Ear rubbing	Not liking what is being said
Fingers (or other objects) in mouth	Anxious
Chin stroking	Making a decision
Eye contact	Authentic
Lack of eye contact	Deceptive
Fidgeting	Deceptive

Of course, even though studies have found that these gestures are normally associated with certain responses or feelings, you should remember that the man who touches his teeth may not really be anxious; he could just be searching for the remnants of his breakfast.

Questioning

You will need to use appropriate questions if you are going to get the most out of a negotiation. You certainly can't rely on the other party telling you everything you need to know. Refer to the chapter on interviewing for more detail on questioning techniques.

Persuasion

As a negotiator, you will be trying to persuade the other side that at least some of your arguments are right.

Getting the other side to see things from your point of view can be as much about the way you speak as what you say. You should be as clear as possible. That means as few pauses and 'um's as possible; avoid complex words and sentences, just as you would if writing a letter.

Good preparation

One of the essential elements of being a good negotiator is being well prepared. To present your case effectively, you need to know it well. You also need to know the law relevant to your case, otherwise you won't be able to respond to allegations made by the other side. Consider the following:

> Of course, you must realise that your case is very weak and *Cheshire and Fifoot* says that the Occupiers' Liability Act 1957 is of little relevance in this kind of situation.

> I don't think that's right.

> Well, I think you're going to face problems there. Let me set out the position as I see it under common law negligence, where establishing a duty is going to be difficult for you.

Compare this:

> Of course, you must realise that your case is very weak and *Cheshire and Fifoot* says that the Occupiers' Liability Act 1957 is of little relevance in this kind of situation.

> I can't accept that. Are you familiar with last month's Court of Appeal decision in *Smith v Jones*? I have a copy here if you would like to see it. Although the facts are somewhat different from ours, one of the judges spent some time discussing the general applicability of the Act and expressly states that it will apply in these kinds of circumstances. That judgment has also been followed in another High Court case.

In the second exchange, due to more thorough preparation, the negotiator is able to take control, rather than losing it.

As we discussed when considering preparing for a negotiation, a very useful exercise is to identify the strengths and weaknesses of your case and the other side's case. You will then be better able to predict the other side's line of attack. Looking at a case from your opponent's point of view will always be useful. Ask yourself, what arguments will they use? How will you respond?

As part of your preparation, you must clarify what it is that your client wants from the negotiation. Is there anything that is not acceptable? If money is involved, does your client have a figure above or below which they will not go? What authority do you have to make an agreement; can anything be agreed before a final check with your client?

A negotiation plan is useful as an agenda for your meeting with the other side. You can draw up a plan before the meeting or agree a plan with the other side.

Self-awareness

The more you are able to watch yourself in a detached way, the easier you will find it to be aware of what is going on in a negotiation. If you are reacting to your opponent's behaviour or becoming emotionally involved, you will see this quickly and will be able to choose to alter your behaviour.

Using information effectively

You will need to be able to process information fairly quickly and efficiently. When reading through the information you have about the case and during the negotiation itself, you will need to assess what is relevant and what is not. You must use the relevant information to strengthen your case as far as you can.

Being realistic

When making assertions about your client's case or the strength of your arguments, you must always be realistic. If you use bluff, or exaggerate your case, you are likely to do more harm than good. Obviously, you will want to use the most beneficial interpretation of the facts; that is fine. But if you step into the realm of exaggeration, you are very likely to lose credibility with your opponent who will then be less likely to be co-operative in the negotiation or believe any of the points you make.

Honesty

You will not be surprised to hear that you must be honest at all times. Dishonesty will not help a negotiation, and is unethical and unprofessional.[12]

Politeness

Stalemates and walk out situations are much more likely to occur when one or both of the parties to a negotiation stops being polite. If you can both maintain your politeness, it will be much easier to remain objective.[13]

Counselling skills

What we mean here is the interaction between you and your client which is necessary to decide how to progress. This will include the decision of whether to negotiate at all, and the identification of realistic objectives and best and worst outcomes. Your relationship with your client is not equal: you are the legal expert. You must be careful never to dominate. You should be realistic and truthful about the chances of success at trial and through negotiation. You need to keep the client as fully informed as you can and remember that you are only acting on instructions.

Learning to negotiate

During your course, if negotiation is taught as a skill, you will undoubtedly be given the chance to practise. This practice will probably be through negotiation exercises. You might also be assessed on your competence as a negotiator. In this section, we will consider how you may be taught and assessed. We hope that this will help you to get as much as you can out of the process.

---

12 Law Society, *Guide to the Professional Conduct of Solicitors*, 8th edn, 1999, London: Law Society, para 19.01: 'A solicitor must act towards other solicitors with frankness and good faith consistent with his or her overriding duty to the client. Any fraudulent or deceitful conduct by one solicitor towards another will render the offending solicitor liable to disciplinary action, in addition to the possibility of civil or criminal proceedings ...'

13 *Ibid*, para 19.01 (continued): 'A solicitor must maintain his or her personal integrity and observe the requirements of good manners and courtesy towards other members of the profession or their staff, no matter how bitter the feelings between the clients.'

How will students be assessed?

Usually, if you are going to be assessed on your negotiation technique, you will be given a problem to negotiate with another student. You will probably be given some advance documentation to read giving the background to the problem. You are likely to be given a certain amount of time to complete the negotiation, maybe about 15 minutes. The negotiation itself will almost certainly be directly observed or video recorded. You might also be asked to submit a written plan and/or an analysis of the negotiation for assessment.

What are lecturers assessing?

Below is an example of the kind of checklist that might be used to assess a negotiation exercise. A tutor would consider whether, and to what extent, you had met each of the set criteria.

Did the student:

(a) Show evidence of thorough preparation?

(b) Show an understanding of the strengths and weaknesses of the case?

(c) Deal well with unexpected information?

(d) Deal well with ethical issues?

(e) Obtain a reasonable result for the client?

If your negotiation plan is assessed, your tutor will be looking for evidence of the first two criteria above being met. You might have been given a suggested format for your plan, in which case you will be expected to use that format.

When assessing your analysis of the negotiation, your tutor will be looking for a realistic assessment of your performance as well as a record of what happened. If you do have to provide an analysis, you should not worry if you did not stick to your original plan. But you should explain why you didn't. You should aim to show in your analysis that you have reflected on your performance and are aware of the things you did well and the things you could improve.

Diana Tribe considers what makes an effective negotiator in her book *Negotiation*.[14] Factors such as the financial outcome for the client, the costs, the number of issues unresolved and the relationship between the parties at the end of the negotiation are highlighted as measures of success.

Improving your performance

Not surprisingly, the best way to improve your legal negotiation technique is to practise. But even practice on its own is not enough. If you continue to practise only, you could just repeat the mistakes you have already made. How can you make sure that you will improve? Only by reviewing what you did and considering what was good, what was bad and how you might have done things differently. You can do this yourself

---

14 Tribe, D, *Negotiation*, 1994, London: Cavendish Publishing.

by doing a simple self-assessment after each negotiation exercise. It is even more useful if you can get constructive criticism from observers or if you can video your performance and reflect on it, as both these techniques give more objectivity.

Studying law, you are often encouraged to look for problems in scenarios. Even as a lawyer, this is an essential task. In a negotiation, if you concentrate on the problem spotting instead of the problem solving, you will never get as far as you might. You have to be aware of the issues, but you also need to take a constructive approach.

FURTHER READING

Fisher, R and Ury, W, *Getting to Yes*, 2003, London: Random House.

Tribe, D, *Negotiation*, 1994, London: Cavendish Publishing.

Ury, W, *Getting Past No: Negotiating Your Way from Confrontation to Co-operation*, 1993, London: Random House.

CHAPTER 10

MEDIATION: THE PROCESS AND
PRACTICE OF MEDIATION AS A FORM
OF DISPUTE RESOLUTION

INTRODUCTION

Mediation is included in this book because the ways in which disputes are resolved have changed radically in recent years. The term 'litigation' has been replaced in many areas by 'dispute resolution', which can include litigation, but also means negotiation, arbitration, mediation and various combinations of all of these.

We have looked at negotiation in detail in Chapter 9. In this chapter, we will explain what mediation is and the skills needed by a mediator as well as giving a little background about other dispute resolution procedures.

What is mediation?

If you're not familiar with mediation, you might have a picture of the mediator running backwards and forwards between two people who have their backs to each other and their arms folded obstinately, trying to get them to turn around and give each other a hug. You won't be surprised to hear that it's not quite like this. For a start, mediation can only happen if the parties want it to, so they need to be willing to negotiate with each other. The mediator is really only there to help that process.

Technically, mediation can be described as the process whereby a neutral third party, the mediator, helps two or more parties to solve a dispute or conflict by facilitating their negotiations. This means that, to understand mediation, you need also to understand negotiation. A mediator does not give any judgment about who is right and who is wrong. So as with most of the skills in this book, the basis of mediation lies in common sense. If two of your friends are arguing over something, it is quite natural for you to intervene and try to help them come to some agreement. If that works, it is better than coming in forcefully with your own opinion which will probably result in you falling out with one or both of them. Mediation is nothing more than this in essence, but certain approaches and methods have been developed for use in a legal context and we will look at those in more detail in this chapter.

As we have mentioned above, mediation is just one form of alternative dispute resolution (ADR). This is a term used to describe procedures that can be used instead of litigation to settle disputes.

Litigation is the whole process of taking a dispute to court, from the issue of the claim to the eventual trial. Court litigation in the UK often doesn't provide the answer that commercial organisations or individuals are looking for. It is adversarial in nature, and if a case goes as far as a court trial, then there will always be a winner and a loser. Even if relations weren't too bad between them before the court action, they inevitably will be after it. Once two parties have done battle in public, any bridges between them will be burnt.

The Civil Procedure Rules 1998 (CPR)[1] which govern the conduct of civil litigation are very strict and they must be complied with; this can add to the expense of taking a case to court. In addition, the outcome of a court trial is not decided by either the claimant or defendant, but the judge applying legal principles and choosing one of the limited remedies available, such as the payment of damages or the imposition of an injunction.

Of course, negotiation is another form of ADR which is very commonly used alongside litigation. It depends a little upon whom you ask, but there are probably about 15 distinct types of ADR.

Two of the most common alternatives which can be used instead of either negotiation or mediation are conciliation and arbitration.

Conciliation is a term that is often used with, or instead of, mediation. Conciliation is used to describe a process where the mediator might be appointed by someone other than the parties, and the process may not be entirely voluntary. It has been used in employment situations in the past where an employer and a union will enter conciliation to try to resolve an industrial dispute.

An arbitrator is a third party appointed to hear both sides' arguments and then reach a decision by which the parties will usually agree to be bound. The parties appoint the arbitrator themselves and agree to be bound by his decision. It is similar to litigation in that the parties don't have control over the outcome in the same way as they do in mediation. But it is supposed to be faster, cheaper and more private than litigation. Arbitration was initially developed to meet the needs of those involved in commercially based disputes and is regulated by the Arbitration Act 1996.[2]

Mediation has come to be seen as an attractive alternative that can work more effectively in some situations. If the parties need to keep some kind of relationship going, whether personal or business, it's much easier to do so after a mediation than after a trial. If they want to save money, time or to take a more flexible approach, mediation can be more useful than court action or even arbitration. Some industries rely heavily on mediation; for example, it is very common in the areas of construction, engineering, insurance and banking, where the average case will be worth millions of pounds. It is also common in family proceedings and is being used more and more in medical negligence cases, neighbour disputes and employment cases. Since the CPR governing the conduct of civil litigation were introduced in 1999, the number of mediations has increased significantly. Under the CPR, part of the court's duty is to encourage the use of processes like mediation. Parties can be given 'time out' from the litigation process to try mediation.[3]

Michael Noone, in *Mediation*,[4] outlines the four principal characteristics of the kind of mediation used as an alternative to litigation. These are that it is:

---

1   CPR 1998 SI 1998/3132.
2   Provision is made under the Arbitration Act 1996, s 9, for a stay of proceedings for arbitration to take place.
3   Under the CPR, requests for a stay of proceedings in order for mediation to take place can be made to the court.
4   Noone, M, *Mediation*, 1997, London: Cavendish Publishing.

(a) accessible – anyone who wants to can use mediation. There is no rigid procedure which all mediations must follow. Being flexible is seen as another characteristic of mediation;

(b) voluntary – anyone taking part in mediation has to agree to do so and can withdraw at any time they want to. They can't be forced to accept any outcome that they don't feel comfortable with;

(c) confidential – because the parties need to feel free to say anything and to be open for a mediation to work, everything disclosed as part of a mediation is confidential;

(d) facilitative – mediation takes a creative and problem solving approach to issues and it is up to the mediator to remain impartial and help the parties come to an agreement.

Some mediators are lawyers, while some come from other professions and bring a particular knowledge of a subject or industry to their work as mediators. Anyone can mediate, but there are professional mediation qualifications which people seeking a mediator will often demand. Nearly all professional mediators will have had specialist mediation training. This is provided by mediation organisations which can also provide mediators on request. These mediators might have some specialist knowledge or background, so someone who has worked in the construction industry might concentrate on construction-based mediations, but it is more important that a mediator is an expert in the process of mediation than in the subject matter of the dispute. If detailed subject knowledge will be needed because the subject of the dispute is so complicated, a mediator without it can always be assisted by a subject specialist.

Facilitative and evaluative styles of mediation

At this point we should just mention one of the main distinctions between approaches to mediation. It is a distinction that will be considered when choosing a mediator as well as the mediator's qualifications, training, knowledge and experience. A distinction is made between the purely facilitative and the evaluative approach to mediation. Some mediators are more evaluative of the subject matter than others. As well as facilitating the process, they will weigh up the arguments on each side, challenge the parties and give a view on positions taken or options raised. They will not act as judge, but they might give an indication when one party's argument on a particular point is weaker than the other's. Other mediators will be purely facilitative, and not go beyond helping the parties to clarify their interests and priorities without giving any opinion on the strength of their cases. The evaluative approach can be criticised on the basis that it is really for the parties to form views on the issues, not the mediator. The more evaluation that goes on, the more the process moves away from being mediation and comes closer to arbitration. Our description of mediation in this chapter assumes a purely facilitative approach.

How is it structured?

Most mediations will follow a fairly standard pattern. There will be an opening meeting between everyone involved, then the parties can go into separate rooms where they can talk confidentially with the mediator. The mediator can move between these rooms and the parties can also periodically come back together to discuss the issues. The use of separate rooms means that open discussions can take place without revealing confidential information to the other parties if that is what is wanted.

How does mediation fit into the legal process?

Mediation can be used outside litigation or alongside it. In pretty much any kind of dispute, from arguments over who's responsible for cutting a dividing garden hedge to million pound commercial problems about luxury liner outfitting contracts, it can be used as an alternative to court action.

If court action is started, mediation can still be used at almost any time, and the courts will be happy to accommodate this in the hope that an agreement will result and a trial be avoided.

Mediation is particularly likely to be encouraged by the courts at the allocation stage, case management conference and pre-trial review. In fact, if mediation is not considered and discussed between legal advisers and clients, legal advisers could be deemed negligent. If it is appropriate but is not used, costs penalties may be imposed by the courts.[5]

Timing can be particularly important to the acceptability and success of mediation. Because the parties have to agree to the mediation, if it is proposed too early, their reaction might be to say: 'There's no way I'm going to sit in a room and talk to X. I don't trust him and I can't believe it will do any good.' Later, although their feelings towards each other might be no kinder, they are likely to be more tired of the argument and more attracted by the prospect of ending the hassle, time and money they are expending on it.

Teaching mediation

Mediation is a skill that is much more rarely taught in law schools than most of the other skills covered in this book. There are a number of reasons for this. In particular, although a lawyer might become a professional mediator, mediation is not a skill that is used on a day to day basis by a solicitor or barrister. It is fair, then, to give it a lower priority than research or interviewing, but it is still a useful skill and, even if it will not be used formally by most of those reading this book, it is more and more likely that there will be some involvement with the mediation process.

We think that you will probably gain a much better understanding of mediation and of the mediators that you might meet if you understand the skills involved. So learning about mediation is useful if you want to become a mediator, if you want to become a lawyer or if you want to work in any area or industry that might make use of the process to settle disputes.

---

5   See *Dunnett v Railtrack plc* [2002] EWCA Civ 303; [2002] 2 All ER 850.

MEDIATION – THE SKILLS NEEDED

As with many legal skills, there are some people who may be better suited to being mediators or who find the mediation skills easier than others. There are some, too, who will be fascinated by the process of helping to bring two sides together and others who will find it hard to get very excited about. Partly it's about learning and experience; partly, it's just personality. However, it is possible to set out the main skills needed in the mediation process and these skills can be developed by almost anyone. These skills are outlined below.

Negotiation skills

Of course it is the parties, not you as the mediator, who are really negotiating. You are just helping them to do that, because mediation is a kind of guided negotiation. But to help them, you do need good negotiation skills too. You need to know about the different approaches to negotiation, and how they can be used by the parties in a mediation to similar effect. You must be a problem solver, and be able to suggest possible offers and counter-offers to each party.

When you are mediating a dispute about how money and assets will be split between a divorcing couple, you can use negotiation techniques like getting at their underlying interests and finding creative solutions to help the couple work through the process. In fact, most mediation settlements will deal with the parties' interests rather than their legal rights or duties. Using your experience of reading body language will also help you manage people. When you see the signs, you can intervene and calm things down before the steam starts to waft from someone's ears or the two sides start threatening each other with physical violence.

Building trust

The parties must feel confidence in the mediation process and the mediator and they should through the process begin to feel some confidence in each other. This confidence comes from trust. For example, the mediator will make sure the parties fully understand the process and make it clear that she is completely neutral at the start. Noone, in Chapter 2 of *Mediation*,[6] gives some examples of how a mediator might build trust in the process, the mediator and between the parties. So, for example, getting the parties to work together on a list of issues might help their relationship with each other.

Maintaining neutrality

It is very important that neither side ever feels the mediator is biased or more sympathetic to one side or the other. Both sides must be treated equally. That doesn't mean you won't have your own thoughts and feelings about the dispute; it just means you won't show them. In truth, you might have taken an instant dislike to the rude company manager or the whining, greasy haired accountant, or you may have very

---

6   *Op cit*, Noone, fn 4.

strong personal feelings about the problem they face, but you must be able to put these aside during the process, or at least hide them and not allow them to affect the way you act. You need to make sure that the *process* is fair and that you are in control of it. But you are not there to make sure that the *agreement* is fair, because they control the agreement, not you. You are there to help them reach an agreement that is acceptable to them, not to you.

You can be challenging and firm, but never judgmental. It will be part of your job to act as a 'devil's advocate' or 'reality checker', particularly in private sessions with each party. You can do this by testing their positions and making sure they can be justified, but that doesn't involve giving your own opinion.

Maintaining impartiality

As well as appearing neutral about the outcome, you must treat the parties impartially. So you need to balance the time you spend with each party, and give them roughly equal time to speak and put their views as far as you can. Sometimes this is not possible, so if you do need to spend more time with one side you should take care to explain why to both, and reassure the other side that it is not due to any bias. You should never say anything that implies blame on either side more than the other and you should avoid giving advice to either party, even by agreeing when one says: 'We will only offer this much, isn't that reasonable?'

Facilitating the process

Part of your job as a mediator is to ensure that the process runs as smoothly as possible. If the atmosphere starts to get tense or hostile, you will need to act to make it more constructive. Everything you do is intended to help the parties reach agreement, so mediators must always be facilitative.

Controlling the process and the people

People involved in a mediation can sometimes behave honestly, calmly and fairly, but they can also sometimes be emotional, selfish, deceitful, rude or bullying. You will need to be able to spot and regulate all kinds of conduct. The parties will need guidance regarding the process, and there may be times when the mediator will need to step in to control their behaviour. How far you let people blow off steam will depend a lot on the individual case, but you will probably get a feeling for when things are about to go too far and you should step in and take control if either side seems to be getting too angry or upset. You need to do it in a way that shows understanding and concern, rather than by getting angry yourself.

You will also act as a chairperson when the parties are talking to each other and should be able to stop one party dominating or two people talking at the same time. To help you do this, you might go over some basic ground rules at the start of the mediation, so that the parties know from the beginning what they are, and are not, allowed to do.

Being adaptable

A mediator might need to adapt the process to the needs of the parties either before or during the mediation. Although you may have a planned structure, you need to be able to change it if it would be to the advantage of the parties.

Being able to listen

A good mediator will need to be able to concentrate on what each party is saying and understand the underlying meaning. You will also need to be able to show the parties that you are actively listening to them. This involves checking understanding by questioning, rephrasing and summarising what has been said, and taking note of body language. We have considered active listening in detail in Chapter 8 of this book.

Being able to question appropriately

A mediator will need to draw out what each party wants by appropriate questioning. There are many different types of questioning and, in mediations, some will be more appropriate than others. Open questions will help you to understand each side's position at the beginning by providing more information than closed questions. So:

> What do you really want?

might be better than:

> Do you want to stay in your flat and wait two months for the damp in your kitchen to be treated or do you want to pay for it yourself and put in a claim for reimbursement?

Hypothetical questions, that is, questions using a scenario, can be helpful in considering options for settlement, and clarifying questions enable the mediator to fully understand the problem.

> So, for example:

> How would you feel about being re-housed immediately in the same area, but in a slightly smaller flat?

This is a hypothetical question, the answer to which will help you understand what exactly it is that the person does want or need. If you are naturally someone who is interested in other people you will find it easier to listen actively and ask appropriate questions. If not, you'll have to think a bit harder about the questions you ask and how you phrase them.

Specialist knowledge

Sometimes the parties might want their mediator to have experience or knowledge in a certain area. It might help you to mediate in a dispute about the level of pension payments from a fund if you know something about how pension funds work. Most mediators would say that it's the mediation skills, not the specialist knowledge, that makes a mediation work. But in particularly complicated cases, it can help to have someone to whom the intricacies of, say, share option schemes or the workings of the international diamond market do not need to be explained. If the parties want an experienced mediator and a specialist, it is possible to have two mediators, one being less experienced but having specialist knowledge of the relevant area.

IS MEDIATION APPROPRIATE?

Mediation is appropriate for most kinds of disputes, but there are some important questions to consider, the answers to which might mean that another way of resolving the problem would be more appropriate.

Do the parties both want to use mediation?

Are the parties at a stage in their dispute when mediation might work? If you try to get two people to mediate when they are very angry with each other, before they have had a chance to even think about how they might deal with a problem, it might not work. If one of the parties, or even their lawyers, are reluctant to use mediation, but you think that it would actually work, you might need to employ a bit of gentle persuasion. See the section below, p 314, on dealing with problems, for some ideas on how to counter a hostile attitude to mediation.

Do the parties want/need to maintain a relationship?

If a husband and wife are trying to agree on who their 10 year old son will live with, or if two companies which have an otherwise very profitable arrangement fall out over a particular issue, their continuing relationship will be very important. The more important it is, the more likely it is that mediation will be a good choice because mediation, unlike litigation, can help important relationships to continue.

Is confidentiality important?

In family cases, this issue will be less important, as most alternatives to mediation will also allow for confidentiality. In commercial disputes, this is not the case. A trial of a commercial problem is very likely to be open to anyone who wants to come in and watch it, including the press. If confidentiality is important or if it will mean that certain information can be more easily discussed, mediation will be particularly attractive.

Is relative cost important?

The actual value of a dispute doesn't make any difference to whether mediation is appropriate. Two drug companies could be arguing over a patent licence worth millions of pounds worldwide or an employee might be arguing with an employer over plans to change the time of her lunch break. What is more important is the cost of mediation compared to the cost of the alternatives, whether those include complicated litigation or a possible strike by union members.

Is speed important?

If those involved are suffering emotionally or financially, a mediated settlement can resolve the problem and possibly end the suffering much faster than litigation. There are no rules or timetables for preparation so, although the parties will want to feel they are ready to mediate, they can almost always get to that stage before they would be ready for a trial.

How many people are involved?

It's easier for a mediator to deal with a dispute between two people or companies, but mediations can involve lots of different people. So just because you have not only the business accused of polluting the river, and the owner of the fish farm whose stock has been affected, but also the insurance company, the Environment Agency and the supermarket which buys the fish, it doesn't mean mediation should be avoided.

What kind of case is it?

Some cases are probably better dealt with through the courts. Occasionally a dispute over a straightforward matter requires a yes or no answer and there is no scope for agreement. It is also important for cases involving novel facts or points of law to be heard by the courts. The law would certainly be poorer if cases like *Attorney General v Guardian Newspapers Ltd* regarding the publication of confidential information, disclosed by Peter Wright in his book *Spycatcher* (1988, Bantam), had not been fully and publicly considered by the courts.[7] This is partly so that a clear precedent can be set which will be useful in other cases, and partly because, if there have been no similar cases before, it will be extra hard to agree on what is fair in this case. In cases where one of the parties is a child, mediation will also not be appropriate. This is, in part, due to the point below.

Is there a large power imbalance?

Although it is the mediator's job to facilitate a fair outcome, this can be very difficult if one party is in a much weaker position than the other. Even in litigation, there will always be advantages in being bigger and better resourced, but it can be easier for the courts to see and mitigate the effects of one party throwing their weight around or intimidating the other.

PREPARATION

The ultimate success of a mediation can easily be jeopardised by lack of proper preparation. The mediator needs to know what they are doing and the parties and their advisers need to be clear about the process and their cases.

---

7   *Attorney General v Guardian Newspapers Ltd (No 2)* [1988] 3 All ER 545.

Before the mediation even begins, it is important that the scene is properly set. If either party or the mediator isn't suitably prepared, it's pretty likely that the mediation is going to run into problems. This means that the parties must be happy with the plan to use mediation and the process should have been explained to them. Obviously, a decision will need to be made about who the mediator is to be, where and when the mediation will take place and what the mediator will be paid. The fee will often be split equally between the parties. Before a mediation, the parties might give the mediator documents to look at which provide information on the case.

Getting an agreement to mediate

The terms on which the mediation will take place should generally be written down before the mediation. If you are a professional mediator or are acting for someone using one, you will probably use a written 'agreement to mediate' which will appoint the mediator, set out the position on legal issues, such as the obligation of confidentiality and the authority of the parties to agree a settlement, and be signed by all the parties.[8] The agreement will also include practicalities like the date and place of the mediation and who will attend. It may also contain details of the kind of mediation that will take place: whether the mediator is going to be facilitative only, helping the parties come to an agreement, or whether the mediator can be evaluative, giving some opinion about the subject or the legal position.

Finally, there will be an agreement about how long the mediation will take. Usually one day is enough. Some mediations might only take an hour or so, while others may involve a number of sessions over days or weeks. It is possible for mediation to deal with only part of a dispute and, in that case, the process might be quicker.

Setting a time limit is useful, because agreements often come when there is some time pressure, though of course, when you aren't very experienced, it is difficult to know how long a particular problem will take to deal with. If it turns out to be necessary, a mediation can keep going over a time limit and even into the night if that's what the parties want.

All these things that need to be agreed can be dealt with through letters or telephone calls, or all together at a preliminary conference. If as a lawyer you are acting for one person who would like to try mediation, you should send the other side a letter proposing mediation and maybe outlining some of the potential advantages. A conference can be useful, because you can explain the mediation process to everyone face to face, and you get the chance to meet the parties and assess their relationship, which will help you prepare for the mediation itself. If you do have a preliminary conference, the opening stage of the actual mediation can be cut down slightly to avoid unnecessary repetition.

Who will come to the mediation?

The parties will always come to a mediation, but what about their lawyers? Will they come too? This depends on the kind of case you are dealing with and on the wishes of

---

8   Noone has included an example agreement in his book, *Mediation* (*op cit*, fn 4).

the parties. It can be really useful, in a family dispute, to get away from the lawyers and mediate on a more emotional and practical, rather than legal, level. On the other hand, in a large commercial dispute, company directors might rightly feel that they need their lawyers there with them for advice and help.

As a mediator, you will have to make sure that any lawyers who do attend are clear about the role they are expected to play. They are there to give assistance to their clients but not to negotiate for them. Ideally, the parties will do all the real talking, not the lawyers. Lawyers are used to the adversarial nature of litigation, and you might have to remind them about the facilitative approach needed in mediation. Lawyers can be very helpful if they prepare all the relevant information for the mediation, discuss the process and possible outcomes with their clients before the session, and advise on what information should be made available to the other side, or the mediator, and when. They can help their clients during the process by giving advice on possibilities for settlement and, afterwards, by drawing up the terms of any settlement.

There might be experts or others who won't be at the mediation, but who it is just possible either side might need to contact for some vital piece of information. If you are planning a big commercial mediation over licence rights to broadcast cable television in China and you find, very late in the evening, that you are close to a settlement but you just need to know about the plans for advertising break content, you will not want to discover that you don't have the home telephone number of your advertising director. If there is anyone who might need to be contacted, the parties should make sure they have contact details, day or night.

Authority to settle

Whoever is there representing the parties, they must have the authority to accept and sign any agreement reached. It's pointless to go through the whole gruelling process only to find that the agreement won't be kept to because the director representing the company had to get the agreement of the whole board and they won't give it.

This is why it's a good idea to deal with the question of authority in the agreement to mediate. By addressing the issue before the mediation starts, you can avoid a lot of problems later on.

Knowing the subject and the background

As a mediator you're not expected to know the details of the case before the mediation, but you will need to have a broad idea of what it is about. You can only get this from the parties or their advisers, and it's really up to you to tell them exactly what you need. You might ask the parties to prepare a case summary or confidential report of the case and their priorities. Using this before the mediation, you can think about possible trade offs to suggest.

It is essential that, during the mediation, you are able to access, record and organise all the information you have efficiently. You will build up a file of notes and other information and you need to be able to lay your hands on the right piece of paper at the right time. The best way to do this is to prepare a file with different sections for the following information:

• the names of all the parties and their advisers;

- the case summaries;
- any chronology;
- any joint statement of issues;
- the agenda;
- your notes on the opening session;
- your notes from private sessions (don't leave this open for the other side to see);
- any personal notes on mediation skills/tactics.

If you are a lawyer, acting as an adviser to a client in a mediation, your preparation on the case itself will be much the same as a preparation for a negotiation or a trial. So, lawyers should be clear about the facts, the strengths and weaknesses of the case, best and worst possible outcomes and alternatives to settlement.

It's a good idea for lawyers to exchange any evidence they think is helpful before the mediation with the other side and, in fact, a mediator might ask them to do this. This way, they won't be springing surprises on each other and the atmosphere of co-operation will not be prejudiced. To do this, the lawyers will need to think about what they will and will not disclose in the mediation. A basic rule to follow is that lawyers and clients should disclose everything unless there's a good reason not to. Lawyers are commonly rather wary of disclosing anything they don't have to, but a mediation will only work if there is an atmosphere of openness, and nearly all disclosures made as part of the mediation will be without prejudice, so the other side won't be able to use them to their advantage in subsequent litigation.

Part of the role of a lawyer will also be to explain the process to their client. They will need to explain how the mediation will work, that the mediator is neutral and that anything said within the mediation will be kept confidential. They should make sure their client understands not just the facts of the case, but the strengths and weaknesses, and the implications of carrying on to a full trial. Knowing this, clients can make a realistic assessment of any offers made.

Preparing a case summary

A lawyer advising a client in mediation will often prepare the case summary for the mediator. Lawyers will probably be given some guidance about what is required, usually a brief statement including the strengths and weaknesses and any relevant documents like contracts or statements from other people involved. Sometimes a mediator might ask for a joint statement of the issues in dispute. If so, the lawyers will have to liaise with each other to produce this.

Lawyers will also need to plan the opening statement for the mediation with their clients. This will be similar, but not exactly the same, as the summary. The actual statement can be made by the parties or by their lawyers. Mediators will often encourage the parties to make the statement, so that they can hear it in the parties' own words and if there is a team on each side, all of them might have something to say as part of the opening statement.

The statement should be short but include:

- a concise chronological description of the problem;
- reference to the strengths of the case;

- reference to any objective standards of fairness that might apply;
- reference to the alternatives should no settlement be reached;
- an acknowledgment of any of the other side's particular strengths;
- an explanation of what is hoped will be achieved through the mediation.

Where will the mediation be?

Figure 10.1

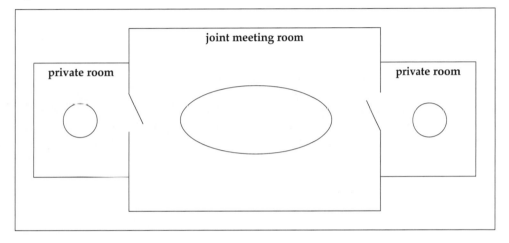

The setting for a mediation can be very important. It is advisable to choose somewhere independent, so that neither party has an advantage, although, if you do this, make sure there won't be any problems if you need to stay well into the night or even come back the next day. The setting should also be comfortable and facilitate discussion, and should be as private as possible. All the rooms will have to be relatively sound proof. It should be possible for the parties to go into separate private rooms for discussions with the mediator. See the diagram above in Figure 10.1.

You will need to consider how the parties will feel about the location the mediation will take place in, whether they will be comfortable and, in particular, how you will arrange the seating in the main joint meeting area. Some mediators prefer a round table, while others go for a long table with everyone from one side on the right and everyone from the other side on the left, with the mediator at the head. If you plan to arrange things this way, put the parties nearest to you, with the advisers at the end of the table – that way, they are less likely to feel left out.

What should those taking part in a mediation as lawyers consider?

The role of those acting as lawyers in a mediation is to give advice and to help negotiate with the other side. During the mediation, they must let the mediator take control of the process. They must employ a creative, problem solving approach. If they are overly aggressive or confrontational, they may stop the mediation working. Remember that the mediation settlement can include anything the parties will agree to and will usually include 'non-legal' remedies. As we will discuss below, lawyers should keep their clients around until the agreement has been written and signed.

THE PROCESS

Most mediations will follow a standard format. There will be an opening joint session followed by private sessions between the mediator and each party, in between which there will be more joint sessions. The mediation will end with a final joint session. However, there are no strict rules about the format of a mediation, and it is up to the mediator to decide exactly how each mediation progresses.

The opening phase

Just before the opening, the parties will be shown into their private rooms and be given a chance to have a final discussion with their lawyers. As a mediator, you should have checked the rooms and made sure that they are as comfortable as possible with enough room for everyone, and access to things like tea or coffee. Although the number of cushions on the chairs and the availability of fresh as well as UHT milk might seem irrelevant, if the parties are not distracted or irritated by any kind of discomfort, they are more likely to concentrate and be happy to put their efforts into the mediation.

You might want to go to see the parties in private before the mediation begins, so that you can introduce yourself, check that they are happy and answer any last minute questions which they might not want to ask in front of the other side.

When you're ready to begin, you should get the parties into the main joint area where everyone will meet at various stages during the mediation. Everything said in that room will be heard by everyone, but it can't be disclosed or used outside the mediation without permission.

The opening phase is an introduction to the mediation itself. Everyone involved will be introduced, and the whole process will be explained by the mediator. It's important that this explanation is comprehensive, but it shouldn't last too long or the parties will start to switch off. You should cover the following:

* who you are, including relevant experience/qualifications;
* the purpose of the mediation;
* the position regarding confidentiality and authority;
* the way the mediation will be structured;
* how long it will take;
* whether any settlement will be binding;
* any other rules – for example, no interrupting;
* whether anyone has any questions.

You need to know exactly what you are going to say, and say it slowly and clearly.[9] You should check to see if anyone has any questions about how the mediation will be conducted.

---

9   Noone gives an example of a mediator's opening statement (*op cit*, fn 4, p 94).

Your job as a mediator at this stage is to instil confidence in the process and in you personally. You have to manage the whole process, so you need to be firm but also reasonably friendly and approachable. You need to make the parties feel that you are there to help all of them find a solution to their problem. This is very important and the whole mediation can fail if you don't do it properly. The parties may be sitting there thinking: 'I'm really nervous about this and I'm not convinced it is going to be of any benefit at all. I don't trust the other side to be open so I must be careful not to give anything away or be forced into agreeing to something I don't want.' You need to at least start to convince them all that they have nothing to lose and a lot to gain, and that you will manage the process so that that happens.

Towards the end of this phase, both parties will be asked to present their case by making opening statements. This is done in a fairly informal way, and some discussion might take place between the parties after the opening statements have been given. It's useful for you, as the mediator, to hear these opening statements, but it also means that each side can start to appreciate the needs and priorities of the other and how they have been affected by the problem. You don't want life histories up to the present; you just want a short explanation of their side of the story. If you set a time limit of 10–15 minutes and tell them that they can bring in details later on, this should help to keep the opening statements to a manageable length. It's better if these statements are planned and written by the parties themselves; possibly with the help of their advisors, but not entirely written by them, because the parties will give the clearest picture of what the problem is really about. The person who initiated the mediation or, if litigation is going on, the claimant, will make their statement first. You should explain why they are first when you ask them to speak. After both sides have made their statements, you might summarise the main issues and then, with everyone's agreement, set an agenda. Summarising the statements lets you show the parties that you have taken in what they have said, allows you to check that you've understood it, and reinforces those important issues to each side.

You will need to make a list of all the issues too, if you're going to come up with a running order for dealing with them. Issues need to be identified for the agenda in neutral terms so 'the nature of the materials used' in a building dispute is obviously more appropriate than 'the builder's use of cheap and nasty bricks'. Anything can go on the list: legal, factual or emotional. You can control the order in the same way as you might do in a negotiation, putting things that are more likely to be agreed at the top, or following some other logical order. As with negotiation there is no 'right' order. Sometimes it helps to agree on something small first to get things moving, but sometimes dealing with the most important issue while everyone's still keen gets results.

Lots of mediators will use a white board to record the issues, and this means that everyone can clearly see what's on the agenda and where they've got to. It also makes it easy to swap things around, rub them out or alter them as you go along.

The middle stage

The structure of the middle stage

This is the most complex stage, when the issues are explored and offers and counter-offers will be made and considered. The parties will either start this phase by going into separate private rooms with their advisers, if they have any, and the mediator to talk in private, or they may start it with a joint session which follows on from the opening phase.

If you start with a joint session, you'll be encouraging the parties to talk to each other rather than through you. What you can do is make sure they keep to the point and don't get bogged down in the less important details but really, you should be taking a back seat. This joint session might flow fairly naturally from the opening statements with a discussion of the issues and then the possible solutions. Your role will be to keep things moving and make sure that the atmosphere is as constructive as possible. If the atmosphere is difficult, you would be wise to keep this stage fairly short. You should ask neutral questions and stay away from particularly sensitive issues until later on. People will always want to talk more about the issues that they feel most strongly about. You need to give them time to do this, so that they feel they have addressed those items properly, but you may need to move them on when you think it is time to consider other issues or solutions. To help you get as full a picture as possible, ask questions of anyone who has not yet spoken.

By the end of the first joint session, you should have a pretty good idea about where the mediation might go and what kind of settlement might be possible. When you have reached this position, and when it seems that the parties have come to a point where there is not much more they can say to each other, you can end the first joint session. You should do this by summarising what has been said, highlighting any points of agreement, then explaining why you think this is a good point to end the joint session. Finally, thank all the parties for their contributions and explain what will happen in the next stage.

If you decide to go straight to the first private session, you will usually go first to the party who made the first opening statement, although it doesn't matter which party you see first, and sometimes you might decide that it is best to see the one who, in the opening session, said they were less confident about the mediation working. You may prefer not to give your reasons for seeing one party first; there is no need, and it can be seen as bias. Finally, try to give some time estimates to the party you are leaving alone for how long you will be in the private session with the other party. Obviously the time you spend with each should be roughly equal, although that may not always be possible. When you do leave one side, you can get them to keep working on something while you are not there or, if you think it would be useful, allow them time to relax.

The private session is your opportunity to have a more full and frank discussion without the threat of interruption or argument, although it's quite possible that the private sessions will begin with each party saying: 'Can you believe what they said? I don't know how they've got the nerve to suggest ...' etc. You need to acknowledge these feelings so they can be got out of the way, but don't agree with them, otherwise you'll be losing your neutrality. You can also use these sessions to stop either party becoming entrenched and hampering the progress of the mediation. As an independent participant, you can see more clearly where problems and blockages exist and so try to uncover the interests behind them and suggest options that might be acceptable to both parties. As the mediator, you will want to go over a number of points with each party. Below is a list of some of the things you should cover:

• Remind them that everything said will be confidential unless they agree otherwise.

- Go over the strengths and weaknesses of their case and the other side's case.
- Consider the objectives and their order of priority.
- Ask what their best alternative to a negotiated agreement is (and what the other side's might be).
- Ask about the details of any prior negotiations.
- Explore whether there is anything that has not yet been considered in detail which would make a difference to any offers or proposals already made; for example, the timing of a payment or the addition of an apology.
- Find out what their future needs will be.
- Find out what they can offer.
- Ask whether they have any questions for you.

Everything said in the private rooms is confidential unless it is agreed that the other side should be told about it. This means that you will get a much better picture of what each side's real interests, problems and bottom lines are, because they will usually be keeping things back from the other side, especially in the early stages. You'll need to take notes of these conversations. That can be difficult because your notes need to be accurate and clear enough for you to use them again, but you can't spend all your time with the parties writing. It's a good idea to check, before leaving one party to speak to the other, that you have an accurate note of what you are permitted to repeat. Another way to help this is to spend a short time between private sessions on your own, checking that your notes are in order. If you find that there is something missing, you can go back and check it before moving into private session with the other party.

In private sessions, you should always begin by reminding everyone that everything said will be confidential. At the end, too, you should double check anything that you have been asked not to pass on to the other side before you go into their private room. One way to make sure that you can keep things separate is to use different notebooks or different coloured pens for joint and private sessions.

If things go really well you might find, after talking to the parties in private only once, that there is enough that is agreed on to bring them back to a joint session and reach an agreement. This would be rare, though. Normally, you'll need at least a few private sessions, possibly with joint sessions in between.

In the private sessions you should be aiming to create a better relationship of trust with the party you are with. Although you have to stay neutral, you can help this process by showing understanding of their position – but try to avoid clichés like, 'I hear what you say', or 'I can feel your anger'.

Building these relationships means you can get the real story behind the things said in the joint sessions. This will help you to form a better understanding of the problem. You'll probably have to ask questions to get at all this information. You might also need to challenge what the parties say, particularly if you think they are making wrong assumptions or have unrealistic expectations. You can use negotiating skills to find out what the parties' underlying interests are, what each party's bottom line is and later, to help them find compromises and creative solutions.

One of the functions of private sessions is for the parties to come up with possible settlement options. They are more likely to come up with ideas in a private session where everything is confidential than in a joint session, although options will be discussed in joint sessions too. These options can be discussed in detail in the private sessions and you can challenge each side's position and encourage them to be open and creative.

During this phase, various large and small items might be agreed. You need to keep a very careful note of everything that is agreed and you might want to make this available to both sides constantly, or at various intervals. Sometimes it's easy for everyone to recognise that an agreement has been reached, but at other times you will be the one who has to see it and point it out.

After these first private discussions with each side, the mediation can progress in a number of ways. You might go backwards and forwards between the private rooms taking offers and counter-offers to each side. The advantage of this is that in private sessions there is more time to consider offers carefully. This is often referred to rather grandly, as shuttle diplomacy. All this means is that, where the parties are really not able to get anything useful from face to face discussions, the mediator will just go backwards and forwards between them in private sessions. If you have to deal with this kind of mediation, your role will be to take each side's settlement options to the other. You'll need to make very sure that the options you are taking are realistic and that the reactions you take back are well considered. Some might say that this is not really true mediation, because the parties are barely negotiating with each other. You might decide that it would be easier to get the parties back together in the main joint area to talk again directly to each other before going back into another private session. This is generally the preferred way to proceed. This toing and froing can go on for as long as you think it's useful.

Managing the middle stage

It is common for a mediation to start with both sides feeling negative towards each other and, at best, unsure about the process itself. Part of your role throughout this middle phase is to try to get them to feel more positive, if not towards each other, then at least about the mediation process. To do this, you need to keep an eye out for any comments or indications from those involved that they are getting something out of the mediation, even if it's just some small new piece of information. You can refer to these positive items later to show the parties that they are getting somewhere.

You will need to manage this stage very carefully and make sure that, throughout, everyone is given a fair chance to put their case. If you think that any specific advice to one or both parties would be useful, you can suggest that technical or legal experts are brought in.

It is not your job as a mediator to give any advice to the parties or express any views about what they should agree to. Even if you do have a strong view, your job is only to help them reach a settlement, not to negotiate for any of them. If it's been agreed that you will take an evaluative approach, you will, if necessary, give your views on certain practical or legal matters and suggest solutions, but that is not the same as imposing the outcome you think is best on the parties.

What you can do is test what has been proposed, or 'reality check'. So, when the employer in a redundancy payment dispute says, 'Why don't we offer half the payment but waive the restraint of trade clauses in the contract?', you will be asking what effect that might have, and whether they would be happy if the employee then began to work for a close competitor.

The end stage

Finally, all the options must be outlined, concessions made and an agreement concluded. This stage might not, in fact, be completely distinct from the middle phase. Concessions might be made fairly early on some items, and the end stages could be just a matter of finalising the details. In other cases, it might not be until the very end that agreement comes on one or all of the major points in dispute. If there is one final sticking point, it can be dealt with in the same way as it might in a negotiation, so you might suggest splitting the difference, coming up with a trade off, throwing in an additional 'sweetener' or any number of other tactics discussed in Chapter 9. The final agreement often won't come until very near the end of the time you've made available for the mediation, and it can be a real struggle to get there, even if things have been going reasonably well. If they haven't, it can be a very stressful 'touch and go' period.

As with negotiations, towards the end of a mediation, things will generally speed up, sessions should become shorter and you will need to work harder to keep the parties to the point. You will also need to take more control and really push the parties to come up with options if they can't agree to proposals already made. Remember too that, as with simple negotiations, some people will hold out until the very last minute before they will agree to accept their bottom line.

It is important that the final agreement, when you get it, is written down clearly and agreed by everyone. It should be read out by the mediator and always be signed before the parties leave, because unsigned agreements are very often not kept to. If it's signed, there can be no re-opening the next day of issues that have been agreed. The parties will be anxious to get things finished off, so if it's a long and complicated agreement you can write down what are called 'heads of agreement', that is, the basic points without the detail, and get those signed; the detail is then added later. If lawyers have been involved in the mediation, they will probably draft the agreement with your help.[10]

The agreement itself, or parts of it, can fall into one of three categories:

(a) Non-binding agreements which are made on trust only. Certainly, an unsigned agreement would fall into this category.

(b) Binding agreements which could be enforced like a contract, through court action. Most people will feel more comfortable with this kind of agreement. There should be a term in the agreement saying that any terms of the settlement can be enforced by taking court action.

(c) Seriously binding agreements which are set out in a court order. This kind of agreement can be made if the parties had already started court action before the mediation. Where the parties are not sure they trust each other, or the consequences of non-compliance would be terribly serious, they might feel more comfortable with this because non-compliance will be contempt of court.

---

10   Noone gives an example settlement agreement in his book (*op cit*, fn 4, p 148).

PROBLEMS IN MEDIATION

Ethics

The three main ethical problems that you might face as a mediator are a conflict of interest, dealing with confidential information or staying impartial.

Conflicts of interest

There is some overlap between a conflict of interest and a lack of impartiality, because if you have an interest that conflicts with that of one of the parties, you will no longer be impartial about the outcome of the mediation. If you have any kind of interest in the outcome of the mediation, you cannot act as a mediator. For solicitor mediators, it is important to check to see if their firm has acted for any of the parties before. If there is any potential conflict, everyone will have to be told, so that they can decide whether a new mediator should be found.

Confidentiality

Confidential information will almost always be given to you during a mediation. Some might also be given by one party to the other. It is best if rules about confidentiality are written down and agreed before the mediation. Generally, you are only free to disclose information which is already public, or which the parties agree you can disclose. The only exception to that might be where you found out something so serious that your duty was overridden by another duty. As an example, if you found out about a serious design fault in new fire safety clothing for firefighters which was being used already, and there was no agreement to allow you to disclose that information, you might do so anyway, as other people's lives might be put at serious risk.

Impartiality

As a mediator, it is vital that you are impartial. That means that, if you have shares in one of the companies in dispute, even if you are not sure that the outcome will affect the share price, or if one of the parties is a second cousin on your mother's side, you will have to tell both parties. Whenever you have any personal interest in the outcome, you must declare this. The parties might agree to let you carry on, but usually they will want someone else to step in.

Impartiality also means that you are not there to help one party or the other. You shouldn't tell one side what your opinion of the issues is. But what if they come to an agreement that you think is very unfair to one of them? There is a delicate line to be drawn here. It is not your job to get the parties to come to the agreement that you think is the best. If they are happy with the settlement, that should be enough. However, if you really think that the parties are moving towards an agreement that is not fair or is maybe just unworkable, you can suggest that they take advice on its legal implications if they don't have legal advisers with them.

Controlling the behaviour of those involved

Sometimes the mediating parties won't quite play the game as you think or hope they should. They might argue on and on about a minor point without really listening to each other, not say anything at all, try to get you to take their side or just like the sound of their own voice too much. You need to take control calmly and clearly and steer them back on course, make it clear that you are impartial or, if they are too quiet, find out why they don't want to speak and see if you can deal with any problem they have.

But how much should you intervene: are there times when you should keep quiet and let the parties get on with it? Partly this will depend on your personality, partly on the particular situation and the people involved. There's a balance to be achieved which really only you can evaluate once you are in the mediation. You shouldn't intervene too much or misuse the control you have, but you do need to manage the parties and move them towards settlement.

Party not talking

There can be different reasons for not talking in a mediation. It can be that someone is just nervous or unsure about what they can or should say. You can usually deal with this by explaining things to them and trying to build their confidence in the process. If one side seem to be trying to take advantage of the mediation only to get information without giving it, you will have to speak to them in private about this. If there is no other reason for their behaviour, you will have to end the mediation.

Walk outs

The most extreme bad behaviour is a threatened walk out of the mediation. You will have to decide how to deal with this in the context of the case. You might have decided that the mediation is not going to work, so it could be the best option, or it might be worth having a short break and trying to persuade the unhappy party to carry on. People are often going to become emotional under the stress of a mediation. One way to help calm them is to explain that what is happening and the way they are feeling is quite normal for the situation. This can help them to take a step back and try again.

Problems from the lawyers

Unfortunately, sometimes the biggest problems can come from legal advisers rather than the parties. If the lawyers think they should be taking control and acting as advocates for their clients, this can make the mediation very difficult. You need to remind them tactfully of the way the process works and their role, that is, as advisers only, in it.

Power imbalances

Generally, the power balance will shift one way and then the other during a mediation. That's fine as long as you manage the process so that it is fair. But what if it becomes obvious that one side has all the power, all the time? Say you suspect the husband has been violent towards the wife and she seems reluctant to say anything that he might not like. If there is anything you can do to change this, like suggesting the weaker side brings in more advisers, then you can do so. What you can't do is start to act as an adviser or advocate for one side, because once you do that, you're no longer impartial. In the end, you might have to end some mediations because it becomes obvious that they just can't work due to the use of greater power by one side over the other.

Reluctance to use mediation

You think mediation was made for this problem, you can see that the chances of a good settlement are high, but one of the people involved is dismissing the idea out of hand. If you can't persuade them it's worth a try, they will fulfil their own prophecy and any attempt to settle will be doomed. How can you respond to their excuses and worries?:

They say there are issues of law involved
so a court trial is needed.

↓

There are always issues of law involved.
That alone is not a reason to litigate rather than mediate.

They say the gap between them and the other side
is bigger than the Grand Canyon.

↓

This is often the case, but over 95% of cases that go into the court system
do settle before the final trial. If you don't even begin the process,
you cannot know exactly how wide or deep that gap really is.

They say that there are too many people involved.

↓

A mediation is easier with only two parties, but so is ordinary litigation.
The question is whether mediation in a multiparty action is more difficult
than litigation in a similar action. Many experienced mediators will
say that mediation is still the better alternative.

They say that litigation has already started, so mediating
now would cause too much delay and expense.

↓

The courts are more than happy to allow a break in litigation for mediation
to take place. If time is a real concern, time limits can be put on how
long mediation will take. Even if the mediation doesn't work, it will not mean
that time or money have necessarily been wasted, because things learnt
through the mediation can help in the litigation.

They say they are bound to win, so why bother?

↓

If they are sure that their case is so good, that means they should get a very
favourable outcome from the mediation and save time and costs.

No agreement

If you're very near to the end of the day and, although there's no agreement yet, you feel that one is not too far off, it's best to just keep going. With the momentum you have, it is still easier to carry on into the night than to stop and start again another time.

If the parties aren't that close, but you still think an agreement is a possibility, you can suggest that the mediation be adjourned for a week or so. Mediation is completely flexible, so as long as the parties are happy with this, there is no reason why it can't be done.

If it really looks like an agreement will not be reached at all, then you should end the mediation. Preferably, this should be with the agreement of both parties, if not, then at least one has to have effectively given up, otherwise it's still worth carrying on. Even where this happens and everyone walks away without an agreement, you must wrap up the mediation in as positive a way as possible. It's very unlikely that nothing has been gained because, at the very least, some issues should have been clarified. In fact, of those cases where mediation ends without agreement, most will settle very shortly afterwards.

THE ADVANTAGES AND DISADVANTAGES OF MEDIATION

Mediation can be seen as a variation of negotiation. The two parties to a negotiation have brought in a neutral third party. This may be because they think they are not able to negotiate usefully, or it may just be because they think their chances of reaching a mutually acceptable solution are increased by taking this approach. It is certainly less likely that one person will be able to use adversarial tactics to force an unfair compromise when using mediation. This means that, in mediation, a weaker party is given some protection. So, mediation has many advantages; it also has some disadvantages. These should be considered before entering any mediation, and we have set them out below.

Advantages

- Mediation shows a high success rate: 75%–95% of cases achieve settlement.
- It gives the people involved a chance to be heard. The parties get a chance to put their side and to think about all the issues. They are allowed to get things off their chests and there are no rules about what they cannot say.
- The mediation process is a fair one. Because the mediator is in control of the process, it's much less likely that one side will be able to dominate the process and take advantage or just not let the other side get the chance to say very much. In negotiation, an aggressive person can sometimes take complete control of the process, but that can't happen in a mediation.
- It can be informal. In family cases, this means legal language is kept to a minimum and people are less likely to feel intimidated. It is quite common for first names to be used even in a commercial mediation. You can set the level of formality to match the situation and get the people involved to feel as relaxed as possible. As the mediator, you might be 'Chris', 'Chris Brown', or even 'Mr or Ms Brown', though almost definitely not Sir or Madam as you could be in a court.

- It is creative. Because a problem solving approach is used by the mediator and encouraged in the parties, creative solutions can be found. There is no limit to the actual solutions the parties can agree to, so explanations and apologies, which are often not possible in litigation, can be part of the package.

- The process can be informative. The parties get the chance to hear the other side and are forced to consider the problem from other perspectives.

- It can be fast. Even a very complex mediation in a high value commercial case with four or five parties can be dealt with in something like three days. It could take at least a week just to deal with all the evidence in a trial of this kind of action, and that is ignoring the months of preparation beforehand.

- Mediation can be satisfying. Because the outcome depends on the parties and how much effort they put in, and because they cannot be forced to accept anything they do not like, the process is much more satisfying than giving evidence at a trial, then letting the lawyers do the talking and waiting for the judge to make a decision.

- Mediation is cheap. Mediators still have to be paid, but their overheads are less than those of the courts and because mediation is faster than litigation, it is also cheaper.

- It is confidential. Most court hearings are open to the public, so anyone can come in and listen to what is going on. This follows a sound principle of open justice, but sometimes parties might prefer to keep information confidential, and that can more easily be done in the context of a mediation. This means that those involved feel more willing to speak openly, and that helps in reaching a settlement.

- The discussions in a mediation are all without prejudice. If there is no agreement and the parties go on to, or back to, litigation they don't need to worry that they have let the other side know too much about their case. Nothing disclosed in the mediation can be used by one party against the other.

- Taking part is voluntary. If anybody changes their mind about being involved, they are free to pull out, and there is always the option of going to court if no agreement is reached.

- The parties have more control in a mediation. In cases like divorce or disputes over children, this can make a big difference to their experience and to the success of whatever agreement results.

- It is convenient. The mediation is arranged for a time and at a place that is convenient for those involved. Unlike a court trial, it will not stop at 5.00 pm if the parties want to carry on.

- Mediation can be used for any kind of dispute. Even if it doesn't involve legal rights, mediation can still help those involved come to an agreement.

Disadvantages

- Even a binding agreement which is written down and signed only has the same level of enforceability as an ordinary contract. That doesn't compare with a court order because, to enforce the agreement, one of the parties will have to do what they were trying to avoid and start litigation. Only a settlement endorsed by a court order will have the same effect as a trial judgment. This will be relatively rare, especially if the mediation did not occur after litigation started.

- The parties have to agree to mediate. If one party wants to be difficult and refuses to start mediation or wants to walk out halfway through, there is not much you can do about it.

- There are some cases where mediation is not going to be appropriate. If someone needs an injunction fast to stop the other side moving assets out of the country, or if a court decision on an important point of law is vital, mediation won't help.

- Because mediation is fast, it is possible for facts that might have influenced the outcome never to come to light.

- You need to get the timing right. Too early, and mediation may not work because one side won't agree to it. Too late, and the advantages of time and cost savings may have been lost.

CONCLUSION

In this chapter, we have described the structure of a mediation and considered the skills needed by an effective mediator. You can see that, because a mediator is facilitating a negotiation, a good knowledge of negotiation skills and practice are essential. Of particular use will be the negotiation skills of active and passive listening, counselling, understanding body language, questioning, self-awareness, using information effectively and being realistic, honest and polite. As well as those, a good mediator must be a good manager of people and be able to appear impartial at all times.

Of all the skills in this book, we have to be realistic and admit that mediation is probably the least likely to be part of your law course and the least likely to be used by you in the early stages of your career. Having said that, it is more and more likely that, if you train to be a lawyer, you will be involved in mediations and need to advise and accompany your clients. What we have tried to do, therefore, is to give you an overview of the subject; enough to start you off if you are learning the skills of mediation and enough, too, to help you if you are involved as a lawyer in the process.

Learning mediation skills

It's still fairly rare for mediation to be taught as a skill in law schools. It's not part of the compulsory syllabus for either the Legal Practice Course or the Bar Vocational Course. However, because its use is growing, its study is bound to grow too, and there are skills courses and elective subjects which do focus on ADR processes such as mediation. If it is taught, it's quite likely to come after some study of negotiation as an understanding of that skill is necessary to practise mediation. If mediation is part of your course, it's likely that you'll be given mediation exercises to practise, and any assessment of your skills will be of your performance in this kind of exercise. The subject matter of the exercises could be almost anything. Some courses will concentrate more on commercial mediation, some on family, and others will include any number of different kinds of cases. An assessment of your performance as a mediator would consider similar items to an assessment of your negotiation skills. So, your preparation, understanding of the issues and ability to deal with ethical problems would be considered. As well as this, you would need to show that you could effectively manage the parties to the mediation and help them towards a settlement. So, the way you interact with them, your impartiality and ability to keep information confidential would be very important.

As with all skills, improving your performance will depend on increasing your experience and your knowledge of mediation. The list of further reading at the end of this chapter will, we hope, help you do this.

FURTHER READING

Brown, H and Marriott, A, *ADR: Principles and Practice*, 2nd edn, 1999, London: Sweet & Maxwell.

Mackie, K and Miles, D, *The ADR Practice Guide – Commercial Dispute Resolution*, 2nd edn, 2000, Haywards Heath: Tottel Publishing.

Nesic, M and Boulle, L, *Mediation: Principles, Process, Practice*, 2001, Haywards Heath: Tottel Publishing.

Noone, M, *Mediation*, 1997, London: Cavendish Publishing.

Palmer, M and Roberts, S, *Dispute Processes – ADR and the Primary Forms of Decision Making*, 1998, Haywards Heath: Tottel Publishing.

Stitt, A, *Mediation: A Practical Guide*, 2004, London: Cavendish Publishing.

Stone, M, *Representing Clients in Mediation*, 1998, Haywards Heath: Tottel Publishing.

CHAPTER 11

INFORMATION TECHNOLOGY

INTRODUCTION

Information technology (IT) is a term that often fills people with apprehension. In its broadest sense it means any form of technology that allows the transfer of information from one person to another or others. Although this term therefore technically applies to radios, televisions and other such appliances, it has nevertheless come to be almost exclusively used when referring to the field of computer technology.

Computers have revolutionised the home and workplace over the past two decades. As a result, the government-appointed body responsible for standards in higher education – the Quality Assessment Agency (QAA)[1] – has laid down benchmark requirements for the provision of IT within educational programmes. These benchmarks aim to standardise the capabilities of graduates leaving higher education institutions. The required levels of IT ability vary according to the particular course, although it is expected that all law students should be able to use the internet to retrieve information and word process documents by the time they graduate. Students following vocational programmes, such as the Legal Practice Course or Bar Vocational Course, will also need to be aware of how IT is used in the professions they are planning to enter.

This chapter will look at the internet, word processing and the uses of IT generally in the field of law. At the end of this chapter some advice will be provided on purchasing a computer.

COMPUTERS IN THE LEGAL WORLD

There are very few solicitors' firms or barristers' chambers that do not use computers in some form or other. Sadly not every legal practice has the means to invest heavily in IT and there are often disparities between the provision of IT amongst legal offices. Computer systems are expensive, especially as networks need to be installed to make full use of the available applications.

When on work experience you may see that some law offices have invested heavily in computers and make full use of the various legal applications that are available. Others, however, are lagging far behind and there are some who still swear by the traditional typewriter and corrector fluid method. Thankfully, these lawyers are few and far between and most now recognise the need to develop IT within the workplace and that the advantages of IT certainly outweigh any disadvantages.

The main aim of IT within the legal office is to save time, as well as providing a better service for the client. The uses of IT in this context can be identified as follows:

---

1   www.qaa.ac.uk.

(a) word processing;

(b) the creation of court documents;

(c) email;

(d) legal research;

(e) the use of case management systems.

Each of these will be examined in turn.

Word processing

Perhaps the most popular computer application within a law office is the word processor. A word processor is in effect nothing more than a very clever typewriter, where the words are typed on to the screen, formatted in a particular way and then printed. Word processors eradicate the need for carbon copy paper and corrector fluid, as multiple copies of a document can be printed or saved to a computer file and typing errors can be corrected on the screen.

Word processors also have the added attraction of allowing for alterations in the appearance of text simply and easily. At the touch of a button, the user can underline text, italicise text, embolden text, or even all three. You can also change the size of the text and the typeface (called a font) so that a document has greater impact. There are numerous fonts that are available on word processors and, although legal documents tend to use the standard font called Times New Roman, many others are available and can often be downloaded freely from the internet.

Word processing for the solicitor

Most solicitors employ the services of a secretary or typist to carry out word processing in the office. Understandably, this is due to cost implications – the hourly rate of a typist is substantially below that of a qualified solicitor. However, the level of IT proficiency within the profession is on the increase, as is the ability of many newly qualified solicitors to touch type. Those intending to enter the legal profession should be aware that touch typing is now considered by some to be an important criterion in the employment of trainee solicitors.

In the law office, the word processor has become commonplace. The days when legal documents would be scripted in the finest copperplate have long since disappeared and now legal documents invariably come in computerised form. This has a number of advantages.

One advantage is that it allows for the creation of letter and document templates. A template is a standard document that can be used time and time again and all word processors can create them. This standard document can be called up each time it is required and then altered slightly to adapt the document to a particular matter. Templates can therefore save a great deal of time, as there is no need to type standard letters or documents repetitively. These templates can cover any aspect of a solicitor's work. For example, it is standard practice for solicitors to send all new clients a 'client care' letter. This letter contains information about the particular solicitor's firm and the levels of service the client can expect. The letter will also contain information on action clients can take if they are dissatisfied with the work that the solicitor has or has not done. Client care letters are often adapted from office templates, which save considerable time and expense in the busy legal practice.

In addition to letter templates, word processors can be used to store a variety of draft legal documents such as contracts, wills or trust instruments. These can be opened and adapted to suit different cases. Again, this saves time and money and avoids repetitive work.

Word processing for the barrister

The paper practice part of a barrister's working life consists mainly of writing opinions and drafting court documents. As with the solicitor's practice, almost all of the paper work a barrister sends out will be in typed form.

Very few standard letters or documents are ever drafted by barristers. As such, the use of document templates is not as important for the barrister as for the solicitor.[2] The real benefit of the word processor for barristers is that it is becoming increasingly common for barristers to do all the word processing themselves, without the aid of a typist. This does not mean that all barristers do not make use of a typist. However, it is becoming more common for junior barristers to undertake any typing themselves. This again highlights the benefit of learning how to touch type for any person intending to practise law.

Word processing packages

There are numerous word processing packages available on the market these days, although surprisingly there are fewer on the market today than there were 10 years ago.[3] The steady increase in the use of Microsoft products has meant that Microsoft's word processor has tended to become the most widespread. Due to the special rates afforded to universities by campus agreements, Microsoft Word is the most common word processing application in higher education institutions. Their current version – Word 2003 – comes as part of the Office 2003 suite accompanying a spreadsheet application (Excel), a database application (Access) and presentation creation software (PowerPoint). However, other word processing packages are available and it should be noted that, when buying a new computer, the word processing software installed on the machine might not be the Microsoft version. If this is the case, do not feel that you should immediately rush out and purchase Office, for there is no need. Most word processing packages are able to read and convert files created on other word processors and although this may lead to some problems with the document's visual appearance, the actual content should remain the same.

Court document creation

Whenever you wish to involve the courts in either a contentious matter or even some non-contentious matters, there are certain court forms that will need to be completed.

---

2   One of the few standard form letters sent out by barristers (or their clerks) is addressed to solicitors, reminding them of outstanding fees.
3   The main packages currently on the market are WordPerfect, Lotus SmartSuite and Microsoft Word.

Before computers, these forms were completed either by hand or typed on a typewriter. Now computer packages are available which allow the completion of the various court forms on screen.

These computer packages display a copy of the blank form on screen and you can complete it by simply typing in the relevant information and printing it off. For lawyers who specialise in litigation, these packages are very useful. Although it is possible to access free packages on the internet,[4] the best of these services cost money, with payment normally being calculated on the number of forms that are held on the computer. There is little doubt that creating court forms on a computer saves time, but for the small high street practitioner who does not specialise in litigation, these premium services may not be worth the expense.

Email

Email has revolutionised our communications system. Essentially, it is a method of communication between people using computers and there is no real difference between email and ordinary mail except that email is in a computer form and therefore intangible, whereas ordinary mail is sent by physical means and is therefore tangible. Email requires a connection to the internet, either by a modem which connects the computer to the internet via a telephone line, or through a network. Most if not all legal offices with a computer system will probably have access to email.

The benefits of email are as follows.

Speed

Email has been described as an instantaneous method of communication. Although it is certainly fast, it is rare these days to find email systems (other than internal ones) that can be said to be truly instantaneous. However, compared with ordinary mail it is far quicker.

Cost

Email is very cheap. Charges are either calculated according to on-line time or on a flat rate charge and the cost does not depend on how many emails are sent. Currently, email is a great deal cheaper than sending a letter by post. Also, there is no difference in the cost of sending an email to a person in England or sending an email from one country to another or from one continent to another.

Attaching documents

Another major advantage of electronic mail is that you can attach documents which are in an electronic format to an email and then send these over the email system. These file attachments make it incredibly simple for lawyers to communicate with one another

---

4   A free court form package is available on the internet called Hot Docs. This can be found at www.capsoftuk.co.uk. Individual forms themselves can be found on the court service website – www.courtservice.gov.uk – under forms and guidance.

and with their clients. Given the fact that much of a lawyer's work involves drafting letters and documents, the benefits are clear. Although in normal circumstances, the only files that are sent over the email system are those that exist in an electronic form as an existing computer file, 'hard copy' documents can be scanned into a computer, saved as a file and then attached to an email in the normal way. This has now led to the electronic instruction of barristers by solicitors with all relevant papers attached and the Civil Procedure Rules provide for the service of documents on opponents by email.

Although of tremendous benefit, there are nevertheless two main disadvantages to email. These relate to the security of the information sent and also the transmission of computer viruses.

Security

For lawyers, one of the major concerns with the use of electronic mail relates to the confidentiality and the security of the email message. Much of a lawyer's work is confidential and as such it is important that he or she can guarantee confidentiality when using email as a method of communication so that unauthorised persons are prevented from viewing it.

As soon as an email is sent, there is always the possibility that it will be intercepted and read by a person other than the one to whom it is addressed. Although the hijacking of emails by technical means does not occur very often, it is possible. Certain security protection systems are available that allow email messages to be encrypted (put into code form) so they can only be read by the person to whom the email is addressed; for example, dual key cryptography.

A further security issue arises when a person receives an email. Although the email will state from whose account it was sent, it is not possible to guarantee that the account holder actually sent the email. It is, after all, plausible that one person has temporarily left their desk and that another person sent an email using the other's account whilst the person was away. This is an important issue when goods are bought and sold over the internet. Given the rise in the levels of e-commerce, and the associated increase in the number of contracts formed over the internet, it is vital to confirm the identity of the contracting parties. Steps have been taken to remedy this dilemma through the introduction of electronic signatures in the form of coded email attachments. Since the Electronic Communications Act 2000, an electronic signature has the same legal force as a normal handwritten signature.

Viruses

Viruses are programs that are specifically written to cause problems with computers and the applications that run on them. There are many types of virus that exist and they can range from those that are completely harmless to those that are designed to be malignant. In order to ensure that no virus can infect a computer, preventative measures need to be taken.

Computer viruses are similar to the ones that infect humans and can spread very easily. The most common method of virus infection at one time arose from the use of infected computer diskettes. However, with the increased use of the internet and email, viruses can be transmitted much more easily.

Despite the potentially destructive threat posed by computer viruses, they are relatively easy to protect against. Protection software can either be purchased from a shop or downloaded from the internet.[5] However, just because virus protection software is installed on a computer, this does not mean that the computer is protected. New viruses are created on a daily basis and therefore it is important to keep any virus software up to date.

There are, of course, simple ways to prevent viruses from infecting a computer; for example, by taking care with the files that are either downloaded from the internet or opened as email attachments. The Melissa virus back in 1999 would not have spread so rapidly if recipients had not opened the Word document attached to the email that read, 'here is the file that you have been waiting for'.[6]

Email for the solicitor

There is little doubt that electronic mail can be of use to solicitors. Clients can be contacted simply and easily and, since email is cheaper than using the postal service, it can allow solicitors' firms to be more competitive. The Law Society has recognised the importance of electronic mail and has published guidelines and suggestions for its use. These guidelines can be found on the Law Society website.[7]

Email for the barrister

Email means that barristers and solicitors can communicate more easily than in the past; allows for the electronic instruction of counsel (where the solicitor instructs a barrister via email); and also the provision of electronic advice (where the barrister emails an opinion to the solicitor). Email guidelines are available for barristers on the Bar Council Website.[8]

Legal research

Computers offer major advantages when used to conduct legal research. There are two ways to conduct legal research using a computer:

(a) research using CD ROM;

(b) research using the internet.

Research using CD ROM

A CD ROM is a compact disk identical to a music compact disk (CD) that contains large amounts of computer data. Each CD ROM can hold over 650 megabytes of information,

---

5   Visit www.download.com for some free downloadable virus protection software.
6   It should be noted that not every computer file can carry a computer virus. Picture files (jpg or gif files) cannot carry a virus and neither can normal word processor files. The files that normally carry viruses are exe, bat and vbs files.
7   See www.lawsociety.org.uk.
8   See www.barcouncil.org.uk

which roughly equates to 450 three and a half inch computer diskettes. Therefore, the main advantage of a CD ROM lies in its capacity to store information.

The fact that a CD ROM is able to hold large amounts of data means printed items that would normally take up a great deal of room, when stored on CD now only take up a fraction of the space. For example, a single CD ROM can contain the *All England Law Reports* from 1935 to date[9] whereas in the library the same printed materials take up almost 10 metres of shelf space. Other CDs available reduce three or four volume practitioner works to a single CD.[10]

CD ROM versions of texts can also prove more accessible than the printed copies. A CD ROM is small and portable and its contents can be accessed – with the right equipment – from virtually anywhere.

A further advantage of storing data on CD ROMs is that finding information on them can be remarkably quick. All legal CDs have search mechanisms enabling the user to find the information that they require relatively quickly and easily.

There is a wide range of legal CDs available on the market today and the majority are aimed at practitioners, thereby allowing the publishers to charge high prices to those who can afford to pay, although student discounts are sometimes available.

Research using the internet

There is little doubt that the internet is a useful tool for conducting legal research as it contains legal databases which include every statute in force; every statutory instrument in force; almost every case ever reported in the UK; and even summaries of those cases that have not been reported. This information does, however, come at a price and the publishers who own the rights to the legal information often charge heavy premiums for access by practitioners.

Internet databases are popular for two main reasons. The first is due to the fact that connecting to the internet is simple and convenient. This can be compared with CD ROM legal research where it is normally necessary to have a copy of the individual CD ROM and install certain files on the computer's hard drive in order to make use of them.

The other major benefit of the internet is that you are able to access up to date information. Although CD ROMs are cheap to produce, updated disks are only available periodically, for example every three months, which means that there is a chance that information contained on the CD ROM is out of date when accessd. The internet, on the other hand, allows the user to get the law correct on the day.

Case management systems

As computers have become more advanced, the complexity of the tasks that they can perform has increased. One way computers have revolutionised the solicitors' legal practice is through the use of what are commonly known as 'case management systems'. Essentially, these systems allow a solicitor to call up a wide range of

---

9   Available from Butterworths.
10   Eg, *Archbold's Criminal Practice*, London: Sweet & Maxwell.

information on a particular client or case. The information that is often available on these systems can include:

(a) Personal information – enabling the solicitor to check for possible conflicts of interest.

(b) Type of work undertaken (for example, personal injury).

(c) Funding details, that is, whether the case is funded on a conditional fee basis or is privately funded, and the balance of the client's account.

(d) Details of the case.

(e) Copies of all documents involved with the matter.

(f) A diary containing an alarm system that notifies the solicitor of important dates.

(g) A timer for the case – a useful function that allows a solicitor to start the timer when he or she starts dealing with a file and stops the timer when the work is done. This allows precise time recording for the client's final bill.

The above list is certainly not exhaustive and different systems may have other functions to those listed above. It is also increasingly popular for the larger firms to have their case management systems tailormade so that they are completely suited to that particular firm.

There are a large number of firms that have adopted case management systems and, although they are expensive, they can save a great deal of time and prevent the generation of excessive paperwork. Systems such as these are becoming vital for firms that wish to hold a Community Legal Service franchise.

BUYING A HOME COMPUTER

Buying a computer can be a complicated process. The following guide will provide some basic advice on what to look for when purchasing a computer.

Do you need a computer?

Many students will have access to a computer either at university, in a public library or through an internet café. There are of course drawbacks when you use a computer that is not your own. For example, even if you are fortunate enough to go to a university or college with 24 hour computer access, there is no guarantee that a computer terminal will be free when required. The simple answer therefore is to buy your own computer.

Buying a computer is expensive and, although computers are a lot cheaper than they were five years ago, they still represent a fairly large outlay of money. Think twice before you buy and ask yourself whether you really need your own computer or whether, with improved time management, you can get all your work done using a computer elsewhere. If you are still convinced that you need to buy a computer, the following information may assist you with your purchase.

Types of computer

There are numerous ways to classify computers. There is the Apple computer (for example the iMac), the personal computer (PC), the desktop computer or the laptop computer.

For the computer novice, there are two things that you need to note:

(1) the type of microchip used in the computer and how fast this chip runs;

(2) the amount of memory that is available within the machine.

Chips

Although it is not strictly correct to state that the faster the computer chip (microprocessor) the better the computer will be, there is a strong link between the two. A computer works on the basis of commands and the faster the chip, the quicker it can process all of the commands to give you the response that you want. For example, if when using a word processor, you use the spell check function, a computer with a fast chip will be able to check all of the words much faster than a computer with a slower chip.

There is often no need to buy a computer with a really fast chip and the computer user should try to work out what it is they want from a computer before purchasing. If all that is required is word processing, then a slower chip will serve just as well. Technology is advancing rapidly and computers are becoming very powerful. However, the most commonly used applications, such as word processors and spreadsheets, are now at the point where a faster chip will do little to improve their performance. The newest and fastest chip will not make a word processor type a letter any quicker nor endow a CV with magical qualities that will guarantee success.

Memory

Computer memory can be separated into two divisions, random access memory (RAM) and the hard drive.

RAM

The larger the RAM within a computer, the better your computer will work: it will be more stable, it will be able to run more applications simultaneously and will run programs faster. Most new computers these days will come with 512 megabytes of RAM, although it is certainly worth choosing a PC (or even upgrading) to have more if you can afford it.

The hard drive

A computer's hard drive is its storage facility. It is the space where you can save documents and pictures and install applications. With hard drive space, the larger the better. It is normal these days for computers to come with around 250 gigabytes of memory and extra hard drive space is probably not worth investing in. Instead ensure that the PC has a writeable CD drive. As seen before, CD ROMs have large capacities and should a hard drive become almost full, the excess can be transferred to a CD ROM. Blank CD ROMs now cost less than 20p and will hold large amounts of data. Writeable CD ROM drives are now standard in computers.

Added issues

It is worth noting that it is possible to balance the processor speed with the computer's RAM. A cheaper computer with a slower processor and more RAM may run as quickly or even quicker than a computer with a faster processor and less RAM.

When buying a computer it is also worth remembering, that given the change in pace of technology, it is almost certainly better to buy a £1,000 computer now and replace it with an equally priced computer after one year, than a £2,000 computer now (unless of course the £2,000 computer has something that you particularly need).

Desktop computers

A desktop computer (desktop PC) is one that is designed to fit on your desk. Essentially it is a large computer that is not portable.

Given their size, desktop PCs are generally cheaper than a laptop as the components do not have to be so small and the design not so compact; however, as most new desktop PCs arrive with LCD (flat) screens the space required for a desktop PC is far less than was previously required.

There are two types of desktop PC: the tower system, where the main unit is housed in a tower, or where the main unit sits underneath the monitor. There is no real difference between the two and you should choose whichever will suit your available space.

When buying a desktop PC there are some aspects that should be highlighted. First, as a general rule, it is better to have a large computer screen. There is little worse than sitting for long periods in front of a small monitor. Fifteen inch LCD monitors often come as standard these days and should be thought of as a minimum requirement.

It is worth considering when purchasing a desktop PC that the ports used for plugging certain peripherals (digital camera, memory stick) into are easily accessible, that is, at the front of the computer as opposed to being at the rear.

Laptop computers

Laptop computers are much smaller than their desktop equivalent and because they are designed to be portable they are significantly more expensive than a comparative desktop model. Laptops do not offer real value for money although portability can be worth paying for. You will, after all, be able to work wherever and whenever you want. If considering a laptop computer, it would be strongly advisable to purchase one with Wi Fi capabilities. Most universities are now Wi Fi enabled, thereby allowing students to access the computer network from 'social' spaces. Whilst, it is possible to purchase a Wi Fi card to plug into a laptop, these can easily be forgotten or lost.

Peripherals

Computers are generally only as good as the extras that can be attached to them and are known as peripherals. Common extras include the following.

Printers

A printer will allow whatever is displayed on a computer to be printed in hard copy. They have fallen in price and it is now possible to get a good printer for less than £75. You can get colour printers and black and white printers. It is worth considering the cost of the ink when purchasing a printer, as the refill cartridges can be expensive.

Scanners

A scanner will allow the user to transfer whatever is on the printed page into a computer file. They can also help turn a PC into a more traditional fax machine – although a scanner is not necessary for this – and allow large amounts of text in hard copy form to be put into a form which can be edited by a computer.

Digital cameras

These will allow the user to take a photograph and then download it into the computer. This is useful for the creation of web pages and also producing professional and interesting documents.

Often when buying a computer the above peripherals may be included in a package deal. If so, remember the cost of these extras will be included in the price and if you do not use them there seems little point in paying for them. It is also possible to buy a printer that is also a scanner and a photocopier. Such a purchase can often be worthwhile.

Where to buy your computer

Once you have decided to invest in your own computer, you will need to consider where to buy it. Computers can be bought either on the high street or by using mail order or e-commerce.

The shop

There are a number of advantages in buying a computer from a shop. First, you will be able to see your computer and it will be easier to picture it in your home. You will also feel more secure as you can return the goods to the shop should they go wrong. However, buying a computer from a shop will generally cost more than if you choose the mail order option. Also some of the budget PCs[11] use poor quality components and therefore things are more likely to go wrong. If you choose to buy from a shop – and certainly it is worth paying a bit more for peace of mind – choose one that has a good reputation.

Mail order

If value for money is what you want, then mail order may be the best way forward.

There is no one good mail order supplier. There are quite a few that often advertise in the major newspapers and these certainly offer good value for money. However, you can find a cheaper deal if you are prepared to look in one of the many computer magazines. Each month at least one of these magazines will produce a buyer's guide for computers. If anyone is considering purchasing a computer then the best advice would be to do some research and see what is the best deal on the market at the time. One word of warning: when buying a computer that is highly recommended in a computer magazine, it is likely that other people will have the same idea as you. Suppliers can often be inundated with large numbers of orders that cause delays. If you are going to buy using mail order then always plan ahead and be prepared to wait a little for delivery.

Another concern when buying by mail order is the support available should anything go wrong. It is worth checking to see what sort of warranty comes with the product and, if necessary, paying extra to have the on-site warranty, so that if anything goes wrong, the company will send a technician to your house to fix it rather than you having to send the computer back to the manufacturer. Whilst this may seem a little more expensive at the time, it is worth serious consideration.

E-commerce

Buying from an e-commerce trader will probably give you the same PCs as those in the shops but at a reduced price as you will not be subsidising the shop's overheads. This can be a useful method of purchase and with the levels of protection now offered by the Consumer Protection (Distance Selling) Regulations 2000, SI 2000/2334, there is little real risk as a 7 day cooling off period exists which should allow you to to return the goods and get your money back.

---

11   At the time of writing, it is possible to get an internet ready desktop PC for under £300 and a laptop for under £400.

USEFUL WEBSITES

Legal professional bodies

Website title	Web address	Website description
Bar Council	www.barcouncil.org.uk	Home page for the General Council of the Bar. Useful information for barristers and pupils. This site also gives the contact details of its personnel.
Law Society	www.lawsociety.org.uk/home.law	Home page for the Law Society. Useful information and contact details are provided.

Search engines

Website title	Web address	Website description
Alta Vista	www.altavista.com	N/A
Ask Jeeves	www.ask.co.uk	N/A
Find law	www.findlaw.com	N/A
Law Crawler	www.lawcrawler.com	N/A
Google	www.google.co.uk	N/A
Law Guru	www.lawguru.com	N/A

Government pages

Website title	Web address	Website description
Acts of Parliament	www.opsi.gov.uk/acts.htm	Full text of Acts from 1996.
Hansard Reports	www.parliament.the-stationery-office.co.uk/pa/cm/cmhansrd.htm	Full report of the goings on in the Houses of Parliament. Database goes back to 22 November 1988.
Houses of Parliament	www.parliament.uk/index.cfm	Home page for the Palace of Westminster. This site gives access to the House of Lords and also the House of Commons.
Judicial Studies Board	www.jsboard.co.uk/	Home page for the body responsible for the training and monitoring of judicial staff.
Department of Constitutional Affairs	www.dca.gov.uk/	Home page for the successor to the Lord Chancellor's Department providing useful information on the administration of justice.
Statutory Instruments	www.opsi.gov.uk/stat.htm	Full text of statutory instruments from 1997.
The Court Service	www.hmcourts-service.gov.uk	Useful site providing information and materials on court structure as well as daily listings of trials, court forms (which can be completed on-line).

Miscellaneous sites

Website title	Web address	Website description
Access to Law	www.accesstolaw.com/default.asp	Portal giving access to a wide range of legal information.
Company Law Club	www.companylawclub.co.uk	Useful website dedicated to company law. Includes a discussion forum on company law issues.
Consillio	www.spr-consilio.com	An interactive magazine for law students. An advanced website containing revision notes, audio lectures and other materials for students.
Crown Prosecution Service	www.cps.gov.uk	Home page for the Crown Prosecution Service.
Daily Law Notes	www.lawreports.co.uk/indexdln.htm	Useful service for students giving summaries of the latest cases heard in England and Wales.
European Court of Human Rights	www.echr.coe.int/	Home page for the ECHR.
Human Rights Web	www.hrweb.org	Information on human rights and human rights issues. Useful links to other human rights resources.
Legal 500	www.legal500.com	Useful website for those people who are interested in Commercial Law. This site also hosts the on-line version of the Legal 500 (the definitive guide to the legal market and lawyers).
International Court of Justice	www.icj-cij.org	Home page for the International Court of Justice. Numerous materials available on-line.

Website title	Web address	Website description
Internet Law Library	www.lawguru.com/ilawlib/index.html	Database full of worldwide legal information categorised by every country. Although not complete for every country, it certainly provides some useful information.
Internet Legal Research Group	www.ilrg.com	An index of more than 4,000 websites dealing with legal issues. Emphasis here is on American law, although there is some useful English legal information.
Law Careers	www.lawcareers.net	Useful website dealing with legal careers.
Law Commission	www.lawcom.gov.uk	Website for this esteemed reforming body. Useful information on legal topics currently under review.
Law Dictionary	www.duhaime.org/dictionary/diction.htm	Duhaime's on-line law dictionary. Useful when your hard copy is too far away to reach.
Lawzone	http://lawzone.thelawyer.com	A website providing news and comment on a variety of legal issues. This site also provides a weekly update by email on the latest news. This is a free service.
Legal Services Commission	www.legalservices.gov.uk	Home page of the body replacing the Legal Aid Board.
The Barrister	www.barristermagazine.com	Independent magazine for legal professionals.
Government Legal Service	www.gls.gov.uk	Government Legal Service website.
Crimeline	www.crimeline.info	Useful criminal litigation updating website.

Website title	Web address	Website description
BAILII	www.bailii.org	Access to freely available British and Irish public legal information.
Online Law	www.online-law.co.uk	Website providing information on lawyers around the country.
Society for Computers and Law	www.scl.org	Home page for the Society. Useful information regarding IT and the law. This page also has a good list of up to date legal resources available on the internet.
The Bar Directory	http://2.sweetandmaxwell.co.uk/bardirectory/website	On-line version of the Bar Directory providing information on all practising barristers and chambers.
The Student Law Centre	www.studentlaw.com	A site dedicated to the law student that answers many student concerns and also gives advice on CVs, etc.
UK Patent Office	www.patent.gov.uk	Home page for the UK Patent Office.
University of Kent Law Library	http://library.kent.ac.uk/library/lawlinks/default.htm	A very useful link site that is updated on a regular basis. This should be the first port of call for anyone wishing to conduct any legal research on the internet.

Legal publishers

Website title	Web address	Website description
Butterworths	www.butterworths.co.uk	
Cavendish Publishing	www.cavendishpublishing.com	
Oxford University Press	www.oup.co.uk	
Sweet & Maxwell	www.sweetandmaxwell.co.uk	

INDEX